# THE ARDEN SHAKESPEARE

THIRD SERIES

General Editors: Richard Proudfoot, Ann Thompson
David Scott Katsan and H.R. Woudhuysen

Associate General Editor for this volume:
George Walton Williams

# KING
# HENRY IV
# PART 1

# THE ARDEN SHAKESPEARE

* Second series

THE ARDEN SHAKESPEARE

# KING HENRY IV PART 1

Edited by
DAVID SCOTT KASTAN

THE ARDEN SHAKESPEARE

LONDON • NEW YORK • OXFORD • NEW DELHI • SYDNEY

THE ARDEN SHAKESPEARE
Bloomsbury Publishing Plc
50 Bedford Square, London, WC1B 3DP, UK

BLOOMSBURY, THE ARDEN SHAKESPEARE and the Arden Shakespeare logo
are trademarks of Bloomsbury Publishing Plc

This edition of *King Henry IV, Part 1*, by David Scott Kastan, published 2002
by The Arden Shakespeare
Reprinted by Bloomsbury Arden Shakespeare 2009, 2010,
2011, 2012, 2013, 2014 (twice), 2015, 2016, 2017, 2018 (twice), 2019 (three times), 2020

The general editors of the Arden Shakespeare have been
W. J. Craig and R. H. Case (first series 1899–1944)
Una Ellis-Fermor, Harold F. Brooks, Harold Jenkins and
Brian Morris (second series 1946–82)
Present general editors (third series)
Richard Proudfoot, Ann Thompson, David Scott Kastan
and H. R. Woudhuysen

A catalogue record for this book is available from the British Library.

A catalog record for this book is available from the Library of Congress.

ISBN: HB: 978-1-9042-7134-5
PB: 978-1-9042-7135-2

Series: The Arden Shakespeare Third Series

Printed and bound in Great Britain

To find out more about our authors and books visit www.bloomsbury.com
and sign up for our newsletters.

*The Editor*

David Scott Kastan is Old Dominion Foundation
Professor in the Humanities at Columbia University,
New York. His publications include *Shakespeare and the
Book*, *Shakespeare after Theory*, and *Shakespeare and the
Shapes of Time*; in addition he has edited *A Companion to
Shakespeare*, *A New History of Early English Drama*
(with John Cox), and *Staging the Renaissance* (with Peter
Stallybrass). He is one of the General Editors of the
Arden Shakespeare.

For MK, who doubled Kate and the Douglas in her first
appearance on stage

# CONTENTS

vii

# Contents

# LIST OF ILLUSTRATIONS

# GENERAL EDITORS' PREFACE

The Arden Shakespeare is now over one hundred years old. The earliest volume in the first series, Edward Dowden's *Hamlet*, was published in 1899. Since then the Arden Shakespeare has become internationally recognized and respected. It is now widely acknowledged as the pre-eminent Shakespeare series, valued by scholars, students, actors and 'the great variety of readers' alike for its readable and reliable texts, its full annotation and its richly informative introductions.

We have aimed in the third Arden edition to maintain the quality and general character of its predecessors, preserving the commitment to presenting the play as it has been shaped in history. While each individual volume will necessarily have its own emphasis in the light of the unique possibilities and problems posed by the play, the series as a whole, like the earlier Ardens, insists upon the highest standards of scholarship and upon attractive and accessible presentation.

Newly edited from the original quarto and folio editions, the texts are presented in fully modernized form, with a textual apparatus that records all substantial divergences from those early printings. The notes and introductions focus on the conditions and possibilities of meaning that editors, critics and performers (on stage and screen) have discovered in the play. While building upon the rich history of scholarly and theatrical activity that has long shaped our understanding of the texts of Shakespeare's plays, this third series of the Arden Shakespeare is made necessary and possible by a new generation's encounter with Shakespeare, engaging with the plays and their complex relation to the culture in which they were – and continue to be – produced.

## THE TEXT

On each page of the play itself, readers will find a passage of text followed by commentary and, finally, textual notes. Act and scene divisions (seldom present in the early editions and often the product of eighteenth-century or later scholarship) have been retained for ease of reference, but have been given less prominence than in the previous series. Editorial indications of location of the action have been removed to the textual notes or commentary.

In the text itself, unfamiliar typographic conventions have been avoided in order to minimize obstacles to the reader. Elided forms in the early texts are spelt out in full in verse lines wherever they indicate a usual late twentieth-century pronunciation that requires no special indication and wherever they occur in prose (except when they indicate non-standard pronunciation). In verse speeches, marks of elision are retained where they are necessary guides to the scansion and pronunciation of the line. Final -ed in past tense and participial forms of verbs is always printed as -ed without accent, never as -'d, but wherever the required pronunciation diverges from modern usage a note in the commentary draws attention to the fact. Where the final -ed should be given syllabic value contrary to modern usage, e.g.

> Doth Silvia know that I am banished?
> (*TGV* 3.1.214)

the note will take the form

214 **banished** banishèd

Conventional lineation of divided verse lines shared by two or more speakers has been reconsidered and sometimes rearranged. Except for the familiar *Exit* and *Exeunt*, Latin forms in stage directions and speech prefixes have been translated into English and the original Latin forms recorded in the textual notes.

## COMMENTARY AND TEXTUAL NOTES

Notes in the commentary, for which a major source will be the *Oxford English Dictionary*, offer glossarial and other explication of verbal difficulties; they may also include discussion of points of theatrical interpretation and, in relevant cases, substantial extracts from Shakespeare's source material. Editors will not usually offer glossarial notes for words adequately defined in the latest edition of *The Concise Oxford Dictionary* or *Merriam-Webster's Collegiate Dictionary*, but in cases of doubt they will include notes. Attention, however, will be drawn to places where more than one likely interpretation can be proposed and to significant verbal and syntactic complexity. Notes preceded by * discuss editorial emendations or variant readings from the early edition(s) on which the text is based.

Headnotes to acts or scenes discuss, where appropriate, questions of scene location, Shakespeare's handling of his source materials and major difficulties of staging. The list of roles (so headed to emphasize the play's status as a text for performance) is also considered in commentary notes. These may include comment on plausible patterns of casting with the resources of an Elizabethan or Jacobean acting company, and also on any variation in the description of roles in their speech prefixes in the early editions.

The textual notes are designed to let readers know when the edited text diverges from the early edition(s) on which it is based. Wherever this happens the note will record the rejected reading of the early edition(s), in original spelling, and the source of the reading adopted in this edition. Other forms from the early edition(s) recorded in these notes will include some spellings of particular interest or significance and original forms of translated stage directions. Where two early editions are involved, for instance with *Othello*, the notes will also record all important differences between them. The textual notes take a form that has been in use since the nineteenth century. This comprises, first: line reference, reading adopted in the text and closing square bracket; then: abbreviated reference, in italic, to the earliest edition to adopt the accepted reading, italic semicolon and noteworthy alternative reading(s), each with abbreviated italic reference to its source.

Conventions used in these textual notes include the following. The solidus / is used, in notes quoting verse or discussing verse lining, to indicate line endings. Distinctive spellings of the basic text (Q or F) follow the square bracket without indication of source and are enclosed in italic brackets. Names enclosed in italic brackets indicate originators of conjectural emendations when these did not originate in an edition of the text, or when this edition records a conjecture not accepted into its text. Stage directions (SDs) are referred to by the number of the line within or immediately after which they are placed. Line numbers with a decimal point relate to entry SDs and to SDs more than one line long, with the number after the point indicating the line within the SD: e.g. 78.4 refers to the fourth line of the SD following line 78. Lines of SDs at the start of a scene are numbered 0.1, 0.2, etc. Where only a line number and SD precede the square bracket, e.g. 128 SD], the note relates to the whole of a SD within or immediately following the line. Speech prefixes (SPs) follow similar conventions, 203 SP] referring to the speaker's name for line 203. Where a SP reference takes the form e.g. 38 + SP, it relates to all subsequent speeches assigned to that speaker in the scene in question.

Where, as with *King Henry V*, one of the early editions is a so-called 'bad quarto' (that is, a text either heavily adapted, or reconstructed from memory, or both), the divergences from the present edition are too great to be recorded in full in the notes. In these cases the editions will include a reduced photographic facsimile of the 'bad quarto' in an appendix.

## INTRODUCTION

Both the introduction and the commentary are designed to present the plays as texts for performance, and make appropriate reference to stage, film and television versions, as well as introducing the reader to the range of critical approaches to the plays. They discuss the history of the reception of the texts within the theatre and scholarship and beyond, investigating the interdependency of the literary text and the surrounding 'cultural text' both at the time of the original production of Shakespeare's works and during their long and rich afterlife.

# PREFACE

I began with the desire to speak with the dead, but in truth what else can a Shakespeare editor do. Not only is this edition an effort to commune with Shakespeare, to attempt to recover his intentions from the ouija board of the surviving texts, but it is also a series of vigorous conversations through the medium of print with all previous editors since Rowe in 1709, or even Heminge and Condell in 1623, seances in type whose benefits are inscribed on every page that follows. No form of scholarly work more obviously reveals itself less as an individual labour and more as a collective activity than an edition of a Shakespeare play. My name on the title-page merely marks my place in the line of editors who have tried to produce a text as 'cur'd and perfect' as Shakespeare 'conceiued' it, but whose efforts will always leave more for the next editor in line to do. My debts to my predecessors are I hope generously registered in the references of this edition. But this acknowledgement is to indicate how inadequate even these references are; for the work of earlier editors, from the earliest to the most recent, not only taught me much about this play but also inspired me with the astonishing evidence of their learning, rigour, imagination, integrity and, above all, their love of Shakespeare.

I end with the desire to speak to the living, publicly to thank my friends and colleagues who have made this edition possible in their different ways. First there is the Arden team: Richard Proudfoot and George Walton Williams read every word of this edition, indeed several times, each time attempting to remedy the gaps in my knowledge, working to clarify my fuzzy thinking, graciously making available their astonishing banks of information and ideas, but most of all always encouraging me and reminding me by their own passion why this project was worth doing. Ann Thompson was the very best of colleagues as together we both strove to finish individual editions while engaged in too many other activities. Linden Stafford was the most remarkable of copy-editors, careful and alert, and caring as much about the edition as anyone other than I could. And Jessica Hodge was inevitably wise, inspiring, patient (most of the time), and always good-humoured and amazingly unflappable (often under circumstances when any lesser mortal would have been flapped). She is for the Arden Shakespeare the *genius loci*.

Other friends generously read, corrected, improved, talked and listened, as this edition lurched towards completion, most notably Tom Berger, David Bevington, John Cox, Barbara Hodgdon, Jean Howard, Barbara Mowat, Eric Rasmussen, Richard Sacks, Bill Sherman, David Yerkes and Steven Zwicker. Still others, who also have heard more about *1 Henry IV* than they ever wished to – David Armitage, Kim Coles, Margreta de Grazia, Jonathan Hope, Claire McEachern, Gordon McMullan (who, unlike Hope, roots for a football team far better than he deserves), Stephen Orgel, Jim Shapiro, John Tobin, David Trotter (who in fact deserves a far better football team to root for) and Peter Stallybrass (who, astonishingly, prefers rugby) – not only offered their considerable founts of knowledge but, no less importantly, gave again and again of their time and friendship, often in restaurants and pubs it must be said (which, while not speeding up the edition, certainly made it much more fun to do). The wonderful Columbia students with whom I have been privileged to work, many already now recognizable in their own right as extraordinary young members of the profession, also must be thanked for their contributions to this both in class and out, as they taught me what I needed to know: Douglas Brooks, Pat Cahill, Alan Farmer, Heidi Brayman Hackel, Jesse Lander, András Kiséry, Zach Lesser, Ben Robinson, Dan Vitkus and Chloe Wheatley. Susan Kastan also deserves thanks; she watched this project begin, sometimes must have despaired that it would ever be finished, and made so much of the work possible to do.

The libraries where I worked and their staffs also should be acknowledged, for none of this was achievable without them: the

Columbia University Library, and especially its rare Book and Manuscript Reading Room, the library of University College, London, the Huntington Library, the British Library and, above all, the Folger Library. The rich holdings of these libraries, the civilized and stimulating environments they create, and most importantly the wondrous knowledge, patience and generosity of their staffs, made work on this edition possible and far simpler and more pleasant than I ever imagined it could be.

And then there is the person to whom this is dedicated, who has taught me more about everything that matters than anyone else on earth from the very moment she was born.

*David Scott Kastan*
*New York*

# INTRODUCTION

## GREAT EXPECTATIONS

In 1784, Thomas Davies, in a collection of essays on Shakespeare's plays, observed that 'in the opinion of Thomas Warburton, and I believe all the best critics, the First Part of Henry IV. is, of all our author's plays, the most excellent' (Davies, *DM*, 1.202). If 'all the best critics' of more recent times have been somewhat less willing to grant *1 Henry IV* absolute pre-eminence in the Shakespeare canon, they have generally shared this admiration. 'No play of Shakespeare's is better than *Henry IV*,' wrote Mark Van Doren in 1939; 'History as a dramatic form ripens here to a point past which no further growth is possible' (Van Doren, 116). A few years later, W. H. Auden exuberantly punctuated Van Doren's enthusiasm in his lectures on Shakespeare at the New School in New York City: 'It is difficult to imagine that a historical play as good as *Henry IV* will ever again be written' (Auden, 101).

The judgements are easily multiplied, but it is worth noting that, although Davies's commendation is specific to 'the First Part', Van Doren and Auden praise a play that doesn't exist: *Henry IV*. Both write about the two plays on the reign of Henry IV as if they formed a single, coherent dramatic conception. The two, however, were written separately and, until recently, were almost always performed independently of one other (see p. 22). And, if they are equally interesting, unquestionably *1 Henry IV* has regularly been the more admired and popular of the two.

Even in its own time, *2 Henry IV* was less well received, never reprinted after its initial publication in 1600 until its appearance in the 1623 Folio. *Part One*, however, was almost immediately both a literary and a theatrical triumph, as successful in the bookstalls of London as it was on the stage. Nine editions were published between 1598 and 1640, making it an early bestseller among all printed playbooks of the period; and in the theatre it seemingly also flourished, probably first performed in the winter of 1596–7 and regularly acted throughout the seventeenth century. In 1640, in a commendatory poem to Shakespeare's *Poems*, Leonard Digges noted that, while Ben Jonson's plays no longer could dependably attract an audience large enough to cover the costs of production, Shakespeare's play was still a certain hit: 'let but *Falstaffe* come, / *Hall* [i.e. Hal], *Poines*, the rest, you scarce shall have a roome / All is so pester'd [i.e. crowded]' (*Poems*, sig. *4ʳ).[1] After the Restoration, Samuel Pepys saw the play acted five times between 1660, when the theatres reopened, and 1668, the first time admittedly disappointed with the performance, his 'expectation being too great' (Pepys, 1.325). Today the play still produces great expectations of pleasure, which usually are fulfilled. It holds a secure place in the theatrical repertory, in school and university curricula, and in the hearts of contemporary playgoers and readers.

No doubt much of its continued popularity has resulted, as Digges suggested, from the comic action, and, in particular, from the character of Falstaff. There are more references to the fat knight up until the end of the eighteenth century than to any other literary character, and, before the last half-century, discussions of Falstaff ('the most substantial comic character that was ever invented', as Hazlitt said, presumably aware of the joke[2]) dominated the criticism of the play. On stage, throughout the eighteenth and nineteenth centuries, *1 Henry IV* was inevitably Falstaff's play, and virtually every great actor of those times took on the role, from Thomas Betterton to James Hackett, Charles Kemble to William Macready, and Samuel Phelps to Herbert Beerbohm Tree. At least one woman played the role: Lydia Webb in 1786.

---

1  Though the lines could be referring to both parts, Poins's far more limited role in *Part Two* makes it likely that they refer only to *1 Henry IV*.
2  William Hazlitt, *Characters of Shakespear's Plays* (1817), 148.

The twentieth century, however, rediscovered, both on stage and in the study, the fact that the play offers more than the remarkable (and oft-remarked) Falstaff. The irrepressible knight strains against but does not overwhelm the design of the play as it now appears on stage and in critical accounts. Indeed today the play is far more likely to be Hal's play than Falstaff's, the story of the seemingly prodigal prince proving himself a worthy heir, with his relationship with Falstaff as the crucial measure of his growth.

What now seems the greatest achievement of the play is precisely its 'mingling of kings and clowns' (Sidney, *Prose*, 114), what A. P. Rossiter sees as the 'deep penetration that emerges from the conflict of serious and comic' (Rossiter, 59). Falstaff is no longer the centre of the play as it is understood today, but merely one pillar (though unquestionably a sturdy one) of its elegant structure. The comedy neither dominates nor is subordinated to the historical plot but is actually part of the same exploration of the historical world as is the overtly political action. Unlike *Richard II* and *King John*, its immediate predecessors among Shakespeare's historical plays, *1 Henry IV* insists that history must be recognized as something more capacious than merely the record of aristocratic motives and actions. The comedy of the tavern world comments on these, with an often withering insight into their compromises and self-deceptions, but, at least as importantly, the comedy assumes its own place within the drama of the nation. When Falstaff tells Hal in the tavern that 'Worcester is stolen away tonight', the reference is of course to the rebellion that is at the centre of the historical action, but he judges its effect in an idiom and a measure impossible to imagine in the earlier histories: 'Thy father's beard is turned white with the news. You may buy land now as cheap as stinking mackerel' (2.4.349–51). As Howard Erskine-Hill says, this 'is not only a sign of human distance from these events: it is a mark of a new kind of interest in them' (Erskine-Hill, 79), the interest of people not directly involved in shaping the serious military and political action of the play but whose daily lives are inevitably changed by the events that swirl beyond their control.

The play sets before us an intricately woven tapestry of high and low characters, of public and private motives, of politics and festivity, of poetry and prose, of history and comedy, of fact and fiction, allowing us to see and hear not only the variegated play world but history itself as a brilliantly polychromatic pageant. More than any other of Shakespeare's history plays, *1 Henry IV* explores and extends the territory that counts as history, and in the process deepens the understanding of the politics that has been its traditional subject as it explores the process by which authority is achieved and the nature of the state in which it is exercised.

In its very amplitude *1 Henry IV* reveals its own compelling design – and one that articulates Shakespeare's most complex and humane version of English history. Arguably the play offers, in J. Dover Wilson's words, 'the broadest, the most varied, and in some ways, the richest champaign in Shakespeare's empire' (Wilson, 15), and that richness is at once the source of the play's unrivalled theatrical energy and the sign of its unique political vision. The title-page of the first surviving edition of *1 Henry IV*, published in 1598, sharply signals the play's complex focus: '*THE HISTORY OF HENRIE THE FOVRTH; With the battell at Shewsburie,* betweene the King and Lord *Henry Percy, surnamed Henrie Hotspur of the North.* With the humorous conceits of Sir *Iohn Falstalffe.*' Almost a table of contents rather than a title, it in fact indicates something essential about the ambitious design of the play. Though the play takes its usual title solely from the name of the King, his story is not, as any reader or spectator must know, the play's primary concern. In the play's full title, three major characters are named, each of whom makes a strong claim upon an audience's attention and even sympathy: the pragmatic King Henry, struggling to rule with his tainted crown; the rebel Hotspur, recklessly committed to his chivalric ideals; the irrepressible Falstaff, with his outrageous, comic vitality.

Unnamed on the title-page, but in fact at the play's dramatic centre, as Samuel Johnson was perhaps the first to note, is the

Prince (Johnson, 4.355), who stands in the middle of this triangulation of forces. His pragmatic father is at one point of the triangle, at the head of the political world that one day must be Hal's own to rule; his self-indulgent father-surrogate Falstaff stands at a second, seemingly offering an escape from the pragmatic calculation of the political world; and at the third is the impetuous Hotspur, whose exuberant heroic commitments stand as an inviting alternative to Hal's apparent scapegrace idleness. Each of the three is in some way attractive to the young Prince, but each also represents something dangerous or debilitating for his development as a future King of England. The play, at least in part, traces the process by which he takes for his own some qualities that each models for him and rejects others.

In this sense, the play is a coming-of-age story; and on the battlefield at Shrewsbury Hal reveals his new-found maturity, displaying the heroism and magnanimity that both give moral authority to the victory of the King's forces and testify to his own emergence as a worthy heir. And there can be little doubt that this centrality was intended. The historical battle at Shrewsbury (see Fig. 1) was dominated by the actions of the King; as Holinshed writes: 'The king in deed was raised & did that daie manie a noble feat of armes, for as it is written, he slue that daie with his owne hands six and thirtie persons of his enimies' (Holinshed, 3.523). Shakespeare, however, de-emphasizes the role of the King and gives Hal a prominence in the climactic battle he did not historically have. At Shrewsbury, according to Holinshed, the historical Prince 'holpe his father like a lustie yoong gentleman' (3.523), but history's Hal didn't save the King, or defeat Hotspur, or free Douglas, the Prince's defining actions at the end of Shakespeare's play.

Hal's glorious demonstrations of his maturity on the battlefield provide the narrative climax of *1 Henry IV*, but the play is no more exclusively a dramatic 'Education of a Christian Prince' (Hawkins, 301) than it is a mere vehicle for the display of Falstaff's wit. The play is always more than Hal's story, just as it is always more than

1 Map of
Shropshire with
the Battle of
Shrewsbury, 1403,
(lower right)
from Speed, *A
Prospect of the
Most Famous Parts
of the World*, 1631

Falstaff's – or more than Hotspur's, or more than the King's – but it is also always no less than all of their stories. The four major roles, unique in Shakespeare's canon in the almost equal sharing of the lines,[1] do define the outlines of the play's brilliant prismatic achievement, and, as productions and indeed critics find their own concerns which force the emphasis of some one character over the others, the particular tenor of a performance or a reading emerges. But even the minor characters in this play are here precisely and memorably imagined, creating the sense of a capacious and fully realized world as they interact with one another and with the central characters of the plot. Indeed, *1 Henry IV* is a play no less about relationships than about character: about subjects and rulers, fathers and sons, nephews and uncles, wives and husbands, and about friends. Hal's transformation from the truant prince of the tavern scenes to the chivalric hero on the battlefield at Shrewsbury is, no doubt, the central trajectory that the play traces, but *1 Henry IV* is concerned as much with the complex social formation of England as it is with the complex moral formation of the king who will one day rule over it as Henry V.

## 'MINGLING KINGS AND CLOWNS': HISTORY, COMEDY AND DRAMATIC UNITY

The very richness that is the defining mark of *1 Henry IV* does, however, complicate our sense of what kind of play this is. It is, of course, conventionally thought to be a 'history play', although Francis Meres, in *Palladis Tamia* (1598) in praising Shakespeare 'for Tragedy', indiscriminately cites as examples 'his *Richard the 2. Richard the 3. Henry the 4. King John, Titus Andronicus* and his *Romeo* and *Juliet*' (Meres, sig. OO2$^r$). For Meres the distinction between the Histories and Tragedies is not so clear, and indeed the early printings of *3 Henry VI*, *Richard II* and *Richard III* refer to

---

1   Falstaff speaks 542 lines; Hotspur, 538; Hal, 514; and King Henry, 338. The four speak 1,938 of the play's 2,857 lines, or 67.6 per cent; see King, table 50, 186.

7

each of these as 'Tragedy'. Nonetheless, *1 Henry IV* was entered in the Stationers' Register on 25 February 1598 as 'The historye of Henry the iiijth', and all the early quartos similarly title it *The History of Henrie the Fourth*. In the 1623 Folio, the play appears as the third of the ten plays grouped as 'Histories'.

It isn't, however, exactly clear what was understood by the generic label – or even if it is a generic label. Though the use of the word '*History*' on the 1598 quarto title-page seems to be a very early example of the term used as a generic designation, two earlier examples necessarily raise doubts about what was intended. The title-page of the manifestly unhistorical *Taming of a Shrew* in 1594 refers to that play as *A Pleasant Conceited History*, and in 1578 the title-page of the two parts of George Whetstone's *Promos and Cassandra* calls it *The Right Excellent and Famous History*, though Whetstone in his dedication more conventionally refers to his own plays as 'two Comedies'. Even *The Merchant of Venice* was first published as *The Most Excellent History*. 'History', in these cases, seems to mean no more than 'story' (Thomas Elyot's Latin–English dictionary of 1538 gives 'story' as the definition of *historia*; and 'story' is of course merely an aphetic form of 'history').

'History' on the quarto title-page of *1 Henry IV* cannot, then, be confidently understood as a specific generic assertion, but the category of 'Histories' in the 1623 Folio is clearly making a generic claim. Ten plays are isolated from the Comedies and Tragedies and given their own parallel generic location and identity within the volume. The ten history plays are not, of course, the only plays on historical subjects that Shakespeare wrote, but what gives the Folio category coherence is a common origin in post-Conquest English history. Coleridge said that 'in order that a drama be properly historical, it is necessary that it should be the history of the people to whom it is addressed' (Coleridge, 219), and indeed the Folio grouping reflects a similar understanding of the particular relationship that such plays can establish with their audience. But, if this is indeed the generic principle at work, the conception may belong more to John Heminge and Henry Condell's editorial labours in organizing the Folio than to Shakespeare's own generic conceptualization. There is no compelling evidence that he thought of his English history plays as generically distinct from the other plays whose source material was historical, like *Macbeth* or *Coriolanus*.

Yet, whether or not Shakespeare had a specific idea of what a history play should be, clearly his dramatic imagination was sharply drawn to English historical subjects. As Shakespeare wrote for his acting companies, history plays became an important part of the ever-increasing repertory of the professional theatres. By the time of the publication of the Folio in 1623, each of the twenty-four monarchs from William the Conqueror to Elizabeth had been represented on stage, and at least one play on English history had been published in twenty-five of the previous thirty years, evidence that history was recognized, if not as an identifiable dramatic genre, at the very least as a valuable repository of plots for the burgeoning theatre industry. No fewer than twenty contemporary playwrights wrote or collaborated on plays on English history, but none composed as many as Shakespeare's ten. *King John* and *Henry VIII* define the chronological limits of Shakespeare's wide dramatic focus, which ranges over 250 years of English history: *King John* opens soon after the King was crowned, an event that took place in 1199; *Henry VIII* ends with the birth of Elizabeth, which occurred in 1544, and looks forward to the reign of King James. The eight other English history plays, often considered as two coherent and related 'tetralogies', cover the tumultuous period between 1397 and 1485. *Richard II*, *Henry IV, Part One* and *Part Two*, and *Henry V*, plus the three *Henry VI* plays and *Richard III*, traverse England's medieval history from the last years of the reign of Richard II to the end of the Wars of the Roses and Henry Richmond's crowning as Henry VII, the first of the Tudor monarchs.

Many, of course, have viewed these eight plays *in toto* as an extended dramatic version of what has been called the 'Tudor Myth'. This is a providential view of England's history that finds the archetypal pattern of innocence, fall and redemption in the turbulent historical period that ended with the coming of the Tudors to power. The Wars of the Roses are seen as a punishment visited by God upon England for Henry IV's unnatural deposition of Richard II, and Richard III as the scourge by which God's anger is expressed and finally exhausted, as England is restored to spiritual and political health.

It was E. M. W. Tillyard who gave this version of English history prominence in *Shakespeare's History Plays* (esp. 234–44), and, if one must grant that the Tudor Myth is in truth the product more of Tillyard's synthesizing historical imagination than of the Elizabethans', one can indeed find the broad outlines of Tillyard's model among Shakespeare's contemporaries. In the preface to *The Civil Wars*, for example, Samuel Daniel writes of 'the deformities of Ciuile Dissension . . . which folowed (as in a circle) vpon that breach of the due course of Succession, by the Vsurpation of Hen. 4; and thereby to make the blessings of Peace, and the happinesse of an established Gouernment (in a direct line) the better to appeare'. The fall from the innocence of an unbroken line of legitimate rule becomes a kind of fortunate fall that makes possible, in Daniel's words, 'the glorious Vnion of Hen. 7: from whence is descended our present Happinesse' (*Civil Wars*, 67).

But to see Shakespeare's eight plays on England's medieval history as a secular cycle of retribution and renewal with England's tribulations ending in Tudor glory is to allow the schema to overwhelm and oversimplify what the individual plays achieve. First of all, there is no evidence that before the middle of the nineteenth century the plays were ever performed sequentially to allow this structure to be visible on stage (see pp. 92–3). A stronger argument, however, against this understanding of the histories is posed by the order of their composition. The two so-called 'tetralogies' (the four-play sequences *1, 2* and *3 Henry VI* and *Richard III*; and *Richard II*, *1* and *2 Henry IV*, and *Henry V* ) do trace the history of England from 1397 to 1485, from the deposition of Richard II to the beginning of the Tudor monarchy after the death of Richard III, which seems to mark the end of God's anger and a new time of grace. But the two halves of this history were not written in the order in which the events unfolded. The four plays written first – the three *Henry VI* plays and *Richard III* – treat the latter part of the history, the period of the Wars of the Roses, the supposed result of the sinful deposition; and only after writing these did Shakespeare turn to the events of 1397–1422 that were its putative cause. Most likely, if Shakespeare had conceived of this history from the first as one extended historical sequence demonstrating God's providential plan for England, he would have written them in the order of the historical events; but, in any case, what is certain is that the plays reached the stage in an order that would have made it difficult for any early theatre-goer to see the putative pattern unfold.[1]

No less disruptive of the assumption that the eight plays are an extended cycle of providential history is that the plays themselves resist, or at least complicate, any suggestion that England's fifteenth century demonstrates the providential romance pattern that Daniel and others found in it. Occasionally characters do invoke the deposition of Richard II as the unnatural origin of England's troubles and see in human events the evidence of God's purposive will. The iterated language of providentialism in these plays cannot be completely ignored or dismissed as irrelevant, as it often is by those who would explain Shakespeare's intentions in the histories in terms of exclusively political concerns. The providentialism serves, if only by its residual force, to indicate a potential context for these issues, to suggest, as so many in Shakespeare's audience would have, that history exists *sub specie aeternitatis*, under the eye of God. But this is not to say that Shakespeare uncritically accepts the providential assertions of his characters. Providentialism in the plays is usually more a rationalization of the past than an explanation for it, a system invoked less

---

1   Wagner's *Ring*, where the libretti were written in reverse sequence, or Proust's *A la recherche du temps perdu*, suggest that sequential composition is not inevitable.

to explain reality than to avoid it. Though characters give it voice, the plays as a whole offer something more complex than the ultimately comforting patterns of coherence and correspondence that some had sought in English history (Ornstein, 1–32; French).

Indeed the eight plays are each so different in their use and conception of history that on that ground alone it is impossible to see them as the individual tesserae of a single grand mosaic. No single model of history emerges from the plays. If they do not uniformly enact or affirm God's providential design, neither do they inevitably assert the truth of a Machiavellian *Realpolitik*: the pious Henry VI is destroyed by a Machiavellian monster, but that monster is in turn undone by what are seemingly the actions of a benign providence (Rackin, esp. 27–30). The plays explore different ways of understanding and ordering the past, and Shakespeare experiments with various formal strategies as he seeks to turn history into dramatic form: chronicle history, homiletic tragedy, saturnalian comedy, the prodigal son play, epic, and these often in improbable mixtures that bring incompatible versions of history into contact and conflict.

Yet, whatever their generic impulse, the plays' very relation to the historical past is problematic. The individual plays can hardly be taken as reliable accounts of the historical material they represent. The opposite has, however, often been asserted. In 1612, Thomas Heywood enthusiastically claimed that such plays 'instructed such as can[n]ot reade in the discouery of all our English Chronicles' (Heywood, *Apology*, sig. F3ʳ). Even in the nineteenth century, the Duke of Marlborough, as Coleridge relates, was 'not ashamed to confess that his principal acquaintance with English history was derived' from Shakespeare's plays (Coleridge, 223). No doubt he speaks for many more now (especially those not from the United Kingdom) whose acquaintance with England's medieval past comes via Shakespeare, but the plays do not attempt in any exacting way to recollect and rehearse that history. In every one of the historical plays, events are selected from the chronicle accounts, sometimes invented, and always shaped, so that what Sidney called the 'bare was' of history is dressed with dramatic purpose and power, or simply cast aside.

Nowhere is this more obvious than in *1 Henry IV*. The historical action is, of course, largely based upon the account of the reign which Shakespeare found in Holinshed's *Chronicles* (see Appendix 1, pp. 340–1). There Shakespeare found the details of the unsettled time of Henry IV, a reign whose precariousness was perhaps inevitable 'sith it was evident inough to the world that he had with wrong vsurped the crowne, and not onelie violentlie deposed king Richard, but also cruellie procured his death' (Holinshed, 3.522). But Shakespeare's play conspicuously compresses and selects events of the reign, ignoring the conspiracy of the Abbot of Westminster as well as the troubled relations with France, and making the revolt of the Percys and their defeat at Shrewsbury the play's central historical spine. Following Samuel Daniel, Shakespeare makes Hotspur the contemporary of Hal (in spite of being three years older than the King), and the young Prince emerges, against the evidence of the chronicle sources, as the hero of the decisive battle (when in fact it was the vigorous activity of his father that led to victory).

These are the sorts of telling reshapings that regularly mark the difference between history and historical drama, in addition to the encounters and speeches that have been invented for historical figures. Like John Marston, Shakespeare has obviously not attempted 'to relate anything as an historian but to inlarge everything as a Poet' (Marston, 2.5). Here Shakespeare's arrangement refocuses the story of the reign of Henry from the chronicles' emphasis upon the King's largely successful efforts to impose order and inspire confidence in his illegitimate rule into the story of the development of Hal from the notoriously prodigal prince to the chivalric hero who will become England's greatest hero-king. But what even more unmistakably demonstrates Shakespeare's limited commitment to historical fact is, of course, how much of the play is given over not to subtly restructured history but to conspicuously invented fiction.

Much of the play is dedicated to the non-historical comic scenes; indeed less of this play is dependent upon historical source material than any other of the histories. One measure of the play's attenuation of its relation to history is that six of the play's nineteen scenes are completely devoted to the comic action and Falstaff appears additionally in three of the thirteen 'historical' scenes. The scene divisions no doubt misrepresent the theatrical rhythms of the play (see p. 119), but a line count similarly reveals that over a third of the play's lines appear in the six exclusively comic scenes, and Falstaff's interactions in the others bring the total of 'comic' lines closer to one half of the play. (And as the comic scenes are virtually all in prose, allowing longer lines on the printed page than the verse of the historical scenes, even this measure may still underestimate the presence of comedy in the play.)

Critics, of course, have long registered the importance of the play's comedy, usually focusing on the character of Falstaff. Indeed, through the nineteenth century, criticism tended to focus on the fat knight to the exclusion of the rest of the play, attracted to his irrepressible vitality and largely unconcerned with how (or even if) the character fitted into the larger dramatic design. Even as they recognized his moral failings, critics inevitably succumbed to his inventiveness and charm. 'For the sake of his wit', wrote Corbyn Morris in 1744, 'you forgive his cowardice, or rather are fond of his cowardice for the occasions it gives to his wit' (Bevington, 3). Modern critics, no less sensitive to the appeal of the comic scenes, have, however, been less concerned with character than with dramatic structure, and for them the Falstaff scenes take importance precisely from their relation to the historical plot. They attempt to show the play's carefully crafted unity, usually by demonstrating how the comic action serves the main plot, functioning as a 'subplot' clarifying the serious concerns of historical action. Fredson Bowers, for example, speaks of 'the mimic world of the underplot' which he sees brought 'into the larger unity as a form of parody of the main plot' (Bowers, 'Theme', 53). The crowns stolen at Gad's Hill and then stolen in turn by some of the original conspirators from their successful partners must comically remind an audience of the stolen crown that Henry wears and which the Percys, who helped him to it, would now remove from his head.

If the early concern with Falstaff ignored dramatic structure, implicitly suggesting by the exclusivity of the focus that his outrageous character has somehow been able to break free of the structure of the play, this later desire to assert the play's formal coherence has inevitably depended upon some hierarchical arrangement, which, however much it works to clarify the meanings of the play's historical action, does so only by subordinating subplot to main plot, commoners to aristocrats, comedy to history. But the actual achievement of the play seems to me less neat and stable than this suggests – not therefore less good or less interesting but less willing to organize its disparate voices into hierarchies than such demonstrations of the terms of its putative unity would allow. The very idea of a comic subplot imposes on the play the very hierarchy of privilege and power that exists in the state upon the play. But the play does not so readily depreciate its comedy. Though Thomas Fuller in 1662 objected to the fact that Shakespeare makes Falstaff merely 'the property of pleasure' for Hal 'to abuse' (Fuller, *Worthies*, 408), and Hal himself admits to using his tavern companions as a political strategy (1.2.185–207), the play itself does not subjugate the fat knight to the Prince's desires or designs. Falstaff's exuberance and excess refuse to be so comfortably subordinated to the Prince's desires and designs. Falstaff's resistance registers materially on the title-page of the early quartos where 'The humorous conceits of Sir John Falstaff' appear with 'the battell at Shrewsburie' as the most notable aspects of the play, and, even more disruptively, the play itself was performed at Whitehall by the King's men on 'New-years night' of 1624–5 as *The First Part of Sir John Falstaff* (Herbert, 52).[1]

---

1 That this was not an entirely anomalous practice is revealed by a notation on a scrap of paper in the Revels Office that has been dated to around 1619: 'nd [sic] part of Falstaff'; see Bentley, 2.1.

If this titular inversion of the traditional relationship of history and comedy no doubt overestimates the importance of Falstaff to the play, it does reveal the inadequacy of the familiar demonstrations of the play's unity (e.g. Brooks & Heilman). The comic plot does more than merely parody the historical action. At very least it gives voice to what is silent elsewhere. To say this is not merely to say that the comic plot includes social elements absent from the so-called 'main plot' or, more pointedly, that the comic plot speaks the reality of class differentiation and domination that the aristocratic, historical plot ignores or idealizes (though no doubt Hal's arrogant joking at the expense of Francis in 2.4 does do this). It is, rather, to say something even more radical: that the very existence of the comic plot serves to raise questions about the nature of history. Comedy here isn't subordinated to history, nor does it compete with history. Rather, comedy is revealed to be part of the very same fabric, exposing the exclusions and biases in our usual definitions of history. The social and generic richness that marks *1 Henry IV* reveals and disrupts the social hierarchies that conventional histories silently assume and reproduce. In *1 Henry IV*, however, history is displayed as something other than aristocratic history – something more expansive, if also more unstable, than the history of what Renaissance historians characteristically called 'matters of state'.

Comedy and history here intermingle, each qualifying the claims of the other but simultaneously endowing it with consequence. John Florio, in his *Second Fruits* (1591), saw this as the very essence of the professional English theatre, where plays were 'neither right comedies, nor right tragedies', but 'representations of histories, without any decorum' (Florio, *Second*, sig. D4ʳ). Florio, of course, is echoing Sidney, who had grumbled that the native drama contained 'neither right tragedies, nor right comedies, mingling kings and clowns, not because the matter so carrieth it, but thrust in the clown by the head and shoulders to play a part in majestical matters with neither decency nor discretion, so as neither the admiration and commiseration, nor the

right sportfulness, is by their mongrel tragi-comedy achieved'
(Sidney, *Prose*, 114). Words like 'mongrel', 'mingle-mangle' and
'gallimaufry' appear again and again to describe, or at least to
protest against, these increasingly common miscegenated forms.
In 1597, probably the year *1 Henry IV* was first performed, Joseph
Hall complained about what he termed the 'goodly *hoch-poch*' that
results 'when vile *Russetings* [i.e. rustics or clowns] / Are match't
with monarchs, & with mighty kings' (Hall, 5). But if matching or
mingling clowns and kings has resulted in something generically
uncertain and ideologically unsettling it has, at least in *1 Henry
IV*, unquestionably resulted in a remarkable play.

## *1 HENRY IV*: ONE PART OR ONE PLAY?

Thinking about the play's genre inevitably raises the question of
its relation to the other plays treating historically contiguous
events. Even if *1 Henry IV* is not part of a grand cycle of eight
plays, or of a smaller tetralogy, or even of a trilogy of Hal/Henry
V plays, its usual title seemingly demands at the very least that we
do see it as part of a two-play sequence. Indeed, in the last forty
years or so, it has been increasingly common for acting companies
to play the two parts of *Henry IV* together (see pp. 93–8), usually
alternating on successive nights but sometimes performed
together on the same day; and once the two plays are thought of
in tandem, whether by a director, an actor, a playgoer or a reader,
the earlier play inevitably looks different than if it were viewed as
an independent entity. Seen in the harsher light of the second
play, the brilliance of the first may seem tawdry; certainly the
social and political satisfactions of its ending seem more fragile
than they do when the play is viewed on its own. There is, however, no evidence that the plays were ever played together in
Shakespeare's time, and certainly the first part was regularly read
on its own. It is necessary, therefore, to assess the relation of the
two plays if we are to understand the achievement of *1 Henry IV*.

All modern editions acknowledge in their various and inter-
changeable titles that the play is the first of two plays that
Shakespeare wrote on the reign of Henry IV: *1 Henry IV*, *The
First Part of King Henry the Fourth*, or, as this edition is titled,
*King Henry the Fourth, Part One*. The earliest printed editions of
the play, however, simply called it *The History of Henrie the Fourth*.
Even after *Part Two* was published in 1600 as *THE Second part of
Henrie the fourth*, editions of the first play still used its original
title.[1] Only in 1623, when the play was published as one of the ten
histories appearing among the thirty-six plays of the Shakespeare
First Folio, was it titled *The First Part of King Henry the Fourth*;
but when the play was next published by itself, in 1639, it again
appeared merely as *The Historie of Henry the Fourth*, with no mention of it being the first of two plays.

There is, however, one early reference to the play as 'the firste
part'. In the Stationers' Register for 25 June 1603, Matthew Law
entered five books, the rights to which he received from Andrew
Wise, including '3 enterludes or playes':

> The ffirst is of *Richard the.* 3
> The second of *Richard the.* 2
> The Third of *Henry the.* 4 *the firste part.*      all kinges
> (Arber, 3.329)

But what this suggests is not that the two plays were seen as two
parts of a single artistic conception but exactly the reverse: that
the plays were understood to be independent and self-sufficient.
Law has acquired only *1 Henry IV*, obviously assuming it would
sell on its own. *2 Henry IV* was already in print, hence the need to
specify which play Law is entering. Wise himself had published *2
Henry IV* in 1600, with William Aspley; and Law, then, might

1   Malone thought the play was first distinguished as *Part One* in the Stationers'
Register, where on 9 January 1598/9 John Wolfe entered *A Book called the First Part
of the Life and Reign of K. Henry the Fourth*. This, however, is not the entry for
Shakespeare's play, as Malone assumed, but rather for Sir John Hayward's history of
the reign, the book for which he was tried and imprisoned for treason. See Malone,
in Steevens[2], 1.300.

have acquired both *1* and *2 Henry IV* together. But he did not take over title to *Part Two*. Perhaps Aspley was unwilling to sell his share when Wise's other titles were acquired by Law, but, as no further edition of *2 Henry IV* was apparently ever published, it is at least as likely that Law simply didn't want the less popular play. Law was a shrewd businessman. *Richard II*, *Richard III* and *1 Henry IV* would all prove bestsellers, each appearing in six or more editions before 1640.

But, if *1 Henry IV* can obviously stand on its own, it is still undeniably the first of the two plays on events of the reign of King Henry IV, and scholars have understandably debated the plays' relationship. Are they each autonomous structures, independently conceived, or are they two halves of a single unit? Was the second play imagined only in response to the successes of the first, or from the beginning was Shakespeare's plan to write two plays on the history of the reign? Is *King Henry the Fourth, Part One* a self-contained entity, or is its 'action', as E. M. W. Tillyard argued, 'patently incomplete', demanding the second part to finish the story and imagined from the first with *Part Two* in mind (Tillyard, 264). Harold Jenkins gave a name to the controversy: *The Structural Problem in Shakespeare's 'Henry the Fourth'*.[1]

A number of critics have argued for seeing the two plays as a single, unified sequence stretching over ten acts. As early as 1765, Samuel Johnson asserted that the two plays must be seen 'to be so connected that the second is merely a sequel to the first; to be two only because they are too long for one' (Johnson, 4.235). In 1779, Capell insisted that both 'plays appear to have been plan'd [*sic*] at the same time, and with great judgment' (Capell, *Notes*, 164). In the twentieth century, J. Dover Wilson similarly argued that *2 Henry IV* 'is a continuation' of the first play, 'which is no less incomplete without it than Part II is itself unintelligible without Part I'. For Wilson the two plays constitute 'a single structure'

---

1   This was Jenkins's inaugural lecture at Westfield College, delivered 19 May 1955 and published the following year by Methuen.

(Wilson, 4). Sherman Hawkins also argues that the two plays depict a unified action, and that Shakespeare 'set out to construct a double play enacting his hero's education in valor and justice' (Hawkins, 301). A. R. Humphreys, the previous Arden editor of *1 Henry IV*, concluded that 'Shakespeare seemingly intended two plays from the outset, or very near it' (*2 Henry IV*, Ard², xxviii), and that commitment virtually dictated that Humphreys take on the editing of *Part Two* as well.

Other critics have vigorously argued the reverse: that each of the plays is coherent and complete in itself, the second undertaken only after the success of *1 Henry IV*. In 1746, John Upton was the first critic to feel any need to insist that 'the plays are independent of each other', and argued energetically that calling them '*first and second parts*, is as injurious to the author-character of Shakespeare as it would be to Sophocles, to call his two plays on Oedipus, *first and second parts of King Oedipus*' (Upton, 58). In the early twentieth century, Tucker Brooke confidently restated that opinion, asserting that *2 Henry IV* was 'an unpremeditated addition, occasioned by the enormous effectiveness of the by-figure of Falstaff', an opinion echoed by M. A. Shaaber, who concluded that the 'immoderate popularity of *1 Henry IV*' forced Shakespeare to write an 'unpremeditated sequel' (Tucker Brooke, 333; Shaaber, 'Unity', 221).

Harold Jenkins sought a middle position, holding that Shakespeare began *Henry IV* thinking of it as one play, but that some time before he completed it he realized he could not fit in the death of the King and the ascension of Hal to the throne, and so he 'improvised', as Jenkins says, an ending in which the battle at Shrewsbury becomes 'a grand finale in its own right' (Jenkins, 21–2). For Jenkins, then, *Henry IV* is 'both one play and two . . . The two parts are complementary, they are also independent and even incompatible' (26). But, if the formulation offers something to everyone, the very fact that the 'structural problem' can only be solved by a paradox suggests its own limitations; and, perhaps more tellingly, the argument assumes more independence of playwriting from play performance than is likely to have been the case. It is unlikely that a play, especially one written by an important member of the company, would be written before the company had seen an outline or a plot from which they could at least estimate casting requirements and any other costs production would entail.

Those who hold that the plays trace a single action make much of the fact that *1 Henry IV* ends with the triumphant battle at Shrewsbury and not Hal's accession as King; those that hold the plays are independent make much of the fact that *2 Henry IV* seemingly forgets the reconciliation of father and son and Hal's emergence as a 'true prince' on the battlefield there. The second objection seems to me the more telling, for it suggests that the plays are not related as a continuous sequence. Even the first play's various anticipations of a future do not prove that the two plays were conceived of together. The King's final speech, looking toward 'such another day' (5.5.42), is a mark of the open-endedness of Shakespeare's history plays themselves (Kastan, *Shapes*, 37–55) rather than necessarily an anticipation of a sequel and seems, like a number of these forward-looking comments, anticipatory, as Paul Yachnin says, only when it is 'in fact fulfilled by a sequel' (Yachnin, 166). Most scholars now believe that the second play was, indeed, begun only after the first achieved its success. The driving logic of *1 Henry IV* – the story of Hal's emergence as a worthy heir – is fulfilled by the ending of the play. If Shakespeare had a sequel in mind as he wrote it, it seems likely it was, as M. A. Shaaber suggests, 'a sequel approximately like the play we know as *Henry V* ' (Shaaber, 'Unity', 221). The death of Henry IV and the rejection of Falstaff could have begun that play as easily as ended a second part of *Henry IV*.

But for whatever reason Shakespeare obviously did write that second part, and, once it was written, *Henry IV* became a two-part play, like *1* and *2 Tamburlaine*. Indeed Marlowe's *Tamburlaine* plays provide an instructive parallel. The prologue to *Tamburlaine, Part Two* admits that 'The generall welcomes Tamburlaine receiu'd, /

When he arriued last vpon our stage, / Hath made our poet pen his second part'; and the two *Tamburlaine* plays were entered together in the Stationers' Register on 14 August 1590 (and a single fee paid) and printed together when they were published that year, again in 1593, and a further time in 1597, both times with the comic scenes '(purposelie) omitted and left out' (sig. A2ʳ). Only in 1605 was *1 Tamburlaine* published alone, and *2 Tamburlaine* was published by itself the following year. *1 Henry IV* received 'generall welcomes' no less enthusiastic than *1 Tamburlaine*, and *2 Henry IV* was written, I suspect, with the same motive as Marlowe's sequel. But, unlike Marlowe's plays, no known early edition publishes the two *Henry IV* plays together, although a catalogue of the books belonging to the second Viscount Conway dated 1640 and now in Armagh Public Library does list 'Henry 4, the first and second parte, 1619'; it is unclear, however, whether this is actually a now unknown edition of the two plays or a nonce collection of the two, as seems most likely since the copyrights of each play belonged to a different publisher (*TLS*, 5 April 2002, 17–18). And, while there are references to the two *Tamburlaine* plays being performed on successive days by the Admiral's men, no early record survives of commercial performance of the two *Henry IV* plays in that manner.

The evidence suggests, then, that *1 Henry IV* should be thought of as imaginatively prior to and independent of *2 Henry IV*. Nonetheless, if *2 Henry IV* was not in mind as Shakespeare wrote *Part One*, it is certain that *1 Henry IV* was in mind as he wrote *Part Two*. It is, then, not surprising to find the two plays related, not only in terms of their shared subject matter but even in terms of their structure. This is not the place to take up *2 Henry IV* at any length; still, the second play seems to me less a continuation than a commentary. *Part Two* does not so much bring the events of *Part One* to conclusion as reimagine the actions of the first play in a more sombre key. Events of *Part One* find their disheartening echo in *Part Two*: the military victory at Shrewsbury, for example, replaced by the cynical policy of John of Lancaster at Gaultree

Forest. The plays together form a 'diptych', as G. K. Hunter has said, 'in which the repetition of shape and design focuses attention on what is common in the two parts' (G. K. Hunter, 237; Dean, 426–30), but the achieved comparison perhaps works not as mere contrast but as pointed critique. The second play revisits and revises the first, exposing the conclusion of *1 Henry IV* as history gilded in the happiest terms Shakespeare was able to imagine.

## UNDERSTANDING POLITICS IN THE PLAY

Seen on its own, however, as it usually has been on stage, in the classroom or in the study, *1 Henry IV* seems neither sentimental nor unrealistic. Hal emerges as a hero at Shrewsbury, having successfully synthesized the forms of public behaviour that Hotspur and the King have differently modelled. He takes from Hotspur his bravery and chivalric magnanimity without the damaging irresponsibility that accompanies it in the rebel, and from his father the pragmatism and responsibility of public office without the despiriting cynicism of the King. Nonetheless, even Hal's clear emergence as a worthy heir does not offer a perfect solution to the political problem the play poses of how to establish and maintain effective rule.

Indeed that difficulty is what drives the plot. The play begins with Henry IV understandably 'shaken' and 'wan with care' (1.1.1). He rules over a nation whose borders are insecure and whose integrity is under attack from within. The same northern nobles that had helped Henry to the throne are now joined by their traditional Scottish enemies in opposing the King in the north; in the west there is a threat from Wales, made more ominous by the fact that the daughter of the Welsh leader has now married a captive Englishman, Edmund Mortimer, who arguably has a better claim to the throne than Henry's own (see commentary on List of Roles and Fig. 3). And Henry's eldest son, instead of serving as a source of comfort for his beleaguered father, serves only to depress him further with the 'riot and dishonour' (1.1.84) that stain the young Prince's reputation.

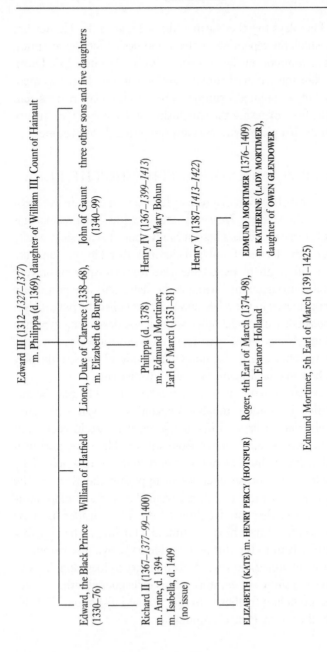

Edward III (*1312–1327–1377*)
m. Philippa (d. 1369), daughter of William III, Count of Hainault

Edward, the Black Prince (1330–76) — William of Hatfield — Lionel, Duke of Clarence (1338–68), m. Elizabeth de Burgh — John of Gaunt (1340–99) — three other sons and five daughters

Richard II (*1367–1377–99–1400*) m. Anne, d. 1394 m. Isabella, d. 1409 (no issue)

Philippa (d. 1378) m. Edmund Mortimer, Earl of March (1351–81)

Henry IV (*1367–1399–1413*) m. Mary Bohun

Roger, 4th Earl of March (1374–98), m. Eleanor Holland

Henry V (*1387–1413–1422*)

ELIZABETH (KATE) m. HENRY PERCY (HOTSPUR)

Edmund Mortimer, 5th Earl of March (1391–1425)

EDMUND MORTIMER (1376–1409) m. KATHERINE (LADY MORTIMER), daughter of OWEN GLENDOWER

2  Genealogical table: the descendants of Edward III (Names of those in the play are in bold small capitals. Italicised dates indicate reigns).

The real source of instability, however, rests in the manner in which Henry has become king. Henry, of course, was crowned not as a son lineally succeeding his father but as a rival noble having dispossessed a lawful monarch. The play is haunted by recollections of the usurpation of Richard II. The Percys, who had sided with Henry against Richard and are certain that they 'Did give him that same royalty he wears' (4.3.55), now nervously consider their success: 'The King will always think him in our debt, / And think we think ourselves unsatisfied, / Till he hath found a time to pay us home' (1.3.281–3). Feeling both unappreciated and vulnerable under the new regime, the Percys have come to regret their role in setting 'the crown / Upon the head of this forgetful man' (1.3.159–60). The one-time rebels become fierce legitimists, rallying behind the claim of Mortimer to the throne (see 1.3.144–6) and reminding Henry of his vow at Doncaster that he returned from his exile 'but to be Duke of Lancaster' (4.3.61).

But, if Henry is less beholden to the Percys than they would wish, he is never 'forgetful' of his passage to the throne; indeed that is the problem. He knows well how he came to wear the crown. Even when Henry explains to his son how he skilfully won the support of the English populace, he unconsciously reveals the uncomfortable truth of his actions: 'I stole all courtesy from heaven / And dressed myself in such humility / That I did pluck allegiance from men's hearts, / Loud shouts and salutations from their mouths, / Even in the presence of the crowned King' (3.2.50–4). The verbs – 'stole', 'dressed', 'did pluck' – reveal the illegitimacy of his present rule, and the adjective 'crowned', which he wishes to undermine the authority of the noun it precedes (establishing Richard merely as a *de facto* King), in fact reminds us of Richard's *de jure* right (see Fig. 2).

In such a world, authority can be little more than the name which power gives itself. Henry's presence on the throne must trouble the familiar notions that kings rule by divine sanction and that political disobedience is as much blasphemy as it is treason. In successfully deposing Richard, Henry exposes the insubstantiality

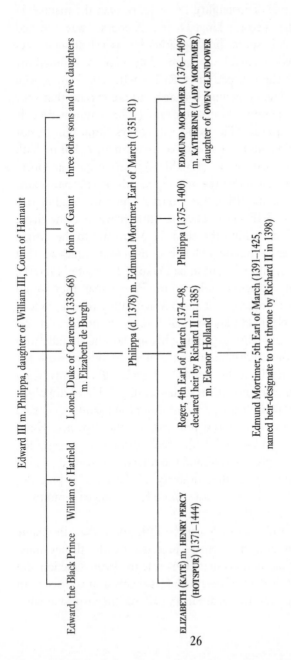

Edward III m. Philippa, daughter of William III, Count of Hainault

Edward, the Black Prince — William of Hatfield — Lionel, Duke of Clarence (1338–68) m. Elizabeth de Burgh — John of Gaunt — three other sons and five daughters

Philippa (d. 1378) m. Edmund Mortimer, Earl of March (1351–81)

Roger, 4th Earl of March (1374–98, declared heir by Richard II in 1385) m. Eleanor Holland — Philippa (1375–1400) — EDMUND MORTIMER (1376–1409) m. KATHERINE (LADY MORTIMER), daughter of OWEN GLENDOWER

ELIZABETH (KATE) m. HENRY PERCY (HOTSPUR) (1371–1444)

Edmund Mortimer, 5th Earl of March (1391–1425, named heir-designate to the throne by Richard II in 1398)

3 Genealogical table: the house of Mortimer (Names of those in the play are in bold capitals.)

of the traditional assertions of sacred majesty, and he now has no meaningful access to the powerful rhetoric of legitimacy that had surrounded the throne. At best such assertions sound tendentious in Henry's mouth. 'Thus ever did rebellion find rebuke' (5.5.1), the victorious King chides Worcester at the play's end, asserting the inevitability of the triumph of legitimate rule; but clearly the precept did not apply to Henry's own rebellion against the lawful Richard. To the degree his claim is true, then, it is only in the sense suggested by John Harington's shrewd epigrammatic observation: 'Treason doth never prosper: what's the reason? / For if it prosper, none dare call it treason' (Harington, sig. K4$^v$). Similarly, a rebellion that does not find 'rebuke' is rarely called a rebellion; with Henry on the throne, few would dare so name his passage to it.

Nonetheless, though Henry's rebellion did prosper, its success alone can neither legitimize the crown nor unify the country. If Henry is indeed, as Blount says, 'anointed majesty' (4.3.40), a king lawfully confirmed and celebrated by the rituals of state (see Fig. 4), his rule can never have the legitimacy of a king lineally succeeding to his throne. Henry thus begins the play looking towards an action that would both heal the torn nation and supply the moral authority his reign lacks. The national integrity rent in civil war would be reformed in common religious purpose. Instead of the 'intestine shock / And furious close of civil butchery' (1.1.12–13) that England has experienced, Henry looks to a purgative and unifying crusade in which English fighting men will 'in mutual well-beseeming ranks / March all one way' (14–15). The proposed crusade to Jerusalem 'To chase these pagans in those holy fields' (24) is, thus, an act of policy every bit as much as the act of penance King Henry had proposed at the end of *Richard II* for his role in the death of Richard (*R2* 5.5.49–50).

And as policy it is good: an attractive fantasy of unity and a plausible strategy for achieving it. But too soon it disappears as an option. As the news of Humbleton reaches the court, the King quickly admits that 'the tidings of this broil / Brake off our business for the Holy Land' (1.1.47–8). 'This broil' sounds heavily here; its unhappy

The right noble Prince Henry the 4.ᵗʰ King of England and
Fraunce: Lord of Ireland. &c. Who died at the age of 46
yeares. in Anno. 1413. after he had raigned 13 yeares.
6 moneths. and 4 dayes. and lieth buried at Canterbury.
Are to be sold by Comp: Holland over against the Exchange.

4   Henry IV, in Henry Holland, *Baziliologia*, 1618

echo of his earlier words mocks Henry's desire for 'new broils / To be commenced in strands afar remote' (3–4). The reality of his divided kingdom overwhelms his hopes of a unified nation; his 'holy purpose to Jerusalem' will indeed be delayed 'awhile' (101–2). Henry already knows of Hotspur's refusal to turn over prisoners that he believes are rightfully his, and his treatment of Worcester in 1.3 reveals how clearly the King recognizes 'Danger and disobedience' (1.3.16) in the attitude of the Percys. The royal 'we' that Henry publicly uses cannot truthfully speak the mutuality of King and country that it is designed to articulate; and, face to face with the refractory northerners, he tellingly begins in the first person: 'My blood hath been too cold and temperate, / Unapt to stir at these indignities, / And you have found me, for accordingly / You tread upon my patience; but be sure / I will from henceforth rather be myself' (1–5). To be himself is to be the King in all his regal majesty, but to be the King in this delegitimized world is to be dependent upon a coercive power that can be displayed rather than upon an authority willingly ceded by loyal subjects. For Henry to be king he must show himself 'Mighty and to be feared' (6), because he knows that he cannot depend upon his subjects' instinctive gift of obedience.

The rebels, if that is the proper term for those who oppose a successful usurper and claim to support the lawfully named heir, are clearly uncomfortable in the new political world they have helped to bring about. Richard is now 'that sweet lovely rose' (1.3.174) and King Henry merely 'this thorn, this canker, Bolingbroke' (175). New circumstances force the revision of old history. Their own role in putting Henry on the throne seems to Hotspur now dishonourable. It remains a source of 'shame', he tells his father and his uncle, 'That men of your nobility and power / Did gage them both in an unjust behalf' (171–2); and it is a shame doubled in that now they 'are fooled, discarded and shook off / By him for whom these shames ye underwent' (177–8). Their opposition to Henry is thus the means by which they may 'redeem' their 'banished honours' and 'restore' themselves 'Into the good thoughts of the world again' (179–81).

For Worcester and Northumberland revisionism is a pragmatic necessity. Well they understand that Henry will never trust them, having so effectively demonstrated their ability to overturn a seated king, and they know their safety now depends upon this king's overthrow. Knowing that Hotspur's chivalric commitments might well demand his allegiance to the King, Worcester provides Hotspur with a justification for the rebellion in his disingenuous question about Mortimer: 'was not he proclaimed / By Richard, that dead is, the next of blood?' (1.3.144–5). And Hotspur immediately seizes on it, finding in Mortimer's claim to the throne an ethical basis to animate his own resentment of the King. When Blount comes to the rebels assembled near Shrewsbury 'with gracious offers from the King' (4.3.30), Hotspur spurns them, rehearsing the history of his family's role in helping him to the 'royalty he wears' (55), insisting that Henry 'deposed the King' and 'Soon after . . . deprived him of his life' (90–1), and finally asserting provocatively (if more provocation were needed) that Mortimer would be Henry's king 'if every owner were well placed' (94).

It is little wonder Blount mutters: 'Tut, I came not to hear this' (4.3.89), but Hotspur's anger will not be quieted. He justifies the rebels' course on the grounds of Henry's actions, which drove them 'to seek out / This head of safety' (102–3), and he even risks the prediction that Henry's compromised title is 'Too indirect for long continuance' (105). If Worcester's initial invocation of Mortimer's claim seems too self-interested to provide a genuine challenge to Henry's legitimacy, Hotspur's passionate *de jure* arguments do raise troubling doubts about Henry's right to rule. Yet significantly Hotspur raises these only to Blount. It is the next morning when Worcester presents Henry with the rebels' grievances, and revealingly he says nothing about Mortimer's superior claim. The resentments that he does speak of are the familiar ones of Henry's forgetfulness of their role in placing him on the throne (5.1.30–71).

The question of Henry's legitimacy is not in fact what motivates the rebellion. For Worcester and Northumberland resistance to the crown is justified pragmatically, based on their realistic evaluation of their vulnerability in the new political order they have ushered in. Their ally, Glendower, never clearly states his reasons for joining with them, and he was fighting against the King before Mortimer married his daughter. 'Three times hath Henry Bolingbroke made head / Against my power', he reminds Hotspur, and each time he 'sent him / Bootless home and weather-beaten back' (3.1.62–5). If his alliance with the Percy family will no doubt advance his son-in-law's claim, Glendower never admits it as a motive. In the proleptic division of the land, Glendower is given all of 'Wales beyond the Severn shore, / And all the fertile land within that bound' (74–5), and presumably his participation is part of his ongoing fight against English attacks on Welsh national integrity. Hotspur alone uses the argument of monarchical right to motivate his participation. The leaders of the rebellion themselves prove no more unified than the country Henry rules over. Not just the thieves at Gad's Hill are unable to be true to one another. The rebels have differing commitments and values, ironically demonstrated both in the embarrassing division of the nation played out upon the map in 3.1 and in the fact that they are unable all to come together to fight at Shrewsbury. If Hotspur indeed is able to unsettle the ease with which an audience accepts Henry's *de facto* rule, the rebels themselves provide no attractive alternative to it.

In *2 Henry IV*, Henry will, of course, admit the 'by-paths and indirect crooked ways' by which he became king (4.5.184–5), but even in *Part One* he is no less clear-sighted about his oblique route to the throne. In 3.2, he rebukes Hal for his 'inordinate and low desires', worrying that the Prince has put his authority at risk. Henry is not worried about the state of Hal's soul but about Hal as the soul of the state. For the King, the issues are political, not moral; what is at stake is the production of power. 'Had I so lavish of my presence been,' he lectures his prodigal son, 'So common-hackneyed in the eyes of men, / So stale and cheap to vulgar company, / Opinion, that did help me to the crown, / Had still kept loyal to possession' (39–43). Henry admits that he made his way to power through calculated manipulations of public opinion, turning his aristocratic aloofness into a political asset: 'By being seldom seen, I could not stir / But, like a comet, I was wondered at' (46–7).

The King understands this new political world where power is unnervingly dependent upon popular support rather than reassuringly derived from divine sanction, but he fears his son does not know this truth. He worries that the Prince has alienated the very opinion upon which effective rule depends, derogating his authority by his tavern carousing: 'thou hast lost thy princely privilege / With vile participation' (3.2.86–7). Hal seems to his father too much like Richard, who lost authority as he 'Grew a companion to the common streets . . . Afford[ing] no extraordinary gaze, / Such as is bent on sun-like majesty / When it shines seldom in admiring eyes' (68–80). The King fears that Hal in his carousing has become similarly familiar, a 'common sight' (88). The irony, of course, is that Hal knows, well before his father's lesson in public relations, precisely what he plays for and how to play. If his father is willing to share his understanding of the necessity to be 'wondered at' in this new world of *Realpolitik*, the Prince has already revealed his own uncanny knowledge of the same fact. In his soliloquy at the end of 1.2, he declares his distance from his tavern friends by admitting, in the exact idiom of his father, that he indulges himself in the tavern precisely so that when he takes on his princely role 'he may be more *wondered at*' (191; my emphasis). His 'loose behaviour' (198) is a tactic, opposite to but designed for the same purpose as his father's calculated reserve, to 'attract more eyes' (204) when he is ready to assume responsibility. Hotspur may well be the child of Henry's desire (as he admits in 1.1.86–8), but clearly Hal is the child of his loins.

Both father and son understand that kingship does not magically reside in the person of the king but in the political relations that bind, even create, king and subject. Neither ever confuses the charismatic claims of kingship with the political relations they would accomplish. Both Henry and Hal understand that kingship is a role that can – indeed that must – be acted. Each reveals his awareness that legitimacy is something that must be forged no less by kings in Westminster than by Falstaff in the tavern. In dispossessing Richard, Henry, no less than the disguised Blount on the battlefield, has only a 'borrowed title' (5.3.23), but he must manipulate the verbal and visual symbols of power as if they were rightfully his own. And Hal will indeed prove a worthy inheritor, not merely on the battlefield at Shrewsbury but in the political intelligence that shows him very much his father's son.

## UNDERSTANDING THE POLITICS OF THE PLAY

How might an Elizabethan audience understand this portrayal of the problems of establishing rule in the political world delegitimized by Henry's usurpation? Perhaps the very ambiguity of the word 'understand' might help us answer the question or at least complicate any of our answers. Literally, the understanders in the amphitheatres of Elizabethan and Jacobean London were those who, as the Swiss visitor Thomas Platter recounted in 1599, paid 'one English penny' to *stand under* the raised platform of the stage, rather than, for an additional fee, to sit above the stage in the galleries (Platter, 166).

Though little is known about the identities of those who assembled in the playhouse yard, the differential price structure suggests that these understanders were largely apprentices and tradesmen. In 1613, Antimo Galli gleefully reported the hostile reception of the Venetian ambassador, Foscarini, who, to save money at the Curtain, chose to stand 'down below among the gang of porters and carters' (Orrell, 171). If this doesn't describe the actual social make-up of the groundlings, it does testify to an actual social prejudice as to how they were perceived. And this class marking of the playhouse yard no doubt contributed to the stereotype that these understanders were the least capable of actually understanding the play they witnessed. They were generalized by Ben Jonson in *The Case is Altered* as a 'rude barbarous crue, a people that haue no braines, and yet grounded iudgements; these will hisse anything that mounts aboue their grounded capacities' (2.7.69–72; Jonson, 3.137). These were the 'vnderstanding Gentlemen o' the ground' at the Hope, whose critical judgement Jonson derides in the Induction to *Bartholomew Fair* (Jonson, 6.14), and the 'Grave understanders' of the Globe, as James Shirley contemptuously terms them, who only 'delight' in 'Bawd'ry', 'Ballads' and 'Target fighting.' (Shirley, sig. D4ᵛ-5ʳ). These understanders were the notorious groundlings that Hamlet says are 'capable of nothing but inexplicable dumb shows and noise' (*Hamlet*, 3.2.10).

It should be said, however, that the contempt for the groundlings that Shirley, Jonson and Shakespeare's Hamlet express does not necessarily articulate the reality of the taste or capacities of those that paid their penny. Not enough is known about the social composition and behaviour of the actual audience that filled the yard of the public playhouses to speak confidently about its make-up, and the playwrights' contempt for these understanders is obviously itself not disinterested. It is far more likely to be a rationalization of a play's failure than an accurate anatomy of its audience, like William Fennor's praise of the 'wits of gentry' that 'did applaud' his play and his excoriation of 'the fooles in th'yard', the 'understanding grounded men' that 'wanting wit (like fooles to iudge) contemn'd it . . . like hissing snakes adiudging it to die' (Fennor, sig. B2ᵛ).

For much the same reason, an anxiety about reception, the drama's understanders, in its intellectual sense, were easily imagined as the very opposite of the physical understanders in the yard. These understanders became precisely that 'fit audience . . . though few' much valued by playwrights, who inevitably felt no less anxious than civic authorities in the face of the diverse public that attended the commercial theatres. In the 1616 folio, Jonson addresses his preface to the *Alchemist* 'to the reader', but, recognizing what Shakespeare's first editors, Heminge and Condell,

called 'the great Variety of Readers', a variety that increasingly
with the spread of literacy reflected a similar range of interests
and abilities as in the heterogeneous playhouse audiences, he
begins aggressively: 'If thou beest more, thou art an
Vnderstander, and then I trust thee' (Jonson, 5.291). But this
'understander' was clearly not the rude and unruly 'understander'
of the playhouse. The understander whom Jonson trusts is a
sophisticated interpreter, much like himself, who recognizes the
'boisterous' and the 'robust' as meretricious and appreciates an art
that is 'polish'd' and 'compos'd'.

Neither of the two meanings of 'understander' can, then, be
confidently taken to define any actual theatre-goer, except in the
most literal physical sense, but the ambiguity does, however, effectively crystallize the various class interests and antagonisms that
Shakespeare's *Henry IV* plays articulate, as well as the ongoing
critical debate about their politics. We can understand the plays'
politics in two senses, from above, so to speak, or from below, be an
understander like Jonson's fit reader, who values the polished and
composed over the boisterous and robust, or be an understander,
like those that filled the playhouse yard, characteristically demanding something more immediately engaging, energetic and various.

From above, the play indeed seems to be the play that E. M. W.
Tillyard saw in the 1940s and that Stephen Greenblatt would see
a half-century later, a play that is purposefully structured, its
disparate elements unified by effectively subordinating comedy to
history, demotic energy to aristocratic control, copiousness to
coherence, or, in the play's well-known names for these dualities,
subordinating Falstaff to Hal (Tillyard, 264–304; Greenblatt,
21–65). From this perspective it is a play about the authorization
of power and the assumption of rule, a prodigal son play as Hal
redeems the time, abandoning the tavern world for the battlefield,
repudiating revel for responsibility, his rejection of Falstaff the
superfluous proof of the new king's fitness to rule.

What differentiates Greenblatt's argument from Tillyard's, however, is that Greenblatt is more suspicious than Tillyard of the

claim of power, though finally no less subject to its charisma, eager to analyse instead of merely reproduce it. Both Tillyard and Greenblatt see the play as the story of Hal's progress to the throne; but, where Tillyard sees the *Henry IV* plays as Shakespeare's attempt to define 'the perfect English King' (Tillyard, 299), Greenblatt sees them not as Shakespeare's idealizing effort to present royalty but as Shakespeare's presentation of Hal's successful manipulations to achieve it. The plays 'confirm the Machiavellian hypothesis that princely power originates in force and fraud even as they draw their audience toward an acceptance of that power' (Greenblatt, 65). Hal's time in the tavern world, then, which has seemed to many a potential subversion of his political destiny and desire, is revealed instead to be the very product of that desire, a carefully calculated intemperance designed to make his 'reformation' the more extraordinary and compelling.

The conversion of the wild prince, a central strand in the chroniclers' account of Henry V,[1] is in Shakespeare's play not a miraculous transformation but a self-conscious strategy. Hal announces from the first that he will only 'awhile uphold / The unyoked humour' of Falstaff's 'idleness' (1.2.185–6). To the degree, then, that Falstaff can be seen as a threat to order, he is a threat that is purposefully conjured to necessitate the exercise of rule, an example of authority's 'constant production of its own radical subversion and the powerful containment of that subversion', in Greenblatt's notorious formulation (Greenblatt, 41). Hal's insistent role-playing, which finds its characteristic form in the tavern, is, then, not to be understood as an evasion or an undoing of power but, rather, as 'one of power's essential modes' (Greenblatt, 46); and the comic plot itself offers, therefore, not a generously humane alternative to the power-seeking impulses of aristocratic history but, rather, their very justification, an antimasque, to

---

1  John Stow, for example, tells the story of Hal's robbery of 'his owne receyvers' (a historical version of the play's Gad's Hill robbery), but concludes that 'after the decease of his father, was never any youth, or wildnes, that might have place in him, but all his actes were sodainely chaunged into gravitie and discreation' (Stow, 547)

5  First page (sig. D5ᵛ) of *1 Henry IV* from the 1623 Folio annotated by a Scottish reader around 1630 (MR 774)

switch dramatic metaphors, that is routed in the face of, and to prove, legitimate authority.

But this is, as the masquing analogy suggests, a royal, or royalist, fantasy of power. It is to accept Hal's version of events as identical with Shakespeare's or, rather, it is uncannily to behave as Hal, to presume that the tavern world exists only for the production of aristocratic pleasure and value. Yet neither the history play nor history itself in fact gives much evidence that containment is ever as efficient or complete as this reading insists. If subversion were always produced by and for power, power would always remain unchallenged and intact; but Henry IV's very presence on the throne argues otherwise.

Nonetheless, differently understood (seen, we might say, from below) the play may have seemed exactly to reverse the authoritarian political valence that Greenblatt and Tillyard find. From the playhouse yard, role-playing may have appeared less productive of power than a challenge to it, and the comic plot may seem indeed to give compelling voice to what aristocratic history would repress. Hierarchy in this view gives way to variety, ceremony to festivity, containment to carnival. Falstaff rules. In the Beaumont and Fletcher folio of 1647, a commendatory poem uses as the very measure of theatrical popularity Falstaff's hold upon the spectators in the yard, offering to 'tell how long / Falstaffe from cracking Nuts hath kept the throng' (Beaumont & Fletcher, sig. f2ᵛ). Falstaff speaks to and for those understanders. His mimicry exposes the narrow self-interests of those in power and those who seek it. His improvisatory clowning challenges the illusionistic representation of history, directly engaging the spectators in the yard, even as the history insists upon their respectful distance.[1]

Though Falstaff is, of course, Sir John, an aristocrat, he continuously reinvents himself as an irrepressible everyman: 'sweet

1   It is Falstaff, of course, who improvises, not the actor playing him (for whom all has been carefully scripted); and indeed it may well have been Shakespeare's insistence that his clowns 'speak no more than is set down for them' (*Ham* 3.2.39) that eventually resulted in Will Kemp's departure from the acting company.

Jack Falstaff, kind Jack Falstaff, true Jack Falstaff, valiant Jack Falstaff', one with 'every man jack' (2.4.463–4). The ideals of his actual social class, as Freud recognized, 'rebound from so fat a stomach'.[1] He is in his massive corporeality Bakhtin's 'material bodily principle' writ large, an image of 'the people . . . constantly growing and renewed' (Bakhtin, 21–2). Falstaff's exuberance refuses to be dominated by any authority, resisting incorporation into or containment within the stabilizing hierarchies of the body politic or indeed of the well-made play.

Though literary history has again and again proved the futility of the effort, Hal attempts to fix Falstaff within the hierarchies of the orderly state. However much the Prince enjoys his slumming, it is clear that Hal would use the fat knight to construct his own political identity. Hal knows himself only a temporary inhabitant of the underworld of Eastcheap, and that only to make his inevitable assumption of responsibility and rule the more remarkable and desired. In the 'play extempore' of 2.4, Hal enacts his accession, deposing Falstaff from the 'joint-stool' that was his throne. Hal is immediately capable of the language and gestures of sovereignty, and, more, immediately aware that rule depends upon the exclusion of those anarchic energies that resist the strategies of incorporation, of subjectification, that are necessary to construct and maintain the unitary state as well as the well-made play. 'Banish plump Jack and banish all the world,' Falstaff warns; and the future is clearly if chillingly etched in Hal's 'I do; I will' (2.4.468).

What can we, then, say about the politics of *1 Henry IV*? How are we to understand it? Does it produce and promote order and authority? Or does it challenge and contest these? Are we witnessing, in the language of political theory, subversion or containment, or, in the play's terms, are Falstaff's unruly energies eventually triumphant or finally banished? The answer is, I take it, it depends. It depends, one might say, on where we stand. This is

---

1 'Jokes and the relation to the unconscious', in *The Standard Edition of the Complete Psychological Works of Sigmund Freud*, ed. James Strachey (1960), 231.

not the same, I would insist, as saying either that the play does both (i.e. the new critical reading that would find political positions held in sympathetic balance but that in fact becomes a refusal of politics, which demands choice, not merely sympathy), or that it does neither (i.e. a post-structural reading that would hold the politics of the drama to be indeterminate and the play merely what might be called an empty site open to endless signification).

Literary texts do have politics, but they are never invariable and essential (Limon, 14–19). They are provoked rather than produced, never monopolized either by authorial intentions or by textual effects. Playing spaces, actors, individual spectators, history itself inevitably compete with the written text for control of its meanings. Plays mean differently at different times, in different places, their politics always newly created within different conditions of representation, for different readers and spectators. Only in the specific historical circumstances of performance can the political meanings and effects of theatrical representation be determined – and even then, unless the audience is impossibly uniform, those meanings and effects are necessarily multiple and often contradictory. The now familiar binary of subversion and containment (like the no less familiar binary of popular and elite) is clearly too idealizing of structure, too dismissive of this density of actual history to serve as anything more than an analytic frame. To recover the actual politics of *1 Henry IV*, we must ask about whose politics and when, try, that is, to comprehend – or at least to imagine – how specific readers and spectators at specific historical moments could and did understand the plays.

This might well mean that the play performed at the Theatre or later at the Globe was available for a wider range of responses than the play performed at court or at an ambassador's house. An elite audience might well respond differently from a popular one (though even those audiences cannot be homogenized in attitude, values or even critical competence). The play's concerns with unifying a nation torn by civil war must have resonated with many who feared what would follow Elizabeth's death, and the King's strategies to produce the desired unity must have seemed familiar in the England of Elizabeth, which similarly sought an imaginary unity in the nation – and indeed in the monarch. The familiar political metaphors of the well-ordered body or the patriarchal family articulated the would-be absolutist state's desire for an integral wholeness, and the various historical and mythological typologies of Elizabeth did the same. Elizabeth, the Tudor Rose, representing the unification of aristocratic factions, was also Deborah, uniting secular and divine authority, and Diana, expressing in her chastity the inviolability of the Queen's body and the body politic.

The various tropes of the integrity of the Virgin Queen and of the nation for which she stood were no doubt demanded by a nation that in sixty years had experienced five forms of official religion and endured four changes of monarch, the reign of each marked by a significant rebellion (and the northern rebellion in 1569–70 led by the very Percy family that some 170 years earlier had opposed Henry IV; see Campbell, 229–35); a nation that now faced further instability as Elizabeth ruled without an heir, over a country whose traditional social and economic structures were under pressure from the stresses and possibilities of a nascent capitalism and a country increasingly aware of itself at war abroad, both in the Low Countries and in Ireland, where English rule was fast collapsing. In the prologue of Dekker's *Old Fortunatus* (1599), an old man speaks of Eliza: 'Some call her Pandora, some Gloriana, some Cynthia, some Belphoebe, some Astrea, all by several names to express several loves. Yet all those names make but one celestial body, as all those loves meet to create but one soul' (Dekker, 1.113). And Nicholas Breton, in his 'Character of Queen Elizabeth', similarly, if more hysterically, finds a radical unity in the representations of the Queen:

was she not as she wrote herself *semper eadem* alwaies one?
zealous in one religion, believinge in one god, constant in
one truth, absolute vnder god in her self, one Queene,
and but one Queene; for in her dayes was no such queene;
one Phoenix for her spiritt, one Angell for her person,
and one Goddese for her wisdom; one alwayes in her
word, one alwayes of the word, and one alwaies, in one
word ELIZABETHA . . . one chosen by one god to be
then the one and onlie Queene of this one kingdome, of
one isle.

(Breton, 2.n.p.)

Not least of the inadequacies of this is that the 'one isle' inconve-
niently contained two kingdoms: England and Scotland, as well as
the conquered principality of Wales; but such fantasies of imperial
unity, however attractive, inevitably occlude the degree to which
their reality is constructed through acts of exclusion and homoge-
nization. In Elizabethan England this was achieved by ideological
configuration and political repression that either violently eliminated
marginal subgroups – vagabonds, gypsies, the Irish – from the articulation of the English nation or discursively arranged them into
stable and stabilizing hierarchies. In *1 Henry IV*, with the rebels
routed, Henry orders his forces to follow up their advantage and
extinguish the remaining pockets of resistance: 'Rebellion in this
land shall lose his sway / Meeting the check of such another day; /
And since this business so fair is done, / Let us not leave till all our
own be won' (5.5.41–4). 'Won' here might well be heard as 'one'.
These were not necessarily exact homophones in late sixteenth-
century London English, though they were moving in that direction. In *Richard II* 'one' and 'done' rhyme (1.1.182–3), and in *All's
Well* 'done' and 'won' rhyme (4.2.64–5). The potential homonyms,
'won' and 'one', would exactly enact the process of unification the
play imagines, verbally reconciling what can usually only be
coerced. 'Winning' is 'One-ing', one could say; but the process of
incorporation inevitably involves a more violent repression of

difference than can comfortably be admitted in a complex society; too often only what is 'won' is 'one'.

Falstaff, in a sense, is the play's mark of resistance to the total-izations of power, massive evidence of the heterogeneity that will not be made one. Revealingly when he imagines his life in the impending reign of Henry V, Falstaff invokes a familiar trope: 'Let us be Diana's foresters, gentlemen of the shade, minions of the moon; and let men say we be men of good government, being governed, as the sea is, by our noble and chaste mistress the moon' (1.2.24–8). This is the exact fantasy of social order in the England of Elizabeth, the Virgin Queen. She was Diana in one of the mythologies that surrounded her, and her loyal subjects would then be 'men of good government, being governed . . . by our noble and chaste mistress'. But for Falstaff this is not a submission to authority but an authorization of transgression; he serves not the monarch whose motto was '*semper eadem* alwaies one' but only the changeable moon, 'under whose countenance we steal'. And it is perhaps, then, not inconsequential that 'Diana' could sound dif-ferently, for it was not only a name for Elizabeth but also a mocking name used for the Irish leader Tyrone, as Thomas Lord Burgh revealed when he vowed to Cecil to "beat the Diana" in the proud traitor's fort' (*CSP Ireland*, 1596–7, 340).

How we understand the politics of the play depends, then, on how much we allow Falstaff to undermine the political drive to unity. Is he the vitalist truth-teller who exposes the life-denying lies of power? Or is he the disruptive force of misrule who threat-ens the hope for social order and coherence? Or reversed: is order a positive or a negative value in the play? Is it the achievement of social harmony or is it the result of repression and coercion? Or is it merely a necessary fact of human society, a compromise with our competing but incompatible desires for freedom and for safety?

## 'UNIMITATED, UNIMITABLE FALSTAFF'[1]

But this brings us directly to Falstaff, and the need to assess his character. And indeed, more than most literary creations, he seems to have a character rather than merely to be one. To many readers and playgoers, Falstaff appears, as he would insist, not as a 'counterfeit', but as 'the true and perfect image of life' (5.4.118). This impression finds perhaps its most extreme voice in Harold Bloom's recent insistence that 'Falstaff is a person, while Hal and Hotspur are fictions' (Bloom, 282). Certainly, it is true that Falstaff seems as if he would have to exist even if there were no plays to present him to an audience. He does appear to us a fully developed and autonomous creature, no mere function of the plays' plotting but a coherent and complex personality that erupts into the play world, and a personality that it cannot easily contain. If, then, he is the most compelling of Shakespeare's characters, it is because he is the character who seems least like a character.

It is of course an illusion, perhaps the very best of Shakespeare's artistic tricks upon us. Falstaff seems to be the authentic source of the language he speaks, but he is, of course, merely an effect of it. He is no more real than any other character in the plays, no more independent of Shakespeare's playmaking genius. No character is real in any play, any more than is the London, or the Venice, or the Elsinore that they apparently inhabit, or the crown that is placed on the head of an actor to mark him as king. All that exists in these play worlds is mere illusion; all is an invention of the playwright's and the players' art. All is made in word and gesture; all serves the playwright's complex design.

It is this knowledge that has made character itself an unfashionable category of Shakespeare criticism. Modern Shakespeareans tend to resist its analysis, usually claiming that focus on character leads us to think of the fictional beings as actual people existing outside of the plays in which they appear. Literary characters, of

1   The phrase is Samuel Johnson's from his endnote to *2 Henry IV* (Johnson, 4.235).

course, do not have lives outside the boundaries of the represented action; nonetheless, the characters that we most value are so compelling, so plausible as human beings, that we imagine that they must have an existence as complete and coherent as our own.

Falstaff is certainly one of these. He is unquestionably the most outrageously animated of Shakespeare's inventions. His vitality seems so essentially his own, rather than a function of the plot, that it inevitably seems actually a threat to the dramatic design rather than an organic part of it. We recognize the characteristic habits of mind; we wait for them and are delighted when we see them. He is indeed, as Dryden saw, 'old, fat, cowardly, drunken, amorous, vain, and lying', but his individuality – and the source of his irresistible grip on our affection – lies elsewhere: 'That wherein he is singular is his wit . . . [h]is quick evasions, when you expect him surprised' (Dryden, 17.59–60).

We may not hold him in esteem, but we always enjoy him. The moralist's response always seems thin. 'The Poet was not so partial as to let his Humour compound for his Lewdness,' said Jeremy Collier (Vickers, 2.88), but just 'so partial' Shakespeare seems to be. Falstaff enacts the escape from responsibility that none of us has quite managed but also that none of us has not more than once wished was possible. His outlandish exaggerations when he is baited into relating the events at Gad's Hill are not lies anyone is expected to believe but evidence of the improvisatory genius that has long delighted his friends (and longer has delighted audiences), as his tale of the 'two rogues in buckram suits' (2.4.185–6) who attacked him turn quickly to four, then seven, then nine and finally eleven. No one has ever more literally recounted an event. But if this is a lie, it is, as Hal says, one so 'palpable' (219) that it cannot possibly be intended to mislead anyone about the truth.

This is precisely why Falstaff, though a palpable liar, delights; he does not intend to deceive – though he is happy enough to profit when he does. And when his actual behaviour at Gad's Hill, his running in fear from the Prince and Poins and roaring like a bullcalf, is exposed, the real issue, even for the Prince, is not his cowardice (that can hardly be in doubt[1]) but again his wit. 'What trick, what device, what starting-hole canst thou now find out to hide thee from this open and apparent shame' (2.4.255–7), says Hal, confident that this time he has him cold. But Falstaff escapes one more time in his audacious insistence that he knew him all along: 'By the Lord, I knew ye as well as he that made ye.'

> was it for me to kill the heir apparent? Should I turn on the true prince? Why, thou knowest I am as valiant as Hercules, but beware instinct. The lion will not touch the true prince; instinct is a great matter. I was now a coward on instinct.
>
> (2.4.260–4)

Indeed, the episode becomes, in the shameless lie, proof not only of Falstaff's instinctive virtue but even of the Prince's legitimacy: 'I shall think the better of myself, and thee, during my life – I for a valiant lion and thou for a true prince' (265–6).

Falstaff cannot be humiliated; he is resilient, always able to recover his poise and regain his comic mastery of the situation. What actually happens doesn't matter; all that matters is how he wittily construes it. Even his own manifest sinfulness becomes the sign of his radical innocence, as he appropriates 1 Corinthians, 7.20: 'let every man abide in the same vocation wherin he was called', which served as the proof text for many Puritans for the confidence that what truly counts in this world is only one's faith in God: ''tis my vocation,' he jokes after Hal reminds him of his wicked behaviour: ''tis no sin for a man to labour in his vocation' (1.2.100–1).

His wit does make him often lovable and always enjoyable – but rarely admirable. At one's most rigorous, one might say with Dr Johnson 'that no man is more dangerous than he that with a will

---

1    Maurice Morgann, however, famously argued the opposite. In his *Essay on the Dramatic Character of Sir John Falsaff* (1777), he devotes himself 'to the vindication of Falstaff's courage' (Morgann, 144).

to corrupt hath the power to please' (Johnson, 4.355). Yet, however clearly we may register Falstaff's moral failings, we inevitably respond to his humour. 'The comic subsumes the moral,' as Ronald Knowles says (Knowles, 17), and perhaps it is because, in comparison with Hal's wit, Falstaff's is the more humane. It does not display the careless insensitivity of Hal's, who isn't ever really funny and enjoys a bit too much the discomfort of others. Think of the difference between Falstaff's jokes and Hal's jest with Francis in the tavern 'to drive away the time till Falstaff come' (2.4.27). Hal gets Poins to stand in some other room and call the Drawer, while the Prince holds him there with his questions. All Francis can do is call out to Poins, 'Anon, anon, sir.' Finally both Hal and Poins call him and, as the stage direction says, '*The Drawer stands amazed, not knowing which way to go.*' Even Poins doesn't quite get the joke. 'What cunning match have you made with this jest of the drawer? Come, what's the issue?' he asks hopefully. And Hal replies only that Francis has 'fewer words than a parrot' and that his whole life is running up and down stairs and totalling up bills (2.4.87–98). If 'the issue' for Hal is that Francis is exposed as unimaginative and inarticulate, 'the issue' for the audience is that Hal is exposed as a snob and a bully, as condescending and cruel. What he accomplishes with his jest is merely to discomfort a waiter in a tavern, paralysing him in confusion and fear.

Falstaff is in a sense the opposite of both Hal and Francis. Unlike Hal's, his jokes are not generally at the expense of others but at his own expense; and, unlike Francis, he is a man of a great many words, and one who will not be fixed by the Prince's designs. His wit is the articulate exercise of a remarkable verbal inventiveness and social intelligence. He may be a liar, a glutton, a coward, a thief, but he is neither a hypocrite nor a fool. He sees the world clearly and his place within it. He laughs at himself as easily as he laughs at those around him. But his wit exists for its own sake, or rather for *his* own sake. If he sees, with growing anxiety, that his access to the court depends upon his ability 'to keep Prince Harry in continual laughter' (*2H4*, 5.1.79), he never doubts that he can.

And if Hal will all too soon cease to find the fat knight funny, banishing him in fact in *2 Henry IV* as he does in play in 2.4 of *Part One*, Falstaff almost never fails to delight an audience. Little of his appeal, however, can be explained through the literary genetics that have been traced. Various literary types have been recognized in his genealogy but none explains his function in the play. He is not Riot or Vanity in some morality play about good government (Ainger, 1.119–55); he is not the *miles gloriosus*, the braggart warrior, in some satire of contemporary social vices (Stoll, 65–108); he is not the Lord of Misrule in some festive comedy (Barber, 192–213); and he's not a court fool, a clown or a buffoon (Welsford, 51–2; Wiles, 116–35). Shakespeare's Falstaff has some relation to all his literary precursors; but his nature will not be found in or explained by any of them. What he is is unmistakably himself, not an imitation of something else. The effort to identify him with some literary or folk tradition emerges from the fact that he plays these roles, 'continually reinvent[ing] himself', as Hugh Grady says, 'through a lengthy series of dramatic improvisations' (Grady, 612). Ironically, by playing roles, he defines his own individuality, becoming something unique and seemingly alive, contained neither by literary tradition nor even comfortably by the plays themselves.

Indeed he is the character most easily imagined outside the plots that nominally contain him. And he has been so imagined: in the eighteenth century a play by William Kenrick, *Falstaff's Wedding* (1760), continues his story from where *2 Henry IV* leaves him; and more than two hundred years later Robert Nye would write a wonderful comic novel, *Falstaff* (1976). But it was apparently always thus. Shakespeare's first editor, Nicholas Rowe, in 1709 reported that Queen Elizabeth had been 'so well pleas'd with that admirable Character of Falstaff in the two Parts of Henry the Fourth, that she commanded him to continue it for one play more, and to shew him in love' (Rowe, 1.viii). It is probably one of those stories just a bit too good to be true, but if it is factual it offers regal confirmation of the point I am making. Plot has become subordinate to character. Falstaff insists that plot is a function of character, rather than, as criticism since Aristotle would have us expect, its source. But even if, as is likely, the story isn't true, if Elizabeth's supposed desire to see Falstaff in love was not in fact what inspired *The Merry Wives of Windsor*, the fact it is told at all also confirms the point, as it seeks some authority for Falstaff's uncanny ability to overwhelm the dramatic structures from which he took life.

No doubt Falstaff is the character easiest to imagine existing outside the plot of the play. But he is, as a result, also the one most difficult to imagine inside the plot of the play. Falstaff never quite fits into the restrictive frames of the history plays in which he appears. He is a conspicuously fictional character in a historical plot, an anarchic comic presence in a focused, political world. The stylistic mark of the difficulty of his incorporation is that he always speaks a supple, kinetic prose where the historical characters speak within the more rigid confines of verse. 'The better we come to know Falstaff', wrote W. H. Auden, 'the clearer it becomes that the world of historical reality which a Chronicle Play claims to imitate is not a world which he can inhabit' (Auden, *Dyer's*, 183). But of course he does – at least in the two *Henry IV* plays; there he indeed inhabits 'the world of historical reality' and inhabits it so fully that the genre of the history play has to broaden to contain him. The very understanding of what counts as history is swollen by his swollen presence. The history play, like history itself, can no longer merely be the story of more conventionally imagined great men and matters of state.

Falstaff is never merely the servant of the historical plot. He exists at its margins, observing, willing to take what it offers, but always as its critic, an unruly presence challenging the fundamental assumptions that motivate the political world. His mockery and parody lessen whatever hold it may have on us. To him, order is less important than freedom, patriotism is less valuable than fellowship, honour is less desirable than laughter. Pleasure not virtue inspires him; individual appetite not social good drives him on.

He is the very antithesis of civic responsibility. He is unimpressed with the claims of good government. Falstaff has no interest in public values; too often, he knows, they are mere cant, masking self-interests as public good. He has no commitment to the state, or to any other abstraction. The rationalizations, the lies, the hypocrisies and, worse, the stupidities of the historical world are relentlessly exposed by Falstaff's alert and irreverent wit. The rebellious Worcester's disingenuous protest that he had 'not sought the day of this dislike' elicits from King Henry a sputtering response: 'You have not sought it? How comes it, then?' And Falstaff, in the only moment in which he shares the stage with the King, responds forthwith to lay bare Worcester's cowardly lie: 'Rebellion lay in his way, and he found it' (5.1.26–8). Falstaff exposes the cynical self-interest of those who seek after power, and he does no less to the self-regarding folly of those who seek after honour. Hotspur's extravagant chivalric commitments are countered by Falstaff's devastating common sense:

Can honour set to a leg? No. Or an arm? No. Or take away the grief of a wound? No. Honour hath no skill in surgery, then? No. What is honour? A word. What is in that word "honour"? What is that honour? Air. A trim reckoning. Who hath it? He that died o'Wednesday. Doth he feel it? No. Doth he hear it? No. 'Tis insensible then? Yea, to the dead. But will it not live with the living? No. Why? Detraction will not suffer it. Therefore I'll none of it. Honour is a mere scutcheon. And so ends my catechism.
(5.1.131–40)

And later, coming upon the dead body of Sir Walter Blount, he concludes: 'There's honour for you' (5.3.32–3).

His critique is telling, but his rejection of public values is not without cost. If his anarchic laughter exposes the historical world's joyless purposefulness, his irresponsibility is a danger not merely to the pretensions of those in power but to the very lives of the innocents who always suffer through the dishonesty and cowardice of their leaders. 'Falstaff betrays and harms no one', claims Harold Bloom in his sentimental defence of the fat knight, 'and does not write with the lives of the other characters, as Iago always does' (Bloom, 288). But Falstaff cannot be let off quite so easily. He has, by his own admission, 'misused the King's press damnably' (4.2.12–13), taking bribes to allow all those with the means to pay to escape impressment and mustering only the 'poor and bare' (68). 'Food for powder, food for powder,' he jokes when Hal says that he 'did never see such pitiful rascals': 'They'll fill a pit as well as better' (63–6). And so they do. 'I have led my raga-muffins where they are peppered; there's not three of my hundred and fifty left alive, and they are for the town's end to beg during life' (5.3.35–8).

In the tavern, Falstaff is irresponsible and funny; on the battle-field his irresponsibility costs innocent men their lives. Neither sentimentalizing Falstaff nor moralizing about him will quite do. What one must say is that he is unquestionably unreliable and self-indulgent, but also that his behaviour marks a commitment to life (at least his own) over a set of thin abstractions that too often deny it. 'Give me life, which if I can save, so,' he says (5.3.60–1); and that is the essence of his philosophy. He wants to live, to enjoy, to indulge; he wanders over the battlefield with a bottle of sack instead of a pistol. If his are not the most noble of aspirations, they are unmistakably and understandably human. Always he is a survivor, suspicious of all values that might put that survival at risk and holding them up to the light of common sense, allowing us at least to see them for what they truly are.

## FALSTAFF AS OLDCASTLE/OLDCASTLE AS FALSTAFF: RADICAL PROTESTANTISM AND RABELAISIAN PLAY

However much Falstaff may have captivated audiences, it is clear that Shakespeare initially intended Hal's fat tavern companion to have another name – and a name which, even erased, continues to haunt the play.[1] As early as the 1630s, Richard James noted:

> in Shakespeares first shewe of Harrie ye fift, ye person with which he vndertook to playe a buffone was not Falstaffe, but Sr Jhon Oldcastle, and that offence beinge worthily taken by personages descended from his title, as peradventure by manie others allso whoe ought to haue him in honourable memorie, the poet was putt to make an ignorant shifte of abusing Sr Jhon Fastolphe, a man not inferior of Vertue though not so famous in pietie as the other, whoe gaue witnesse vnto the truth of our reformation with a constant and resolute martyrdom, vnto which he was pursued by the Priests, Bishops, Moncks, and Friers of those dayes.
>
> (Schoenbaum, 143)

Apparently objecting to the defamation of the well-known Lollard martyr, the fourth Lord Cobham (as Oldcastle became through his marriage to Joan Cobham in 1408), William Brooke, the tenth holder of the title,[2] seemingly compelled Shakespeare to alter the name of Sir John, acting either in his own right as Lord Chamberlain (as Brooke was from 8 August 1596 until his death on 5 March 1597) or through the intervention and agency of the Queen (as Rowe claims: 'some of the Family being then remaining, the Queen was pleas'd to command him [i.e. Shakespeare] to alter it' (Rowe, 1.ix).

Pale traces of the original name can perhaps still be seen in the modified text. Hal refers to Falstaff as 'my old lad of the castle' (1.2.40), the colloquial phrase for a roisterer seemingly taking its

---

1 For a fuller account of the implications of the name change, see Kastan *SAT*, 93–108. See also Taylor, 'Fortunes'; Taylor, 'Cobham'; Honigmann; Goldberg; Sams; Fiehler; Scoufos

2 Following the *DNB*, most commentators identify William Brooke and his son Henry as the seventh and eighth Lords Cobham, but see *Complete Peerage*, 3.341–51, where they are identified as the tenth and eleventh holders. See also the genealogical tables in McKeen, 2.700–2.

point from the name of its original referent; and a line in Act 2 – 'Away, good Ned. Falstaff sweats to death' (2.2.105)[1] – is metrically irregular with Falstaff's name but arguably not with the tri-syllabic 'Oldcastle' (and the image itself is grotesquely appropriate for a man who notoriously did virtually sweat to death, being hanged in chains and burned at St Giles Fields, the spectacular martyrdom grimly memorialized in one of the woodcuts in Foxe's *Acts and Monuments*; see Fig. 6). Also, in the quarto of *2 Henry IV*, a speech prefix at 1.2.114 has 'Old.' for 'Falstaff', a residual mark somewhat like phantom pain in an amputated limb;[2] and, of course, the Epilogue insists that 'Oldcastle died a martyr,

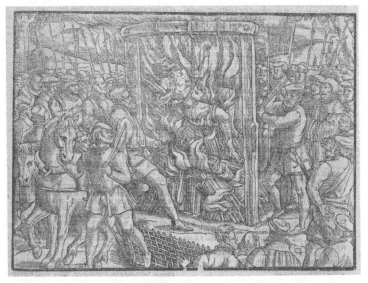

6  The martyrdom of Sir John Oldcastle, from Foxe, *Acts and Monuments*, 1583

1  Stanley Wells says that this is 'the only verse line in which [Falstaff's] name occurs' and notes that it 'is restored to a decasyllable if "Oldcastle" is substituted for "Falstaff" ' (Wells, 72). But it is worth observing that at least in the early editions this is not 'a verse line' at all. In all the early quartos, as well as in the Folio, the line appears in a prose passage. Pope was the first to reline the passage as verse; see Pendleton, 62–3.
2  The text's 'Old.' could, however, stand for 'Old man' ('I know thee not, old man') rather than 'Oldcastle'.

and this is not the man' (29–30), a disclaimer that is meaningful only if it might reasonably have been assumed on the contrary that indeed 'this' might well have been 'the man'.

It seems certain that Shakespeare, in *1 Henry IV*, originally called his fat knight 'Oldcastle' and under pressure changed it.[1] The printing of the quarto in 1598 was perhaps, as E. K. Chambers suggested, demanded from the company as proof of Shakespeare's willingness to respond to the concerns of the authorities (Chambers, *Stage*, 1.382). Oldcastle thus disappeared from the printed texts of the play, though it is less certain that he disappeared in performance. At least in private performances 'Oldcastle' seems to have survived, even as late as 1638 (see p. 80). Rowland White, for example, reports a performance by the Lord Chamberlain's company in March of 1600 for the Flemish ambassador, apparently at Lord Hunsdon's house, of a play referred to as *Sir John Old Castell*. Though some have thought this to be *The First Part of the True and Honorable History of the Life of Sir John Oldcastle* by Drayton, Hathaway, Munday and Wilson, it was almost certainly Shakespeare's *1 Henry IV* rather than the play belonging to the Admiral's men, which was unquestionably still in that company's possession (and so unavailable to the Lord Chamberlain's men) at least as late as September 1602, when Henslowe paid Dekker ten shillings 'for his adicions' (Henslowe, 216).

Yet, whatever play was performed for the ambassador, clearly the character we know as Falstaff was sometimes known as Oldcastle, which can only prove the longevity on stage of

---

1   The available evidence, however, does not allow us to say precisely why 'Oldcastle' disappeared from the text of *1 Henry IV*. An influential family seems unquestionably to have objected to the name 'Oldcastle', but it is less certain that the elimination of that name was a result of the operations of a process we can confidently and precisely identify as censorship. Certainly there is no record of such an action. We do not in fact know that the replacement of 'Oldcastle' with 'Falstaff' was an effect of direct governmental interference rather than an example of the inevitable compromises that authors make with and within the institutions of dramatic production. In the absence of documentation, we cannot tell whether we have a text marred by forces beyond the author's control or a text marked by the author's effort to function within the existing conditions in which plays were regularly written and performed.

Shakespeare's first intention. In Nathan Field's *Amends for Ladies*, published in 1618, Seldon asks, obviously referring to Falstaff's catechizing of honour in Act 5 of *1 Henry IV*: 'Did you never see / The Play, where the fat knight hight *Old-Castle*, / Did tell you truly what this honour was?' (sig. G1ʳ). Presumably Field, for one, did see that play with 'Falstaff's' catechism in Oldcastle's mouth, as seemingly did Jane Owen, who in 1634 similarly recalled 'Syr Iohn Oldcastle, being exprobated of his Cowardlynes' and responding: 'If through my persuyte of Honour, I shall fortune to loose an Arme, or a Leg in the wars, can Honour restore to me my lost Arme, or legge?' (Martin, 185–6).

What, then, are we to make of Oldcastle's tenacious presence in *1 Henry IV*? What are our obligations to the ghostly Oldcastle, who has not quite been exorcized? Gary Taylor, of course, has argued that at very least this should mean that editions of *1 Henry IV* should return 'Oldcastle' to the play, restoring 'an important dimension of the character as first and freely conceived' (*TxC*, 330).[1] And notoriously the complete Oxford text (Oxf) does just that, though even the individual Oxford *1 Henry IV*, edited by David Bevington (Oxf¹), does not follow the lead. Still, it is useful to be forced to think about the original act of naming. The critics who have commented on the 'Oldcastle' name have usually focused on the perceived slight to the honour of the Cobham title and speculated either that Shakespeare aggressively framed an insult to William Brooke (usually, it is argued, because of Brooke's putative hostility to the theatre[2]); or

---

1  John Jowett has argued, on somewhat similar grounds, that 'Peto' and 'Bardolph' were names 'introduced at the same time as Falstaff', and that their original names, Harvey and Russell (present in Q1 at 1.2.154), like Falstaff's, should be restored in modern editions (Jowett, 325–33).

2  J. Dover Wilson, for example, argues that Cobham was 'a man puritanically inclined and inimical to the theatre' (Wilson, 'Origin', 13). See also Chambers, *Stage*, 1.297. William Green, however, has demonstrated that during Cobham's term as Lord Chamberlain 'not one piece of legislation hostile to the theater was enacted' and, in fact, between 1592 and his death in 1597, Lord Cobham 'was absent from every meeting of the Council at which a restraining piece of theatrical legislation was passed' (Green, 113–14).

that Shakespeare actually intended no offence but chose his character's name unluckily, as Warburton argued in 1752: 'I believe
there was no malice in the matter. *Shakespear* wanted a droll name
to his character, and never considered whom it belonged to'
(Warburton, 4.103).

It seems, however, unlikely that Shakespeare set out to mock or
goad Lord Cobham, not least because, if indeed the play was written, as seems almost certain, in late 1596 or early 1597, Cobham,
who became Lord Chamberlain in August 1596, was a dangerous
man to offend; and no one has put forth any credible motive for
the pragmatic Shakespeare to engage in such uncharacteristically
imprudent behaviour (Fehrenbach, 87–101).[1] But Warburton's
formulation can't be quite right either: that Shakespeare '*never*
considered' (my emphasis) to whom the name 'Oldcastle'
belonged. If the play does not use the fat knight to travesty the
Elizabethan Lord Cobham, certainly it does use Sir John to travesty Cobham's medieval predecessor. Contemporaries seemed to
have no doubt that Shakespeare's character referred to the Lollard
knight. The authors of the 1599 *Sir John Oldcastle* consciously set
out to correct the historical record Shakespeare had distorted: 'It
is no pampered glutton we present, / Nor aged Councellour to
youthfull sinne, / But one whose vertue shone above the rest, / A
Valiant Martyr, and a vertuous Peere' (Prologue, 6–9; Corbin &
Sedge). Thomas Fuller similarly lamented the travestying of the
Lollard martyr by 'Stage poets', and was pleased that 'Sir John
Falstaff hath relieved the memory of Sir John Oldcastle, and of
late is substituted buffoon in his place' (Fuller, 4.168). George
Daniel, in 1649, was another who saw through Shakespeare's fic-
tion, like Fuller commending 'The Worthy S$^r$ whom Falstaffe's
ill-us'd Name / Personates on the Stage, lest Scandall might /
Creep backward & blott Martyr' (G. Daniel, 4.112).

1  Honigmann, however, argues that the play was indeed intended 'to annoy the
   Cobhams' and 'to amuse Essex' (Honigmann, 127–8), and suggests that the play 'was
   written – or at least begun' in the first half of 1596 'before Lord Cobham became
   Lord Chamberlain' (122).

If Shakespeare's fat knight, however named, is readily under-stood to 'personate' the historical Oldcastle and 'blott martyr', one might well ask what is at stake in his presentation as a 'buffoon'. Whatever Oldcastle was, he was hardly that.[1] Oldcastle had served the young Prince Henry in his Welsh command but had remained a relatively undistinguished Herefordshire knight until his marriage, his third, to Joan Cobham, the heiress of the estate of the third Baron Cobham. At last wiving wealthily, Oldcastle became an influential landowner with manors and considerable landhold-ings in five counties. He was assigned royal commissions and was called to sit in the House of Lords.

However, for all his new-found political respectability, Oldcastle remained theologically unsound. Clearly he held hetero-dox views. He was widely understood to be a protector of heretical preachers, and was himself in communication with Bohemian Hussites and possibly sent Wycliffite literature to Prague. Perhaps inspired by the decision of the council at Rome early in 1413 to condemn Wycliffe's work as heretical and certainly encouraged by the newly crowned Henry V's need for ecclesiastical support, the English church began vigorously to prosecute the Lollard hetero-doxy, and Oldcastle himself was tried before Archbishop Arundel in September of 1413 and declared a heretic. Oldcastle was, how-ever, given forty days to recant his heresy, no doubt because of his long friendship with the King, and during this period of confine-ment he succeeded in escaping from the Tower. Following his escape, a rebellion was raised in his name and an attack on the King was planned for Twelfth Night. The King learned of the uprising and surprised and scattered the insurgent troops mus-tered at Ficket Field. Oldcastle fled and remained at large for three years, hiding in the Welsh marches. On 1 December 1417 news of his capture reached London. Oldcastle was carried to the

1 The best account of Oldcastle's life is still that of W. T. Waugh (Waugh, 434–56, 637–58). See also the entry on Oldcastle in the *DNB* written by James Tait. The fol-lowing paragraphs are indebted to both, and also to Strohm, 132–48.

capital, brought before parliament, indicted and condemned. He was drawn through London to the newly erected gallows in St Giles Field. At least as legend has it, there Oldcastle promised that on the third day following his death he would rise again,[1] whereupon he was hanged in chains and burned, as Francis Thynne writes, 'for the doctrine of wiclyffe and for treasone (as that age supposed)' (McKeen, 1.22).

Although it took considerably longer than three days, Oldcastle was finally resurrected. As the English Reformation sought a history, Oldcastle was rehabilitated and restored to prominence by a Protestant martyrology that found in his life and death the pattern of virtuous opposition to a corrupt clergy that underpinned the godly nation itself. Most powerfully in the five Elizabethan editions of Foxe's *Acts and Monuments* (1563–96), Oldcastle emerged, as Foxe writes, as one 'so faythfull and obedient to God: so submiss[iv]e to his kyng: so sound in his doctrine: so constant in his cause: so afflicted for the trueth: so ready & prepared to death' that he may 'worthily be [ad]orned with the title of a martyr, whiche is in Greek as much as a witnes bearer' (Foxe, 569).

One might, then, easily echo the question raised in 1752: 'could *Shakespeare* make a pampered glutton, a debauched monster, of a noble personage, who stood foremost on the list of *English* reformers and Protestant martyrs, and that too at a time when reformation was the Queen's chief study?' And the author, identified only as P.T., concludes that Shakespeare could not: ''Tis absurd to suppose, 'tis impossible for any man to imagine' (P.T., 459–61), and he then undertakes to explain away the evidence that Falstaff ever was Oldcastle in Shakespeare's play. But since that evidence seems as incontrovertible as the evidence that Oldcastle, as P.T. says, 'stood foremost on the list of *English* reformers and Protestant martyrs', one must assume that Shakespeare

---

1 See *DNB*, 14.986. Stow, in his *Annals of England* (1592), reports that 'the last words that he spake, was to sir Thomas of Erpingham, adjuring him, that if he saw him rise from death to life again, the third day, he would procure that his sect might be in peace and quiet' (Stow, 572).

deliberately engaged in the very character assassination P.T. finds impossible to imagine.

So the question must be asked: why? Gary Taylor, committed to the original and the restored presence of Oldcastle in the play, has argued that it was precisely Oldcastle's notoriety as a proto-Protestant hero that demanded Shakespeare's travesty. (Taylor, 'Fortunes', 99). John Speed, in *The Theatre of the Empire of Great Britain* (1611), had objected to the presentation of Oldcastle as 'a Ruffian, a Robber, and a Rebell' by the Jesuit Robert Parsons (writing as N.D.), complaining that his evidence was 'taken from the Stage-plaiers' and railing against 'this Papist and his Poet, of like conscience for lies, the one euer faining, and the other euer falsifying the truth' (Speed, 637). Marshalling evidence that purports to establish Shakespeare's sympathy to Catholic positions if not Shakespeare's commitment to the Catholic faith itself, Taylor, like Speed, takes the caricature of Oldcastle to suggest at very least Shakespeare's 'willingness to exploit a point of view that many of his contemporaries would have regarded as "papist"'. Noting other dramatic facts that admit of such an interpretation, Taylor concludes: 'In such circumstances, the possibility that Shakespeare deliberately lampooned Oldcastle can hardly be denied' (Taylor, 'Fortunes', 99).

Certainly it can hardly be denied that Shakespeare has deliberately lampooned Oldcastle, but the 'circumstances' in which Shakespeare was writing and in which his play would be received are arguably more complex than Taylor allows. Whether or not Shakespeare was a Catholic or Catholic sympathizer,[1] Shakespeare's audience in 1596 or 1597 was far more likely to see the lampooning of Oldcastle as the mark of a Protestant bias rather than a papist one, providing evidence of the very fracture in the Protestant community that made the accommodation of the Lollard past so problematic. Lollardy increasingly had become

---

1  I remain unpersuaded that Shakespeare was a Catholic, though, for one of the more compelling examples of the many recent arguments for a 'Catholic Shakespeare', see Honigmann, *Lost*, 126.

identified not with the Protestant nation but with the more radical Puritans, the 'godly brotherhood', as some termed themselves, who had tried and failed to achieve a 'further reformation' of the Church of England. If in the first decades of Elizabeth's rule the Lollards were seen (with the encouragement of Foxe) as the precursors of the national church, in the last decades they were seen (with the encouragement of Bancroft and other voices of the Anglican polity) as the precursors of the nonconforming sectaries who threatened to undermine it. As Milton would later say to those orthodox churchmen who attacked the reformers, those who 'were call'd Lollards and Hussites' are 'now by you term'd Puritans, and Brownists' (Milton, 1.788).

Under the leadership of John Field (the father of Nathaniel Field, the author of *Amends for Ladies*), nonconforming Protestants had in the 1580s attempted the establishment of presbyterianism by parliamentary authority, but by the mid-1590s the government, led by Whitgift's rigorous promotion of uniformity and the Queen's continuing insistence 'upon the truth of the reformation which we have already' (Neale, 2.163), had succeeded in its campaign against the radicals (Collinson, 'Field', 335–70). Christopher Hatton's appointment as Lord Chancellor, as Thomas Digges remembered, marked a change of policy whereby not merely papists but 'puritans were trounced and traduced as troublers of the state' (quoted in Collinson, 388), and, by the early 1590s, forward Protestantism, conceived of by the government as a threat to the polity, was in retreat, at least as a political movement. The 'seditious sectaries', as the 1593 'Act to retain the Queen's subjects in obedience' (35 Eliz. c. 1, in Tanner, 197–200) termed the nonconformists, were driven underground or abroad; and advanced Protestantism, even as its evangelical impulse thrived, was, in its various sectarian forms, thoroughly 'discredited', as Claire Cross has written, 'as a viable alternative to the established Church in the eyes of most of the influential laity who still worked actively to advance a further reformation' (Cross, 152). Whatever Shakespeare's own religious leanings, then, certainly most members of his audience in 1596 would most likely have viewed the travesty of a Lollard martyr not as a crypto-Catholic gesture but an entirely orthodox commitment, designed to reflect upon the nonconformity that the Queen herself had termed 'prejudicial to the religion established, to her crown, to her government, and to her subjects' (quoted in Neale, 2.163).

It is in this context that a sometimes confusing aspect of Falstaff's characterization must be understood. One of Falstaff's characteristic speech patterns is his parody of the conventicle style of many of the reformers. It is his 'damnable iteration' (1.2.87) of scripture, rather than Hal's, that is most evident in the play; roughly half of the play's biblical citations issue from his mouth (Shaheen, 137). He speaks in the familiar godly idiom of 'vocation' and 'saint' (1.2.79–101). He wishes he were a 'weaver' so that he 'could sing psalms' (2.4.127), a well-recognized enthusiasm of the godly community. Scholars have long noted the presence of such stereotypically reformist markers, and argued that in these moments Falstaff parodies the 'scriptural style of the sanctimonious Puritan' (Hemingway, 37–8). Scholars see the contradiction between Falstaff's bacchanalian appetites and the Puritan rhetoric and conclude that his language must therefore be parodic.

But if Falstaff was himself initially Oldcastle, and at least to some readers and viewers still recognizable in his original form, the functioning of this parody becomes complex. Falstaff would become, then, both the proto-reformer and the mocker of reform. Perhaps it is better to see, as Kristin Poole has recently argued, that 'Falstaff does not, therefore, parody the self-styled saints in a determined, willfull way. Rather Falstaff – in and of himself – is a parodic representation of a "puritan"' (Poole, 37).

This perhaps seems an implausible assertion. Certainly Falstaff is not a type of the precise, dour, life-denying Protestant saint who in his virtue would have no more cakes and ale. But there was another caricature of the Puritan. In response to a series of polemical pamphlets attacking the national church from the 'Puritan' left, putatively by 'Martin Marprelate', the authorities produced pamphlets of their own, caricaturing their pseudonymous antagonist as a gluttonous and irresponsible Rabelaisian figure, a fitting image for the unnervingly proliferating voice of further reform that circulated (not least in alehouses) and one that Poole argues provides at least some of the genetic material of Shakespeare's Falstaff. If his original name gave more immediate purchase to the parody of religious nonconformity, even as Falstaff the fat knight embodies the dangerous, carnivalesque qualities that were attributed to Marprelate by his orthodox foes (Collinson, 391–6; McGinn, 85–8). But, more than merely taking on these characteristics, Falstaff uncannily recirculates them. If the historical Oldcastle must inevitably colour Shakespeare's Falstaff, giving particular meaning to his carnival energies, increasingly Falstaff came to colour Oldcastle: by the end of the sixteenth century the fifteenth-century martyr inevitably becomes 'fatte Sir John Oldcastle' (*Meeting*, sig. B4ᵛ), historical fact giving way to the compelling dramatic reality that had – more or less – preserved him on stage.[1]

## COUNTERFEITING AND KINGS, CREDIT AND CREDIBILITY: ECONOMIC LANGUAGE IN THE PLAY

Falstaff is certainly one locus of the play's insistent concern with counterfeiting, and not least as the character itself counterfeits his own historical forebear. Falstaff also, of course, counterfeits both the King and Hal in the improvisations in the tavern, and on the battlefield he counterfeits death to avoid it. There, however, he brilliantly rationalizes that 'to counterfeit dying when a man thereby liveth is to be no counterfeit' (5.4.116–17). But even his

---

1  Womersley points out that John Foxe in speaking about the calumnies that circulated about Oldcastle imagines that he could have been presented as 'some grandpaunch Epicure of this world', though Foxe admits this was not a strategy that was used (Wormersley, 3) and Womersley notes that this hint is not picked up by any later writer, unless by Shakespeare. Womersley, who is primarily interested in *Henry V*, is responding to Everett, for whom Falstaff's bulk is the mark of the resistent reality of his character.

appeal to 'life' as a source of authenticity is undone by his sense of himself as 'the true and perfect image of' it (118), and, no doubt, it will occur to some viewers or readers that the character of Falstaff is being counterfeited by an actor, even as that character is insisting that his own acting is no counterfeit.

But there are other counterfeiters in the play, not least in the play's recurring scenes of mimicry – Hal of both Francis and Hotspur, Hotspur of the popinjay, and, of course, Hal and Falstaff alternating in the roles of King and Prince. But counterfeiting is perhaps most obvious on the battlefield at Shrewsbury, where the rebels encounter multiple nobles 'Semblably furnished like the King himself' (5.3.21). Douglas's response to these various counterfeits is brutally to dispatch each in turn as he seeks to discover an authentic royalty: 'Now, by my sword, I will kill all his coats. / I'll murder all his wardrobe, piece by piece, / Until I meet the King' (26–8). But although he works his way through the King's 'wardrobe' with murderous efficiency, when at last he does 'meet the King', Douglas is unable to recognize the monarch. 'What art thou / That counterfeit'st the person of a king?' he wearily asks when he comes upon the King in the field; and Henry replies: 'The King himself, who, Douglas, grieves at heart / So many of his shadows thou hast met / And not the very King.' But Douglas has been misled before, and nothing in Henry's person leads Douglas to accept the King's assertion at face value. The Scot replies with understandable scepticism: 'I fear thou art another counterfeit' (5.4.26–34).

The language of difference here – 'shadows', 'counterfeit' – clearly implies an authentic regal presence against which these imperfect representations can be measured; however, on the battlefield at Shrewsbury the King cannot be distinguished from his shadows. Henry's majesty can be effectively mimed. In *The Merchant of Venice*, Portia confidently asserts that 'A substitute shines as brightly as a king / Until a king be by' (*MV* 5.1.94–5), but, when Douglas is face to face with Henry, the King's majesty shines no more brightly than any of the counterfeits Douglas has killed. Although Douglas admits to Henry that 'thou bearest thee like a king' (5.4.35), royal bearing proves no guarantee of royalty. But the implications of the episode are not merely that Henry unheroically adopts a strategy in the interests of his safety, prudently manipulating appearances to deceive the enemy. They are far more disturbing: that kingship itself is always and only a counterfeit, a role, an action that a man might play. Or, rather, that kingship lacks an authentic identity that can be counterfeited. Even Henry can bear himself only '*like* a king' (my emphasis). Falstaff's instruction to 'Never call a true piece of gold a counterfeit' (2.4.478–9) proves inapplicable as a political metaphor; in the political world of the play no 'true piece of gold' can be found and counterfeits therefore pass as current.

But the play's reiterated language of counterfeiting is not only metaphoric. Though indeed it helps structure the play's concern with political authority, it takes particular meaning in relation to the play's pervasive concern with economic issues and its constellation of economic language (Levine; Fischer; Lander). The only reference to actual economic conditions in Shakespeare's England may be in the Carrier's remark that Robin Ostler 'never joyed since the price of oats rose' (2.1.12–13), a register of the dearth and inflation that marked the late 1590s, but economic terms and concepts are everywhere. Falstaff points to the carbuncles on Bardoll's face as a potential source of payment for his own tavern debt: 'Let them coin his nose; let them coin his cheeks' (3.3.78). Hotspur, too, thinks of coins in his contemptuous dismissal of 'half-faced fellowship' (1.3.207). The image emerges, of course, from his unwillingness to share honour's 'dignities', but the language he finds for his contempt is numismatic – a reference to the profile portraits of monarchs that began to appear on coins, probably particularly the facing profiles of Mary and Philip on the shilling minted in 1554. The play refers explicitly to 'coin' and 'coinage': to 'angel', 'crowns', 'denier', 'marks', 'noble', 'penny', 'pounds', 'shillings', and 'sovereigns'. Indeed there are more numismatic references in *1 Henry IV* than in any other play by Shakespeare.

This reiterated language of coinage does more than merely provide texture for the economic concerns of the play. Coinage specifically focuses attention upon the relation of value and political authority that is so central in the play (Lander). Coins assume value in two different ways: either from the substantial value of the metal or from the nominal value of the currency. In 1626, Robert Cotton remarked these two distinct sources of valuation: 'One the Extrinsick quality, which is at the King's pleasure . . . to name; the other the Intrinsick quantity of pure Metall, which is in the *Merchant* to value' (McCulloch, 6). The economy of monarchical prerogative is contested by an economy of market value. The cost of the metal in the coin may counter the monarch's assertion of its worth.

From the very beginning of her reign, Elizabeth's economic policy was designed to realign the values of coin and metal after the debasement of the currency in her father's time – to ensure that the valuations of the monarch and the market were the same (Gould). At her death, she was almost as renowned for her commitment to the reform of the coinage as for her commitment to the reform of religion (the epitaph on her tomb listing it third among her accomplishments). The play, however, written near the end of her reign, registers the impossibility of achieving any exact correlation of metallic and nominal worth, and perhaps also the economic and political instability of which this is both symptom and symbol. Royal command and market value will always be at odds. Coins themselves are vulnerable to normal deterioration (wear) and purposeful degradation (clipping or counterfeiting), debasements of currency that force the two valuations apart. The cost of minting itself will always ensure that the metallic value of the coin is somewhat less than its face value. After Bardoll lets Falstaff know that his accumulated debt has now reached 'an angel', the fat knight jokes, 'An if it do, take it for thy labour; an if it make twenty, take them all. I'll answer the coinage' (4.2.7–8).

But Falstaff can no more 'answer' the coinage, that is, establish and secure its value, than can the King or the Prince.

Falstaff's characteristic scepticism makes him an unlikely source for a theory of stable monetary value. The man who knows that the wars have made 'land now as cheap as stinking mackerel' (2.4.350–1), must know that contingencies affect the value of currency too. An angel is worth not what Falstaff declares it is, or even the value established in law; it is worth what those who use the coin assume it is. In part this will be a function of the value of the precious metal of which it is minted, but to observe this is merely to displace the question of value from the coin to the metal, from the monarch to the market. Either way, the coin is worth what the community agrees upon as its value. Interestingly, when Vernon seeks a language for the glorious appearance of the Prince before Shrewsbury, he describes Hal looking like an 'angel' (4.1.107). Clearly Vernon's image is religious ('dropped down from the clouds') but in this play the numismatic sense is always there to be heard – and to disrupt the claim of value with the thought that this too may be one more counterfeit.

Hal has from the first understood the value of deceptive appearances. In his soliloquy in 1.2 he has made it clear that his princely debasement was merely a ploy to make his emergence into public life seem the more remarkable. His prodigal past is to serve as the 'sullen ground' against which his 'reformation' will 'show more goodly' (1.2.202–4). A number of critics have observed the marketing strategy at work here, finding Hal behaving uncomfortably 'like a clever Elizabethan shopkeeper'. Hal conceals his true worth, counterfeiting prodigality to allow the ultimate revelation of 'his princely assets . . . [to] bring a double profit' (Ornstein, 138). But why should his glorious chivalric appearance at Shrewsbury seem any more real than his tavern identity?

Both the Prince and the King understand that political value, like commercial value, is a function of social desire. And that desire can be manipulated. Henry established his value by letting Richard serve as his 'foil', as his son would term it (1.2.205), carefully withholding his own public appearances even as 'the skipping King' (3.2.60) made his regal presence 'cheap', 'common-hackneyed in the eyes of men' (3.2.40–1). Hal establishes his authority the same way, differing only in that he uses his own apparently prodigal behaviour as the foil to make his assumption of responsibility every bit as 'wondered at' (1.2.191; 3.2.47) as his father's 'seldom but sumptuous' manifestations (3.2.58).

Value can be produced by manipulating appearances – and perhaps must be so produced when value is not natural or intrinsic. The very means of Henry IV's assumption of the throne ensures that political value, in any case, must be negotiated differently than in the world where the crown is a matter of patrilineal transfer. The Prince is able to use his position as 'heir apparent' to receive credit in the taverns of London; in his inevitable picking up of the tab, he has paid 'so far as my coin would stretch, and where it would not I have used my credit' (1.2.52–3). But in the political realm his credit may not be much better than Falstaff's in the tavern. Hal's political credit, undermined by his father's path to the throne and by his own apparently prodigal behaviour, must be established, and to that end he has pledged to do his part by 'throw[ing] off' his 'loose behaviour' in order to 'pay the debt [he] never promised' (198–9). But such paying back may not succeed. To fulfil his obligation to the future, he must betray his relationship with his past, a betrayal that may itself erode the trustworthiness he seeks to establish by it.

Still, it is a carefully calculated trade-off, and the cost–benefit analysis could not have been undertaken by a better accountant. Hal has always kept his eye upon the balance sheet, and tellingly uses its idiom to express his political intelligence. If his father believes him lacking in chivalric capital in contrast to Hotspur's wealth of honour, Hal assures his father that the northern rebel is merely the Prince's 'factor', whose chivalric energies work only to 'engross up glorious deeds on [Hal's] behalf'. Hal then promises to 'call [Hotspur] to so strict account / That he shall render every glory up' or Hal will 'tear the reckoning from his heart'

(3.2.147–52). Hal will force Hotspur to pay his debts as the means of redeeming his own.

Heroic action is thus commercialized by the language of the play, becoming part of the process by which 'royal power is pragmatically produced in, and to some extent by, an economy of credit and negotiation' (Engle, 127; Levine). Falstaff will seek endlessly to avoid paying his debts; he likes not 'that paying back' (3.3.178) and would postpone paying even the debt/death he owes to God (5.1.126–7). Henry IV, however, as Hotspur says, 'Knows at what time to promise, when to pay' (4.3.53), and Worcester says that 'The King will always think him in our debt . . . Till he hath found a time to pay us home' (1.3.281–3). But Hal understands that his own political ambitions will be fulfilled as he arranges to 'pay the debt [he] never promised', establishing credit as he reveals himself 'better than [his] word' (1.2.199–200).

Hal's commercialization of the public arena is not merely a mark of the play's demystification of politics but is in fact an indication of how to succeed in this new world. In seeing his behaviour as a matter of good credit, Hal finds a way to turn his personal liabilities into strengths ('to make offence a skill', 1.2.206) and to free himself from his father's debt to the Percys. Only those who pay what they owe will thrive in a world where sovereignty is no longer a value that inheres unproblematically in the crown but must depend upon both credit and credibility.

What makes rulers sovereign in this new world, like that which makes coins 'current' (2.3.90), is finally the nation's willingness to accept them as such. Counterfeiting, in both realms, undermines confidence both in kings and in the coins issued in their name (and often virtually *with* their name – 'sovereigns', 'crowns', 'nobles' – and with their portraits, as coinage became the most significant site of royal portraiture). The strategic decision to put counterfeits of the King on the battlefield at Shrewsbury of course protects Henry but risks debasing the crown, making it all too apparent that kingship is subject to the same crisis of value that Tudor coinage suffered as it was debased by royal policy in the reign of Henry VIII and counterfeited not infrequently through-out the Tudor period. Hal, however, appears at Shrewsbury self-consciously as himself. Having begun the play as merely the 'shadow of succession' (3.2.99), Hal marks his reformation by his triumphant appearance in his royal identity: 'It is the Prince of Wales that threatens thee, / Who never promiseth but he means to pay' (5.4.41–2). He has kept his promise to 'Be more [him]self' (3.2.93); at Shrewsbury he gloriously shines forth, perhaps as a heavenly 'angel' who will dispense justice upon a rebellious crew but unmistakably as an 'angel' that will now pass current in the marketplace that is the public world.

## 'WHAT IS THAT WORD "HONOUR"'?

Falstaff's question is a crucial one in *1 Henry IV*, in which the reiterated language of honour has seemed to some the very source of the play's unity (Jorgensen, 43; Council, 36). Falstaff's own answer is profoundly sceptical: 'Honour' is no more than 'A word', and the word is no more than 'Air' (5.1.133–5). Honour is illusive, if not illusory. 'Who hath it? He that died o'Wednesday' (135–6); it is 'insensible' to the dead (137), and, for the living, indefensible from 'detraction' (138–9).

Unsurprisingly, then, Falstaff will not risk much for such an insubstantial conception of honour. He will ignominiously coun-terfeit death to escape an encounter with Douglas, repudiating the chivalric commonplace that 'a man of honour should alwaies pre-ferre death, before infamous safetie' (Romei, sig. O3ʳ). Of the honour that leads men to risk their lives or that accrues to those who do so, Falstaff dismissively claims that he will have 'none of it' (139), knowing that the 'better part of valour is discretion' (5.4.118–19). But honour that might be purchased more cheaply does in fact interest him. His scepticism does not prevent him from taking credit for Hotspur's death and thereby to 'look to be either earl or duke' (142). If he is certain that honour is nothing worth dying for, he is no less certain that it is something that will help him live.

But the honour that Falstaff claims on the battlefield is, of course, a matter of recognition rather than of action, an external bequest of reward and reputation rather than an internal principle of behaviour. His decidedly *dishonourable* actions, stabbing the dead Hotspur in the thigh and then lying about his achievement – along with Hal's willingness to gild that lie – are what win him honour in the public world (an honour that in *2 Henry IV* will lead Colevile of the Dale to surrender at the very sight of him: 'I think you are Sir John Falstaff and in that thought yield me'; *2H4* 4.3.16–17). This honour is indeed 'but a word', even if it proves effective in the world.

At the opposite extreme from Falstaff's scepticism is Hotspur's passionate devotion to 'bright honour' (1.3.201). In place of the fat knight's deflating nominalism, Hotspur displays a committed essentialism that sees honour as something objective, almost material, something that indeed he might 'pluck . . . from the pale-faced moon' or from 'the bottom of the deep' (201–4). He welcomes the opportunity to test and display his valour, never fearing 'danger' so long as 'honour cross it' (194–5). The news that neither his father nor Glendower will join the rebel forces at Shrewsbury seems to Douglas 'the worst tidings that I hear of yet' (4.1.126), but to Hotspur their absence provides an opportunity for glory, as their diminished ranks will lend 'a lustre and more great opinion' to their 'enterprise' (77–8). Understandably he is seen by others as 'the king of honour' (4.1.10) and 'the theme of honour's tongue' (1.1.80). But, if Falstaff's understanding of honour selfishly underestimates its value, Hotspur's, no less selfishly, overestimates it. Honour becomes an obsession that overwhelms any other consideration – even success. It is no wonder he so infuriates his pragmatic father and uncle: 'Imagination of some great exploit / Drives him beyond the bounds of patience' (1.3.198–9).

Falstaff and Hotspur may then be taken, as many critics have suggested, as two extremes in the understanding of honour: one deficient in its conception, one excessive (Hunter, 86–8; Brooks & Heilman, 377–8). Robert Ashley, writing about the same time the play was written, speaks of those who are 'so eager in the desire' for honour 'that they had more need of a brydle to restraine them from their over hote pursuit, then of spurrs to pricke them forward' (Ashley, 49). Hotspur needs the bridle to restrain him, so eagerly does he pursue honour; for Falstaff, if honour might sometimes be the spur that 'pricks him on', he is always aware that the pursuit of honour might 'prick him off', leaving him vulnerable on the field of battle (5.1.129–30). Yet, if they are at opposite poles, there are obvious similarities between them. Both are irresponsible and self-indulgent. Both are interested in what glory can be taken from the battlefield, though Hotspur alone is willing to risk his life in its pursuit. But he also risks the lives of those who would follow him in his appetite for glory ('Die all; die merrily', 4.1.133), as Falstaff sacrifices his troops to his appetite ('food for powder, food for powder', 4.2.64–5).

Hal, then, in this schematic view, comes to exemplify an Aristotelian mean between the two extreme positions represented by Falstaff and Hotspur (Ribner, 175). Until Shrewsbury, Hal has largely been 'kept aloof from the intricate demands of honour that so compel Hotspur and repel Falstaff' (Council, 49). But on the battlefield Hal reveals how fully he understands its claims. The Prince avoids both the careless pursuit of personal honour and the cowardly exploitation of unearned reputation. He acts courageously and behaves chivalrously; he defeats Hotspur, but he allows Falstaff to claim the credit, unconcerned with the world's report. Earlier he had vowed to claim Hotspur's honours for himself, forcing the exchange of Hotspur's reputation for his own 'indignities' (3.2.146), and even on the battlefield he vows to Hotspur that 'all the budding honours on thy crest / I'll crop to make a garland for my head' (5.4.71–2). But in the event he does not challenge Falstaff's insistence that the honours belong to him.

In the terms in which Hal initially conceives of honour, he reveals the pragmatism that has marked his behaviour from the first. As he promises to redeem his reputation, he thinks of it as an 'exchange' of his dishonour for Hotspur's 'glorious deeds' (3.2.145–6). Honour, as Lars Engle has written, is a 'commodity which, like money, can move all at once from one person's possession to another's', and 'Hal means to profit by the exchanges he enters into' (Engle, 111). But when the moment comes in which he tears 'the reckoning from [Hotspur's] heart' (3.2.152), the achievement itself is its own reward. Hotspur, of course, feels the deprivation in precisely the terms we would expect: 'I better brook the loss of brittle life / Than those proud titles thou hast won of me' (5.4.77–8). Hal, however, instead of cropping Hotspur's favours, graciously covers Hotspur's face with his own (5.4.95), and the 'proud titles' he has won he immediately cedes to Falstaff's lie.

At Shrewsbury, Hal reveals how fully he has internalized the conception of honour; he demands neither renown nor reward. Even the magnanimous treatment of the captured Douglas, unlike Hotspur's insistence on keeping his prisoners 'To his own use' (1.1.93), he allows to come from his brother's mouth: 'Then, brother John of Lancaster, / To you this honourable bounty shall belong', ordering: 'Go to the Douglas and deliver him . . . ransomless and free' (5.5.25–8). Once a 'truant . . . to chivalry' (5.1.94), Hal comes to embody a conception of honour far more compelling than Hotspur's, which reveals itself finally to be no less a 'scutcheon' (5.1.140), no less superficial and trivial, than that of Falstaff.

But this is perhaps all a bit too neat. The play does unmistakably set up Falstaff's and Hotspur's conception of honour in opposition, and it does allow Hal (unhistorically) to display his preeminent worthiness at Shrewsbury. Indeed the play offers on the battlefield a perfect emblem of the schema we have traced. In 5.4, Hal stands triumphant between the fallen bodies of Hotspur and Falstaff, his position the very sign of his successful synthesis of the extremes they represent. For a brief moment the play sets before us that satisfying image. But Hal then exits and Falstaff gets up, destroying the emblem with his own irrepressible refusal to be subordinated to any principle of order. In rising and stabbing Hotspur's body, he undoes the reassuring dialectic – and history's judgement – that would insist upon Hal's triumph. Hal leaves and, as Sigurd Burckhardt cleverly notes, 'Falstaff *remains*, the bulky remainder of a division that was calculated as $2 \div 2 = 1$, but which would not come out even' (Burckhardt, 147–8). If Hal tries to re-establish the symmetry, urging Falstaff to bear Hotspur on his back and promising to 'gild' Falstaff's lie 'with the happiest terms I have' (5.4.158), the dialectic is then revealed to be as much a function of Hal's desire as a structural fact of the play. Shakespeare, perhaps, at one stage intended to have Hal clearly emerge as a middle way from between two discredited extremes, but a logic deeper than that of plot insisted it could not be so simple.

## WOMEN IN THE PLAY

In 1817, Mrs Elizabeth Inchbald declared that 'This is a play which all men admire and which most women dislike' (Hemingway, 395); and Francis Gentleman in 1773 had already provided a likely explanation for Inchbald's observation, remarking the play's 'want of ladies, and matter to interest female auditors' (Odell, 2.41). Indeed the play, like most of the histories, describes a world of predominately male activity, with woman pushed to the margins. But in fact they are pushed further in *1 Henry IV* than in any other of these plays. Women speak fewer lines in this play than in any of the other nine, merely 3.47 per cent of the total number of lines. In only one other history, *Henry V*, do women speak fewer than 9.5 per cent of the lines; in *Richard III* they speak more than 22 per cent (Howard & Rackin, 217–18). Unsurprisingly excluded from court and the battlefield, the few women in *1 Henry IV* are limited to the tavern and the households of rebels. The female characters in the play are the Hostess and the wives of Hotspur and Mortimer, and one of these, Mortimer's wife, speaks nothing but Welsh. 'Their presence functions', as Barbara Hodgdon says, 'primarily to separate public from private domains' (Hodgdon, 155).

One could possibly make an argument that, even though women are excluded from the court and the battlefield, the places where male power is most obviously wielded, these marginal spaces allow women to 'regain some of the subversive power they had in the first tetralogy' (Howard & Rackin, 164). Certainly the tavern world, presided over by the Hostess, serves in some sense as an alternative to and a critique of the political world. Its popular energies are tied to social transgression: drunkenness, thievery, even rebellion itself, as the comic robbery at Gad's Hill is not merely of crowns 'going to the King's exchequer' (2.2.53) but parallels the robberies of crowns that are at the centre of the political action. And, at very least, the play-acting in the tavern serves to degrade royal authority by exposing its self-interest and, more radically, by suggesting how clearly it is constituted by acting (Kastan, *SAT*, 115–18).

Perhaps unsurprisingly, then, the other locations where women are seen and can be heard – Wales and Hotspur's castle on the northern border – are places of rebellion, and the role of women there, if not subversive of established order, does threaten the established terms of masculine virtue. Wales is clearly marked as a place of subversion and female power. 'Welshwomen' commit the 'beastly shameless transformation' upon the bodies of the dead English soldiers (1.1.43–6 and 44n.), an image of emasculation that is replayed in a more gentle key in 3.1 where Glendower's daughter appears as the cause of Mortimer's defection from his loyalty to Henry, robbing him of his manhood and honour. Even in his new alliance, with his 'blood' charmed by his wife (3.1.213), he becomes 'as slow / As hot Lord Percy is on fire to go' to war (258–9). The spoken Welsh of the scene marks Wales as alien (even less assimilable to English desire than France in *Henry V*, where the ultimate English victory is anticipated by the English the French nobles speak). Glendower's magic may be all bluster, but his daughter's language, even though it is unintelligible to her husband, is indeed 'ravishing' (206), and keeps Mortimer from exerting his claim to the throne. His notable absence (4.4.21–2) from Shrewsbury perhaps saves his life but costs him his place in history.

In Hotspur's castle, another place where rebellion is fostered, the play's other woman appears, and, like Mortimer's wife, Kate is also a threat to her husband's public success. The tenderness between them is usually clear on stage, as Kate tries, like Portia in 2.1 of *Julius Caesar*, to get Hotspur to share his 'business' (2.3.77) with her. She fears that 'Mortimer doth stir / About his title' and that he has sent for Hotspur 'To line his enterprise' (78–80); but Hotspur parries her efforts to get him to admit what takes him away, refusing her claim to know anything of his intentions: 'I must not have you henceforth question me / Whither I go, nor reason whereabout. / Whither I must, I must' (99–101). Unlike Mortimer, Hotspur is not seduced from the world of masculine honour that calls him: 'This is no world / To play with mammets and to tilt with lips' (87–8). And Kate, for all her charm, finally must bow to her husband's will as he departs without her: 'Will this content you, Kate?' asks Hotspur, promising she can follow him the following day; 'It must, of force', she tellingly replies (113). For all of Kate's intelligence and spirit, she is in Hotspur's eyes and heart 'But yet a woman' (105) and therefore not worth the full commitment that perhaps might have saved him from his death or at least made his life less 'brittle' (5.4.77). Mortimer listens to the silken music of Wales; Hotspur hears a different tune: 'Sound all the lofty instruments of war, / And by that music let us all embrace' (5.2.97–8).

Women thus offer consequential, imaginative alternatives to the public world of politics and rebellion – the anarchic, carnival world of the tavern and the passionate, domestic world of the household – but that public world always dominates. If the women ensure the recognition of social domains excluded from aristocratic history, they are finally most notable in this play for their small number and few words, and for their inability to act or speak in any public arena. Their marginalization, however, comes at a heavy price. In 1975 Emrys James played the King in a production at Stratford (see pp. 97–8), and based his characterization on the fact that there were 'no women in his world at all', which had left him unable to express emotion, alienating him from his son and even from his nation (Mullin, 22). Only metaphorically do women participate in the historical action, and then tragically, suffering its consequences rather than shaping them: England itself is a mother who, by virtue of the civil wars, has had to 'daub her lips with her own children's blood' (1.1.6).

## THE PLAY IN PERFORMANCE

We know *1 Henry IV* was written by early 1598. It was entered in the Stationers' Register on 25 February 1598, and praised by Francis Meres in *Palladis Tamia*, which was published that year (see p. 7). It is impossible to know exactly how much earlier the play was first acted, but a date for performance in early 1597 ' seems likely, which would make the likely venue the Theatre in Shoreditch, where the Lord Chamberlain's men, Shakespeare's company, had played since they were formed in 1594. Although their lease for the Theatre formally expired on 25 March 1597, negotiations for renewal had begun, and the company possibly continued to use the venue on sufferance, or perhaps switched their playing to the Curtain. Both theatres, however, were closed by Privy Council order in late July of that year (Chambers, *Stage*, 4.322–3). After the enforced closing, the company travelled in the south-west, playing in Bath in the summer (*REED: Somerset*, 1.17), the Guildhall in Bristol in September (*REED: Bristol*, 150) and in Marlborough (Chambers, 2.321). When they returned to London later in the autumn after the closing order was rescinded, the Chamberlain's men apparently played at the Curtain, as the Theatre seemingly never reopened. 'The vnfrequented Theater', as a contemporary satire noted, stood unused in its 'darke silence, and vast solitude' (Guilpin, sig. D6$^r$). The Globe, of course, was not built until the summer of 1599.

The play is well suited for any of the large outdoor London amphitheatres in which the play was performed in its first few years, and even for the various makeshift venues in which it would have been played while on tour. It makes no unusual staging demands. The discovery of Falstaff asleep in 2.4 was accomplished probably by pulling aside a hanging suspended from the front of the gallery or a traverse curtain draped across the opened stage doors. Otherwise, the large stage serves the play well, allowing the flow of the battle scenes in Act 5, as well as the pomp of the court scenes. Pillars, like those at the Globe, would provide places for Hal and Poins to hide in 2.2 as they watch the robbery. The multiple stage doors would allow actors to enter as others exited, permitting a rapidly paced production, and the unlocalized Elizabethan playing space demanded at most that a few props be placed or rearranged on stage to define the new location. The play requires no props that would not normally be available, needing little more than would be found in any well-stocked property room: masks, purses, coins, daggers, swords, shields, a crown, a throne, stools, tables, chairs and drinking vessels; and it necessitates no costumes that would not already be in the company's wardrobe, as it was played essentially in 'modern dress' (i.e. Elizabethan rather than medieval costume): boots, doublets and hose, various loose fitting jackets, a robe for the Archbishop and probably for Glendower, gowns for the boys playing the female parts, armour for the soldiers, and a distinctive tabard for the King and his counterfeits to wear at Shrewsbury.

The play's thirty-four speaking roles can be comfortably performed through doubling by a company of seventeen, including three boys for the female roles (see Appendix 4). Beyond the normal demands of the script on the talents of the actors, it does require two who can speak passable Welsh, including one boy who also must be able to sing (3.1.240). The original casting is not known, but it seems likely that Richard Burbage played Hal. Augustine Phillips may have played the King, and William Sly, Hotspur (Baldwin, 228, list II), though it is at least possible that Shakespeare himself played the King. John Davies of Hereford, in an epigram published in 1610 addressed 'To our English Terence, Mr. Will: Shake-speare', seemingly suggests that Shakespeare's most identifiable roles were monarchs: 'Had'st thou not plaid some Kingly parts in sport, / Thou hadst bin a companion for a king' (*Scourge*, sig. F7ᵛ).

Who initially played Falstaff is no more certain. Malone stated that he had seen a tract (whose title he had forgotten) that Falstaff was first played by John Heminge, one of the two friends and fellow actors who oversaw the 1623 Folio (Boswell–Malone, 3.187), but it seems more probable that the role was originally played either by Will Kemp, as David Wiles suggests (Wiles, 116–35), or by Thomas Pope, who also played clown roles for the company. Kemp was, of course, one of the great comic actors, but Pope too was recognized as one of the leading clowns of the era, as John Taylor's list attests: '*Tarlton, Lanum, Singer, Kempe* and *Pope*' (J. Taylor 1630, sig. 2Fᵛ). Pope may well have played Buffone in Jonson's *Every Man Out of His Humour* (Baldwin, 439–40), a character described, not unlike Falstaff, as 'A Publike, scurrilous, and prophane Iester; that . . . will swill up more sack at a sitting than would make all the Guard a posset' (Jonson, 3.423–4), a characterization which might suggest that Falstaff was his role too (and perhaps also Sir Toby Belch in *Twelfth Night*). Wiles argues that Buffone was played by Robert Armin (Wiles, 146–7), who had replaced Kemp as the company's major clown some time in 1599, but Armin is not listed among 'The principall Comoedians' who 'first acted' in the play in the list in the 1616 Jonson folio (sig. P4ᵛ). Only six actors are listed and parts are not assigned, but it is hard to believe that the actor playing Buffone would not be among these. Also, the similarity of characterization in the two parts strongly suggests that Buffone and Falstaff were played by the same actor once Jonson's play reached the repertory, and, although Kemp might well have played Falstaff, Armin seems a less likely candidate for that role on account of his notoriously diminutive stature – which further indicates that Pope, if he did not originate the role, probably succeeded Kemp in playing it (and played Buffone as well).

We do know that John Lowin later assumed the role of Falstaff, a fact which might also buttress Pope's claim to having played the role of the fat knight. James Wright reports in 1699 that 'before the wars Lowin used to act with mighty applause, Falstaff' (Chambers, *Stage*, 4.371). Lowin joined the company from Worcester's men some time in 1603, soon after Pope left it (Pope's name does not appear in the patent of 19 May 1603 when the Lord Chamberlain's men were re-formed as the King's men, and neither does Lowin's, though Lowin is named in the cast of *Sejanus*, a King's men play first acted in 1603). In essence, Lowin replaced Pope in the company, presumably taking on most of Pope's roles in the repertory. Perhaps the part of Falstaff was originally Kemp's, until he left the Chamberlain's men in 1599, and then passed to Pope, or perhaps it was Pope's all along, before it became Lowin's.

Yet, whoever acted the part, the character was certainly appealing to the groundlings of the amphitheatres. Thomas Palmer, as we have seen, took as a telling measure of theatrical popularity 'how long / Falstaff from cracking nuts hath kept the throng' (Fletcher, sig. f2$^v$). But Falstaff – and the rest of the play – appealed to elite audiences as well, and indeed the only certain early performances of *1 Henry IV* took place in aristocratic locales – and, interestingly, with titles different from the one we know for the play, but which help to explain its popularity. In March 1600, Lord Hunsdon entertained the Flemish ambassador, Ludovik Verreyken, with a play referred to as *Sir John Old Castell* (see p. 54), but which was clearly Shakespeare's play (rather than the *Sir John Oldcastle* belonging to the Admiral's men) with Hal's comic companion identified not only as the titular character but by his original name (Chambers, *Stage*, 1.220). In the winter of

1612–13, the play was one of the twenty plays performed by the King's men for the celebration of the marriage of the Princess Elizabeth and Frederick, the Elector Palatine, but identified in the Chamber Accounts as 'the Hotspur' (Chambers, *Stage*, 2.217; 4.180); and a performance at Whitehall on 'New-years Night' 1624–5, which again elevated the fat knight to titular prominence but this time as he had been rechristened: *The First Part of Sir John Falstaff* (Herbert, 52). The variant titles reveal the complex focus of the play, which might allow any of its major characters pre-eminence in performance, and it is worth recalling that Q1 allows 'Henry Percy, surnamed Henrie Hotspur of the North' and '*Sir* John Falstaff' to share the title-page with 'Henrie the Fovrth'.

A performance of 'Olde Castell' performed at court on 6 January 1631, like the 'ould Castel' performed on 29 May 1638, also seems likely to be Shakespeare's play rather than the Oldcastle play written for the Admiral's men (McManaway, 119–22). Another planned seventeenth-century aristocratic performance doesn't seem to have come off. In the Folger Library is a bound manuscript of fifty-five leaves that is a conflation of the two *Henry IV* plays. The manuscript was owned by Sir Edward Dering (1598–1644), and indeed he seems himself to have undertaken the abridgement (though most of the text is in the hand of a scribe, with Dering's corrections; see pp. 349–50). A scrap of paper preserved with the MS contains eight lines to be added to the King's speech at 1.1.20, on the back of which is a list of eight characters from John Fletcher's *The Spanish Curate* matched with the names of various relatives and friends of Dering who presumably were to be cast in the parts for an amateur production. The *Henry IV* conflation must have been similarly intended for a performance about 1622, but Dering never completed his preparation of the manuscript. Still, the Dering MS points not only to the popularity of the play but also to a mode of early theatrical activity that has almost totally disappeared from view.

One additional pre-Restoration production should be noted. During the Interregnum, with the theatres officially closed, at least an excerpt of *1 Henry IV* was played, a popular 'droll' entitled *The Bouncing Knight, or the Robbers Robbed*. The short playlet, a conflation of the Falstaff scenes, was later printed and partially illustrated in an anthology of 'select pieces of drollery' published in 1662: *The Wits, or Sport upon Sport*. On the frontispiece of *The Wits*, various plays' characters from the drolls are shown on an indoor stage, most prominently Falstaff and the Hostess (see Fig. 7). The droll itself is an adaptation of *1 Henry IV*'s 2.4, 3.3, 4.2, 5.1 and 5.3. Clearly it was made from a printed quarto of the play, since it reproduces Q's erroneous speech prefix *'Ross.'* at 2.4.168, 170 and 174, although, as in Q, *'Bardol'* appears later (and *'Ross.'* even appears among the names of the characters). *The Bouncing Knight*, however, and the other performances mentioned above, are the only specific indications of the pre-Restoration performance history of *1 Henry IV*. If this history is disappointingly thin, it must be said that it is hardly more so than that for any other play of the period, and even in its sparseness it is revealing, at the very least testifying that almost immediately the play became Falstaff's (or the tenacious Oldcastle's) play, or sometimes Hotspur's, but rarely the story of the prodigal Prince or the King burdened by history, the two versions of the play that have dominated the play's recent stage history.

This aspect didn't change after the theatres reopened in 1660 (though Oldcastle finally disappeared), and the play instantly became a staple of the theatre season. The play was one of those belonging to Thomas Killigrew in the new theatrical environment of Restoration England, which split the repertory between Killigrew's King's company and William Davenant's Duke of York's men. It was performed at least three times in that first year of renewed playing, including the production on 8 November 1660 that initiated the new theatre in Vere Street. The performance there on 31 December was that which occasioned Pepys's already-mentioned disappointment at seeing the play, his 'expectation being so great', though he admits that the fact of his having just read the play 'I believe did spoil it a little' (Pepys, 1.325).

7  Frontispiece of Kirkman, *The Wits*, 1662

Nonetheless, the following year Pepys attended another production and on that occasion found it 'a good play', and he would see it twice more in the next few years, especially enjoying on 2 November 1667 at Drury Lane 'contrary to expectation . . . Cartwright's speaking of Falstaffe's speech about "What is Honour"' (Pepys, 8.516).

In 1682, when the two theatre companies merged, the play was produced again, and Colley Cibber recalled with great pleasure 'the fierce and flashing fire' of Thomas Betterton's Hotspur (Cibber, 87). In 1700 Betterton produced the play at the Theatre in Little Lincoln's Inn Fields, this time playing Falstaff to great acclaim (at sixty-five years old, Betterton was no doubt better suited to that role than to a reprise of his earlier Hotspur). One correspondent enthusiastically reported that 'the critics allow that Mr Betterton has hitt the humour of Falstaff better then any that have aimed at it before' (Thorn-Drury, 48). His success led him to revive the production in eight of the next ten years before his death in 1710.

If, however, Betterton's acting was striking, his approach to the playing text showed an unusual restraint. Unlike most post-Restoration adaptations of Shakespeare's plays, which aggressively rewrote them to bring them into line with contemporary taste and expectation, Betterton altered almost nothing, confining his revision to cuts. Betterton eliminated much of 1.1, reducing the King's opening speech to ten lines; removed Lady Percy and Glendower's daughter from 3.1, ending the scene with the drawing of the indentures; cut all of 4.4 and the first fifty-six lines of 5.4, and reduced 5.5 to the first nine lines and the last eleven. In essence, he did not do much more than any modern director does with a Shakespeare play, seeking cuts that will clarify the conception of the play and speed up its playing. Betterton streamlined the historical action while leaving the Falstaff material largely intact, and the published text was significantly entitled *K. Henry IV with the Humours of Sir John Falstaff. A Tragi-comedy* (1700). His success with the play allowed it to avoid the radical 'Newmodelling', as Nahum Tate terms his adaptation of *King Lear* (1681), that most of Shakespeare's plays suffered to make them acceptable to the polite audiences of the day. Indeed *1 Henry IV* was one of the few Shakespeare plays, along with *Hamlet*, *Julius Caesar* and *Othello*, successfully to resist the Restoration and Augustan 'improvements'.

Throughout the eighteenth century, *1 Henry IV* remained a favourite on stage. In the first half of the century over 214 performances were recorded and no doubt there were more (Hogan, 1.460). James Quin supplanted Betterton as the next great Falstaff (see Fig. 8), though, like Betterton, he too first appeared in the

8  James Quin as Falstaff, London, between 1721 and 1751

play as Hotspur (in 1718–19). In 1721–2, he took on the role of the fat knight for the first time and performed the role for the next thirty years until he retired in 1751. David Garrick played Hotspur to Quin's Falstaff at Drury Lane in 1746, though as Thomas Davies noted: 'The person of Garrick was not formed to give a just idea of the gallant and noble Hotspur.' Quin's Falstaff, however, was a success, 'the most intelligent and judicious Falstaff since the days of Betterton'. Less jovial than Betterton's, Quin's Falstaff displayed a 'satire and sarcasm' new to the role, at least in part a reflection of 'the surliness of [the actor's own] disposition' (Davies, *DM*, 1.250). Quin was the first to cut the 'play extempore' from 2.4, a cut which productions followed into the middle of the nineteenth century and which Francis Gentleman heartily endorsed in 1773, saying that it 'rather choaked and loaded the main business' and was 'dreadfully tedious in representation' (Bell, 4.41). Interestingly, Abraham Lincoln, a devotee of Shakespeare both in the study and on the stage, invited the American actor James Hackett to the White House after a performance in 1863, particularly eager 'to know why one of the best scenes in the play, that where Falstaff & Prince Hal alternately assume the character of the King, is omitted in the representation'. 'Hackett says', reported John Hay, Lincoln's Secretary of State, 'it is admirable to read but ineffective on stage, that there is generally nothing sufficiently distinctive about the actor who plays Henry to make an imitation striking' (Hay, 139).

In the second half of the century, the play was only a little less popular than in the first, 149 performances being recorded (Hogan, 2.717) and productions in all but twelve of the fifty seasons. It was played for the first time in America in New York on 18 December 1761, with David Douglass as Falstaff and Lewis Hallam as Hotspur, and seventeen additional productions were mounted before the end of the century. On both sides of the Atlantic the playing text was generally shaped much like Quin's, and again it was Falstaff who elicited most of the commentary. John Henderson was probably the greatest of the Falstaffs of this

era, playing the role first at the Haymarket in July 1777 and regularly after that until his death in 1785. Henderson's Falstaff was
'frolicksome, gay and humorous', a self-conscious rejection of the
'impudent dignity' that Quin had brought to the role (Davies,
*DM*, 1.252), and much loved. A bit of contemporary doggerel
held that 'When Henderson resigned his breath / Jack Falstaff
also died' (Winter, 338). But of course Falstaff lived on.
Henderson was followed by others: James Dance, John Palmer
(the younger), Edward Shutter and John Fawcett, Jr, probably the
best of these. J. Dover Wilson's observation is apt: 'the part was to
the stage of those days what Hamlet is to ours – a part which no
actor can be satisfied without attempting' (Cam[1], xxxvii).

Into the nineteenth century the play was still largely defined by
the character of Falstaff. In 1802 at Drury Lane in London,
Stephen Kemble, the brother of J. P. Kemble, took on the role
with apparent success, as his portrayal held the stage until 1820
and a number of his innovations (like Falstaff's discovery asleep
at the beginning of 1.2) held the stage for many decades (see Fig.
9). Not all, however, were captivated by his performance. Kemble
was a large man and notoriously 'he played Falstaff without stuffing', as J. R. Planché recalled (Salgado, 180). Notwithstanding, as
Hazlitt noted in a review in *The Examiner* in October, 1816, 'Every
fat man cannot play a great a man', concluding, 'We see no more
reason why Mr Stephen Kemble should play Falstaff, than why
Louis XVIII is qualified to fill a throne, because he is fat, and
belongs to a particular family' (Hazlitt, *Works*, 5.340).

Nonetheless, Falstaff continued to dominate the play. Kemble
was succeeded by Robert William Elliston and Samuel Phelps as
the best known of the English Falstaffs, but the American James
Henry Hackett was the equal of any on the English stage (Fig. 10).
Taking on the role first in May 1832, in a production at
Philadelphia's Arch Street Theatre (with Charles Kean as
Hotspur), he played Falstaff regularly on both sides of the
Atlantic until his retirement in 1870. Hackett's Falstaff showed
the character's 'powerful mind, which has been corrupted by

9  Stephen Kemble (1758–1822) as Falstaff

10   James H. Hackett (1800–71) as Falstaff, *c*. 1850

sensuality and self-indulgence', wrote William Winter, who had often seen him act the part. The corruption had often been the basis of performance, but Hackett also captured Falstaff's 'boundless resources of mirth and wit, his prodigious vitality, his acute knowledge of human nature and of the world' (Winter, 361). Not all were so taken with the actor, however. In a production in Edinburgh, he made at least one enemy in the cast, who during a performance 'pricked a hole in his false abdomen. . . . He continued to decrease in size till at last there came a rush of wind and the stomach disappeared all together, the actor finishing the scene the best he could and the audience convulsed with laughter' (Wallack, 194–6).

A significant shift in the perception of the play began arguably in 1815 with William Macready's performance of Hotspur at the Theatre Royal in Bath, a role he continued in until 1847. Queen Victoria requested a revival in 1849, but Macready, no doubt wisely, declared himself too old for the part. Macready's Hotspur was volatile but always graceful and intelligent, and he commented that he had discovered 'the vast benefit derived from keeping vehemence and effort out of passion' (Macready, 1.85). The success of Macready's Hotspur had the effect of refocusing attention upon the historical action, and the movement beyond seeing the play as a mere vehicle for a comic Falstaff continued in 1824, when Charles Kemble produced a spectacular *1 Henry IV* at Covent Garden in May. What was most remarkable about this production was less the acting than the set and costumes, which strove almost obsessively for an authenticity to the represented history. The playbill announced that 'Every character will appear in the precise Habit of the Period; the whole of the Dresses being executed from indisputable authorities, viz. Monumental Effigies, Painted Glass, &c.' The King's costume was based on the funeral effigy in Canterbury Cathedral, for example, and for others reference was made to 'The Sumptuary laws passed during the Reign of Henry IV' and portraits and various illuminated manuscripts 'in the Royal, Harleian, and other Collections' (Odell, 2.173–4).

That the production was not a great success was a function of the fact that the acting was not found to be the equal of the splendid costumes and sets, but the very effort, as with Kemble's *King John* earlier that year, re-established the play as a history play, and established its history as of genuine theatrical interest.

In the second half of the century, the play had fewer consequential productions. In part this was because the play did not really lend itself to the age's delight in spectacular stagings. The very thing that allowed *1 Henry IV* to be so successful on the Elizabethan stage, the simplicity of its staging demands (see p. 77), seemingly frustrated the English theatre impresarios who were eager fully to test and display the theatrical resources at their command. The play largely dropped out of the repertory. In 1888 Frank Marshall could say that for some time the play had been 'virtually dead to the stage' (Sprague, *Stage*, 51) and two years later a reviewer would similarly lament that 'to the present generation *1 Henry IV* is practically unknown' (*Atheneum*, 5 April 1890). There had been, however, at least one notable production: a magnificent staging of the play at Drury Lane by Samuel Phelps, mounted to celebrate the tercentenary of Shakespeare's birth. Thirteen painted scenes provided a dazzling backdrop for the production, the most spectacular being that for the 'field of Battle near Shrewsbury' (see Fig. 11), allowing a 'brilliant effect', reported the *Illustrated London News* (2 April 1864), that 'roused the audience to repeated plaudits'. Reviewers were pleased (though one commented that Phelps's Falstaff 'could use a little more stuffing'), but found the production 'distinguished' not least by the fact that 'The great Glendower scene, hitherto omitted, was supplied' (Odell, 2.299), as well as the 'play extempore', which Phelps had first restored in 1846 but had omitted again in 1856.

The last important nineteenth-century production took place in 1896. Herbert Beerbohm Tree produced the play at the Haymarket Theatre and played a witty and good-natured Falstaff of enormous girth aided by a wicker structure strapped on to his

11 The Battle of Shrewsbury in the 1864 Drury Lane production, from the *Illustrated London News*, 30 April 1864

chest. In one sense, this production stands as a fitting end to the play's nineteenth-century performance history. It was marked, like so many productions of the century, by the fascination with scenic elaboration and by the almost inevitable domination of the play by Falstaff's personality. In another sense, however, the production signalled the end of those traditions and the beginning of recognizable modern ones, in that the play was 'accepted from Shakespear mainly as he wrote it', as George Bernard Shaw noted as 'the chief merit of the production' which he otherwise disliked (Shaw, 105), and in its commitment to an acting style more psychologically realistic and textually based than had been usual on stage. In 1914, Tree mounted the play again at His Majesty's Theatre, a production that has become noteworthy for the introduction of a stage tradition in which Hotspur falters as he attempts to vocalize certain letters. Matheson Lang's stammer (which Tree had first heard in a German production; Lang, 120) gave rise to a host of stuttering Hotspurs, based, however, on a misunderstanding of the reference in *2 Henry IV* 2.3.24 to Hotspur's 'speaking thick', which in fact means merely that he spoke quickly.

In the twentieth century, the play continued to reveal how much more it is than a Falstaff play, not least from the fact that increasingly companies began to perform the histories in clusters. The first known cycle of histories was produced in Germany in the 1860s by Franz Dingelstedt. Working on the histories since 1851, when he first directed *1 Henry IV*, Dingelstedt organized a sequence of seven histories played one a day throughout the week for a Shakespeare birthday celebration in Weimar in 1864 (Williams, 153–4). In England it would take until the first decade of the twentieth century for the plays to be performed in sequence and systematically thought of in relation to one another. In 1905–6 in Stratford-upon-Avon, Frank Benson produced *Richard II*, *1* and *2 Henry IV* and *Henry V*, sometimes in severely cut and rearranged texts (which often made more use of *Henry IV Part Two* than *Part One*), though in May 1905 he performed the four plays of the so-called 'second tetralogy' on consecutive days. W. B. Yeats saw a sequence of histories at Stratford in 1901 and noted with delight how much was gained from 'the way play supports play' (Yeats, 96–7), though in fact that year *Henry IV Part One* had been omitted in favour of *Part Two* only as the bridge between *Richard II* and *Henry V*.

On 23 April 1921, for the anniversary of Shakespeare's birthday, Barry Jackson staged both parts of *Henry IV* at the Birmingham Repertory Company, and, to mark the opening of the Memorial Theatre in Stratford-upon-Avon on Shakespeare's birthday in 1932, the two plays were again performed in tandem as a matinee and evening performance (an occasion that saw Prince Edward, who would become the uncrowned King Edward VIII, fly in to see the plays). In 1951, for the Festival of Britain, *Richard II*, the two parts of *Henry IV* and *Henry V* were directed by Anthony Quayle in repertory, sharing a single set. In 1964, for the 400th anniversary of Shakespeare's birth, the Royal Shakespeare Company (RSC) outdid even that, producing its own version of Dingelstedt's extended cycle of histories in 1864, by performing Shakespeare's drama of the contiguous history from the end of the reign of Richard II to the coming of the Tudors to power at the end of *Richard III* in seven plays, achieved with some cuts and sutures in the *Henry VI* plays that reduced the first tetralogy to a trilogy (which had opened on its own the previous summer). In 1987–8, in its second season, the English Shakespeare Company toured the contiguous histories, also in a seven-play sequence with the *Henry VI* plays reduced to two.

But even though few companies have been willing to devote a single season to all the histories, or even to a four-play tetralogy, increasingly they have staged the two *Henry IV* plays together in a single season (and sometimes with *Henry V*, comprising a three-play 'Henriad'). Clearly the understanding of *1 Henry IV* that has come from seeing it in relation to other histories makes it difficult to perform it any longer as the comedy of Falstaff or the romantic tragedy of Hotspur, the two modes that dominated its early stage history. It becomes less easy to sentimentalize either of these characters, as the sequence clearly focuses attention upon Bolingbroke's political ambitions and uneasy command and finally upon Hal's emergence as king (incidentally revealing that Shakespeare wrote more lines for Hal/Henry V than for any other of his characters). Seen in the context of the other histories, *1 Henry IV* becomes a play about the nature and costs of political success, and one that, in the delicate balance of its sympathies, nicely catches the modern age's own ambivalences.

If the play performed by the Old Vic Company at the New Theatre in London in 1945 or even in 1951 in Stratford understandably took the high road in regard to the play's politics in the context of the experience of the Second World War, both productions successfully drew upon the play's implicit tensions by allowing no one character to dominate the performance. In 1945, John Burrell directed a brilliant cast – Laurence Olivier as Hotspur, Ralph Richardson as Falstaff, Nicholas Hannen as King Henry and Michael Warre as Hal – in a sober, intelligent production in which the court scenes, as many critics noted, were as compelling as the tavern scenes, no small achievement given the universal delight that Richardson's Falstaff produced. In 1951, again an extremely talented cast – Richard Burton as Hal, Harry Andrews as King Henry, Anthony Quayle as Falstaff and Michael Redgrave as Hotspur – allowed the play's political vision to come to the fore (see Fig. 12). Quayle's Falstaff was too corrupt ever to be fully lovable, never seducing either the audience or Hal, who from the first displayed 'a gloomy sense of his destiny' in Burton's remote and melancholic performance (McMillin, 43).

In 1955, at the Old Vic, Douglas Seale successfully directed both parts of *Henry IV* in productions that also revealed the dramatic power inherent in the play's structural balance. The *New York Times* (15 May 1955) praised Seale for the integrity of his production and refusal to 'let the wildness of the comedy distract him from the earnestness of Shakespeare's inquiry into the critical problems' of Henry IV's England'. Robert Hardy's Hal began

12   Anthony Quayle as Falstaff and Richard Burton as Hal in the Stratford
     Memorial Theatre production of 1951

in aimlessness and moved quickly to responsibility, his chilling 'I
do; I will' in the play-acting in the tavern leaving no doubt about
either his or Falstaff's future. Paul Rogers's Falstaff was funny but
never carefree, his wit always marked by his awareness of how vulnerable his situation was. The characterization, as one critic
noted, 'may lose a little in boisterous fun . . . but it gains enor-
mously in irony and pathos' (*Punch*, 11 May 1955). Seven years
later, Seale again directed the play, but this time on the other side
of the Atlantic at the Festival Theatre in Stratford, Connecticut.
Again, the centre of the production was in the relation of Falstaff

(Eric Berry) and Hal (James Ray). After Falstaff pleads that to 'banish plump Jack' would be to 'banish the whole world', there was a long pause before Ray's Hal answered as if in a daze, 'I do', and then he rose and walked towards Falstaff and said firmly, 'I will.' Berry's Falstaff's smile froze, reported Dunbar Ogden, 'in a terrible grimace. He turned away. Then back. And out of the depths of his being rose a forced, choked chuckle. He stamped his foot, laughed heartily, embraced Hal; and Falstaff was back in his role again' (Ogden, 538).

But increasingly Falstaff would not be allowed any simple way back to prominence, as the political vision of the play darkened. The Royal Shakespeare Company's production of *1 Henry IV* as part of their grand cycle of histories for the quatercentenary of Shakespeare's birth in 1964 took place on a stark set that reminded many of a stone and steel cage, a striking metaphor for 'the mechanism of power' that co-director Peter Hall saw operating in all the histories (Addenbrooke, 127). Eric Porter's King was tired and careworn, while Ian Holm's Hal was detached and self-contained, acting 'from the outside', as one reviewer criticized the performance (Evans, 'Behaviourism', 137), though perhaps that says more about the characterization than about the actor. Hugh Griffith's Falstaff was often funny but clearly had no real place in the dispiriting world of power politics in which he hoped to make his way. Perhaps some involved in the opening were aware of the strain between the grim logic of the production and the spectacular circumstances of performance, with the many dignitaries in attendance including the Duke of Edinburgh and the President of the World Bank (McMillin, 65).

Performances through the 1960s continued to emphasize in various ways how much *1 Henry IV* had become Hal's play. Productions were defined now not by the interpretation of Falstaff but by the conception of the Prince; and Hotspur, who had once successfully competed for prominence, dwindled progressively to a comic blusterer, perhaps because his chivalric energies were no longer intelligible in an age of high-tech warfare.

Falstaff, of course, could not be forgotten and was often memorably acted, as by Stacy Keach in New York in 1968 at the Delacorte Theater in Central Park. In Gerald Freedman's unfussy and finely calibrated direction, Falstaff was revealed as almost an innocent, at least as having come fully to believe the lies he has been telling: 'He has not corrupted Prince Hal,' noted the reviewer in the *New York Times* (30 June 1968); 'Hal (look of injured innocence) has corrupted him'. Sam Waterston's adolescent Hal was, however, at the core of Freedman's understanding, as the Prince was by turns fascinated and repelled by Keach's Falstaff, while trying unsuccessfully to hold at bay the burdens of responsibility that he knew awaited him.

There were inevitably exceptions to the general refocusing of the play upon politics and political men. In Stratford, Ontario, in 1965, Stuart Burge directed both *Henry IV* plays as two halves of a single conception, the second play, however, retitled *Falstaff*, officially 'to prevent ticket-buyer confusion' (Leiter, 195), but clearly a sign of its focus. Though the historical action was intelligently conceived and well acted, the comedy dominated. As one reviewer observed: 'instead of a history play relieved by comedy, we now have a comedy sprinkled with a bit of history' (*Saturday Review*, 28 August 1965). Falstaff here was a mischievous rogue, whose 'fondness for Prince Hal's company is not based on a hope of eventual preferment but on the irresistible fact that the heir apparent is a "sweet wag"' (*New York Times*, 30 June 1965). A decade later, the RSC would mount the play and again as part of an extended sequence. Tellingly, however, this was not the second tetralogy but a Falstaffiad, composed of the two *Henry IV* plays, *Henry V* and *The Merry Wives of Windsor*. Terry Hands directed the plays consciously to de-emphasize the politics that the 1964 Hall–Barton production found so central. 'Shakespeare goes far beyond politics,' wrote Hands; 'Politics is a very shallow science' (Trussler, 55). But Falstaff was only incidentally the way beyond the political. Hands's production was a study in domestic psychopathology, probing the tortured relationship of father and son. Alan Howard's Hal could evince a boyish charm but was obviously insecure and wary, while Emrys James's King was a 'snarling, sardonic, guilt-laden autocrat' (*The Times*, 25 April 1975). Brewster Mason played Falstaff as an amiable and dignified gentleman down on his luck. Never really threatening Hal's commitment to the public world, and to many critics never really funny, at most this Falstaff provided Hal with some emotional comfort as the Prince sought respite from his volatile and abusive father and too clearly revealed his own potential for the sadism he had learned at home (see Fig. 13).

In 1982, *1 Henry IV* was chosen to open the Barbican Theatre in London, as it had been in 1932 to open the Shakespeare Memorial Theatre in Stratford. Trevor Nunn directed both parts of *Henry IV* in a style manifestly derived from the great success the company had enjoyed with *Nicholas Nickleby*. The spectacular multi-level scaffolding not only allowed the same exhilaratingly hyperactive staging but here also brilliantly articulated the strains and fractures of the English nation (see Fig. 14). Clearly Nunn was interested in the play as a portrait of a society divided along class and ideological faultlines, though the emotional centre of the production was with Gerard Murphy's Hal, as he was forced to choose 'between his cold, hard conscience-stricken father and the warm, generous embrace of his spiritual father in the gargantuan shape of Falstaff' (*Guardian*, 8 May 1982). If this was a familiar enough conception of the play, it took energy from the crisp emotional tensions that were produced between Murphy's adolescent Hal, Joss Ackland's appealing Falstaff and Patrick Stewart's austere King (Fig. 15).

In 1986, the newly formed English Shakespeare Company chose *1 Henry IV* as its first play, and toured throughout that summer and the next with it as one of a sequence of histories. Directed by Michael Bogdanov, the production was edgy and iconoclastic, focusing as much on the nation that could be formed only in violence as on characters all too capable of it, unable to find or express authentic emotion. The social strains were evident in

13 Brewster Mason as Falstaff, Alan Howard as Hal and Maureen Pryor as Mistress Quickly in the Royal Shakespeare Company at Stratford, 1975

14 John Napier's set for the 1982 Royal Shakespeare Company production, with Gerard Murphy as Hal (extreme left) and Patrick Stewart as King Henry (extreme right)

15  Patrick Stewart as King Henry in the Royal Shakespeare Company production at the Barbican, 1982

the production's eclectic costumes: Michael Pennington's Hal in jeans and hiking boots, Patrick O'Connell's King in a Victorian frock-coat, John Woodvine's Falstaff in a green velvet smoking jacket with checked trousers (and a 1940s double-breasted suit and an army poncho for the robbery scene). The psychological sterility of this world was revealed in Pennington's cold and manipulative Prince, who, shockingly, as Hotspur chivalrously returned to him the sword the rebel had knocked away in their duel, quickly picked it up and swiftly stabbed Hotspur from behind. This Hal was no hero, and the production ended with him exiting alone, having proved nothing to the world, indeed with both his brother and his father crediting Falstaff's claim to having killed Hotspur and convinced the Prince is a coward and liar. A solitary figure to the side of the stage played a mournful tune on a flute as Hal exited, a lament for all that had been lost – and perhaps for how little there was to be won.

In 1991 and in 2000, *1 Henry IV* was again a featured part of the RSC repertory. The earlier production, directed by Adrian Noble, sharply juxtaposed the excesses of the tavern with the calculation of the court. Julian Glover's King was neither infirm nor tired, as so often he has been played, but firmly in control of the political world. The worldly commitments of the historical action mocked the set's articulation of a sacred space, with its massive cross formed by the rear panels, candles burning on the sides of the stage, and a suspended reliquary in the shape of a church. In opposition, Robert Stephens's dandyish Falstaff presided over a tavern that seemed almost hellish with its bold red décor and with smoke rising from a trap. The two controlling figures, however, seemed more alike than different, both isolated and melancholy in their respective spheres. Hal, in Michael Maloney's performance, moved uncertainly back and forth between them, attractive in many ways, but disturbingly unready to choose between them. In 2000, Michael Attenborough directed the play at the Swan Theatre in Stratford-upon-Avon. This was an impressively intelligent production, in which Desmond Barrit's Falstaff displayed a genuine affection for the boyish young prince (William Houston), who slowly revealed his potential to lead. But it was David Troughton's arrogant and anguished King Henry who dominated the play, purposefully struggling with the burdens of rule, symbolized by the heavy crown sitting uncomfortably on his head and at which Troughton periodically tugged in an effort to get it off (see Fig. 16).

On television, the play has been arguably seen by more viewers than have seen the play in the entirety of its theatre history. In 1979, the second season of the BBC Shakespeare (seen in the US on PBS in 1980), David Giles directed a straightforward performance of the play, taking advantage of the realism of the medium and the assumptions of the BBC series style to produce the play almost as historical documentary. The small screen, however, struggled to contain the enormous energies of the play, most obviously in the tavern and on the battlefield. Still, the acting was clean and intelligent, especially Anthony Quayle's Falstaff, who revealed the anxiety behind his joking too often missed by more obviously comic Falstaffs, and David Gwillim's Hal, who behind his easy playboy attractiveness could be seen to face his future as king with both dread and desire. The one problematic performance was Jon Finch's King Henry, which was marked (marred?) by the visual evidence of leprosy crusting around his mouth and nose, and his continuous twitching and scratching in his discomfort.

Two memorable films also demand to be noted as part of the play's remarkable performance history, though neither is actually *1 Henry IV* but each a highly idiosyncratic adaptation: Orson Welles's *Chimes at Midnight* (1966, entitled *Falstaff* in the US) and Gus Van Sant's *My Own Private Idaho* (1991). Welles's film is the story of Falstaff's rejection in a conflation and rearrangement of *1* and *2 Henry IV*, though it draws also on *Richard II*, *Henry V* and *The Merry Wives of Windsor*. The title, *Chimes at Midnight*, reveals the nostalgia of the project, a lament not only for Falstaff but for what Welles called 'the death of Merrie England' (McMillin, 92). The film takes both its strength and its limitations from Welles's over-identification with the fat knight. Sentimental

16 David Troughton as King Henry in the Royal Shakespeare Company
production at the Swan Theatre, Stratford, in 2000

it is, but not precisely in the way often seen on the stage. Welles's Falstaff is not a jolly Falstaff. At most he plays the clown. For Welles, the film is a tragedy of a man who lives in a world of historical necessity that must repudiate him, but it is a film which only becomes tragic from the fact of Falstaff's collaboration in his own sacrifice. The film ends with the image of Falstaff's coffin and a voice-over of a passage from Holinshed (3.583) insisting that Henry V was '(so humane withall) that he left no offense vnpunished or friendship vnrewarded'. If one irony here is obvious enough, perhaps another is no less intended: that history gets the final word.

Van Sant's evocative film about street hustlers in the Pacific Northwest has an even more uneasy relation to Shakespeare's plays; indeed it is as much an adaptation of Welles's film as of Shakespeare's play. Like *Chimes at Midnight*, which Van Sant admits as the source of his interest in Shakespeare's characters, the focus is largely on the relationship of Falstaff and Hal, or, in Van Sant's version, Scott (Keanu Reeves), the delinquent son of the sickly mayor of Portland, and Bob (William Richert), an older gay man, addicted to cocaine and adolescent boys and waiting for Scott's twenty-first birthday to share in the money Scott will inherit when his father dies. A seedy hotel for derelicts is the film's equivalent of the tavern in the play. At the end of the film, Scott, who has gone off to Italy, returns in triumph with his foreign bride, clearly no longer a participant in the underworld in which we first met him. The world of conventional expectations has claimed him as one of its own, though, as with Shakespeare's play, the character was never really at risk from his slumming. The film's title, derived from a song by the B-52s called 'Private Idaho', points to a world of liberating imagination that no one in the film can finally live in or even find. The hustlers' world is depressing but perhaps offers more genuine emotion than the straight world which Scott embraces, as Van Sant measures the psychic costs of Scott's predictable transformation.

If the two films are marked as much by their wilful appropriation of Shakespeare's *Henry IV* plays as by their powerfully individual response to them, they also show the continued availability and vitality of those plays. Particularly in *1 Henry IV*, Shakespeare has constructed a world so rich in its variety and so carefully nuanced in its sympathies that directors in whatever medium can shape a performance to make it speak compellingly to different interests in and understandings of that complex field of demand and desire that we call history. The record of that engagement testifies to the fact that *1 Henry IV* not only remains one of Shakespeare's most appealing plays but also stands as one of every age's most important.

## THE PLAY ON THE PAGE:
## THE TEXT OF *1 HENRY IV*

On 25 February 1598, the Clerk of the Stationers' Company noted that Andrew Wise 'Entred for his Copie vnder thandes of Mr Dix: and mr Warden man a booke intituled The historye of Henry the iiijth with his battaile of Shrewsburye against Henry Hottspurre of the Northe wth the conceipted mirth of Sr Iohn ffalstoff' (Arber, 3.105). There is no evidence of how Wise came into possession of the manuscript, but, once he registered it with the Stationers' Company, the title belonged to him. Wise published two editions of the play in the year in which he registered the title, a sign of its remarkable popularity. Only about one-third of all the plays that were printed before 1640 ever reached a second edition, and only twelve achieved it in the same year as the first.

Nonetheless, in spite (or perhaps because) of their popularity, the two editions of 1598 have now almost entirely disappeared. Only three copies of one of these are known: a copy now in the British Library (missing sig. K4 and most of sig. E4); one in the Huntington Library in San Marino, California (sharply cropped), and one in the library of Trinity College, Cambridge. Their title-page (see Fig. 17) slightly varies the wording of the Stationers' Register entry: 'THE

# THE
# HISTORY OF
## HENRIE THE
### FOVRTH;

With the battell at Shrewsburie,
*betweene the King and Lord*
Henry Percy, furnamed *Collated*
Henrie Hotſpur of
the North. *Perfect.*
*D. 1827.*

*With the humorous conceits of Sir*
Iohn Falſtalffe.

*First Edition .*

AT LONDON,
Printed by *P. S.* for *Andrew Wiſe*, dwelling
in Paules Churchyard, at the ſigne of
the Angell. 1598.

17   Q1 title-page, 1598

/ HISTORY OF / HENRIE THE / FOVRTH; / With the battell at Shrewsburie, / *betweene the King and Lord* / Henry Percy, sur-named / Henrie Hotspur of / the North. / *With the humorous conceits of Sir* / Iohn Falstalffe.' Of the other edition of 1598, only a fragment survives (see Appendix 5). James Halliwell found it in the mid-nineteenth century in the binding of a copy of William Thomas's *Rules of the Italian Grammar* (1567), and it is now in the collection of the Folger Library. The remnant of this edition con-sists only of the sheet on which the 'C' gathering was printed (which corresponds to 1.3.200 to 2.2.108 in most modern editions).

The edition with the three surviving copies is usually referred to as Q1, that is, the earliest (complete) quarto of the play; the fragment is generally known as Q0. Both were printed in the shop of Peter Short, as can be ascertained from the common stock of type that appears in the two editions, and both are, by contempo-rary standards, remarkably well printed. On the basis of the number of 'typographical and textual peculiarities' that the two texts share, Charlton Hinman concluded that the 'immediate dependence of one on the other is unquestionable' (Hinman, viii). One text must have been printed from the other, and Q0 seems to be the original from which Q1 was printed. Although there are numerous variations between the two editions, only one is sub-stantive: Q0 has 'How the fat rogue roard' (2.2.108), where Q1 has only 'How the rogue roard', the omission itself suggesting Q1's dependence, as it is far more likely that a compositor would omit a word than add one.

The rest of the differences are almost all unremarkable spelling and punctuation variants (indicating that, although both editions were printed in the same shop, the texts were set by different com-positors (Craven, 393–7). Q1, however, has one more line per page than Q0, and in other ways conserves space (e.g. by crowding prose speeches) so that it fits the play on to exactly ten sheets – seventy-eight pages plus the one for the title with the verso blank. (In a quarto, four pages would be printed on each side of the sheet of paper, which would then be folded to allow the pages to appear in the proper order.) Extrapolating from the Q0 fragment, it is clear that it would have demanded perhaps an additional half-sheet to print the play. Paper was the most expensive of a publisher's production costs apart from the labour, and, especially for a playbook (which from the publisher's point of view was no more than a cheap pamphlet), any publisher would be eager to save whatever paper was possible. That Q1 is more economical in this regard than Q0 is a second reason why scholars seem confident that it is dependent upon Q0 rather than the other way round. It is unlikely that a printer would deliberately expand the text on the page to use more paper. Even with the first edition a publisher would try to use as little paper per copy as possible, but it would be easier to calculate space savings in an edition set from printed copy than in one set from a manuscript, especially in a play with so much prose.

If pragmatic concerns shaped the printing in the shop of Peter Short, where both of the 1598 quartos were produced, considerable care for the text is also evident: the two editions are, as $Cam^2$ notes, 'among the most carefully printed quartos of any play by Shakespeare' ($Cam^2$, 199). Seemingly the Q1 edition was set by formes, the outer formes set first. But, as P. H. Davison was apparently the first to notice, its headlines establish that two skeletons were used in alternate sheets: one for both formes of A, C, E, G and I, and another for both of B, D, F, H and K. (On $D1^v$ and $D2^r$ and on $D3^v$ and $D4^r$, the running titles have been reversed, the recto title on the verso page and vice versa.) Davison has argued that the headline pattern suggests two compositors working with separate presses (Davison, 251–3; see also Jackson, 'Two'). Susan Zimmerman, however, in an analysis based on compositorial preferences in capitalization, spelling and punctuation, concludes 'that only one compositor set the text for 1H4' (Zimmerman, 221).

Still, one must wonder about the unmistakable evidence of two skeletons, especially as most of the books emerging from Peter Short's printing house before 1598 have only one. The simple solution – that two skeletons implies two compositors working on separate presses with a goal to speed production – is undeniably appealing, but if this were the case one would expect to find that the two skeletons were used alternately to achieve the desired time savings. However, each skeleton is used twice, and then the other is used twice and so on, a pattern of imposition seemingly used in other plays, for example Lyly's *Sapho and Phao* (1584) (RP). Zimmerman may then be right, confirming the earlier assertion of Hinman that Q1 was set by a single compositor (Hinman, ix), for this procedure offers little benefit from an additional compositor. A single compositor may indeed have set the play, working, as Zimmerman says, 'from outer A to outer B, inner A to inner B, and so forth' (Zimmerman, 238), a process that makes some sense if the goal was *not* to speed production. In 1598, Short was almost exclusively printing short books in small formats, thus requiring less composition and more press work from his shop. The odd procedure of printing *1 Henry IV* might then actually be the result of a desire to slow composition to keep everyone occupied, and, if so, might well be what permitted the unusually carefully printed text, as type could be held in forme while corrections were made (Bland). If all this, however, is necessarily speculative, what Zimmerman's work certainly shows is how much more we need to know about the usual practices of the early modern printing house.

Nonetheless, the procedures of the printing house are not of any obvious literary interest and have usually been of concern only to analytic bibliographers and historians of printing. Increasingly, however, editors and even critics have begun to recognize how the process of a text's materialization affects what is made present to be read. In the case of *1 Henry IV* interest in the compositors has come largely from editors who have found in the two 1598 quartos a pattern of formalizing colloquialisms (e.g. 'All is one for that' at 2.4.149, which F renders as 'All's one for that' ) and are in search of its source. J. Dover Wilson argued that these demonstrate the 'interference of a compositor or master printer'

(Cam[1], 104), hence some of the interest in the presswork of Q0 and Q1, though there is no reason to think that the language does not reflect the practices of the person who prepared the manuscript that reached the printing house – or even of Shakespeare himself, who might well have been happy to allow an actor to find the appropriate rhythm of the line (see 1.3.123n.).

Later editions of the play – the quartos of 1599 (Q2), 1604 (Q3), 1608 (Q4), 1613 (Q5), 1622 (Q6), 1632 (Q7) and 1639 (Q8), and the Folio text of 1623 (F1) – are all derived from the 1598 quartos. Though Q2 claims on its title-page to be 'Newly corrected by *W. Shake-speare*' (see Fig. 18), for the first time identifying the play as Shakespeare's, the assertion is a marketing ploy rather than a bibliographic fact. Q2 is closely based on Q1; what differences exist are not the result of the author's corrections or revisions but of the normal procedures of a printing house whereby some effort would be made to correct obvious errors while inevitably allowing some new ones to creep in. As Q2 was set from Q1, so Q3 was set from Q2, and Q4 from Q3, Q5 from Q4, and the 1623 Folio text was set from Q5. None of the editions is an exact reprint of its predecessor, but none has access to any independent authority. Q5 does correctly assign 1.3.200–7 to Hotspur where the previous texts give the lines to Northumberland, and it emends Worcester's line at 5.2.3 from 'Then are we all under one' to the far more sensible 'Then are we all undone', the reading followed by all modern editors; but neither of these corrections suggests an authoritative hand at work, only an alert corrector or master printer.

F1, however, does demand additional attention. In the Folio, *1 Henry IV* appears on sigs d5$^v$ to f6$^r$ (pp. 46–73, though what should be 47 is misnumbered 49, with the page numbers continuing successively from the mispagination). The Folio text was clearly set from a copy of Q5, unsystematically correcting, as Alice Walker noted, only some 26 of the more than 200 errors that had by then crept into the text (Walker, 52), but it does show some

THE
# HISTORY OF
## HENRIE THE
### FOVRTH;

With the battell at Shrewsburie,
*betweene the King and Lord* Henry
Percy, *surnamed* Henry Hotspur of the North.

*With the humorous conceits of Sir*
Iohn Falstalffe.

Newly corrected by *W. shake-speare.*

## AT LONDON,
Printed by *S. S.* for *Andrew Wise,* dwelling
in Paules Churchyard, at the signe of
the Angell. 1599.

18  Q2 title-page, 1599

unmistakable signs of editorial involvement. It differs more substantially from Q5 than, for example, Q2 differs from Q1.

The Folio text more or less successfully removes the oaths that the 1606 Act to Restrain Abuses of Players (3 Jac. I, c. 21) had ordered expurgated, a procedure almost certainly not undertaken in the printing house. If it had originated in the printing house, '*1 Henry IV* would be, in terms of the First Folio, inexplicably unique' (Taylor & Jowett, 65). After the Act of 27 May 1606, no doubt the playing text of *1 Henry IV* was subjected to expurgation to bring performance of the play into compliance with the law. Taylor and Jowett conclude that the expurgation in the Folio text 'derives from the [playhouse] manuscript, rather than the folio editors' (65). But 'the availability and use of the manuscript' (65) by the Folio editors, so obvious to Taylor and Jowett, seem less inevitable to me. The Folio expurgation may only reflect the attention of Heminge and Condell in preparing the play for the press from Q5, which served for copy. The two former colleagues of Shakespeare were perhaps aware that the old profanity could offend the Master of the Revels (still George Buc as the Folio was being prepared, but his imminent replacement certain) or maybe they were merely seeking to bring the printed text in line with the play as it had been performed and would be known to the Folio's readers.

Whatever the motive, it would not have been a demanding job, and indeed could easily have been done as other necessary editorial acts were performed. Common oaths like 'zounds' are removed in F, and other changes are made to reflect the mandated removal of profanity from the stage: Q's 'God giue thee the spirit of perswasion' (1.2.144) becomes in F 'maist thou haue the Spirit of perswasion'; even Q's 'I could sing psalmes, or anything' (2.4.127) is altered to F's 'I could sing all manner of songs'. But F also adds act and scene divisions, provides some needed exits absent from Q while also omitting some no less necessary ones that Q includes, and regularizes some speech prefixes. In addition, it undertakes a certain amount of metrical regularization, both marking some elisions, so that, for example, F's version of Q5's 'Then let not him be slandered with reuolt' (1.3.112) has 'sland'red', and sometimes adding a syllable to 'complete' a line, as at 1.1.28, where Q5's 'But this our purpose is twelue month old' becomes the decasyllabic 'But this our purpose is a twelue month old'. In a few places, however, there are readings that seem to involve more substantial revision of the quarto text, and some scholars have argued that Q5 was collated by the Folio editors with a manuscript version of the play, perhaps the acting company's promptbook (the term is, of course, an anachronism, but is still a useful designation for a copy of an acting text marked for performance; see Long, however, for the limitations for Shakespearean editors of the familiar label). Wilson, for example, argues that F's reading 'President' (i.e. precedent) at 2.4.32 for Q's 'present' establishes 'a firm link between the F. *1 Henry IV* and the Globe prompt-book', as it is a reading 'most unlikely to have occurred to the unaided intelligence of a printer or scrivener' (Cam[1], 106). The link, however, does not seem quite as firm as Wilson suggests. The copy of Q5 from which F was printed could have been corrected by the Folio editors, who may well have recalled the proper reading, and there are numerous examples in other plays of 'printers and scriveners' divining what seem authorized readings from copy that makes less than perfect sense.

Other F readings have been offered as evidence that Q5 was collated with some authoritative manuscript. Oxf[1] accepts F's 'Made me to answer' for Q's 'I answered' at 1.3.66, confident that the F reading 'can only be explained as an authorial alteration' (*TxC*, 333), though it is hard to see why the Oxford editors are so certain the alteration is 'authorial'. It is indeed unlikely to be compositorial, but why it might not be scribal or editorial is unclear to me. One might indeed wish to preserve this reading, thinking it Shakespearean, but assurance that it is so seems unattainable. The same argument applies to other places where Oxf[1] prints F readings, as at 1.3.211 or 1.3.134 (see commentary).

The Folio's alterations of Q5 need not have resulted from anything more than an aggressive editorial hand and do not clearly
imply access to an alternative authority for the text itself. If, as
some editors have suggested, the Folio editors had access to the
marked-up promptbook in addition to Q5, one would expect at
the very least that F would supply necessary stage directions
where they are absent from Q5 and amplify or clarify those which
are clearly inadequate for performance; but F does not. Whatever
the habits of prompt copy, one would expect it to be clear about
what characters are on stage; if the bookkeeper's prompt copy had
been consulted for F, one would expect, for example, that
Westmorland would not appear in the entry direction beginning
5.1, though he does in Q (see commentary).

Even those who hold that F was printed from a copy of Q
marked up after being compared with some form of prompt copy
admit that this was at best 'a desultory collation' (Walton, 236). The
example given above (p. 114) of F's metrical regularization of 1.1.28
is telling, for, while F successfully regularizes the imperfect pentameter line of Q5, it does so without reference to the authoritative
Q1 reading, which collation with a playhouse manuscript presumably would have offered: 'But this our purpose now is twelue month
old'. What this suggests is that the preparation of the Folio text did
not include careful collation of Q5 with some authoritative manuscript, but rather involved nothing more than normal editorial
attention from one or both of the volume's editors, probably John
Heminge and Henry Condell but possibly, as Ernst Honigmann has
argued, Ralph Crane (Honigmann, *Texts*, 171–8). But whoever
assumed the task of preparing the texts for the Folio, even though,
as M. A. Shaaber wrote, 'the job was neither thoroughly nor altogether competently done', it was undertaken with 'the same
purpose as the operations of any editor, to make good the obvious
defects of the text and to put it in as intelligible form as possible for
the reader' (Shaaber, 'Problems', 113).

What seems clear, then, is that, as *1 Henry IV* gets republished
after the first edition in 1598, all later texts are essentially based

upon their predecessors. Q0, therefore, becomes the only authoritative text of the play (though the Folio 'alterations' do demand careful consideration, if only because Heminge and Condell, if they were indeed the Folio editors, had experience of the play in performance). Q0, as we've seen, survives only in the fragment covering 1.3.200 to 2.2.108. For the rest of the play Q1 must serve to remedy its incompleteness. Happily Q1's treatment of the Q0 material suggests how carefully it was set from its predecessor. It makes only one error – the omission of 'fat' at 2.2.108 – and two substantive alterations: it corrects Q0's 'whip' to the appropriate 'whipt' (1.3.237) and at 2.2.35 changes Q0's 'my owne flesh' to 'mine owne flesh' seemingly to regularize Falstaff's idiom (cf. 'thine owne heire apparent garters' seven lines later). Even Q0's authority is, of course, no more than relative, but, since all later editions ultimately derive from it, it is here that an editor must begin. But how close this takes us to Shakespeare's original is impossible to say with confidence.

No holograph manuscripts of any of Shakespeare's plays are known to exist (with the possible exception of the 147 lines known as 'Hand D' in the *Sir Thomas More* manuscript). What we have are printed texts, like that of *1 Henry IV*, that were set from manuscripts now lost, which reached a publisher in some unknown way, from some unknown source, representing some unknown state of the play. Bibliographers, however, inevitably wonder about the manuscripts that lie behind the first printed texts of the plays. Were they in Shakespeare's own hand? And, if so, what stage of his writing do they represent – were they early drafts or final revisions? Were they the manuscript copies that the company itself would have kept annotated for performance? Were they copies prepared by a scribe, perhaps for a collector? Or were they copies that were prepared after one or more actors tried to recall the play which they had performed? Each of these might easily be the source of the manuscript that found its way to the printing house and served as the text from which the play was set in print. And, if we knew with certainty the nature of the underlying manuscript, we might speculate more confidently about how closely the printed play represents the intentions of its author.

But it is again worth saying that none of these manuscripts survives. Editors must, therefore, work backwards from the printed texts, searching for clues (such as the consistency of speech prefixes, or the specificity of stage directions) that might reveal the nature of the underlying manuscript. In the case of *1 Henry IV*, the manuscript seems to have been unusually clean; certainly Q0 and Q1 give the impression of reliability, revealing almost nothing of the kind of confusion present in some printed playbooks that seemingly stems from the imperfect nature of the manuscripts from which they were printed. Indeed it has been plausibly argued that the manuscript of *1 Henry IV* was brought to the publisher by the acting company to let the publication advertise their compliance with the request or demand that Oldcastle's name be changed (see p. 54). This manuscript would have changed all the appearances of 'Oldcastle' to 'Falstaff' in the text as well as in stage directions and speech prefixes. Probably it was also at this time that 'Bardoll' and 'Peto' replaced 'Rossill' and 'Harvey', two other names that might have given offence, though this revision was incomplete. Poins refers in QF to 'Falstaffe, Haruey, Rossill, and Gadshil' at 1.2.154, and speech headings remain for '*Ross.*' in Q1–5 at 2.4.168,170 and 174, which were changed in F to '*Gad.*'.[1]

What kind of manuscript was turned over to the printer? The fact that the quartos' entrances and exits are often insufficiently specific to cue performance suggests that the manuscript copy was not the theatre company's prompt copy (which the actors would have been unlikely to turn over eagerly to the printer in any case, given how new a play *1 Henry IV* was in 1598). Some of the printed texts' omissions of entrances and exits of certain characters (notably Bardoll) not merely point to the fact that the underlying manuscript

---

1   See Jowett, 324–33; and Fredson Bowers, 'Establishing Shakespeare's Text: Poins and Peto in *1 Henry IV*', *SB*, 34 (1981), 189–98.

did not specify them but also suggest that they might not all yet have been worked out, indicating to some scholars that the manuscript was Shakespeare's own working draft. Thus Wilson, for example, argues that 'we have every encouragement to believe, in short, that the "copy" used for Q0 and entered on 25 February 1598 was Shakespeare's own manuscript' (Cam[1], 104).

Q0 seems, however, more likely to have been set from a scribally prepared transcript. MacD. P. Jackson argues convincingly that the occurrence of verbal preferences in the printed text that contrast markedly with those appearing in those of Shakespeare's plays that scholars generally agree were printed from authorial manuscripts strongly suggests the intervention of a scribe here: where, for example, *2 Henry IV* ('obviously set from foul papers', as Jackson says) prints '*between*' nine times and never uses the variant form of the connective, '*betwixt*', *1 Henry IV* reverses this almost exactly, printing '*betwixt*' seven times, and never using '*between*'; and, where *2 Henry IV* and indeed all the 'good Shakespearian quartos published before *Hamlet* Q2', regardless of which printing house was responsible for the play, show an almost exclusive preference for 'pray thee' over the colloquial 'prithee', *1 Henry IV* is strikingly anomalous: 'pray thee' appears twice in Q1 and 'prithee' (usually spelled 'preethee') twenty-two times (Jackson, 'Two', 188; Jackson, 'Copy', 353). Perhaps, too, the name changes themselves argue against the manuscript being in Shakespeare's hand. It seems unlikely that Shakespeare would have found his own time well spent on such a scribal task or that he would have forgotten to emend the old names, at least those in the text in 1.2. It is difficult not to conclude that a scribal manuscript, rather than an authorial one, underlies the printed text of *1 Henry IV*. Q1 and the surviving sheet of Q0 are, then, as close as we can get to Shakespeare's hand in this play. If the authentic version keeps receding frustratingly beyond our reach, or, rather, if the very notion of authenticity does, nonetheless we do have in the case of *1 Henry IV* printed versions that are fine and revealing examples of the process of turning a play into a playbook.

## EDITORIAL PROCEDURES

This edition is based on the two quartos of 1598, using the fragment Q0 for the 301 lines of text that it covers (1.3.200–2.2.108) and Q1 for the rest of the play. All substantive changes from these editions are recorded in the textual notes, along with their source. The 1623 Folio has also been carefully considered, since its editors would have had practical experience of the play, and among its accepted readings are the act and scene divisions absent from all the quartos (with the addition of a scene at 5.3 unmarked in the Folio too). Other editions, including the seven additional pre-1640 quartos and the Dering manuscript, have also provided readings adopted here and noted.

I have, however, departed from Q0 and Q1 only when they are evidently in error. In this I have perhaps been more conservative than many editors, but, while emended texts sometimes produce better sense than the original, we cannot be sure it is Shakespeare's sense. The two editions of 1598, in fact, offer few insoluble problems; both are, for playbooks, carefully printed, Q0 apparently from a clean manuscript copy and Q1 from Q0 (see pp. 106–8, 118).

The text presented here, as in all Arden editions, modernizes the spelling and punctuation of the originals. Old forms of words are retained; old spellings or phonetic variants are modernized (thus, 'leathern' is retained at 2.4.68, but 'cristall' becomes 'crystal' in the same line) – though the distinction is often hard to maintain (e.g. is 'holla' a variant spelling or variant form of 'holler'?). Punctuation is brought into line with modern practice, which substitutes for the largely elocutionary pointing of the sixteenth and seventeenth centuries a punctuation designed to clarify the logical relations between grammatical units.

In most regards such modernization is an unobjectionable procedure. It allows the play to be read without the largely artificial obstacle of unfamiliar spelling forms and punctuation practices. If the spelling and punctuation of the early texts accurately preserved Shakespeare's own orthography, a stronger case might be made for its retention. Printing-house compositors setting the text would not, however, generally feel bound to follow the spelling and punctuation of their copy, especially as these had not yet been fully standardized. But, if the spelling and punctuation of the early texts, then, reflect mainly the idiosyncratic habits of the printing-house compositors (who were setting the play from manuscripts which themselves offer no guarantee of being in Shakespeare's hand), an old-spelling edition provides a mere illusion of authenticity and a distraction for most readers.

In general modernization is a straightforward process, as one can see with reference to Fig. 19, which is a reproduction of sig. A3$^r$ of Q1. Words whose spelling has changed or become standardized over time are presented here in their familiar modern forms. It seems unproblematic to print for Q1's 'plaines' in the seventh line the modern 'plains', or, for 'enuy' in the fifteenth line, 'envy'. It is, of course, not without interest that words could be spelled variously and that 'u' was used medially for 'v' (as was 'i' for 'j'), but that interest is not primary for most readers of this edition. And, for those for whom this linguistic or typographic interest is central and the text a significant archive of historical linguistic or printing practice, a facsimile of the original will, in any case, be of far greater value than an edited old-spelling edition. So one confidently renders Q's 'smothe' as 'smooth', 'tooke' as 'took', and 'cald' as 'called'.

But the issues are not always so straightforward. Proper names create a particular difficulty. Q1's 'Holmedons plaines' in the seventh line clearly refers to the place of the battle in 1402 between the Percys and a Scottish invasion force. The modern name of the Northumberland town is 'Humbleton'. Editors have tended here to retain the early spelling, while modernizing other place-names in the text (e.g. St Albans, for Q's 'S. Albones'). Perhaps the inconsistency is untroubling, since this is after all a play rather than a historical account. None of these places can properly be said to exist, except as part of Shakespeare's imaginings, and Humbleton, or Holmedon, is sufficiently unfamiliar to most

*of Henrie the fourth.*

Staind with the variation of each foile,
Betwixt that Holmedon and this feat of ours:
And he hath brought vs smothe and welcom newes,
The Earle of *Douglas* is discomfited,
Ten thousand bould Scots, two and twenty knights
Balkt in their own bloud. Did sir Walter see
On Holmedons plaines, of prisoners Hotspur tooke
Mordake Earle of Fife, and eldest sonne
To beaten Douglas, and the Earle of Athol,
Of Murrey, Angus, and Menteith:
And is not this an honorable spoile?
A gallant prize? Ha coosen, is it not?          In faith it is.
   *West.* A conquest for a Prince to boast of.
   *King.* Yea, there thou makst me sad, and makst me sinne
In enuy, that my Lord Northumberland
Should be the father to so blest a sonne:
A sonne, who is the theame of honors tongue,
Amongst a groue, the very straightest plant,
Who is sweet fortunes minion and her pride,
Whilst I by looking on the praise of him
See ryot and dishonour staine the brow
Of my young Harry. O that it could be prou'd
That some night tripping fairy had exchang'd,
In cradle clothes our children where they lay,
And cald mine Percy, his Plantagenet,
Then would I haue his Harry, and he mine:
But let him from my thoughts. What think you coose
Of this young Percies pride? The prisoners
Which he in this aduenture hath surprizd
To his own vse, he keepes and sends me word
I shal haue none but Mordake Earle of Fife.
   *West.* This is his vncles teaching. This is Worcester,
Maleuolent to you in all aspects,
Which makes him prune himselfe, and bristle vp
The crest of youth against your dignity.
   *King.* But I haue sent for him to answere this:
And for this cause a while we must neglect
Our holy purpose to Ierusalem.

                    A.3                              Coosen

19   Q1 sig. A3$^r$, 1598

121

readers that no spelling prompts instant recognition. Nonetheless, 'Holmedon' appears on no modern map, and the argument that the modern form of the name disrupts the metre of the line depends on knowing how 'Holmedon' was pronounced. Editors reason backwards from the line to assume it has two syllables, but Holinshed's forms – 'Homildon' or 'Homeldon' – suggest it has three; and the modern Humbleton, in fact, is often pronounced by local residents with a collapse of the three medial consonants to produce a word (almost) of two syllables, 'Hum-blton'. Little then seems gained by retaining an idiosyncratic form of a place-name in an edition which otherwise is committed to modernization.

On this same logic, personal names and titles are rendered here in their modern forms. Simple archaisms are adjusted: e.g. 'Canturburie' becomes 'Canterbury' (1.2.120), and 'Mighel' becomes 'Michael' in 4.4. Q's 'Athol' (line 9 in Fig. 19) is normalized to 'Atholl'. Where there is a *DNB* reference for a historical figure represented in the play, that form of the name is adopted; thus, Q's 'Westmerland' becomes 'Westmorland' and 'Blunt' becomes 'Blount'. 'Murrey' (in line 10 of Fig. 19) is in most editions modernized as 'Murray', but the reference is to the Earl of Moray (see 1.1.73 and note) and that is the form adopted here. No significant pronunciation difference results from the modernization (and, in this case, clarification) of the name. Similarly, 'Mordake' (line 8) is rendered in its familiar modern form of 'Murdoch'.

More complicated is the case of Owen Glendower, as the name appears in its familiar anglicized form. The historical figure was Owain ap Gruffydd, who took the cognomen Glyndwr from the name of the manor of Glyndyfrdwy (see List of Roles, 12n.). It is tempting to restore the Welsh form of his name. In part the issue is metrical, since 'Glendower', which is the form consistently adopted by Q, is seemingly pronounced with two syllables (e.g. 1.3.101), closer indeed to the Welsh pronunciation than to the usual English trisyllabic pronunciation.

But arguably more problematic is that the anglicizing can be thought to perform linguistically the political domination the historical Glyndwr so passionately resisted. Welsh identity becomes textually subordinate to English desire. (Interestingly in this regard, the very word 'Welsh' comes from an Old English word meaning 'foreign'.) This is not an inconsequential concern either politically or editorially, but this edition retains the familiar anglicization precisely on the grounds that for Shakespeare 'Glendower' exists as he is written. 'Glendower' is Holinshed's Glendower or Daniel's; that is, a 'Glendower' already written not only into English spelling but into English history. The play, in fact, demonstrates an unusual interest in and respect for the Welsh language, and Shakespeare's company had at least two Welsh-speaking actors. In 3.1, where the play requires Welsh to be spoken, Shakespeare has not transliterated the language (or the compositor has declined to set it), but it would have been spoken on stage (see 3.1.193 SD and Fig. 20). The sounds of Welsh are heard by an audience, but Welsh is not visible on the printed page.

In another case, I have altered a sanctioned name, though this might better be thought an example of 'unmodernizing' than of the modernizing I have been discussing. The character usually referred to as 'Bardolph' is here 'Bardoll' (see List of Roles, 19n.). Though Bardolph has the virtues of both familiarity and consistency with the two other plays in which the character appears, it seems clear that once Shakespeare settled on a name for the character he called him 'Bardoll' (or 'Bardol' as it is spelled four of the twelve times the name appears). He is nowhere referred to as 'Bardolph' or 'Bardolfe' in any of the sixteenth- and seventeenth-century quartos of *1 Henry IV*, the first of the plays in which the character appears. Except in one case at 2.4.290 (TLN 1,255), where 'Bardol' appears, F does regularize (modernize?) the name as 'Bardolph', bringing it into line with the spelling in *2 Henry IV*, *Henry V* and *Merry Wives*, but it is hard to see why an edition of *1 Henry IV* based on the two 1598 quartos would follow suit. All that could justify the spelling 'Bardolph' in such an edition is

47

Mor: In faith, my lord, you are too wilful-blame,

And since your coming hither have done enough

To put him quite beside his patience;

You must needs learn, lord, to amend this fault:

Though sometimes it show greatness, courage, blood,-

And that's the dearest grace it renders you,-

Yet oftentimes it doth present harsh rage,

Defect of manners, want of government,

The least of which haunting a noble man

Loseth men's hearts, and leaves behind a stain

Upon the beauty of all parts besides.

Hot: Well, I am school'd: good manners be your speed!

Here come our wives, and let us take our leave.

Mor: This is the deadly spite that angers me;

My wife can speak no English, I no Welsh.

Gle: My daughter weeps: she'll not part with you;

She'll be a soldier too, she'll to the wars.

Mor: Good father, tell her that she and my aunt Percy

Shall follow in your conduct speedily.

Gle: Tydd ddewr, fy merch.

Rhaid i filwr ateb ei alwad.

Cei ddilyn yn fy ngofal i gyda'th Fodryb

Persi, ac fe weli dy Fortimer annwyl yn fuan eto.

L.M: Ond pwy wyr na welaf mohono byth.

O, fy nhad, gadewch i mi fynd gydag ef.

Nid oes arnag ofn yn wir.

Gle: Na, nid lle i wragedd yw rhyfeloedd, fy ngeneth i.

Rhaid i ti aros a chanlyn gyde mi.

L.M: Nis gallaf aroshebddo.

Mae'n rhaid i mi gael mynd, a chaiff neb fy

ngwahardd chwaith.

Gle: She is desperate here; a peevish self-will'd harlotry,

one that no persuasion can do good upon.

L.M: Syll f'annwylyd, i ddwfn fy llygaid,

20 Page of Welsh text from the promptbook for the Royal Shakespeare production of 1964

124

tradition, and, if that were reason enough, there would be no need to edit. I leave the implications for editing the three other plays to future editors but will confess that in *2 Henry IV* where confusingly there is a Lord Bardolph, 'Bardoll' is particularly appealing, though, unlike *1 Henry IV*, that play's quarto does not authorize it.

The facsimile page also allows us to see some of the issues in modernizing punctuation. Not having a manuscript in Shakespeare's hand makes it impossible to know how closely the quarto's punctuation represents Shakespeare's practice; the inevitability of compositorial influence (and, possibly, also of scribal influence, if the manuscript copy was not in the author's hand) undermines any assumption that the printed punctuation reveals Shakespeare's own habits of punctuation or somehow indicates how the lines are to be spoken.[1] Though the punctuation of Q is rarely 'seriously misleading', in Wilson's phrase (Cam[1], 112), the facsimile page reveals habits of pointing quite different from our own, marked in the main by a heavier dependence on commas than modern usage recommends. Sometimes these are used in Q to mark a desirable pause, as, for example, the comma after 'himselfe', five lines up from the bottom of the page. Sometimes, as in line 3 after 'newes', the comma serves where modern usage demands a heavier stop (in this case a full point or a colon). In other places, however, where we would expect a comma to clarify the logical relationships (e.g. after 'knights' in line 5, where its absence seemingly restricts the following phrase to the knights and not, as I take it the thought is, to all 10,000 Scots), the text has none, perhaps omitted in the manuscript in the confidence that the natural impulse to pause at line end would clarify the issue. It is impossible to respect both the largely

---

1 Audrey Stanley, in 'Acting *Henry IV, Part I* and the quarto text', *On-Stage Studies*, 3 (1979), 65–75, argues that Q's punctuation serves as a useful guide for actors in delivering the verse. Though many of her examples are suggestive, both the tendentiousness of her selection of passages and her lack of attention to printing-house practice vitiate the claim that Q1 can serve as a reliable index to the intended rhythms of a line.

rhetorical principles of late-sixteenth-century pointing and our own age's more syntactic punctuation. With the necessity to choose, the Arden series has opted for modern habits of punctuation, as they at least work to clarify the logical relationships within the lines, offering the reader the kind of help one expects from a scholarly edition.

A further issue for an editor of the play, though one that is not evident on the facsimile page, is that *1 Henry IV* has a number of lines printed as prose in the quartos that many editors have relined as verse. It is often difficult to differentiate rhythmical prose from verse with varied metrical principles. Merely because it is possible to realign the text to produce a number of consecutive lines each with ten syllables is not enough to justify the change. I am tempted to these changes only when the logic for verse can be seen in the text and when the rhythms of what is now to be read as verse seem compelling. The argument for verse is strengthened in those cases where the page on which the disputed text appears gives evidence of crowding, so that the prose setting may result from the compositor's need to save space, probably because the copy was inexactly 'cast off'. This is the necessary procedure in the printing of books set by formes of estimating how much text will be taken by pages not yet printed. For example, in printing a book in a quarto, the compositor would typeset sheets of eight pages, with pages 1, 4, 5 and 8 printed together on one side of the sheet and then pages 2, 3, 6 and 7 printed together on the other. The sheet would eventually be folded twice to get the pages in the correct order for reading. Although the compositor could set page 1 directly from his copy, he would have to estimate how much text would be taken by 2 and 3 to know where he should start on page 4. Sometimes he over- or underestimated, necessitating either crowding or spreading out the text on page 3 to compensate; see 3.1.3–11n.).

In the actual treatment of the verse lines, I am similarly cautious. On the same principle that I, like most modern editors, resist the Augustan tendency to add syllables to a line to regularize the metre, I am reluctant to mark their elision in the text. Shakespeare's metrical practice is not nearly as regular in this play as such procedures would demand (see Appendix 2). The elision of syllables needed to regularize the verse line is indicated only when it is clearly indicated by Q0–1 spellings (e.g. 'there thou makst me sad, and makst me sinne' at 1.1.77; l. 14 in Fig. 19), or where the line seemingly requires it and the elided form has itself clearly been established in contemporary usage (e.g. 'o'erruled' at 4.4.17 for Q1's 'ouerrulde'). Otherwise the word is spelled out (e.g. 'flowerets' at 1.1.8, rendering Q1's 'flourets', where the pronunciation of the Q reading is unclear), as the flexibility of English stress and pronunciation permit various ways of understanding and realizing the metrical principle of particular lines (cf. 3.1.49n.).

In accordance with normal Arden practice, in the commentary I indicate sounded '-ed's in the final syllable of past tense and participial verb forms where these seem to me certain from the metrical structure of the line, and also record unpredictable and unfamiliar pronunciations when these seem clear. Given the flexibility both of Shakespeare's verse and of English pronunciation, I am, however, reluctant to work backward from the normative verse line to conclude that certain words were necessarily pronounced with the number of syllables apparently required where this produces idiosyncratic pronunciations otherwise unsupported. For example, I do not suggest, as have some editors (e.g. Kittredge), that 'Douglas' should suddenly be pronounced with three syllables at 5.2.32, though I do say that Glendower is pronounced with two syllables, mainly on the consistent evidence of the verse (e.g. 3.1.85), but also because there is other evidence of this disyllabic pronunciation (e.g. *Mirror*, 'Owen Glendower', 121, 11.6–7, where 'Glendour' rhymes with 'slender').

I have regularized speech prefixes throughout; thus Q0–1's various forms for the Prince – '*Pr.*', '*Pri.*', '*Prin.*', '*Prince*' – become uniformly 'PRINCE'. The only significant variant in Q concerns Hotspur; in 4.1, in place of the usual '*Hot.*', on ten occasions *'Per.'* appears, the abbreviation of Percy almost certainly a function of the compositor needing an alternative form for the SP because of having run out of capital 'H's. Both *'Hot.'* and *'Per.'* are here regularized to 'HOTSPUR'.

If speech prefixes are easily dealt with, stage directions pose greater difficulty. I have retained all SDs from Q and taken some from F, where F further clarifies the action. The F SDs are recorded in the textual notes and bracketed in the text. Sometimes there are minor changes in wording from the early forms of these SDs, and these changes too are recorded. QF's SDs, however, need to be supplemented. Numerous exits need to be supplied, as well as some entrances. In some of these cases, the exact moment when the character exits or enters is unclear. Even when the entrance is specified this can be the case. For example, in 5.2.27, Vernon says to Worcester, 'Here comes your cousin.' Q's entry for Hotspur, however, is placed at the end of Worcester's previous speech. Possibly this means that Hotspur is meant to be visible to the audience before Vernon begins to speak, but more likely the reason the SD appears where it does in Q is that Worcester's final line takes up only half the available space and there is room for the SD, where Vernon's line ends at the margin. The opposite set of spatial concerns seems to determine Worcester's entrance at 1.3.128. Here Northumberland's line announcing the arrival of the character precedes Q's *'Enter Wor'*. Yet here, too, one cannot be confident that the placement of the SD on the quarto page indicates the desired staging, because Northumberland's previous line reaches all the way to the margin, and even uses '&' for 'and' to prevent the line from turning over. The half-line, 'Here comes your uncle', leaves plenty of room for the compositor to set the SD. An editor must decide where such entry directions belong, but the printed text may mislead. Where I have moved a direction from its place in Q I have collated the change in the textual notes.

While in general QF are, as Alice Walker wrote, 'not, on the whole badly equipped as regards stage directions' (Walker, 55), inevitably many actions remained unspecified. Wherever I have included SDs that do not originate in the early texts these are placed in square brackets. I have not, however, tried to remedy QF's reticence about staging by aggressively specifying action in the text itself, in the main because I don't believe it is the role of an edition to block the play. Directors and actors have theatrical imaginations far better suited to this task than most editors. The role of an editor is to establish the text of the play as accurately as is possible, enabling readers to understand what is said, by whom and to whom and who else is on stage at that moment, and to indicate only those actions that are required to clarify the text.

Therefore I do add a direction at the end of 2.4 for the Prince to pull the arras closed, though no action is specified in QF, since some means must be provided for Falstaff to leave the stage before the rebels appear in 3.1. It is possible that Peto closes the arras, though to me the gesture seems more dramatically effective if it is Hal's, but what seems certain is that the arras is not left open as the Prince and Peto depart, leaving Falstaff visible as the rebels enter. The action, however, is not implicit in the language, so a stage direction must be provided. On the other hand, at the beginning of 3.1, Hotspur invites Mortimer, Glendower and Worcester to 'sit down' (4), and then Glendower in response says, 'Sit, cousin Percy' (6). It does not seem to help a reader in any way to specify after Hotspur's invitation '*They sit*', or after Glendower's line to add '*Hotspur sits*' or some such. Readers will have no difficulty imagining the action, and directors will no doubt find interesting ways of choreographing the edgy stage business that the SDs can only limit. In truth, it isn't necessary that they do sit, or, if they do, precisely when they do; and a director might choose to make the *refusal* of the invitation the point of focus. If they do sit, then the SD is unnecessary, and if they don't (or do it later) it is misleading. In either case, such a direction offers little aid to a reader of the play.

An even clearer example of why I resist adding a direction where the language seemingly invites one comes in the very line in which Glendower asks Hotspur to 'sit'. In 3.1.6, after Hotspur has forgotten the map, Glendower replies, 'here it is.' 'Here' obviously calls for some gesture, but exactly what action accompanies the line is uncertain. Glendower might spot the map somewhere on Hotspur's person and pull it out; he might point to it already unrolled on a table; he might pull it out rolled from inside his own jacket. There are numerous ways of enacting the moment, and even a bracketed SD would suggest to a reader more confidence about the specified action than any editor can possibly have. One could perhaps provide a stage direction carefully worded so that none of the various possibilities is excluded (e.g. *'He reveals the map'*), but this tells a reader nothing more than the line itself does.

But, if the naked line on the page does not reveal the required action, it only confirms the fact that certainty is something all editors must learn to live without. Consider, for example, the main textual problem revealed in Fig. 19. Speaking of the captives taken prisoner by Hotspur, the King concludes: 'And is not this an honourable spoile? / A gallant prize? Ha coosen, is it not?' (lines 11–12). Some six spaces to the right a phrase floats on the page: 'In faith it is.' The following line has the new speech prefix: *'West.'* and the line: 'A conquest for a Prince to boast of.' The difficulty, of course, is posed by the unattached phrase. Seemingly it belongs to Westmorland, as an answer to the King's question, but it is not impossible that the King enthusiastically answers his own question and Westmorland responds only with the line following Q's SP (a reading that perhaps has the virtue of emphasizing the apparent dig in Westmorland's use of the word 'Prince'). Or perhaps the floating line could be split. The King could say: 'is it not in faith?' But, if either seems somewhat less likely than the usual arrangement of the text, the actual form of Westmorland's response is itself problematic. Does he say (as in this edition), 'In faith, it is: a conquest for a prince to boast of' (1.1.76), or some such grammatical arrangement that recognizes the two parts of the utterance as grammatically independent; or is the full point following 'is' a compositorial error, and the line actually 'In faith, it is a conquest for a prince to boast of' (with the emphasis on 'is')?

There is no way to be sure what Shakespeare wrote here, and editors can only arrange the text according to their understanding of the logic of the language, of the relationship between the characters, of the usual processes of the printing house, and what little we know of the usual form of dramatic manuscripts.

In this example perhaps we see both the frustrations and the pleasures of editing a play. We too often think of editing as an activity that is mechanical and objective; it is neither. Even a brilliant editor like Wilson, who must have known better, would sometimes juxtapose the shifting 'sand' of 'literary judgement' and the bibliographic 'rock of fact' (Wilson, 'Copy', 185). But, in the face of what cannot be recovered from the past, those seemingly solid rocks of fact easily crumble into all too shifty grains of sand, and literary judgement becomes in the final analysis what every editor must depend upon. Editing is a mode of critical engagement with the play, though of course one ideally informed with relevant historical knowledge about the theatre, about the playwright, about the language of the period and about the various activities that enabled a play written to be acted to become a text to be read. At almost every moment editors are required to be critics, and their critical judgements construct the text that we read. The attractive solidity of the modern published edition on a bookshelf or open on a desk asserts far more certainty about what is on the page than its editor can possibly feel. Our editions inevitably belie the provisional nature of the edited text, overstating the authority of what is set forth in the impressive physical form in which they appear. The sheer number of editions alone makes this point, but, even so, they remain (at least for this editor) profoundly satisfying acknowledgements of both the effort involved in their making and the long and honourable history in which they take their place.

21  Map of Britain showing principal places mentioned in the play

# KING HENRY IV
## PART ONE

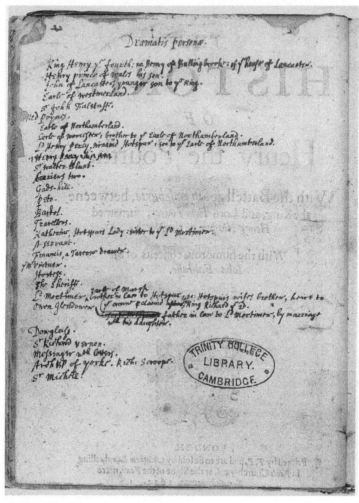

22 Manuscript list of roles in Q6, 1622

# LIST OF ROLES

KING Henry the Fourth

PRINCE Henry of Wales (Hal *or* Harry) }
Lord John of LANCASTER } *sons of King Henry*

Earl of WESTMORLAND

Sir Walter BLOUNT            5

Thomas Percy, Earl of WORCESTER

Henry Percy, Earl of NORTHUMBERLAND    *his older brother*

Henry Percy, *known as* HOTSPUR    *Northumberland's son*

LADY PERCY (Kate)    *Hotspur's wife*

Lord Edmund MORTIMER    *Lady Percy's brother*    10

LADY MORTIMER    *his wife*

Owen GLENDOWER    *Lady Mortimer's father*

Earl of DOUGLAS

Sir Richard VERNON

Richard Scrope, ARCHBISHOP of York            15

SIR MICHAEL    *a member of the Archbishop's household*

Sir John FALSTAFF

Edward (Ned) POINS

BARDOLL

PETO            20

HOSTESS (Mistress Quickly)

FRANCIS    *a drawer*

VINTNER

GADSHILL

1 CARRIER (Mugs)            25

2 CARRIER (Tom)

CHAMBERLAIN

OSTLER

SHERIFF

Two TRAVELLERS            30

MESSENGERS

SERVANT

Lords, Soldiers, Attendants, Travellers

LIST OF ROLES not in QF; first provided by Rowe, though a number of surviving copies of the early quartos have contemporary hand written lists added by readers (see, e.g., Fig. 22).

1 KING Henry IV (1367–1413), Henry Plantagenet, son of John of Gaunt (see Fig. 2), and, before becoming king, often referred to by the surname 'Bolingbroke' (Q's spellings 'Bullingbrooke' at 1.3.136 and 'Bullenbrooke' at 1.3.244 indicate the approximate pronunciation), from the name of the castle in which he was born near Spilsby in Lincolnshire. He was named Duke of Hereford in 1397, and Duke of Lancaster upon his father's death in 1399. He became king in October 1399, helped to the throne with the support of the Percys. The chronicle accounts show his reign troubled from the first, in part 'sith it was euident inough to the world, that he had with wrong vsurped the crowne, and not onelie violentlie deposed king Richard, but also cruellie procured his death' (Holinshed, 3.522). Rumours were circulated that Richard was still alive in an effort to focus the discontent, and the Percys' rebellion broke out in early 1403.

2 PRINCE Harry (1387–1422), eldest son of Henry IV and his first wife Mary Bohun. He was created Prince of Wales at the time of his father's coronation and became Henry V at his father's death in 1413. Stories circulated even during his lifetime of his wild youth miraculously to be redeemed in his maturity, although at the time the play presents him revelling with his tavern friends, he was actually engaged in battles against Welsh insurgents. He was sixteen at the time of the battle of Shrewsbury, where, 'although he was hurt in the face with an arrow', as Holinshed reports, he 'holpe his father like a lustie yoong gentleman' (3.523); but did not play the decisive role that Shakespeare provides for him in the play.

3 LANCASTER John Plantagenet (1389–1435), the third son of King Henry IV, called 'Lancaster' from the place of his birth; he was a young teenager during the events represented by the play, and there is no evidence that he was present at Shrewsbury. He was made Constable of England in 1403, Duke of Bedford in 1411, and served as Regent of France under Henry VI. He died at Rouen in 1435.

4 WESTMORLAND Ralph Neville (1364–1425), first Earl of Westmorland, a title created by Richard II in 1397; he nonetheless sided with Henry against Richard and was appointed Lord Marshal of England with Henry's accession. His first wife was Henry's half-sister, and he remained loyal to the Lancastrian cause. He was made Knight of the Garter and was granted many of the estates of the Percys following their defeat at Shrewsbury in 1403 .

5 BLOUNT Sir Walter (1347?-1403), a nobleman from Derbyshire, the son of Sir John Blount and his first wife, Iseult Mountjoy. In 1367 (the year Henry IV was born) Blount accompanied John of Gaunt and Edward, the Black Prince, on the failed Spanish Expedition to restore Peter IV to the throne of León and Castile. In 1392 he became Chamberlain of Gaunt's household. A loyal Lancastrian, he was waiting at Ravenspur with an escort of armed retainers in July 1399 when Henry returned from exile. He died at the battle of Shrewsbury, at which he had served as King Henry's standard-bearer. QF spelling 'Blunt' indicates the pronunciation of his name.

6 WORCESTER Thomas Percy (1344?-1403), Earl of Worcester and leader of the rebellion of the northern barons against Henry IV in 1403; he was the younger brother of Northumberland and, therefore, Hotspur's uncle. He accompanied Richard II on his two Irish expeditions, and, upon Henry's landing at Ravenspur, he accompanied the King to Wales. He was reconciled with Henry and, at the new king's accession, Worcester was appointed assistant to the King's second son Thomas, who had been appointed High Steward of England in spite of his youth (Holinshed, 3.509). Nonethe-

less, Holinshed reports that Worcester's 'studie was euer (as some write) to procure malice, and set things in a broil' (Holinshed, 3.521). With Northumberland and Hotspur, he led the rebellion of 1403, having begun 'to enuie [the King's] wealth and felicitie' (3.521). He was captured at the battle of Shrewsbury and beheaded, the head 'sent to London, there to be set on the bridge' (3.524). S. Daniel spells the name 'Worster', indicating the approximate pronunciation, always with two syllables.

7 NORTHUMBERLAND Henry Percy (1341–1408), named the first Earl of Northumberland at the coronation of Richard II, at the request of John of Gaunt. In 1398 he refused Richard's order to attend him in Ireland and a sentence of banishment was proclaimed, after which he joined Bolingbroke in Yorkshire in 1399, helping him to achieve the crown (cf. 4.3.54–77). He was named Constable of England when Henry became king. Northumberland, however, soon turned against the King and was one of the leaders of the rebellion of the northern barons in 1403, although he did not fight at Shrewsbury. He was pardoned for his part in the events portrayed by the play, but he raised another army and was beheaded after his forces were defeated at Branham Moor in 1408, his head then being sent to London and displayed on Tower Bridge.

8 HOTSPUR Henry Percy (1364–1403), eldest son of Northumberland, was knighted by Edward III in 1377, and renowned, as Holinshed says, 'as a capteine of great courage' (Holinshed, 3.522); although Shakespeare presents him as the contemporary of the Prince, he was in fact nearly twenty-three years older than Hal and almost three years older than the King. 'Hotspur' was a nickname given him for his fearless behaviour on the battlefield fighting against the Scottish border clans in the late 1380s. He joined with his father and uncle Worcester in rebellion

against King Henry in 1403, and, according to Holinshed, he was killed at Shrewsbury, by unnamed soldiers fighting for the King (Holinshed, 3.523). Several days after the battle, his body was beheaded and quartered; his head was displayed on a gate in York, the quarters placed for view in London, Bristol, Chester and Newcastle.

9 LADY PERCY 'Kate' in this play, though actually Elizabeth Mortimer (1371–1444?) and 'Elianor' in Holinshed, older sister of Sir Edmund Mortimer (see next and Fig. 3) and wife of Hotspur.

10 MORTIMER Edmund Mortimer (1376–1409), son of the third Earl of March and younger brother of Lady Percy. Mortimer married the daughter of Glendower after the English were defeated at the battle of Brynglas (or Nesbit) on 22 June 1402. Historically, this Mortimer was neither an Earl of March nor the heir presumptive to the crown. Shakespeare, however, following Holinshed and Samuel Daniel (see p. 13), has in places conflated him with his nephew, the fifth Earl of March, who was recognized as heir presumptive by Richard II in 1398 (cf. 1.3.144–5), after the death of his father, Roger, the fourth Earl of March, who had earlier been proclaimed heir in 1385. See Fig. 3.

12 GLENDOWER anglicized spelling of *Glyndwr*, the cognomen taken by Owain ap Gruffydd (1359?-1416?), a wealthy landowner in north-east Wales, from the name of 'the vallie by the side of the water of Dee', as Holinshed writes (3.518), which was known as 'Glindourwie' (actually Glyndyfrdwy). Glendower was the leader of the Welsh rebellion for independence (1400–10), and he was proclaimed Prince of Wales by his supporters in 1400. He entered into an alliance with the Percys in their revolt against Henry IV, but was not present at Shrewsbury. He continued to fight for Welsh independence, but suffered reverses, including the capture of his wife and daughters in 1408. He was

included in a general pardon issued by Henry V at his accession in 1413, which he refused. After 1415 nothing is known about him, and a later tradition has him starving to death in the mountains. In *2H4*, Warwick refers to his death (3.1.99). Glendower is seemingly pronounced in the play with two syllables (Glìn-dour; cf. 3.1.85, 4.4.15, 5.5.40, etc., where 'glen-dow-er' would produce a hypermetrical line). On the anglicization of the spelling, see pp. 122–3.

13 DOUGLAS Archibald (1369–1424), fourth Earl of Douglas, called 'the Douglas' as the mark of his leadership of his clan; he was defeated by forces led by Hotspur at Humbleton in September 1402, but at the outbreak of the rebellion the Percys persuaded him to join with them by the promise that he would be given control of Berwick and part of Northumberland. He fought with them at Shrewsbury but was captured, remaining the prisoner of the King until he was freed in 1408. He was killed in 1424 at the battle of Verneuil by English forces led by John of Lancaster, then Duke of Bedford.

14 VERNON Richard, Baron of Shipbrook (1345?-1403), from a Norman family that had been granted land in Derbyshire. Holinshed describes him as 'one of the chiefteines' (3.523) of the Percys' army. While fighting against the King, he was captured by the King's forces at Shrewsbury, and on the Monday following the battle he, along with Worcester, was beheaded.

15 ARCHBISHOP Richard Scrope (1346?–1405), appointed Archbishop of York by Richard II in 1398; although he assisted at the coronation of Henry IV, he sided with the Percys in their rebellion against the King. Shakespeare follows Holinshed in identifying him as the 'brother to the lord Scroope, whom king Henrie had caused to be beheaded at Bristow' (Holinshed, 3.522; cf. 1.3.266); in fact he was a cousin of William Scrope, Earl of Wiltshire, who was executed by Henry Bolingbroke in 1399 (cf. *R2*

3.2.141–2). The Archbishop was taken prisoner by the King's forces under Ralph Neville, Earl of Westmorland, at Gaultree Forest (cf. *2H4* 4.2) in 1405; he was executed at York and buried in York Minster.

17 FALSTAFF Sir John, originally called by Shakespeare 'Sir John Oldcastle', the name of a Protestant martyr burned in 1417, and changed before the play was printed in response to some protest after the play was performed (see pp. 51–62); the name *Falstaff* possibly was suggested by the name of Sir John Fastolf, a fifteenth-century knight who appears in Shakespeare's *1H6*, though the name probably also points at the reality behind the braggart-warrior's boasts and his eventual rejection: i.e. fall staff (and perhaps with some glance at 'shake-spear').

18 POINS a fictional character, first name Edward (Ned), who is a friend of the Prince. In *2H4* 2.2.67, he refers to himself as 'a second brother' (i.e. a gentleman with no money, as opposed to the eldest son who would inherit), and seemingly he, unlike Bardoll or Peto, is imagined as coming from a noble family. The name belonged to a noble Gloucestershire family descended from the Barons Poyntz, who had been influential in the reign of Edward I. Sir Nicholas Poyntz (d. 1567) was active at court in the latter part of the reign of Henry VIII, and had his portrait painted by Holbein. Thomas Wyatt's 'Of the Courtier's Life Written to John Poins', as the poem is entitled in Tottel's miscellany, seemingly addresses a cousin of Nicholas, who was also prominent at Henry's court.

19 BARDOLL All the early quartos consistently use this spelling (or 'Bardol' in four of the twelve times the name appears) for the name of Falstaff's companion, rather than the 'Bardolph' of the Folio. The character does reappear in *2H4* (as well as in *H5* and *MW*) where he is consistently called 'Bardolph', although this may be a sophistication from the rebel lord of that name who

also appears in that play. 'Bardoll' and 'Bardolph' are variants of the same name; however, in *1H4* Shakespeare clearly preferred the form used here (see pp. 123–5). Shakespeare seems originally to have called the character 'Russell', the family name of the Earls of Bedford, probably changing it at the same time he changed Oldcastle to Falstaff. See 1.2.154n.

20 PETO a fictional character, who is one of the Prince's tavern friends. He reappears only briefly in *2H4*, entering as a messenger at 2.4.354. Shakespeare seems originally to have named the character 'Harvey' (see 1.2.154n.) and changed it, as he did Bardoll's name, at the time Oldcastle was changed to Falstaff. Peto is a Warwickshire family name, and William Peto was a prominent clergyman in the reigns of Henry VIII and Mary, elected Cardinal in 1557 and appointed Legate in England, though declining both positions because of age. Florio, in *Queen Anna's New World of Words* (1611), defines *'peto'* as *'goate-eyde, rouling-eyde, one that with a grace roules his eyes from one corner to another. Also looking a squint upward.'*

21 HOSTESS Mistress Quickly (3.3.92), the landlady of the tavern in Eastcheap and married to 'an honest man' (3.3.93); she reappears in *2H4* and also in *H5*, where 'Nell Quickly' is now married to Pistol (2.1.18–19). In *MW*, a Mistress Quickly is the housekeeper of Doctor Caius (1.2.2–5).

24 GADSHILL The 'setter' who arranges the robbery in 2.2. Shakespeare takes his name from the nickname of Cutbert Cutter, a thief in *The Famous Victories*, who is nicknamed 'Gad's Hill' because he is well known as 'a taking-fellow upon Gad's Hill in Kent' (2.57). See 1.2.119n.

# KING HENRY IV,
# PART ONE

**1.1**     *Enter the* KING, Lord John of LANCASTER,
            Earl of WESTMORLAND, *with others.*

KING

So shaken as we are, so wan with care,
Find we a time for frighted peace to pant
And breathe short-winded accents of new broils
To be commenced in strands afar remote.

---

1.1 The quartos are not divided into acts
and scenes. F does provide act and
scene divisions, and, with the exception of one scene in Act 5 not marked
in F, these are followed here.

0.1 In no stage direction in the play does
Shakespeare specify the location of a
scene, and too precise an effort on the
part of editors to indicate locations mis-
represents the practices of Elizabethan
stagecraft, which allowed the spoken
language to establish place whenever an
exact sense is required. Nonetheless,
editors have for the convenience of
readers generally indicated where the
action takes place either by added SDs
or, as here, in headnotes. 1.1 is clearly
set in a public room at the palace; cf. 65,
'this seat of ours'.

0.2 Most editors, beginning with Capell
(and as in Dering), have added Walter
Blount to the assembled nobles, but
this edition follows the QF stage directions in which he is not included; see
62n.

1 The King's first words give voice to his
troubled position; *we* is the royal plural pronoun, and both the King and his
England are *shaken* by the political
instability following the deposition of
Richard II. Holinshed describes the
insecurity of the new King's rule:
'What pleasure or what felicitie could
he take in his princelie pompe, which
he knew by manifest and fearfull experience to be enuied and maligned to
the verie death' (Holinshed, 3.519).

2 **Find we** let us find
**frighted** frightened; cf. *Luc* 1149:
'poor frighted deer'

3 **breathe ... accents** speak while short
of breath (*accents* = words, speech)
**broils** battles; cf. *Civil Wars*, 1.1: 'I
Sing the ciuill Warres, tumultuous
Broyles'.

4 **strands afar remote** distant shores
(i.e. the Holy Land, to which Henry
has pledged to go on crusade at the end
of *R2* 5.6.49–50); cf. 28 and note.

---

TITLE] THE HISTORY OF HENRIE THE FOVRTH; *Q*   1.1.4 strands] *(stronds), Dyce*

No more the thirsty entrance of this soil     5
Shall daub her lips with her own children's blood;
No more shall trenching war channel her fields,
Nor bruise her flowerets with the armed hoofs
Of hostile paces. Those opposed eyes,
Which, like the meteors of a troubled heaven,     10
All of one nature, of one substance bred,
Did lately meet in the intestine shock
And furious close of civil butchery,
Shall now in mutual well-beseeming ranks

5  **thirsty entrance** parched openings, thirsty mouth; cf. *3H6* 2.3.15: 'Thy brother's blood the thirsty earth hath drunk', itself based on Genesis, 4.11, where Cain is reminded how the earth 'opened her mouth to receive thy brother's blood'.
6  **daub** smear, coat
7  **trenching** ploughing (*OED* trench *v.* 3b); it is *war* itself that Henry recognizes as *trenching* English *fields*, avoiding any attribution of responsibility for its brutality.
8  **flowerets** small flowers; i.e. the young men who are vulnerable in battle; probably pronounced with two syllables as the Q1 spelling 'flourets' perhaps suggests. In 1975 at Stratford (see p. 98), Emrys James conceived of his characterization of the King as someone 'who talks not of *flowers*, but *flow'rets* – somehow a harsher, harder word, a word used by somebody who doesn't often talk or think about flowers, except as underfoot in a battlefield' (Mullin, 23).
    **armed** armèd
8–9  **armed . . . paces** gait of the enemy's armoured horses
9  **opposed** opposèd
    **opposed eyes** eyes of those in conflict

10  **meteors . . . heaven** The image is of disorderly meteors disrupting the well-ordered heavens. Meteors, as David Person writes, were believed to be the result of 'dry and moist vapours and exhalations extracted from the earth and waters; and from thence elevated to the regions of the ayre, where they are fashioned' and then exhaled into space; 'they never appeare but some bad event doth followeth thereon' (*Varieties*, sig. E1ʳ).
11  The claim here that *All* are composed of the same elements applies both back to the meteors and the heavens (10) as well as forward to the opposing sides in the civil war (12).
12  **intestine** internal, civil; Bullokar defines 'intestine warre' as 'ciuill war'.
13  **close** hand-to-hand fighting
    **civil** i.e. within the same community, as in the phrase 'civil war'; though, as Mahood (26) points out, 'the split second hesitation' in which one considers and rejects the more familiar meaning, 'polite', adds 'piquancy to the phrase'; cf. *RJ* Prologue 4: 'civil blood makes civil hands unclean'.
14  **mutual . . . ranks** focused and orderly military formations

5 entrance] Entrails *F4;* bosom *Dering*

141

March all one way and be no more opposed                          15
Against acquaintance, kindred and allies.
The edge of war, like an ill-sheathed knife,
No more shall cut his master. Therefore, friends,
As far as to the sepulchre of Christ
(Whose soldier now, under whose blessed cross               20
We are impressed and engaged to fight)
Forthwith a power of English shall we levy,
Whose arms were moulded in their mothers' womb
To chase these pagans in those holy fields
Over whose acres walked those blessed feet,                    25
Which fourteen hundred years ago were nailed
For our advantage on the bitter cross.
But this our purpose now is twelve month old,

15 **all one way** Henry desires a nation unified in common purpose instead of the nation he rules over sundered by dissension; see pp. 23–9.

16 **allies** The usual meaning is 'relatives' (cf. *RJ* 3.1.114: 'the Prince's near ally'), a meaning the context supports, rather than the more modern sense of 'confederates' or 'partners'; however, as *kindred* appears just before, either this is tautological or, more likely, it means 'those related through marriage', 'in-laws' (*OED* ally I †1).

17 **edge** sword
**ill-sheathed** ill-sheathèd

18 **his** its (Shakespeare generally uses the older form, 'his', for the neuter genitive)

19 **sepulchre** tomb

21 **impressed** impressèd: conscripted; the King speaks as if he has been *impressed* to undertake the crusade, though, in the civil wars that will

instead be fought, he is the one who impresses soldiers; cf. 4.2.11–47.
**engaged** personally committed, pledged by oath

22 **power** army
**levy** raise and conduct; Gosson's *School of Abuse* refers to 'Scipio before he levied his force too the walles of Carthage' (Gosson, 33; cited in Ard²).

25 **blessed** blessèd

28 **twelve month old** According to Holinshed, the promise to undertake a crusade 'to recouer the citie of Ierusalem from the Infidels' was made only 'the fourteenth and last year of King Henries reign' and then not to unify his country in common purpose but to counteract the discord among European nations, determined 'to destroie one another . . . rather than to make war against the enimies of the christian faith' (Holinshed, 3.540). At the end of *R2*, Henry had promised to

16 allies] all eyes *Q4*   23 mothers'] *(mothers), Theobald;* Mother's *F4*   26 fourteen hundred] *(1400.), F*   28 now . . . month] is twelue month *Q4–5;* is a tweluemonth *F*

And bootless 'tis to tell you we will go.
Therefor we meet not now. – Then let me hear 30
Of you, my gentle cousin Westmorland,
What yesternight our Council did decree
In forwarding this dear expedience.

WESTMORLAND

My liege, this haste was hot in question,
And many limits of the charge set down 35
But yesternight, when all athwart there came
A post from Wales, loaden with heavy news,
Whose worst was that the noble Mortimer,
Leading the men of Herefordshire to fight
Against the irregular and wild Glendower, 40
Was by the rude hands of that Welshman taken,

undertake 'a voyage to the Holy Land, / To wash this blood off from my guilty hand' (5.6.49–50). This is the promise that is now *twelve month old*, though a strict time scheme would note more than two years passing between Richard's deposition and death in 1399 and the battle at Humbleton, announced in this scene, in 1402.

29 **bootless** useless (because you already know it); it is not until 47–8 that Henry publicly admits that present dangers make it impossible to undertake his proposed crusade.

30 **Therefor** for that reason (rather than 'therefore', meaning in consequence of that)

31 **cousin** not a precise indication of relatedness, but a more general indication of courtesy and respect; see, however, List of Roles, 4n.

33 **this dear expedience** this vital enterprise or expedition (i.e. the proposed crusade); cf. *AC* 1.2.182–3: 'I shall break / The cause of our expedience to the Queen.' *Expedience* clearly carries the sense of urgency as Westmorland's *this haste*, 34, makes clear.

34 **liege** liege lord, the superior to whom service and allegiance are owed
**hot in question** vigorously debated

35 **limits . . . down** responsibilities assigned

36 **But** as recently as, only
**all athwart** frustrating our purposes

37 **post** messenger
**heavy** serious, important

38 **Mortimer** Hotspur's brother-in-law, Edmund Mortimer, who was in fact the uncle of the Edmund Mortimer who had been proclaimed heir to the throne by Richard II; Shakespeare, following Holinshed, conflates these two Edmund Mortimers here and throughout the play; see List of Roles, 10n., and Fig. 3.

39 **Herefordshire** usually pronounced with three syllables, probably Hàr-furd-shir

40 **irregular and wild** Both words mean roughly the same thing: rebellious or lawless, though *irregular* carries, in this context, the particular sense of not observing the rules of war; i.e. using guerrilla tactics.

41 **rude** uncivilized

30 Therefor] *(*Therefore*)*, *Ard²*

143

A thousand of his people butchered,
Upon whose dead corpse there was such misuse,
Such beastly shameless transformation,
By those Welshwomen done, as may not be                                    45
Without much shame retold or spoken of.

KING

It seems then that the tidings of this broil
Brake off our business for the Holy Land.

WESTMORLAND

This matched with other did, my gracious lord,
For more uneven and unwelcome news                                         50
Came from the north, and thus it did import:
On Holy Rood Day the gallant Hotspur there
(Young Harry Percy) and brave Archibald,

42 **butchered** butcherèd
43 **corpse** corpses; corpse functioned as a plural form in English well into the eighteenth century.
44 **shameless transformation** disgraceful mutilation; Holinshed (actually Abraham Fleming, but 'Holinshed' is used throughout this edition to refer to the chronicle; see Patterson) writes that the 'shameful villanie used by the Welsh women towards the dead carcasses was such as honest eares would be ashamed to heare, and continent toongs to speake thereof' (3.520); nonetheless later he does speak of it. Finally deciding that there is 'little reason whie it should not be imparted in our mother Tongue', he relates how the Welsh women 'cut off their privities, and put one part thereof into the mouthes of euerie dead man, in such sort that the cullions hoong downe to

their chins; and not so contented, they did cut off their noses and thrust them into their tailes as they laie on the ground mangled and defaced' (3.528).
48 **Brake** the archaic past tense of 'break'; inevitably the word is heard as 'break' but Westmorland's *did* in 49 confirms this as a past-tense verb.
49–55 **This ... met** Shakespeare collapses the time between two discrete events as an intensification of the pressures felt by the King. Mortimer's capture in fact was on 22 June at Pillith, three months before the battle at Humbleton, which was fought on 14 September 1402.
51 **thus ... import** this was its substance
52 **Holy Rood Day** 14 September; a church festival commemorating the Roman emperor Heraclius' recovery of a piece of the cross on which Jesus was crucified

42 A thousand] And a thousand *F*   43 corpse] *(corpes), Boswell-Malone*   49 did] like *Q3–F*
lord] *(L.), F*   50 For] Far *Q5–F*   51 import] report *Q5–F*

That ever-valiant and approved Scot,
At Humbleton met, where they did spend          55
A sad and bloody hour,
As by discharge of their artillery
And shape of likelihood the news was told;
For he that brought them, in the very heat
And pride of their contention, did take horse,          60
Uncertain of the issue any way.

KING

Here is a dear, a true industrious friend,
Sir Walter Blount, new lighted from his horse,
Stained with the variation of each soil

54 **approved** approvèd: tested, battle-hardened
55 **Humbleton** Northumbrian town near Wooler, pronounced here and at 70 with two syllables (Hòlm-dun). QF print 'Holmedon'; Holinshed's form is 'Homildon' or 'Homeldon'. On the treatment of place-names, see pp. 120–2.
56 The short line has been variously treated by editors, who often readjust the lineation. Nonetheless, the incomplete verse line here, as it is in QF, seems appropriate, as Westmorland hesitates after delivering the unwelcome news, perhaps in response to some gesture from the King or merely awaiting the King's response.
57 **artillery** can refer to any machine for discharging missiles (like catapults and bows), although here seemingly refers to guns; victory in the battle, according to Holinshed, was achieved 'with violence of the English shot' (3.520), which Shakespeare apparently understood in its modern sense (cf. 1.3.63; 2.3.52). Elsewhere, however, Holinshed says, that the victory was won 'with

such incessant shot of arrows' (2.254).
58 **shape of likelihood** likely conjecture
59 **them** i.e. the *news*, 58; Elizabethan usage generally treated 'news' as plural.
59–60 **heat . . . contention** in the midst of the battle; *heat* and *pride* mean roughly the same thing here (*pride* = height).
60, 63 **horse** the first of many references to horses and horsemanship in the play; see Levin.
61 **issue** outcome
**any way** either way
62 **Here** here at court; many editions have Blount already present or have him enter with this line (*Here*, then, marking the King's gesture towards him), but the early texts have no entry for him, he has no lines in the scene, the description of his person would be unnecessary if he were visible to the audience, and in any case the King obviously already knows what news Blount has brought from the battlefield.
63 **new lighted** recently dismounted
64 **variation . . . soil** the various kinds of soil

62 a dear] *Q4c–F;* deere *Q1–3, Q4n*    a true] and true *Q5–F*    64 Stained] Strain'd *F, Dering*

Betwixt that Humbleton and this seat of ours;                    65
And he hath brought us smooth and welcome news.
The Earl of Douglas is discomfited.
Ten thousand bold Scots, two-and-twenty knights,
Balked in their own blood, did Sir Walter see
On Humbleton's plains. Of prisoners Hotspur took        70
Murdoch, Earl of Fife and eldest son
To beaten Douglas, and the Earl of Atholl,

66 **smooth . . . news** The phrase balances the 'uneven and unwelcome news', 50, earlier. Holinshed does not indicate who delivered the news of the victory to the court, but Shakespeare allows Blount to bear it, seemingly to establish the theme of Blount's reassuring service to the King. In fact the messenger was Nicholas Merbury, who was granted an annual retainer of £40 by the King for the good news he brought (Tyler, 1.169).

67 **discomfited** defeated

68 **two-and-twenty** In Holinshed (3.520) the number is twenty-three, the change here either a mere slip or perhaps a decision to add another hard 't' to the line, instead of the 'th-' of the source. The number appears two additional times in the play: at 2.2.16 and 3.3.188, both times spoken by Falstaff and part of the verbal texture linking the historical plot to the comic action.

69 **Balked** heaped up (balk = ridge between two furrows), but with some sense of *balked* as hindered or thwarted

71–3 Holinshed writes that among the prisoners were 'Mordacke earle of Fife, son to the gouernour Archembald earle Dowglas, which in the fight lost one of his eies, Thomas erle of Murrey, Robert earle of Angus, and (as some writers haue) the earles of Atholl &

Menteith, with fiue hundred other of meaner degree' (Holinshed, 3.520). Following Holinshed, Shakespeare makes two errors: (1) Murdoch, the Earl of Fife, was the eldest son, not of Douglas, but of Robert Duke of Albany (Shakespeare being misled by the absence of a comma after 'gouernour'); (2) Menteith was not a separate nobleman but another title that Murdoch held.

71 **Earl** Pope, followed by many editors, adds 'the' before *Earl* to make a ten-syllable line, in spite of its absence from QF. Shakespeare often varies the dominant iambic pentameter of his verse, and in general this edition does not add syllables merely to standardize the metre of a line, nor does it suggest idiosyncratic pronunciations, as, for example, Malone, proposing that *Earl* here would be pronounced 'as a disyllable'; see Appendix 2.

72 **Earl of Atholl** Walter Stewart (1360?–1437), the second son of Robert II's second marriage (to Euphemia Ross), only became Earl of Atholl in 1404; at the time of the battle in 1402 the earldom was vested in his father. The chronicles, however, mention Atholl's presence, proleptically referring to Stewart by the title he would soon assume.

66 welcome] welcomes *F*

Of Moray, Angus, and Menteith;
And is not this an honourable spoil,
A gallant prize? Ha, cousin, is it not? 75

WESTMORLAND
In faith, it is: a conquest for a prince to boast of.

KING
Yea, there thou mak'st me sad and mak'st me sin
In envy that my lord Northumberland
Should be the father to so blest a son,
A son who is the theme of honour's tongue, 80
Amongst a grove the very straightest plant,
Who is sweet Fortune's minion and her pride;
Whilst I, by looking on the praise of him,
See riot and dishonour stain the brow
Of my young Harry. O, that it could be proved 85

73 **Moray** i.e. the Earl of Moray, Thomas Dunbar, the fifth earl. Editions have followed the QF spelling 'Murrey' and modernized this as 'Murray'. As 'Murray' is the family name of the seventeenth-century holders of the earldom of Atholl, the confusion should be avoided. The earldom of Moray takes its name from the ancient kingdom of Moray, which once stretched from the west coat of Scotland opposite the isle of Skye eastward to the river Spey, and now survives as the name of the Scottish county. The earldom was established in 1312 by a grant from Robert I. No significant pronunciation difference results from the modernization.
**Angus** George Douglas, the first Earl of Angus, by a grant from Robert II in 1389; Holinshed mistakenly refers to him as Robert in the account of Humbleton (3.520), though in the

*History of Scotland* it is correct: 'George, earle of Angus' (Holinshed, 2.254).
74, 80 **honourable spoil, honour's tongue** the first of the play's references to honour, here appropriately associated with Hotspur; see pp. 69–73.
76 **prince** Westmorland may not be fully aware of how this word might affect the King, although an actor, as at the Old Vic in 1955, might give an 'unmistakable insinuation' by stressing 'prince' (Wood & Clark, 159).
77 The monosyllables of the line, as well as the personal pronouns in place of the royal 'we', suggest how *sad* the King becomes, thinking of his profligate son.
82 **minion** favourite, darling; as GWW observes, at 1.2.25 Falstaff refers to himself and his followers as 'minions of the moon'; the image links these as subject to chance and change. Also compare *Mac* 1.2.19: 'valour's minion'.

73 Moray] *(Murrey)* 76 WESTMORLAND In . . . is] *Pope;* In . . . is *QF* is: a conquest] *this edn;* A conquest *Pope; West.* A conquest *QF* 79 to] of *Q5–F* 82 Fortune's *(fortunes), F*

That some night-tripping fairy had exchanged
In cradle clothes our children where they lay,
And called mine 'Percy', his 'Plantagenet';
Then would I have his Harry, and he mine.
But let him from my thoughts. What think you, coz,          90
Of this young Percy's pride? The prisoners
Which he in this adventure hath surprised
To his own use he keeps, and sends me word
I shall have none but Murdoch, Earl of Fife.

WESTMORLAND
This is his uncle's teaching; this is Worcester,          95
Malevolent to you in all aspects,

86–8 These lines play on the folk belief that fairies would sometimes substitute deformed creatures for infants, which they would take to fairyland; Shakespeare, following S. Daniel, makes Hal and Hotspur contemporaries. Daniel has 'young *Hotspur*' (4.34) and 'Young *Henrie*' (4.48) as foils for one another, although historically Hotspur was almost twenty-three years older than Prince Hal (and nearly three years older than King Henry). *Plantagenet* = the dynastic surname of the royal family from the reigns of Henry II to Richard III.
90 **from** be out of
91–4 **The prisoners . . . Fife** Cf. Holinshed: 'The King demanded . . . such Scotish prisoners as were taken at Homeldon and Nesbit [but] there was deliuered to the kings possession onelie Mordake earle of Fife, the duke of Albanies sonne, though the king did diuerse and sundrie times require deliuerance of the residue' (3.521).

Chivalric custom held that 'Euery man shall haue liberty to ransome his prisoner taken in warres at his owne pleasure . . . [but] if the prisoner be a Prince or a great man, then the Generall is to haue the prisoner to make what commodity hee can of him for the benefit of his Prince and countrey' (Sutcliffe, sig. ZZ2ʳ). Henry here is asking for more than is his by custom.
92 **surprised** captured (*OED* surprise *v.* 2b)
95 **Worcester** See List of Roles, 6n. Holinshed calls him 'the procuror and setter foorth of all this mischeefe' (3.523).
96 maliciously disposed to you in every respect
**aspects** aspècts, carrying an astrological sense of the influence a planet might exert over individuals in its various phases in relation to the earth; cf. *WT* 2.1.106–7: 'I must be patient till the heavens look / With an aspect more favourable'.

87 lay] say *Q2*   88 'Percy'] *Folg²*; Percy *QF*   'Plantagenet'] *Folg²*; Plantagenet *QF*   94 Murdoch] *(Mordake)*

148

Which makes him prune himself and bristle up
The crest of youth against your dignity.

KING

But I have sent for him to answer this,
And for this cause awhile we must neglect                    100
Our holy purpose to Jerusalem.
Cousin, on Wednesday next our Council we
Will hold at Windsor. So inform the lords,
But come yourself with speed to us again,
For more is to be said and to be done                        105
Than out of anger can be uttered.

WESTMORLAND     I will, my liege.                            *Exeunt.*


**1.2**     *Enter* PRINCE *of* Wales *and* Sir John FALSTAFF.

FALSTAFF     Now, Hal, what time of day is it, lad?
PRINCE     Thou art so fat-witted with drinking of old sack,

---

97 **prune** preen, as a bird its feathers (cf.
*crest*, 98)

99 In Holinshed the Percys rather than
the King initiate the confrontation,
when they 'came to the King vnto
Windsore (vpon a purpose to prooue
him)' (3.521).

106 **out . . . uttered** can be said angrily in
public; proverbial: cf. 'nothing is well
said and done in passion' (Tilley,
N307).
**uttered** utterèd

1.2 The specific location of the scene is
not apparent from the text, though
editors have variously imagined it in
the Prince's apartment (Theobald), in
a tavern (Staunton), or in a room in the
palace (Capell). Holinshed speaks of
the prince's 'house' as a separate residence in London (3.539).

1   **Now . . . lad** Many productions, since
Stephen Kemble first introduced the
stage business in 1804 (Sprague, *Stage*,
53), have Falstaff asleep and waking
with the entrance of the Prince, giving
point to the question about what time
it is. Falstaff's intimacy with the
Prince is immediately evident in his
use of *Hal* and *lad*. In 1765, Voltaire
objected to this familiarity (which
could never happen 'in Corneille'):
'How has Bishop Warburton refrained
from blushing in commenting on the
infamous grossness of this passage'
(Hemingway, 25).

2   **fat-witted** dull-witted (cf. 'fat-
brained' *H5* 3.7.133), but of course *fat*
applies in another sense to Falstaff.
**sack** a Spanish white wine

---

102–3] *T. Johnson; QF line* hold / Lords: /     103 So] and so *F*     inform] informer *Q5*     1.2.0.1 *Enter Prince of Wales, Sir Iohn Falstaffe, and Pointz. F*

and unbuttoning thee after supper, and sleeping upon
benches after noon, that thou hast forgotten to demand
that truly which thou wouldst truly know. What a devil          5
hast thou to do with the time of the day? Unless hours
were cups of sack, and minutes capons, and clocks the
tongues of bawds, and dials the signs of leaping-houses,
and the blessed sun himself a fair hot wench in flame-
coloured taffeta, I see no reason why thou shouldst be so       10
superfluous to demand the time of the day.

FALSTAFF    Indeed you come near me now, Hal, for we
that take purses go by the moon and the seven stars,

4  **forgotten** neglected
4–5  **demand that truly** ask correctly
about that which you would really know
5–11  **What . . . day** Hal incredulously
asks why Falstaff should care what
time it is, since time is the measure of
order and limitation that Falstaff's way
of life suggests is completely irrelevant. Ard² cites Nashe, *Summer's Last
Will and Testament*: 'What haue we to
doe with scales and hower-glasses,
except we were Bakers or Clock-
keepers? I cannot tell how other men
are addicted, but it is against my profession to . . . keepe any howers but
dinner or supper' (Nashe, 3.247; also
cited Cam).
7  **capons** roosters castrated and subsequently fattened for eating
8  **dials** sundials ('dials' can sometimes
mean 'clockfaces', as at 5.2.83, but
here, where Hal has just used *clocks*, 7,
as the previous item in his catalogue of
temporal terms irrelevant to Falstaff, it
must refer to the older instrument for
calculating time)
    **leaping-houses** brothels
9–10  **flame-coloured taffeta** bright
red, silk dresses often identified with
prostitutes; cf. 'your taffeta punk' in
*AW* 2.2.21. In Barry's *Ram Alley*, after

a prostitute is sued by her 'bawd' for
'five-weeks' loan of a red taffety gown',
the prostitute protests: 'I got her in
that gown in six week space / Four
pounds and fourteen pence' (sig. G1ʳ).
11  **superfluous** needlessly concerned,
but also self-indulgent
12  **you . . . me** you almost have it right
13  **go . . . moon** i.e. work at night, and so
have nothing to do with the time of
*day* (6). Falstaff's *go by* incorporates
various meanings, including 'walk by
the light of', 'navigate by' and 'tell
time by' (and see next note). Such
punning is characteristic of Falstaff,
whose language is as capacious as his
appetite.
    **seven stars** the group of stars in the
constellation Taurus, known as the
Pleiades (from the seven daughters of
Atlas and Pleione); cf. Dekker, *The
Magnificent Entertainment*: 'the seauen
Starres, called the *Pleaides*' (Dekker, 2.
301.1,565–6). The Moon and the
Seven Stars might also be an inn name
(Skelton refers to a London tavern
called 'the seuen starres' in 'Colin
Clout', Skelton, sig. Q3ᵛ), in which
case *go by* would also mean 'stop in at'
or 'pass in front of'.

4  after noon] in the afternoone *F*    10  be so] be *Q2–5*

and not by Phoebus, he, 'that wand'ring knight so fair'.
And I prithee, sweet wag, when thou art a king, as God    15
save thy grace – 'majesty', I should say, for grace thou
wilt have none –

PRINCE    What, none?

FALSTAFF    No, by my troth, not so much as will serve to
be prologue to an egg and butter.      20

PRINCE    Well, how then? Come roundly, roundly.

FALSTAFF    Marry then, sweet wag, when thou art king, let
not us that are squires of the night's body be called
thieves of the day's beauty. Let us be Diana's foresters,
gentlemen of the shade, minions of the moon, and let    25

---

14 **Phoebus** god of the sun, Apollo
   **'that . . . fair'** stock phrase from some unidentified ballad or chivalric romance
15 **wag** an affectionate term, literally a mischievous boy
16 **'majesty'** an increasingly common honorific for a monarch in the sixteenth century; Falstaff is perhaps acknowledging this terminological shift by which 'your majesty' gradually came to supersede 'your grace', which by the middle of the seventeenth century had almost completely disappeared from courtly vocabularies. Camden says 'Majestie' became dominant 'in the time of King *Henry* the eight' (Camden, 131).
   **grace** a fourfold pun: the standard term of respect for royalty; a theological term for unmerited divine assistance; social charm; the blessing before a meal (and, predictably, it is the last of

these upon which Falstaff continues to play)
20 **an . . . butter** a light meal, not requiring an elaborate blessing
21 **roundly** to the point, plainly (*OED* 4), but also a comment on Falstaff's size
22 **Marry** a mild oath, derived from the Virgin Mary
23 **squires . . . body** A squire of the body was a personal attendant on a nobleman; here the word-play is obvious enough (night–Knight).
24 **thieves . . . beauty** i.e. those who waste the daylight in sloth (with a play on 'beauty' and 'booty')
   **Diana's foresters** servants of Diana, goddess of the moon; cf. *Cym* 2.3.70: 'Diana's rangers'.
25 **gentlemen . . . shade** ironic phrase derived from respectable title for attendants of the royal household: e.g. Gentlemen of the Chapel Royal; **shade** darkness
   **minions** servants; cf. 1.1.82.

---

14 'that . . . fair'] *Oxf¹*; that . . . fair *QF*    15 a king] king *Q2–F*    16 'majesty'] *this edn;* maiestie *QF*
19 by my troth] *om.* F

151

men say we be men of good government, being
governed, as the sea is, by our noble and chaste mistress
the moon, under whose countenance we steal.

PRINCE   Thou sayst well, and it holds well too, for the
fortune of us that are the moon's men doth ebb and          30
flow like the sea, being governed, as the sea is, by the
moon. As for proof now: a purse of gold most
resolutely snatched on Monday night and most
dissolutely spent on Tuesday morning, got with
swearing 'Lay by!', and spent with crying 'Bring in!',      35
now in as low an ebb as the foot of the ladder, and by
and by in as high a flow as the ridge of the gallows.

FALSTAFF   By the Lord, thou sayst true, lad – and is not
my hostess of the tavern a most sweet wench?

26–8 **men . . . steal** Falstaff provides one
more iteration of the terms of his
ignoble service, but his reference to his
'noble and chaste mistress the moon',
like his reference to Diana, 24, echoes
the familiar language of praise surrounding Elizabeth, the Virgin Queen;
see pp. 41–2.

26 **of good government** another quibble, meaning both 'well behaved' and
'living under a good ruler'

28 **countenance** face, but also authority or
patronage; cf. 'The Moone, patronesse
of all purse-takers' (Wilkins, sig. F3ᵛ;
cited Ard¹). Perhaps the word also plays
on the near homophone 'continence',
following the mention of Falstaff's
*chaste mistress.*
   **steal** in the double sense of 'moving
stealthily' and of 'robbing' (Pope prints
'we – steal', perhaps registering a stage
tradition of Falstaff hesitating before
he finally admits to the truth about his
motives after all the witty euphemisms
that have preceded)

29 **holds well** is apt
33–5 **resolutely . . . dissolutely** the play
on 'resolve/dissolve' and their deriva-
tives was common; cf. *E3* 2.2.166–8:
'Resolved to be dissolved'.
35 **'Lay by!'** lay aside your arms (a high-
wayman's command)
   **'Bring in!'** a call to a tavern waiter for
service
36–7 **now . . . gallows** i.e. at one moment
our fortune is as low as the foot of the
ladder (leading to the gallows); at the
next it is as high as the crossbar at the
top; proverbial: 'He that is at low ebb
at Newgate may soon be afloat at
Tyburn' (Dent, E56), the point being
that good or bad fortune equally leads
a thief to the same end.
37 **ridge** crossbar for the hangman's
noose
38–9 **and . . . wench** Falstaff's abrupt
change of subject may reflect his discomfort with the Prince's discussion of
hanging.

32 proof now:] *Collier;* proofe. Now *QF*   35 'Lay by!',] *Ard²;* lay by, *Q;* Lay by: *F*   'Bring in!',] *Ard²;* bring in, *Q;* Bring in: *F*   38 By the Lord] *om. F*

PRINCE    As the honey of Hybla, my old lad of the castle –        40
and is not a buff jerkin a most sweet robe of durance?

FALSTAFF    How now, how now, mad wag? What, in thy
quips and thy quiddities? What a plague have I to do
with a buff jerkin?

PRINCE    Why, what a pox have I to do with my hostess of        45
the tavern?

FALSTAFF    Well, thou hast called her to a reckoning many
a time and oft.

PRINCE    Did I ever call for thee to pay thy part?

FALSTAFF    No, I'll give thee thy due; thou hast paid all        50
there.

PRINCE    Yea, and elsewhere, so far as my coin would
stretch, and where it would not I have used my credit.

FALSTAFF    Yea, and so used it that were it not here

---

40 **Hybla** ancient Sicilian mountain
town, near the modern Melilli, famous
for its honey
**old . . . castle** a carouser (Dent,
C124.1), though possibly more particularly one who ends up being pun-
ished (*castle* = stocks); cf. Harvey, sig.
G3ʳ: 'some old Lads of the Castell,
haue sported themselues with their
rappinge bable'; but clearly also a pun
on Oldcastle, Shakespeare's original
name for Falstaff; see pp. 51–62.
41 **buff jerkin** tight, leather jacket, often
worn by sheriff's officers (*buff* comes
from 'buffalo')
**robe of durance** long-wearing garment (*durance* = long-lasting quality);
and also prison gear (*durance* = forced
confinement); Sanderson, however,
suggests also a sexual pun, as in Sir

John Davies's epigram 'In Katum 8':
'Thy pleasure's place like a buffe-
jerkin lasteth, / For no buffe-jerkin
hath beene oftner worne, / Nor hath
more scrapings' or more dressings
borne.' The sexual meaning may well
be confirmed by the context in which
Hal and Falstaff are discussing the
hostess.
43 **quiddities** quibbles, precise distinctions
**What a plague** a colloquial intensification of 'what', as in 45; cf. Abbott, 24.
45 **pox** venereal disease
47 **called . . . reckoning** asked her for
the bill (but also both 'demanded she
explain herself' and 'engaged in sex
with her')
54–5 **here . . . heir apparent** The word-
play depends on the fact that 'here'
and 'heir' were similarly pronounced.

---

40 the . . . Hybla] is the hony *F*    54 it not] it *F*

apparent that thou art heir apparent – but I prithee, 55
sweet wag, shall there be gallows standing in England
when thou art king? And resolution thus fubbed as it is
with the rusty curb of old Father Antic the law? Do not
thou, when thou art king, hang a thief.

PRINCE   No, thou shalt. 60

FALSTAFF   Shall I? O, rare! By the Lord, I'll be a brave
judge!

PRINCE   Thou judgest false already. I mean thou shalt
have the hanging of the thieves and so become a rare
hangman. 65

FALSTAFF   Well, Hal, well, and in some sort it jumps with
my humour as well as waiting in the court, I can tell you.

PRINCE   For obtaining of suits?

FALSTAFF   Yea, for obtaining of suits, whereof the
hangman hath no lean wardrobe. 'Sblood, I am as 70

---

**56–7 shall . . . king** Falstaff's enquiry
reverses the action from *Famous
Victories*, where the Prince boasts that
'when I am King' there will be 'no
such things' as 'prisoning', 'hanging'
and 'whipping' (5.10–11).

**57 resolution** determination, commitment
**fubbed** cheated

**58 old . . . law** Falstaff caricatures the law
as an elderly buffoon;
**Antic** clown

**60 No, thou shalt** How Hal says *No* cru-
cially affects how an audience understands the relation of Prince and
Falstaff. It can be playful or cruel, part
of their shared joke or an anticipation of
the inevitable end of their relationship.

**61 rare** splendid (*OED* rare †c)
**brave** fine, excellent

**66 in some sort** in some undefined manner (*OED* sort n.2 3c)

**66–7 jumps . . . humour** suits my inclination (*jumps* may well have been suggested by the fact that the hanged man
'jumps' when the noose is tightened)

**67 waiting . . . court** i.e. waiting for
favours from the King

**68 obtaining of suits** playing on two
meanings of 'obtaining suits': having
one's legal petition granted; receiving
the clothing of the condemned crimi-
nal, a perquisite of the hangman's job;
cf. Brome, *A Mad Couple Well Matched*
(1653): 'I will do some notorious
death-deserving thing, though these
cloaths go to the hangman for't'
(Brome, *Five*, sig. B3ʳ).

**70 lean wardrobe** small amount of
clothing (but with a play on 'wardrope'
or 'warrope', a now obsolete word for a
thick rope used for hauling heavy
objects, *OED*)
**'Sblood** mild oath (by Christ's blood)

---

57 fubbed] fobb'd *F*   58 law?] *F*; law, *Q1–2*; law: *Q3–5*   59 king] a King *Q4–F*   61 By the Lord]
*om. F*   70 'Sblood] *(*Zbloud*); om. F*

melancholy as a gib cat or a lugged bear.

PRINCE    Or an old lion or a lover's lute.

FALSTAFF    Yea, or the drone of a Lincolnshire bagpipe.

PRINCE    What sayst thou to a hare, or the melancholy of
Moorditch?    75

FALSTAFF    Thou hast the most unsavoury similes and art
indeed the most comparative, rascalliest, sweet young
prince. But Hal, I prithee trouble me no more with
vanity. I would to God thou and I knew where a
commodity of good names were to be bought. An old    80
lord of the Council rated me the other day in the street
about you, sir, but I marked him not; and yet he talked
very wisely, but I regarded him not; and yet he talked
wisely and in the street too.

PRINCE    Thou didst well, for wisdom cries out in the    85
streets and no man regards it.

71 **melancholy . . . cat** proverbial expression for melancholy (Dent, C129)
**gib cat** tom cat (*OED* gib sb.¹ 2)
**lugged** baited, abused; bear-baiting was a familiar entertainment in late Elizabethan London.

72 **old lion** presumably *melancholy* because now weak
**lover's lute** the melancholy of lovers was proverbial

73 **drone . . . bagpipe** possibly a reference to the sound of an actual instrument; cf. 'Lincolnshire bells and bagpipes', which Moryson cites as proverbial (3.463), but perhaps a metaphor for a tedious speaker (i.e. windbag).

74 **hare** The hare was itself thought to be, as Turberville writes, 'one of the moste melancholike beastes that is' (sig. K8ᵛ); and the meat of the hare was proverbially thought to produce melancholy in those that ate it (cf. Dent, H151); yet, as Fynes Moryson

notes, 'howsoever Hares are thought to nourish melancoly, yet they are eaten as Venison, both rosted and boyled' (Moryson, 4.171).

75 **Moorditch** foul drainage ditch north of the City of London, between Bishopsgate and Cripplegate; John Taylor refers to 'moody, muddy, Moorditch melancholy' in J. Taylor, *Penniless*, 129; cited by Malone.

77 **comparative** adept in making comparisons, often of a derogatory sort; at 2.4.238–41, Falstaff displays his own ability to generate *base comparisons*, and at 3.2.67, the King uses the word to describe mockers. See also *LLL* 5.2.831–2: 'a man replete with mocks, / Full of comparisons and wounding flouts'.

80 **commodity** supply

85–6 **wisdom . . . it** echoes Proverbs, 1.20, 24: 'Wisdom crieth without . . . and no man regarded.' The omission of *wisdom . . . and* from F responds no

76 similes] *Q5;* smiles *Q1–4, F*    77 rascalliest] rascallest *Q4–F*    79 to God] *om. F*    85–6 wisdom . . . and] *om. F*

FALSTAFF    O, thou hast damnable iteration and art indeed
    able to corrupt a saint. Thou hast done much harm
    upon me, Hal; God forgive thee for it. Before I knew
    thee, Hal, I knew nothing, and now am I, if a man        90
    should speak truly, little better than one of the wicked.
    I must give over this life, and I will give it over. By the
    Lord, an I do not, I am a villain. I'll be damned for
    never a king's son in Christendom.

PRINCE    Where shall we take a purse tomorrow, Jack?        95

FALSTAFF    Zounds, where thou wilt, lad. I'll make one; an
    I do not, call me villain and baffle me.

PRINCE    I see a good amendment of life in thee, from
    praying to purse-taking.

FALSTAFF    Why, Hal, 'tis my vocation, Hal; 'tis no sin for    100
    a man to labour in his vocation.

doubt to the 1606 Act against blasphemy on stage; see p. 113.

87 **damnable iteration** repeatedly quoting (religious texts) for wicked ends

88 **saint** a term used by radical Protestants for one of the godly (and here not referring to one of those formally canonized by the Catholic Church)

91 **one . . . wicked** a conventional expression of one's sinfulness; cf. Dent, W333.1.

93, 96 **an** if; see Abbott, 101, 103.

96 **Zounds** a strong, though common oath (by Christ's wounds)
    **where . . . lad** Falstaff rushes to accept the Prince's idea, much relieved at the change of topic from the previous 35 lines, with their focus on the hangman; Cumberland's acting edition of 1826 says that 'Falstaff eagerly shakes hands with Prince' (Sprague, *Actors*, 84).

97 **baffle** treat contemptuously, disgrace. Literally 'baffle' was a technical term for a dishonoured knight's formal degradation; a baffled knight would

have his armour confiscated and he (or sometimes only his shield as a symbol) would be publicly suspended upside-down; cf. Falstaff's offer to Hal to 'hang me up by the heels' (2.4.424–5) if the Prince can play the part of the King better than Falstaff has. It is easy to forget that Falstaff is a knight, and could indeed be formally baffled. Also see *1H6* 4.1.1–47, where Sir John Fastolfe is 'degraded', his Garter emblem removed, and he is ultimately banished for his cowardice in deserting Talbot.

98 **amendment of life** reformation, repentance; cf. Matthew, 3.8: 'worthie amendment of life' (Geneva translation; Bishops' Bible has 'worthy of repentence'); Noble cites also the Exhortation in the Communion Service to 'confess yourselves to Almighty God, with the full purpose of amendment of life' (Noble, 61).

100 **'tis my vocation** i.e. it is the activity to which God has called me; an ironic echo of a familiar Protestant theme, based on 1 Corinthians, 7.20: 'Let

89 upon] vnto *Q2–F*    90 am I] I am *F*    92–3 By the Lord] *om. F*    93 an] *(and), Pope*
96 Zounds] *om. F*

*Enter* POINS.

Poins! Now shall we know if Gadshill have set a match.
O, if men were to be saved by merit, what hole in hell
were hot enough for him? This is the most omnipotent
villain that ever cried 'Stand!' to a true man.                    105

PRINCE    Good morrow, Ned.

POINS    Good morrow, sweet Hal. – What says Monsieur
    Remorse? What says Sir John Sack and Sugar, Jack?
    How agrees the devil and thee about thy soul, that thou
    soldest him on Good Friday last for a cup of madeira        110
    and a cold capon's leg?

every man abide in the vocation
wherein he was called'; cf. Middleton's
*Family of Love* (sig. D3ʳ): ''Tis my
vocation, boy; we must never be weary
of well-doing.'
100–1 **'tis no . . . vocation** Falstaff per-
verts the Protestant commonplace by
using it to justify his thieving; cf.
Nashe, *Christ's Tears over Jerusalem*
(1593): 'He held it as lawful for hym
(since al labouring in a mans vocation
is but getting) to gette wealth as wel
with his Sword by the High-way side,
as the Laborer with his Spade or
Mattocke' (Nashe, 2.64; cited in Ardˡ).
102 **Gadshill** See List of Roles, 24n., and
119n. below.
    **set a match** planned a robbery
103 **saved by merit** i.e. earned salvation
through good works (and not by faith
alone, as most Protestants believed,
based on their understanding of
Romans, 3.28: 'we hold that a man is
justified in faith, without the deeds of
the law'); cf. *LLL* 4.1.21–2: 'my beauty will be saved by merit! / O heresy in
fair, fit for these days!'
    **hole** dungeon, prison cell; cf. *The
Puritan*, 3.4.197: 'The hole shall rot
him.'

105 **true** honest
107–8 **Monsieur Remorse** Poins is
mocking Falstaff's pretended piety
and repeated claims that he will amend
his life, e.g. 92–3 or 2.2.15–17.
108 **Sir. . . Sugar** a teasing reference to
Falstaff's taste in drink; the desire for
sweeter wines, achieved by adding
sugar, was seen as a sign of old age; cf.
Thomas Dekker, *The Shoemaker's
Holiday*: 'olde age, sacke and sugar will
steale vpon us ere we be aware'
(3.3.23–4; Dekker, 1.55). Some editors, however, have printed 'Sir John
Sack, and Sugar Jack', following Q1's
punctuation as suggesting 'a balance of
elements' (Camˡ, 203); but Dering
reads 'Sʳ Iohn Sacke & suger'; and cf.
*Humour's Blood* epi. 22: 'When signeur
*Sacke & Suger* drinke droun'd reeles'
(sig. B6ʳ).
110 **Good Friday** the Friday before
Easter Sunday and the most rigorous
fast day of the year; cf. *KJ* 1.1.234–5:
'Sir Robert may have ate his part in me
/ Upon Good Friday and ne'er broke
his fast.'
    **madeira** a strong, fortified white wine
produced on the island of Madeira, in
the Atlantic off the coast of North-

101.1 *om. F*    102 Poins] *as SP Q4–F*    match] Watch *F*    105 'Stand!'] Ardˡ; stand, *QF*
108 Sack . . . Jack] *Q5;* Sacke, and Sugar Iacke *Q1–4;* Sacke and Sugar: Iacke *F*

157

PRINCE  Sir John stands to his word. The devil shall have
his bargain, for he was never yet a breaker of proverbs;
he will give the devil his due.

POINS [*to Falstaff*]  Then art thou damned for keeping      115
thy word with the devil.

PRINCE  Else he had been damned for cozening the devil.

POINS  But my lads, my lads, tomorrow morning by four
o'clock early, at Gad's Hill, there are pilgrims going to
Canterbury with rich offerings and traders riding to      120
London with fat purses. I have vizards for you all; you
have horses for yourselves. Gadshill lies tonight in
Rochester. I have bespoke supper tomorrow night in
Eastcheap. We may do it as secure as sleep. If you will
go, I will stuff your purses full of crowns; if you will      125
not, tarry at home and be hanged.

West Africa. The usage is anachronis-
tic, as Portuguese explorers first landed on Madeira in 1419, and the island
was soon after settled. Portuguese sea-
men imported the grapevines, and the
wine quickly became popular throughout Europe. This is the earliest citation
in the *OED*.

113 **he** i.e. Falstaff
　　**a . . . proverbs** one who ignores
　　proverbial wisdom (and itself prover-
　　bial, cf. Dent, P615.1)
114 **give . . . due** i.e. pay what is owed;
　　the phrase is proverbial (cf. Dent,
　　D273) but usually is applied somewhat
　　less literally, meaning 'acknowledge
　　the good points even of the devil'.
117 **Else** otherwise
　　**cozening** cheating
119 **Gad's Hill** hill 27 miles south-east of
　　London on the old Dover road near
　　Rochester in Kent; notorious as a
　　favourite spot for highwaymen to
　　operate ('Gads-hill, very dangerous',
　　Dekker and Webster, *Westward Ho*,

2.2.226; Dekker, 2.343), often robbing
pilgrims on their way to Canterbury.
The usual spelling is as one word, but
most editions, as here, have divided it
to differentiate the place-name from
the proper name, *Gadshill* (102), that
Shakespeare gives the 'setter' who
helps in the robbery in 2.2.
119–20 **pilgrims . . . Canterbury**
Canterbury Cathedral, particularly the
shrine of Thomas Becket in the north-
west transept, was a common pilgrimage destination in pre-Reformation
England.
121 **vizards** masks
122 **lies** lodges
123 **bespoke** ordered
124 **Eastcheap** market street near London
　　Bridge, setting for tavern scenes
　　**secure** safely
125 **crowns** silver coins valued at five
　　shillings; the planned theft of *crowns* has
　　a particular resonance in a play whose
　　titular hero has usurped the crown he
　　wears. See pp. 14–15.

115 SD] *Oxf*　117 had been] had *F*　123 tomorrow night] to morrow *F*

FALSTAFF   Hear ye, Yedward, if I tarry at home and go
   not, I'll hang you for going.

POINS   You will, chops?

FALSTAFF   Hal, wilt thou make one?                    130

PRINCE   Who? I rob? I a thief? Not I, by my faith.

FALSTAFF   There's neither honesty, manhood nor good
   fellowship in thee, nor thou cam'st not of the blood
   royal, if thou darest not stand for ten shillings.

PRINCE   Well then, once in my days I'll be a madcap.    135

FALSTAFF   Why, that's well said.

PRINCE   Well, come what will, I'll tarry at home.

FALSTAFF   By the Lord, I'll be a traitor then, when thou
   art king.

PRINCE   I care not.                                     140

POINS   Sir John, I prithee leave the Prince and me alone.
   I will lay him down such reasons for this adventure that
   he shall go.

FALSTAFF   Well, God give thee the spirit of persuasion
   and him the ears of profiting, that what thou speakest    145
   may move and what he hears may be believed, that the
   true prince may, for recreation sake, prove a false thief,

---

127 **Yedward** a midlands dialectal form
of Edward, Poins's first name
129 **chops** fat cheeks
130 **make one** join in
133–4 **blood royal** royal descent (but
Falstaff is playing with *royal* as the
name of a coin valued at *ten shillings*)
134 **stand for** means both 'fight for' and
'be valued at'
138–9 **I'll . . . king** The historical Oldcastle, the name by which Falstaff's
character was originally imagined, did
turn traitor against Henry V; see p. 57.
143 **shall** with full force of 'can't choose
but', 'must'

144–6 **Well . . . believed** Falstaff parodies familiar pulpit oratory on the topic
of the efficacy of the spirit of God.
147 **recreation sake** a common formulation with *sake* meaning 'for the purpose
of' or 'with regard for'; cf. Abbott, 31
(and as at 2.1.69, 71; 5.1.65).
**false thief** Falstaff means something
like 'one who plays false', in opposition
to the *true prince* he mentions earlier in
the line; but Hal indeed proves a *false
thief* in exposing Falstaff's cowardice
and by eventually giving back the
stolen money.

131 by my faith] *om. F*   138 By the Lord] *om. F*   144 God give thee] maist thou haue *F*
145 him] he *F*

for the poor abuses of the time want countenance.
Farewell. You shall find me in Eastcheap.

PRINCE   Farewell, the latter spring; farewell, All-hallown   150
summer.                                           [*Exit Falstaff.*]

POINS   Now, my good sweet honey lord, ride with us
tomorrow. I have a jest to execute that I cannot manage
alone. Falstaff, Peto, Bardoll and Gadshill shall rob
those men that we have already waylaid – yourself and   155
I will not be there – and when they have the booty, if
you and I do not rob them, cut this head off from my
shoulders.

PRINCE   How shall we part with them in setting forth?

POINS   Why, we will set forth before or after them and   160
appoint them a place of meeting, wherein it is at our
pleasure to fail. And then will they adventure upon the

148 **the poor . . . countenance** the age's
vices are not approved or valued (by
those in power), a parody of familiar
complaints that good deeds go unrec-
ognized and unrewarded
150 **latter spring** unseasonable spring-
like weather in the autumn
150–1 **All-hallown summer** St Martin's
summer or Indian summer; unseason-
ably warm weather around All Saints'
Day (1 November, the day following
All-Hallows Eve or Hallowe'en); both
this and *latter spring* are Hal's personifications of Falstaff as an old man
behaving like an adolescent.
154 ***Peto, Bardoll** QF have 'Haruey,
Rossill' here, Shakespeare's original
names for these characters and probably changed, though obviously incom-
pletely in the manuscript, at the same
time that 'Falstaff' replaced 'Oldcastle'
(see p. 117); most editors have followed
Theobald in substituting 'Bardolph'
for 'Harvey' and 'Peto' for 'Rossill' (i.e.

Russell). Wilson (Cam[1]), however,
notes that '*sir Iohn Russel*' in the quarto entry direction in *2H4* at 2.2.0 is
replaced by '*Bardolfe*' in F, though he
does not follow the implications of this
for his emendation of Q, still main-
taining Theobald's rearrangement.
Melchiori, however, in his edition of
*2H4* for Cambridge, convincingly
argues that 'Russell' must have been
the original name of 'Bardolph', suggesting further that the form 'Rossill'
was 'chosen deliberately in order to
play on the Italian *rosso* for red', in reference to Bardoll's 'formidable red
nose' (Melchiori, 5n.; see also Jowett).
157–8 **cut . . . shoulders** Cf. *Ham*
2.2.156: 'Take this from this if this be
otherwise.'
159 **part with** get away from
161–2 **wherein . . . fail** i.e. at which we
will conveniently fail to show up
162 **adventure upon** stumble on, discover

151 SD] *F2*   154 Peto, Bardoll] *Cam[1]*; Haruey, Rossill *QF*; Bardolfe, Peto *Theobald*   157 head off]
head *Q3–F*   159 How] But how *F*

160

exploit themselves, which they shall have no sooner achieved but we'll set upon them.

PRINCE   Yea, but 'tis like that they will know us by our   165
horses, by our habits and by every other appointment to be ourselves.

POINS   Tut, our horses they shall not see. I'll tie them in the wood. Our vizards we will change after we leave them, and, sirrah, I have cases of buckram for the   170
nonce, to immask our noted outward garments.

PRINCE   Yea, but I doubt they will be too hard for us.

POINS   Well, for two of them, I know them to be as true-bred cowards as ever turned back, and for the third, if he fight longer than he sees reason, I'll forswear arms.   175
The virtue of this jest will be the incomprehensible lies that this same fat rogue will tell us when we meet at supper: how thirty at least he fought with, what wards, what blows, what extremities he endured; and in the reproof of this lives the jest.   180

PRINCE   Well, I'll go with thee. Provide us all things necessary and meet me tomorrow night in Eastcheap.

---

166 **habits** clothing
   **appointment** gear, trapping, accoutrement
170 **sirrah** familiar form of 'sir', often used to address an inferior but here suggesting the intimacy of Poins with the Prince
   **cases of buckram** rough suits or overalls made of coarse linen
171 **nonce** occasion
   **immask** conceal
   **noted** well-known
172 **doubt** fear (here perhaps sarcastic)
175 **forswear** swear to give up
176 **incomprehensible** infinite, unlimited (a word well suited for the immoderation of behaviour and great size of Falstaff)
178 **wards** defensive postures or

manoeuvres
180 **reproof** refutation, denial
181 **thee** Hal's shift from the second person form previously used by Poins, *yourself*, 155, is significant, marking the Prince's reassertion of his social superiority, which was temporarily levelled in their planning of the jest; this reassertion is evident also in the imperatives that follow: *Provide* and *meet*, 181, 182.
182 **tomorrow night** The robbery has been planned for the following day, and many editors, following Capell, have changed this to 'to-night'; but Hal is not referring to the robbery but confirming the dinner arrangements for the next evening that Poins refers to at 123–4.

165 Yea] I *F*   172 Yea, but] But *F*   177 this same] this *Q5–F*   180 lives] lyes *Q2–F*

There I'll sup. Farewell.

POINS     Farewell, my lord.                     *Exit Poins.*

PRINCE

I know you all, and will awhile uphold             185

The unyoked humour of your idleness.

Yet herein will I imitate the sun,

Who doth permit the base contagious clouds

To smother up his beauty from the world,

That, when he please again to be himself,            190

Being wanted, he may be more wondered at

By breaking through the foul and ugly mists

Of vapours that did seem to strangle him.

If all the year were playing holidays,

To sport would be as tedious as to work;           195

But when they seldom come, they wished-for come,

And nothing pleaseth but rare accidents.

So when this loose behaviour I throw off

And pay the debt I never promised,

By how much better than my word I am,            200

By so much shall I falsify men's hopes;

And, like bright metal on a sullen ground,

---

185–207 the play's only verse soliloquy, and one that sets the tone of all performances. Hal may be rationalizing his prodigal behaviour, as Johnson thought: 'a great mind offering excuses to itself' (Johnson, 4.123); or revealing his 'political calculation' in using his tavern life is 'an instrument of policy', as in Traversi, 58; or facing an uncomfortable truth about his life, as at the Old Vic in 1955, when Robert Hardy's Hal 'dropped back into a chair and with a sigh of sadness and regret admitted to himself, "I know you all . . ."' (Wood & Clark, 159).

185 **I . . . all** In *2H4*, the now King Henry V rejects Falstaff: 'I know thee not, old man' (5.5.47).

    **uphold** put up with (and also support)

186 **unyoked humour** unrestrained behaviour

187 **the sun** traditional symbol of royalty (and in contrast with Falstaff's talk about the moon at 12–28)

188 **contagious** infectious, noxious (reflecting a belief that clouds and fogs carried diseases; cf. *MND* 2.1.90: 'contagious fogs')

191 **wanted** lacked, missed

197 **rare accidents** unusual occurrences

199 **debt** The language of debt and repayment runs throughout the play; see pp. 64–9.

    **promised** promisèd

201 **falsify men's hopes** prove people's expectations false

202 **sullen ground** dull background

My reformation, glittering o'er my fault,
Shall show more goodly and attract more eyes
Than that which hath no foil to set it off.                    205
I'll so offend to make offence a skill,
Redeeming time when men think least I will.                   *Exit.*

**1.3**   *Enter the* KING, NORTHUMBERLAND, WORCESTER,
          HOTSPUR, Sir Walter BLOUNT, *with others.*

KING

My blood hath been too cold and temperate,
Unapt to stir at these indignities,
And you have found me, for accordingly
You tread upon my patience; but be sure
I will from henceforth rather be myself,                        5

---

205 **foil** contrast (like the plain background upon which a jeweller might place a jewel to 'set off' the brilliance of the stone)

**set it off** show it to best advantage

206 i.e. I will use my misbehaviour for my own advantage

207 **Redeeming time** making up for wasted time; a Scottish reader about 1630 noted in a copy of the 1623 Folio that this was: 'The princes resolution to giue a time to debauch and then convert to vertue' (Yamada, 112; see Fig. 5). Hal's phrase certainly takes something from Ephesians, 5.16: 'redeeming the time, because the days are evil' (as Jorgensen has fully discussed, 52–69), but, while contemporary audiences might well have understood the phrase in its Pauline sense of taking full advantage of the time allowed us on earth to ensure our salvation, Hal's interest is more secular, concerned rather with renewing his sullied reputation than his tarnished soul. 'The time will come', he promises, when

Hotspur will be forced to 'exchange / His glorious deeds for my indignities' (3.2.144–6); and Henry acknowledges his son's success: 'Thou hast redeemed thy lost opinion' (5.4.47).

1.3 The dialogue does not specify the scene's time or location, although clearly the action takes place at court. At 1.1.102–3 the King has said his council will meet on *Wednesday next* at Windsor, and some editors locate this scene there. What is clear is that the opening dialogue marks some midpoint in a heated conversation between Worcester and the King; possibly they enter with the King already speaking to indicate the ongoing conversation.

2 **Unapt to stir** not inclined to be aroused

3 **found me** found me so

5 **myself** i.e. my regal self; cf. *H5* Prologue 5: 'the warlike Harry, like himself'; in this play, the Prince uses the same phrase at 3.2.92–3, promising his father that he will 'hereafter . . . Be more myself'.

205 foil] soile *Q4–F*   207 SD] *om. F*   1.3.0.2 *with*] *and F*

163

Mighty and to be feared, than my condition,
Which hath been smooth as oil, soft as young down,
And therefore lost that title of respect
Which the proud soul ne'er pays but to the proud.

WORCESTER

Our house, my sovereign liege, little deserves          10
The scourge of greatness to be used on it,
And that same greatness, too, which our own hands
Have holp to make so portly.

NORTHUMBERLAND [*to the King*]

My lord –

KING

Worcester, get thee gone, for I do see          15
Danger and disobedience in thine eye.
O sir, your presence is too bold and peremptory,
And majesty might never yet endure
The moody frontier of a servant brow.
You have good leave to leave us. When we need          20
Your use and counsel we shall send for you.     *Exit Worcester.*
[*to Northumberland*] You were about to speak.

---

6  **condition** natural disposition
7  **smooth . . . down** The King's con-
    ventional similes undermine the credi-
    bility of his account of his behaviour
    as gentle and unthreatening.
8  **title of** claim to
10 **house** family
11 **scourge of greatness** punishment by
    those in power (and, although
    Northumberland does not intend it,
    hints also at the punishment due to
    ambitious subjects, as *scourge* tends to
    imply an instrument of divine chas-
    tisement)
13 **holp** archaic past tense of verb 'help'
    **portly** majestic, imposing (though
    with sense of overweight, cf. 5.1.62,
    linking the King to Falstaff, who calls
    himself *portly* at 2.4.410)

16 **Danger** mischief, harm (*OED* 4)
17 **peremptory** imperious, overbearing
19 **moody frontier** threatening aspect
    (*frontier* = military fortification; 'front' =
    forehead)
    **servant brow** subject's frown (but an
    insult to Worcester in referring to him
    as a *servant*)
20 **good leave** full permission
21 **use and counsel** help and advice
22 **You . . . speak** This line is often
    spoken in the theatre as if daring
    Northumberland to continue Worces-
    ter's defiance, as at Stratford-upon-
    Avon in 1951, when Harry Andrews's
    Henry turned sharply to Northumber-
    land and menacingly said: 'You . . .
    were . . . about . . . to . . . speak'
    (Wilson & Worsley, 70–1).

14 SD] *Oxf*   21 SD] *not in F*   22 SD] *Rowe*

NORTHUMBERLAND                                   Yea, my good lord.
　Those prisoners in your highness' name demanded,
　Which Harry Percy here at Humbleton took,
　Were, as he says, not with such strength denied          25
　As is delivered to your majesty.
　Either envy, therefore, or misprision
　Is guilty of this fault and not my son.
HOTSPUR
　My liege, I did deny no prisoners.
　But I remember, when the fight was done,                 30
　When I was dry with rage and extreme toil,
　Breathless and faint, leaning upon my sword,
　Came there a certain lord, neat and trimly dressed,
　Fresh as a bridegroom, and his chin, new reaped,
　Showed like a stubble-land at harvest-home.              35
　He was perfumed like a milliner,
　And 'twixt his finger and his thumb he held
　A pouncet-box, which ever and anon
　He gave his nose and took't away again
　(Who therewith angry, when it next came there,           40
　Took it in snuff) and still he smiled and talked;

25 **with such strength** so emphatically
26 **delivered** reported
27 **envy** malice
　**misprision** misunderstanding
31 **dry . . . toil** parched with thirst after the fierce fighting
33 **neat and trimly** refined and elegantly (the '-ly' of *trimly* covers both words, as in *fair and evenly* at 3.1.101)
34 **new reaped** recently clipped (as opposed to the unkempt beard of a soldier)
35 **stubble-land at harvest-home** close-cut crop-stalks left in the fields after the harvest has been completed
36 **perfumed** perfumèd. Thomas and Dudley Digges in *Four Paradoxes, or Politic Discourses* contemptuously refer

to captains 'perfumed perhaps with Muske and Syvet' standing upwind from their 'stinking' troops (Digges, sig. B3ʳ).
　**milliner** vendor of fashion accessories (originally referring to a merchant importing fancy goods from Milan)
38 **pouncet-box** small box with perforated lid, a pomander, used to hold various pleasantly scented materials
40 **Who therewith angry** which (i.e. *his nose*) became angry when the *pouncet-box* was not there to be smelled
41 **Took . . . snuff** inhaled; but the phrase also means 'took offence' (*OED* snuff *sb.*¹ 4)
　**still** continually

26 is] he *Q5;* was *F*   27 Either envy, therefore] Who either through enuy *F*   28 Is] Was *F*

And, as the soldiers bore dead bodies by,
He called them 'untaught knaves', 'unmannerly'
To bring a slovenly unhandsome corpse
Betwixt the wind and his nobility.                              45
With many holiday and lady terms
He questioned me, amongst the rest demanded
My prisoners in your majesty's behalf.
I then, all smarting with my wounds being cold,
To be so pestered with a popinjay,                             50
Out of my grief and my impatience
Answered neglectingly, I know not what –
He should or he should not – for he made me mad
To see him shine so brisk, and smell so sweet
And talk so like a waiting gentlewoman                         55
Of guns, and drums, and wounds, God save the mark!
And telling me 'the sovereignest thing on earth'

43 **untaught** coarse, unsophisticated
46 **holiday and lady** refined and lady-like
47 **questioned** engaged in conversation (*OED sb.* 2†) rather than 'interrogated'
49 **cold** unattended to (*OED* II †14, though no example before 1703 is given)
50 **with** by
   **popinjay** parrot; figuratively, a vain prattler
51 **Out . . . grief** as a result of my pain (*OED* grief *sb.* 5)
52 **neglectingly** negligently (first *OED* citation)
55 **so like** so much like
   **waiting gentlewoman** woman of a well-born family in attendance on a great lady
56 **Of . . . wounds** At the New Theatre in London in 1945, Laurence Olivier,

who had adopted a stammer for his Hotspur, hesitating slightly before all words beginning with 'w', 'delivered the line: *of guns, and drums, and w-w-w* . . . , stamping the ground to loosen the word from his mouth. Finally in a convulsion of contempt it sprung out: *w-w-wounds – God save the mark*' (Tynan, 50). Stage tradition, beginning with Matheson Lang's Hotspur in Beerbohm Tree's 1914 production, has often had Hotspur stuttering, seemingly based on a misunderstanding of a line in *2H4*, where he is described as 'speaking thick, which nature made his blemish' (2.3.24; 'thick' actually here means 'quickly' as in *Cym* 3.2.56: 'say and speak thick').
   **God . . . mark** an exclamation of irritation or impatience; *mark* = cross?
57 **sovereignest** best, most effective

42 bore] bare *F*   43 'untaught knaves'] *this edn;* vntaught knaues *QF*   'unmannerly'] *this edn;* vnmanerlie *QF*   44 corpse] *(coarse)*   46 terms] tearme *F*   47 amongst] among *Q3–F*
53 or he] or *F*   57 'the . . . earth'] *this edn;* the . . . earth *QF*

Was 'parmaceti' for an inward bruise,
And that it was great pity, so it was,
This 'villainous saltpetre' should be digged                    60
Out of the bowels of the harmless earth,
Which many a good tall fellow had destroyed
So cowardly, and but for these 'vile guns'
He would himself have been a soldier.
This bald, unjointed chat of his, my lord,                      65
I answered indirectly, as I said,
And I beseech you, let not his report
Come current for an accusation
Betwixt my love and your high majesty.

BLOUNT [*to the King*]

The circumstance considered, good my lord,                      70
Whate'er Lord Harry Percy then had said

---

58 **'parmaceti'** corruption of 'sperma-
ceti', the fat from the head of a whale
(Latin, *cetus*) used to treat bruises and
minor wounds; cf. Hawkins's *Voyage*:
'wee corruptly call *parmacittie*; of the
Latine word *Sperma Ceti*' (*South Sea*,
46)*;* Bullokar says that it is 'used in
Physicke against bruisings of the
bodie'.
60 **saltpetre** potassium nitrite, a central
ingredient in gunpowder
62 i.e. which had destroyed many a good
tall fellow
**tall** valiant
63 **vile guns** like *villainous saltpetre*, 60,
the phrase here expresses the disappointment of the popinjay that modern warfare is no longer the heroic
activity it was before the invention of
gunpowder; *vile* and *villainous*, in their
etymological roots that link them to
the French *villain*, i.e. peasant, reveal
the class bias of the remark.
65 **bald, unjointed chat** trivial, incoher-

ent chatter
66 **I answered** F has 'Made me to answer',
a reading that Oxf prints, since, as the
editors argue in *TxC*, 333, it 'can only
be explained as an authorial alteration'.
Indeed it does seem to be a deliberate
alteration of Q (since it is hard to see
how a compositor would misread copy
to produce the F reading or would feel
it necessary to adjust Q on the basis of
what is there), but it is not obvious why
it is necessary for the revision to be
'authorial' (i.e. Shakespeare's); it might
be an actor's innovation or an unautho-
rized scribal revision, perhaps after
erroneously starting the line with an
'M', influenced by the 'my lord' that
ended the previous line.
**indirectly** casually, in an offhand
manner
68 **Come current** be accepted at face
value
71 **had said** may have said

---

58 'parmaceti'] *this edn;* Parmacitie *QF*    60 This] That *F*    'villainous saltpetre'] *this edn;* villanous
saltpeeter *QF*    63 'vile guns'] *this edn;* vile guns *QF*    64 himself have been] haue been himselfe
*Q4–5*    66 I answered] Made me to answer *F*    67 his] this *Q2–F*    70 SD] *Oxf*    71 Whate'er Lord]
What e're *Q2–5;* What euer *F*

To such a person, and in such a place,
At such a time, with all the rest retold,
May reasonably die and never rise
To do him wrong or any way impeach                                  75
What then he said, so he unsay it now.

KING

Why, yet he doth deny his prisoners,
But with proviso and exception:
That we at our own charge shall ransom straight
His brother-in-law, the foolish Mortimer,                           80
Who, on my soul, hath wilfully betrayed
The lives of those that he did lead to fight
Against that great magician, damned Glendower,
Whose daughter, as we hear, that Earl of March
Hath lately married. Shall our coffers then                         85
Be emptied to redeem a traitor home?
Shall we buy treason and indent with fears

---

74 **May reasonably die** may well be forgotten
75 **impeach** discredit, make subject to
blame
76 **so** provided that
77 **yet** still, even now
**he** The King does not respond directly to Hotspur but speaks of him in the
third person.
78 **proviso and exception** terms and
conditions (*exception* probably pronounced with four syllables as, similarly,
the '-tion' endings at 146, 149, 267)
79 **charge** expense, cost
80 **brother-in-law** Hotspur was married
to Edmund Mortimer's older sister,
Elizabeth ('Kate' in Shakespeare's
play); see List of Roles, 9n., and Fig. 3.
83 **that great magician** Perhaps Shakespeare derives this from Holinshed's
report of how Glendower '(as was
thought) through art magike' brought

on extreme weather to force the King's
army to retreat (Holinshed, 3.520).
84–5 **Earl . . . married** The Edmund
Mortimer who was sent to Wales, and
who married Glendower's daughter,
was not the Earl of March, but his
uncle, another Edmund; Shakespeare
follows the mistake in Holinshed and
in S. Daniel; see Fig. 3.
86 **redeem** ransom
87 **indent with fears** make a pact (i.e. an
indenture) with cowards; many editors
have understood *fears* as 'those who
must be feared', but the context makes
it clear that the King is objecting to
paying for the return of a man who has
refused to fight. A Scottish reader
about 1630 noted in his copy of the
1623 Folio: 'a traitor will not receiue
mortall wounds in his kings seruice'
(Yamada, 113–14).

---

77 yet he] yet *F*   81 on] in *Q3–F*   83 that] the *Q3–F*   84 that] the *Q2–F*

When they have lost and forfeited themselves?
No, on the barren mountains let him starve;
For I shall never hold that man my friend 90
Whose tongue shall ask me for one penny cost
To ransom home revolted Mortimer.

HOTSPUR

'Revolted Mortimer'!
He never did fall off, my sovereign liege,
But by the chance of war. To prove that true 95
Needs no more but one tongue for all those wounds,
Those mouthed wounds, which valiantly he took
When on the gentle Severn's sedgy bank,
In single opposition, hand to hand,
He did confound the best part of an hour 100
In changing hardiment with great Glendower.

---

89 **starve** die a lingering death, by freez-
ing or famine

92 Cf. Holinshed (3.520): 'The King was
not hastie to purchase the deliuerance
of the earl March, bicause his title to
the crowne was well inough knowen
and therefore suffered him to remain
in miserable prison, wishing both the
said earl and all other of his lineage out
of this life, with God and his saints in
heauen.'

**revolted** treasonous.

93 **Revolted Mortimer** In 1784,
Thomas Davies, no doubt recalling
productions that he had seen, noted
that 'These two words should be spoken loudly and passionately, from a
sudden impulse, which the impetuous
Hotspur could not restrain' (Davies,
*DM*, 1.215–16).

94 **fall off** change allegiance

95–107 **To . . . combatants** Some commentators (e.g. Wilson, Cam[1]) have
been surprised by Hotspur's 'ornate'

language here, especially given his
expressed contempt for poetry (cf.
3.1.124–31); but Hotspur readily displays imaginative gifts in his exuberant
thinking about warfare or honour (cf.
200–7 and 200–6n.).

97 **mouthed** mouthèd: gaping (but also
'articulate' or 'eloquent', as in *JC*
3.2.221–2: 'put a tongue / In every
wound of Caesar')

98 **Severn's sedgy bank** the reed-
bordered banks of the Severn; 'sedge'
is a tall, grass-like rush. The Severn
flows south-westerly from Shrewsbury
to the Bristol Channel; see 3.1.72 and
Fig. 21.

99 **opposition** combat; cf. *Cym* 4.1.13:
'more remarkable in single opposi-
tions'.

100 **confound** consume, waste

101 **changing hardiment** exchanging
valiant blows; alternating in their bravery (the phrase expresses the give-and-
take of hand-to-hand combat; cf. *Cym*

---

89 mountains] mountaine *Q2–F* starve] sterue *Q4–F* 93 'Revolted Mortimer'!] *this edn;*
Reuolted Mortimer: *Q;* Reuolted *Mortimer? F* 96 tongue for] *Hanmer;* tongue: for *Q;* tongue. For
*F* 98 sedgy] *(siedgie), F4 (*Sedgie*)

Three times they breathed, and three times did they
    drink,
Upon agreement, of swift Severn's flood,
Who, then affrighted with their bloody looks,
Ran fearfully among the trembling reeds           105
And hid his crisp head in the hollow bank
Bloodstained with these valiant combatants.
Never did bare and rotten policy
Colour her working with such deadly wounds,
Nor never could the noble Mortimer           110
Receive so many, and all willingly.
Then let not him be slandered with revolt.

KING

Thou dost belie him, Percy; thou dost belie him.
He never did encounter with Glendower.
I tell thee, he durst as well have met the devil alone    115
As Owen Glendower for an enemy.
Art thou not ashamed? But, sirrah, henceforth
Let me not hear you speak of Mortimer.
Send me your prisoners with the speediest means,
Or you shall hear in such a kind from me         120

---

5.4.75–6: 'Like hardiment Posthumus hath / to Cymbeline perform'd')

**102 breathed** paused to catch breath

**106 crisp head** wavy or rippled surface (personifying the river), playing on *head* as the pressure of water against the bank (*OED* 17)

**107 Bloodstained** bloodstainèd

**108 bare ... policy** miserable and malicious cunning; *bare* might mean 'barefaced', as some editors assume, but *Colour* in the next line seems to contradict this (though Hotspur in his passion is certainly capable of failing to notice a contradiction). F prints 'base', but there is no reason to emend Q.

**109 Colour her working** disguise its real nature

**110 Nor never** The doubled negative here strengthens the negation.

**112 slandered with revolt** falsely accused of treason

**113 belie** misrepresent

**117 sirrah** here asserts Hotspur's subordinate position; see 1.2.170.

**118 you** The speech begins with the King addressing Hotspur as *thou*, but now shifts to the more formal *you*, indicating the reassertion of his own authority, and similarly at 123 he shifts to the royal 'we' from the first-person pronouns of the first ten lines of the speech.

**120 kind** manner (*OED* 8a)

108 bare] base *F*   112 not him] him not *F*

As will displease you. – My lord Northumberland,
We license your departure with your son.
[*to Hotspur*] Send us your prisoners, or you will hear
    of it.

        *Exit King* [*with all but Hotspur and Northumberland*].

HOTSPUR

An if the devil come and roar for them
I will not send them. I will after straight                125
And tell him so, for I will ease my heart,
Albeit I make a hazard of my head.

NORTHUMBERLAND

What, drunk with choler? Stay and pause awhile.


        *Enter* WORCESTER.


Here comes your uncle.

HOTSPUR                    'Speak of Mortimer'?
Zounds, I will speak of him, and let my soul                130
Want mercy if I do not join with him.
Yea, on his part I'll empty all these veins

---

123 **you . . . it** In Restoration productions, Ned Kynaston's Henry ominously whispered his last line and 'so convey'd a more terrible menace in it than the loudest intemperance of voice could swell to' (Cibber, 1.126). F changes Q's 'you will' to 'you'l', one of several cases where F contracts the forms in Q and which some editors follow. Here, however, although the contraction allows the line to be read with ten syllables if 'prisoners' is pronounced as usual with two, the metre of the first part of the line is still irregular. Dramatically the contraction seems inappropriate, and perhaps raises doubts about whether

F's contractions in general can be safely regarded as original readings that Q has sophisticated.

124 **An if** even if (for *an* or 'and' as an intensification of the conditional use of 'if', see Abbott, 103, 105)
    **devil . . . roar** The image of the roaring devil derives from 1 Peter, 5.8, where the devil is described as a 'roaring lion'; cf. *H5* 4.4.68: 'this roaring devil i'th' old play'.

125 **after straight** follow immediately
127 **make a hazard** put at risk
128 **choler** anger
131 **Want mercy** fail to find God's mercy; i.e. be damned

121 you] ye *F*   123 you will] you'l *F*   SD1] *Oxf*   SD2 *with . . . Northumberland*] *Capell subst.*   124 An] *(And), Capell*   127 Albeit . . . a] Although it be with *F*   128.1 *om. Q5*   129 'Speak of Mortimer'] *this edn;* Speak of Mortimer *QF*   130 Zounds] Yes *F*   132 Yea . . . part] In his behalfe, *F*

And shed my dear blood drop by drop in the dust,
But I will lift the down-trod Mortimer
As high in the air as this unthankful King,                    135
As this ingrate and cankered Bolingbroke.

NORTHUMBERLAND [*to Worcester*]

Brother, the King hath made your nephew mad.

WORCESTER

Who struck this heat up after I was gone?

HOTSPUR

He will forsooth have all my prisoners;
And when I urged the ransom once again                         140
Of my wife's brother, then his cheek looked pale
And on my face he turned an eye of death,
Trembling even at the name of 'Mortimer'.

WORCESTER

I cannot blame him: was not he proclaimed

---

133 **shed . . . dust** The alliterative 'd's, with the lines' monosyllables and stresses (dèar blòod dròp), produce the sound of what is described.

134 **down-trod** F has 'downfall', which Oxf prints, believing that 'the acceptable but unusual past participle form' results from 'authorial annotation' (*TxC*, 333). Even if the reading does come from some annotated copy of Q5, there is no certainty that Shakespeare was the annotator. It could easily be a scribal alteration, and it is not obvious that the reading is any way an improvement; indeed it might be seen as misleading, since *down-trod* properly suggests, as GWW observes, that Mortimer has been pushed down rather than merely careless or unfortunate, as 'down-fall' would imply (cf. *Mac* 4.3.4: 'downfall birthdom').

136 **ingrate** ungrateful
    **cankered** diseased, rotten

**Bolingbroke** Hotspur contemptuously refuses to refer to Henry as King, using instead the surname, Bolingbroke, taken from the name of the castle in Lincolnshire in which he was born; Q's spelling here, 'Bullingbrooke', gives the approximate pronunciation.

139 **forsooth** in truth (though here the tone is derisive, and the implication is 'now will he?')

142 **eye of death** look of mortal fear; Johnson glossed this as 'an eye menacing death'; the context, however, makes it clear that the King's unmanly fear, rather than any threat he poses, is what Hotspur notes.

144–5 **proclaimed . . . blood** repeats the historical error of 84: Roger Mortimer, Earl of March, was proclaimed heir apparent in 1385; he was killed in Ireland in 1398 and the claim passed to his son Edmund, who was then recognized as heir apparent by Richard II.

---

133 in the] i'th *Q5–F*   134 down-trod] downfall *F*   135 in the] in'th *Q5;* i'th *F*   137 SD] *Rowe*
143 'Mortimer'] *this edn;* Mortimer *QF*   144 not he] he not *F*

172

By Richard, that dead is, the next of blood?                145
NORTHUMBERLAND

He was; I heard the proclamation.

And then it was when the unhappy King

(Whose wrongs in us God pardon!) did set forth

Upon his Irish expedition,

From whence he, intercepted, did return                     150

To be deposed and shortly murdered.

WORCESTER

And for whose death we in the world's wide mouth

Live scandalized and foully spoken of.

HOTSPUR

But soft, I pray you; did King Richard then

Proclaim my brother, Edmund Mortimer,                       155

Heir to the crown?

NORTHUMBERLAND    He did; myself did hear it.

---

(This is, at least, the account Holinshed and other Elizabethan chroniclers report; modern historians are increasingly sceptical about whether or not either Mortimer was ever formally named heir.)

147 **unhappy** unlucky

148 **wrongs in us** injuries we inflicted on him; *in us* = caused by us (*OED* in 24), though easily heard as 'done to us'. The Percys had supported Bolingbroke against Richard II. Northumberland's remorse for these acts is seemingly merely rhetorical rather than something deeply felt; Wilson (Cam¹) says 'the old fox gives a sanctimonious smirk'.

149 **Irish expedition** Richard II had undertaken an expedition to Ireland in May 1399 hoping to put an end to the raids of the 'wild Irish' who 'dailie wasted and destroied the townes and villages within the English pale' (Holinshed, 3.496); cf. *R2*, where Richard's 'Irish wars' (2.1.155) take him from England just as Bolingbroke returns from exile.

150 **intercepted** interrupted (in the midst of his campaign against the Irish)

151 **deposed . . . murdered** Richard was formally replaced on the throne on 30 September 1399 and died in the following January. Whether he abdicated or was deposed became a matter of contention, as indeed did the issue of whether Henry was responsible for his death.

**shortly** soon after

**murdered** murderèd

152 **world's wide mouth** general repute

155 **my brother** i.e. brother-in-law; Mortimer was in fact the nephew of Hotspur's wife and in this play calls her *aunt* at 3.1.192.

155 brother, Edmund] brother *Q2–F*

HOTSPUR

    Nay, then I cannot blame his cousin King
    That wished him on the barren mountains starve.
    But shall it be that you that set the crown
    Upon the head of this forgetful man          160
    And for his sake wear the detested blot
    Of murderous subornation – shall it be
    That you a world of curses undergo,
    Being the agents or base second means,
    The cords, the ladder, or the hangman rather?     165
    O, pardon me that I descend so low
    To show the line and the predicament
    Wherein you range under this subtle King!
    Shall it for shame be spoken in these days,
    Or fill up chronicles in time to come,         170
    That men of your nobility and power
    Did gage them both in an unjust behalf
    (As both of you, God pardon it, have done)
    To put down Richard, that sweet lovely rose,
    And plant this thorn, this canker, Bolingbroke?    175
    And shall it in more shame be further spoken
    That you are fooled, discarded and shook off
    By him for whom these shames ye underwent?
    No! Yet time serves wherein you may redeem

---

158 **on . . . starve** refers back to the King's remark at 89

161 **detested blot** disgraceful blemish

162 **murderous subornation** instigation to murder

164 **base second means** mere instruments or agents

165 **hangman** Cf. 1.2.63–5, where the Prince says that in his reign Falstaff shall be *a rare hangman*.

167 **line . . . predicament** degree and category (but also *line* = rope; *predica-ment* = dangerous situation)

168 **Wherein you range** in which you are ranked (or, into which you stray)

170 **chronicles** historical accounts

172 **gage them both** pledge themselves **behalf** cause

175 **canker** dog-rose, a wild, hedge rose rather than the cultivated garden rose (cf. *MA* 1.3.25–6: 'I had rather be a canker in a hedge than a rose in his grace'), though with sense of *canker* = ulcer

158 starve] staru'd *F*   161 wear] wore *F*   166 me] if *Q5–F*

Your banished honours and restore yourselves          180
Into the good thoughts of the world again,
Revenge the jeering and disdained contempt
Of this proud King, who studies day and night
To answer all the debt he owes to you
Even with the bloody payment of your deaths.          185
Therefore, I say –
WORCESTER            Peace, cousin, say no more.
And now I will unclasp a secret book,
And to your quick-conceiving discontents
I'll read you matter deep and dangerous,
As full of peril and adventurous spirit              190
As to o'erwalk a current roaring loud
On the unsteadfast footing of a spear.
HOTSPUR
If he fall in, good night. Or sink or swim,
Send danger from the east unto the west,
So honour cross it from the north to south –        195

182 **disdained** disdainful (an adjective formed on the same principle as 'bearded' or 'aged', that is, by adding '-ed', meaning 'characterized by', to a noun, rather than a passive participle)
184 **answer** repay
185 **deaths** pronounced similarly enough to *debt* to suggest a play with that word in the previous line; cf. 5.1.126–8, where Falstaff puns unmistakably; proverbially (cf. Dent, G237) one's death repays a debt owed to God, though here Bolingbroke would *answer* his debts with the deaths of others.
186 **say –** In many productions, Worcester restrains Hotspur's arm, which is reaching for his sword, and, as at Stratford-upon-Avon in 2000, then anxiously looks around as if to ensure they are alone.
188 **your . . . discontents** dissatisfac-

tions that lead you quickly to see the point
191–2 **to . . . spear** to use an unsteady spear as a bridge to cross a fast-rushing river; the weapon-bridge was a convention of medieval romance, as in Chrétien de Troyes's *Erec and Enid* (l.308): 'The bridge across the cold stream consisted of a polished gleaming sword.'
193 **If . . . night** i.e. If he falls in, it is over; he dies.
**Or . . . swim** whether he sinks or swims, i.e. either way; a proverbial expression of indifference to the outcome (Dent, S485)
194–5 i.e. even if the situation is dangerous it is all right, as long as it provides the opportunity to win honour
195 **So** as long as
**cross** encounter, meet; oppose

184 to you] you *Q5;* vnto you *F*    189 you] your *Q5*

And let them grapple. O, the blood more stirs
To rouse a lion than to start a hare!

NORTHUMBERLAND [*to Worcester*]

Imagination of some great exploit
Drives him beyond the bounds of patience.

HOTSPUR

By heaven, methinks it were an easy leap                    200
To pluck bright honour from the pale-faced moon,
Or dive into the bottom of the deep,
Where fathom-line could never touch the ground,
And pluck up drowned honour by the locks,
So he that doth redeem her thence might wear,               205
Without corrival, all her dignities.
But out upon this half-faced fellowship!

---

197 Cf. *TC* 3.2.88 and *Cor* 1.1.171, where
  the strength of lions and the weakness
  of hares are similarly juxtaposed.
199 **patience** self-control
200 SP *Neither Q0 nor Q1 indicates a
  change of speaker here; Q5 first supplies the speech prefix for Hotspur,
  and all editors have followed in repair-
  ing what must be merely an omission.
200–6 **By . . . dignities** Hotspur's extravagant commitment to honour is paro-
  died in the induction of Beaumont and
  Fletcher's *Knight of the Burning Pestle*;
  the Grocer's apprentice Rafe displays
  his acting ability by 'speaking a huffing
  part' closely based on Hotspur's
  speech: 'By heaven, methinkes it were
  an easie leap / To plucke bright honour
  from the pale faced Moone, / Or dive
  to the bottome of the sea, / Where
  never fathame-line touch't any ground,
  / And plucke up drowned honor from
  the lake of hell' (Induction, 74–8;
  Bowers, 1.13). This speech also marks
  the beginning of the Q0 fragment,
  which serves as the control text for this
  edition from this point until the end of

2.2 (see Appendix 5).
203 **fathom-line** weighted line for mea-
  suring the depth of water (a fathom =
  six feet)
204 **drowned** drownèd
205 **redeem** rescue
206 **corrival** partner, sharer; cf. the similar use at 4.4.30.
207 **out upon** away with
  **this . . . fellowship** this unsatisfying
  partnership; Hotspur's meaning is
  clear enough, even if the image is
  opaque: he doesn't want to share
  honour with anyone; any such shared
  honour would be *half-faced*, i.e.
  incomplete, thin, skimpy, as at *2H4*
  3.2.262–3: 'this same half-faced fellow
  Shadow'. The image, as Capell first
  suggested, seemingly comes from the
  profile face on a coin, possibly the double profiles of Mary and Philip on the
  shilling minted in 1554. Hotspur's *this*
  generalizes the observation (i.e. this
  kind of) but perhaps also glances
  specifically at the Percys' former
  alliance with the King.

196 O, the] the *Q5–F*   198 SD] *Folg²*   200 SP] *Q5–F*

176

WORCESTER [*to Northumberland*]

    He apprehends a world of figures here

    But not the form of what he should attend.

    [*to Hotspur*] Good cousin, give me audience for a while.    210

HOTSPUR

    I cry you mercy.

WORCESTER          Those same noble Scots

    That are your prisoners –

HOTSPUR              I'll keep them all.

    By God, he shall not have a scot of them;

    No, if a scot would save his soul he shall not.

    I'll keep them, by this hand.

WORCESTER          You start away                215

    And lend no ear unto my purposes.

    Those prisoners you shall keep.

HOTSPUR           Nay, I will; that's flat.

---

208 **apprehends** conceives; cf. *MND* 5.1.19–20: 'if it would but apprehend some joy, / It comprehends some bringer of that joy'.

    **figures** images; also, figures of speech

209 **form** actual substance

    **attend** think about

210 **a while**. F prints 'a-while, / And list to me.' Here *TxC* argues that the Folio reading cannot be 'convincingly explained except as an authorial revision', and Oxf therefore follows F. If it could be proved that Shakespeare was the reviser, the change from Q0 would be harder to resist; but the half-line is an unnecessary repetition of thought of the previous phrase, and it disrupts the two sets of half-lines that follow. It does not seem impossible that the phrase originated in the printing house, perhaps from misunderstanding the relation of the half-lines here, confused by

Q's printing of Worcester's lines at 211–12 as a single line; but, even if it appeared in a manuscript which was collated with Q5 before the printing of F, it could be a phrase introduced by an actor, or even one added and then marked for deletion, as easily as being an authoritative line somehow missed out in Q1.

211–12 **Those . . . prisoners** Worcester's calculated plans get interrupted by Hotspur's wild enthusiasm.

213 **scot** small quantity or payment (as at 214), here also playing on the obvious meaning, 'Scotsman'

217 **shall** must (more strongly affirmative here than usual in modern English)

    **will** asserts Hotspur's own wish and intention in response to Worcester's *shall*

---

208 SD] *Oxf*    210 SD] *Oxf*    a while] a-while, / And list to me F    211–12 Those . . . prisoners] *F; one line Q*    213 God] heauen *F*    scot] *(Scot), Cam²*    214 scot] *(Scot), Davison*

He said he would not ransom Mortimer,
Forbade my tongue to speak of Mortimer;
But I will find him when he lies asleep,                                          220
And in his ear I'll holler 'Mortimer!'
Nay, I'll have a starling shall be taught to speak
Nothing but 'Mortimer' and give it him
To keep his anger still in motion.

WORCESTER   Hear you, cousin, a word.                                            225

HOTSPUR

All studies here I solemnly defy,
Save how to gall and pinch this Bolingbroke
And that same sword-and-buckler Prince of Wales
(But that I think his father loves him not
And would be glad he met with some mischance,                                    230

---

218–21 Cf. Marlowe, *Edward II*, 2.2.125–7: 'Cousin, an if he will not ransom him, / I'll thunder such a peal into his ears, / As never subject did unto his king' (Marlowe, 3.31, first cited by Malone).

222 **starling** small, mottled black bird, common in England (not introduced into the US until the nineteenth century, when they were imported with other varieties to allow the US to have all the birds mentioned by Shakespeare), which can be trained to imitate human speech

224 **still** continually

226 **studies** interests, pursuits
    **defy** renounce

227 **gall and pinch** i.e. irritate, torment (*gall* = rub sore)

228 **sword-and-buckler Prince** an insult suggesting that the Prince is a mere poser, unworthy to be taken seriously as a soldier: with the introduction of the rapier and dagger in the 1580s, the sword and buckler (i.e. small

shield with a short, sharp pike extending from the centre) went out of fashion for the arms carried by gentlemen. In 1602, William Basse wrote *Sword and Buckler, or, Serving-man's Defence*, which refers to 'our ancient Sword and Buckler vaine' (sig. B4ʳ). A character in Davenant's *News from Plymouth* (1673) looks back to a time 'when Sword and Buckler was in reputation' (3.1.23; Davenant, 4.141). Stow in the *Annals* (1631) reports the 'common fighting' at Smithfield, 'during the time that sword and Buckler were in use' and 'when every Servingman, from the base to the best, carried a buckler at his back, which hung by the hilt of his sword' (sig. 4L1ᵛ). The use of sword and buckler came to be identified with lower-class ruffians, and the phrase came to carry the sense of swaggering (like the similar 'swash-buckling'), as in Fletcher's *Bonduca*: 'the boy speaks sword and buckler' (4.2.59; Bowers, 4.212).

---

221 holler] *Oxf¹*; hollow *Q0–2*; hollo *Q3–4*; hallow *Q5*; holla *F*  'Mortimer!'] *Ard²*; Mortimer: *QF*
223 'Mortimer'] *Ard²*; Mortimer *QF*

I would have him poisoned with a pot of ale).
WORCESTER
    Farewell, kinsman. I'll talk to you
    When you are better tempered to attend.
NORTHUMBERLAND [*to Hotspur*]
    Why, what a wasp-stung and impatient fool
    Art thou to break into this woman's mood,                    235
    Tying thine ear to no tongue but thine own!
HOTSPUR
    Why, look you, I am whipped and scourged with rods,
    Nettled and stung with pismires, when I hear
    Of this vile politician Bolingbroke.
    In Richard's time – what do you call the place?              240
    A plague upon it. It is in Gloucestershire.
    'Twas where the madcap duke his uncle kept,
    His uncle York, where I first bowed my knee
    Unto this king of smiles, this Bolingbroke.
    'Sblood, when you and he came back from
        Ravenspur.                                               245

---

231 **pot of ale** On stage, Hotspur often
    contemptuously emphasizes *ale*, as the
    mark of Hal's plebeian tastes and
    behaviour.
233 **better ... attend** in a better mood to
    listen
234 **wasp-stung** irritable; F reads 'Waspe-
    tongu'd', but Hotspur's response at
    237–8 confirms the Q reading.
238 **Nettled** irritated (nettle = coarse
    plant, *Urtica*, with stinging hairs)
    **with pismires** by ants
239 **politician** used here contemptuous-
    ly, meaning something like 'schemer'
    or 'intriguer'
240–2 **what ... kept** Hotspur, in his irri-
    tation, cannot focus on small details.
242 **madcap duke** Edward Langley,
    Duke of York and fifth son of Edward

III, who served as regent while
Richard II was conducting his military
campaign in Ireland in 1398–9; there's
nothing *madcap* about York in
Shakespeare's treatment of the Duke
in *R2*, but Holinshed describes him as
'a man rather coueting to liue in pleasure, than to deale with much busi-
nesse, and weightie affaires of the
realme' (3.485).
    **kept** lived
243–4 **where ... smiles** Cf. *R2* 2.3.41–4,
where Hotspur tenders Bolingbroke
his 'service'.
245 ***Ravenspur** the modern Spurn Head,
a spot on the thin promontory that hooks
into the mouth of the Humber, the old
name 'Ravenserespourne', from '*spurn*,
"a spur, a projecting piece of land", in

231 him poisoned] poyson'd him *F*    234 SD] *Oxf¹*    wasp-stung] waspe-tongue *Q2–5;* Waspe-
tongu'd *F*    237 whipped] whip *Q0*    240 do you] de'ye *F*    245 'Sblood] *(Zbloud); om. F*

179

NORTHUMBERLAND    At Berkeley castle?
HOTSPUR    You say true.
    Why, what a candy deal of courtesy
    This fawning greyhound then did proffer me!
    'Look when his infant fortune came to age',                    250
    And 'gentle Harry Percy', and 'kind cousin'.
    O, the devil take such cozeners!

the early spelling with the place-name *Ravenser*', was recorded in 1399 (Mills, 'Spurn Head'); Holinshed says that Bolingbroke, returning from France, landed in Yorkshire, 'at a place sometime [i.e. formerly] called Ravenspur, betwixt Hull and Bridlington' (3.498). Holinshed's 'sometime' suggests that the name Spurn Head had already by the late sixteenth century supplanted the older name. In 1617, Moryson writes: 'Spurnehead . . . is a place made famous by the landing of Henry the fourth' (Moryson, 4.159). Usually Ravenspur has been identified as a seaport on the Humber, which some time in the fourteenth century was submerged by the action of the sea (e.g. Oxf[1]). This identification, however, seemingly results from a confusion of Ravenspur and what was indeed a port town, later submerged, Ravenser or Ravenser Odd. Holinshed notes that Edward IV later landed 'at a place called Ravenspurgh, euen in the same place where Henrie erle of Derbie, after called king Henrie the fourth landed', and that 'for the first night [the King] was lodged in a poore village, two miles from the place where he first set foot on land' (Holinshed, 3.679). If Ravenspur were itself the port town, Edward would have had no need to go further to lodge after landing; and Shakespeare at 4.3.77 refers to 'the naked shore at

Ravenspur', indicating that he too does not imagine Ravenspur as a seaport. See Monsarrat.

246 **Berkeley Castle** Northumberland supplies the name of the castle in Gloucestershire that York visited en route to Wales (cf. *R2* 2.2.118); Q's spelling, 'Barkly', indicates the pronunciation.

247 **You say true** i.e. that's right (said as if it did not much matter in any case)

248 **Why . . . courtesy** 'look how much saccharine flattery'; for the involuted word order, cf. Puttenham, *Art of English Poesy*, where he talks about the 'misplacing and preposterous placing of words' and gives as an example 'A corrall lippe of hew' for 'a lippe of corrall hew' (sig. 2F1[r]).

249 **fawning greyhound** Shakespeare often yokes dogs and flattery; see Spurgeon, 195–9; but here Hotspur has, perhaps characteristically, muddled the image, since it derives from the habit of pet dogs begging sweetmeats, but in this usage the dog is proffering the treat.

250 **'Look . . . age'** what Bolingbroke is alleged to have promised to his supporters upon his return to England; see *R2* 2.3.66: 'till my infant fortune comes to years'.

**Look when** as soon as, whenever

252 **cozeners** swindlers (with obvious quibble on *cousin*, 251)

248 candy] caudie *F*    250 'Look . . . age'] *Ard²*; Looke . . . age *QF*    251 'gentle . . . Percy'] *Ard²*; gentle . . . Percy *QF*    'kind cousin'] *Ard²*; kind coosen *QF*    252–4] *this edn*; *QF line* me, / done. / againe, /

    – God forgive me. Good uncle, tell your tale;
    I have done.

WORCESTER     Nay, if you have not, to it again;
    We will stay your leisure.

HOTSPUR               I have done, i'faith.     255

WORCESTER

    Then once more to your Scottish prisoners.
    Deliver them up without their ransom straight,
    And make the Douglas' son your only mean
    For powers in Scotland, which, for divers reasons
    Which I shall send you written, be assured     260
    Will easily be granted. [*to Northumberland*] You,
       my lord,
    Your son in Scotland being thus employed,
    Shall secretly into the bosom creep
    Of that same noble prelate well beloved,
    The Archbishop.

HOTSPUR          Of York, is it not?

WORCESTER              True, who bears hard    265
    His brother's death at Bristol, the Lord Scrope.
    I speak not this in estimation
    As what I think might be, but what I know
    Is ruminated, plotted and set down,
    And only stays but to behold the face     270

---

255 **stay** wait for
258 **the Douglas' son** i.e. Murdoch (who was not in fact Douglas's son; see 1.1.71–3n.); *the* before a family name signifies that the person is the head of the clan.
258–9 **mean / For powers** agents for raising forces
259 **divers** various
263 **into . . . creep** win the confidence
265 **Of . . . not?** Hotspur eagerly fills in information that is not needed; or, per-

haps, he isn't quite sure which archbishop, being so deeply absorbed in his own concerns.
**bears hard** is deeply affected by
266 **His . . . Scrope** William Scrope, Earl of Wiltshire, executed at Bristol by Bolingbroke in 1399 (*R2* 3.2.141–2), was in fact the Archbishop's cousin; the error is Holinshed's (3.522).
267 **in estimation** as guesswork
270–1 **stays . . . occasion** awaits the opportunity

---

254 I] for I *F*    to it] too't *F*    255 We will] Wee'l *F*    i'faith] insooth *F*    261 granted . . . lord,] *Theobald subst.;* granted you my Lord. *Q0–1, Q4;* granted you, my Lord. *Q2–3, Q5–F*    265 is it] is't *F*

Of that occasion that shall bring it on.

HOTSPUR

I smell it. Upon my life, it will do well.

NORTHUMBERLAND

Before the game is afoot thou still let'st slip.

HOTSPUR

Why, it cannot choose but be a noble plot –

And then the power of Scotland and of York          275

To join with Mortimer, ha?

WORCESTER                          And so they shall.

HOTSPUR

In faith, it is exceedingly well aimed.

WORCESTER

And 'tis no little reason bids us speed

To save our heads by raising of a head;

For, bear ourselves as even as we can,          280

The King will always think him in our debt,

And think we think ourselves unsatisfied,

Till he hath found a time to pay us home.

---

271 **shall** must

272 **smell it** catch the scent (as a hunting dog), i.e. see what you mean

**well** F prints 'wond'rous well', but here the Folio addition seems almost certainly to be compositorial, an effort, as *TxC* argues, 'to facilitate and disguise space-wasting' at the bottom of the page mainly due to the line break now required by the additional word (*TxC*, 333).

273 You always unleash your hounds before the quarry is in sight. Q5 and F print 'game's a-foot', a colloquial contraction for Q's 'game is afoote', which may very well reflect how an actor would speak the line but is unnecessary as an emendation.

275 **power** army

277 **aimed** devised

278–9 **reason . . . head** The first syllable of *reason* was pronounced 'ray', so Worcester's 'raising' is one of the two word-plays in the lines, the other being the punning on *heads* to mean both 'lives' and 'armies'.

280–3 This voices the deepest fear of the Percys: that, because they have helped Henry to the throne, he will feel that his debt to them is so enormous that it can never be satisfied; see *R2* 5.1.59–65.

280 **even** correctly, balanced

283 **pay us home** repay us in full (with the same double sense as 'get even with'); i.e. Henry will settle the debt by killing them.

---

272 it. Upon] it: / Vpon *F*    well] wond'rous well *F*    273 game is] game's *Q5–F*

And see already how he doth begin
To make us strangers to his looks of love.                    285

HOTSPUR

He does; he does. We'll be revenged on him.

WORCESTER

Cousin, farewell. No further go in this
Than I by letters shall direct your course.
When time is ripe, which will be suddenly,
I'll steal to Glendower and Lord Mortimer,                    290
Where you and Douglas and our powers at once,
As I will fashion it, shall happily meet
To bear our fortunes in our own strong arms,
Which now we hold at much uncertainty.

NORTHUMBERLAND

Farewell, good brother. We shall thrive, I trust.                    295

HOTSPUR [*to Worcester*]

Uncle, adieu. O, let the hours be short
Till fields and blows and groans applaud our sport!    *Exeunt.*

## 2.1          *Enter a* Carrier *with a lantern in his hand.*

289 **suddenly** speedily, soon
290 **steal to** go off to (but the word
    inevitably carries some negative conno-
    tation as he goes off to plan the rebel-
    lion against the King, as well as mark-
    ing the parallel between the rebellion
    and the robbery at Gad's Hill)
    **Lord** Q0 and Q1 both print 'Lo:',
    which Q2 misunderstands as an inter-
    jection and prints as 'loe', a reading
    followed by Q3–5 and F. Rowe first
    prints 'Lord', which all modern edi-
    tions follow.
291 **our . . . once** all our forces together
293 ***bear our fortunes** carry our fate;
    Q0 has 'beare out', a not impossible
    reading, which would mean 'take
    responsibility for', but it is strained,

especially without the 'our' which the
idiom seemingly requires.
296–7 The couplet sounds Hotspur's
    characteristic enthusiasm for military
    action; it is mere *sport* for him; but
    note the irony of what follows: not the
    martial encounter that Hotspur too
    eagerly seeks, but the two carriers with
    their mundane concerns.
2.1 The action is set in an inn yard, some-
    where near Rochester on the road
    between London and Canterbury.
    This scene, along with 4.4, has often
    been cut in performance. Francis
    Gentleman, in his introduction to
    Bell's acting edition of 1773, objected
    to the 'low' humour of the scene,
    which he found 'so indecent that it

288 course.] *Johnson;* course *QF*    290 Lord] *(Lo:), Rowe;* loe *Q2–F*    293 bear our] beare out *Q0*
296 SD] *Oxf*    297 SD] *exit F*

1 CARRIER    Hey-ho! An it be not four by the day, I'll be
    hanged. Charles's Wain is over the new chimney, and
    yet our horse not packed. – What, ostler!

OSTLER [*within*]    Anon, anon!

1 CARRIER    I prithee, Tom, beat Cut's saddle; put a few          5
    flocks in the point. Poor jade is wrung in the withers,
    out of all cess.

*Enter another* Carrier.

2 CARRIER    Peas and beans are as dank here as a dog, and

should be cast aside; nay, and might be
without any injury to the plot'.

0.1 **Carrier** one who carries and delivers
goods; carriers established more or less
regular schedules at inns; John
Taylor's *The Carrier's Cosmography*
(1637) lists the London inns where the
carriers stayed, for the ease of those
who wanted to send packages or letters
into the country; e.g. 'A Carrier from
*Reygate* in *Surrey* doth come evry
Thursday (or oftner) to the Falcon in
Southwark' (sig. C3ᵛ).

1 **by the day** in the morning

2 **Charles's wain** Charlemagne's
wagon, the constellation in the northern sky, *Ursus Major*, known today as
the Big Dipper, the Plough or the
Great Bear; cf. Thomas Browne, *The
Garden of Cyrus*: 'the two starres in
*Charles's* Wain never leave pointing at
the Pole-star' (Browne, 308).

**new chimney** Harrison, in his
*Description of England*, remarks among
the three things that were now
'marvellously altered' from earlier
times 'the multitude of chimneys lately
erected' (Harrison, 201).

3 **ostler** groom or stableman (derived
from hosteller = innkeeper)

4 **Anon** in a second, coming

5 **Tom** possibly the Ostler, as in most
editions, but at least as likely the
Second Carrier, as here. The First
Carrier, who is addressed by name,
*Mugs*, 43, by his companion, would
certainly know the other Carrier's
name but would not necessarily know
the name of the new groom at the inn;
and the care of the saddle, which is
what he talks with *Tom* about, would
usually be its owner's concern.

**beat Cut's saddle** Beating the saddle
would soften the leather and even out
the lumps. *Cut* is the horse's name
here, derived from 'cut', a shortened
form of 'curtal', referring to a horse
with a docked tail.

5–6 **put . . . point** stuff some wool under
the saddle pommel (for padding)

6 **jade** nag
**wrung . . . withers** chafed between
the shoulders

7 **out . . . cess** excessively, extremely
(*cess* = measure, assessment)

8 **dank . . . dog** wet as a dog; alliteration
rather than logic drives the simile (like
'right as rain'), and, as Wilson (Cam¹)
notes, *dog* is used as an intensifier in
phrases like 'dog-tired'. Emending to
something more obviously wet (e.g. a
'bog' or 'frog') is unnecessary.

2.1.1 An it] an't *F*    4 SD] *Theobald*    6 Poor] the poore *F*

that is the next way to give poor jades the bots.
This house is turned upside down since Robin Ostler      10
died.

1 CARRIER     Poor fellow never joyed since the price of oats
rose; it was the death of him.

2 CARRIER     I think this be the most villainous house in all
London road for fleas. I am stung like a tench.      15

1 CARRIER     Like a tench? By the mass, there is ne'er a king
christen could be better bit than I have been since the
first cock.

2 CARRIER     Why, they will allow us ne'er a jordan, and
then we leak in your chimney, and your chamber lye      20
breeds fleas like a loach.

---

9   **next** nearest, quickest
    **bots** parasitical worms (from eating feed on which the worms' eggs have been laid)
10  **house** inn
12  **joyed** was cheerful
12–13 **price . . . rose** This reference to the rise in the price of oats has been used by some to establish a specific date for the writing of the play, usually late in 1596; in fact, prices of oats rose consistently between 1594 and 1598 because of shortages from a series of disastrous harvests caused by excessive rainfall, and therefore the reference is not precise enough to fix a date for composition.
15  **tench** carp-like fish with markings as if it has been repeatedly stung by fleas; in Cumberland's acting edition of the mid-nineteenth century, the stage direction for the Carrier reads: '*Catches fleas, and examines them by the light of his lantern*' (GD, 25).
16  **By the mass** a mild oath; *mass* = the sacrament of the Eucharist. In Earle's *Microcosmographia* (1628), it is described as 'an olde out of date innocente othe', yet it was omitted from Folio text of *1H4*

seemingly in response to the 1606 Act against blasphemy on stage.
16–17 **king christen** Christian king. The Carrier is suggesting that even a king, who presumably has the best of everything, could not have better flea bites than he has.
18  **cock** cock-crowing; though the times of the cock-crow were conventionally set, the first at midnight
19  **jordan** chamberpot
20  **leak . . . chimney** urinate in the fireplace; Andrew Boorde warns, 'Beware of emptying of pysse-pottes, and pyssing in chymnes' (Boorde, 236–7; cited Ard²). *Your* here and in *your chamber lye* is a colloquialism for the indefinite article, marking unsophisticated speech.
    **chamber lye** urine
21  **loach** a small freshwater fish sometimes thought to harbour fleas or other parasites; cf. Pliny, 'some fishes there be, which of themselues are giuen to breed fleas and lice' (Pliny, 9.47); though the reference may simply be to the loach's fecundity (i.e. this place breeds fleas as fast as loaches breed).

---

9 that] this *F*   10 Ostler] the Ostler *F*   14 be] to be *Q5;* is *F*   16 By the mass] *om. F*   17 christen] in Christendome *F*   19 they] you *Q5–F*

1 CARRIER   What, ostler! Come away, and be hanged!
Come away!
2 CARRIER   I have a gammon of bacon and two races of
ginger to be delivered as far as Charing Cross.                    25
1 CARRIER   God's body, the turkeys in my pannier are
quite starved! What, ostler! A plague on thee, hast thou
never an eye in thy head? Canst not hear? An 'twere not
as good deed as drink to break the pate on thee, I am a
very villain. Come, and be hanged! Hast no faith in thee?    30

*Enter* GADSHILL.

GADSHILL   Good morrow, carriers. What's o'clock?
1 CARRIER   I think it be two o'clock.
GADSHILL   I prithee, lend me thy lantern to see my

---

22 **Come away** come away from where
you are; i.e. come here, come along
**and be hanged** a proverbial tag line,
which serves as mild intensifier (Dent,
H130.1)
24 **gammon of bacon** leg of smoked
ham
**races** roots (*OED* race *sb.²* 6)
25 **Charing Cross** then a village west of
London. Cherringe, its original name,
derived from OE 'cierring', i.e. turning, from the bend either in the
Thames at that point or, more likely, in
the main road to the west; the *Cross*,
erected by Edward I in 1290, marked
the last resting place of the coffin of
his Queen Elinor before she was buried
in Westminster.
26 **turkeys** an anachronism; turkeys were
imported to England from Mexico in
the 1520s; Baker in his *Chronicle of the
Kings of England* (1643) says that about
1524 'it happened divers things were
newly brought into England, wherupon
this Rime was made: Turkies, Carps,

Hoppes, Picarrell and Beere / Came
into ENGLAND all in one yeere'
(Baker, sig. 3L1ʳ).
**pannier** large basket, often, as here,
one of two that could be draped over a
horse's back
27 **starved** emaciated; cf. Shallow
described as a 'starved justice' in *2H4*
3.2.299–300; 'starved' can also mean
frozen, perished with cold, and some
editors have suggested this as its meaning; but there is no other evidence in the
scene that the night is particularly cold
(and the date, at least of the historical
action, is some time in September).
28 **An** if
29 **as . . . drink** i.e. a damned good thing;
proverbial (Dent, D183.1)
**break . . . thee** bloody your head
30 **Hast** have you
32 **two o'clock** The scene begins with the
Carrier announcing it is 'four by the
day', 1; possibly his statement here is a
slip, or, more likely, the Carrier, suspicious of Gadshill's interest, lies to him.

---

24 races] *(razes)*, Dyce   26 God's body] *om. F*   29 deed] a deed *Q4–F*   on] of *Q5–F*
31, 32 o'clock] *(a clocke)*, *Theobald*   32 SP] *Hanmer (1 Car.)*; *Car: QF*

gelding in the stable.

1 CARRIER    Nay, by God, soft. I know a trick worth two of          35
that, i'faith.

GADSHILL *[to Second Carrier]*    I pray thee, lend me thine.

2 CARRIER    Ay, when, canst tell? 'Lend me thy lantern,'
quoth he. Marry, I'll see thee hanged first.

GADSHILL    Sirrah carrier, what time do you mean to          40
come to London?

2 CARRIER    Time enough to go to bed with a candle, I
warrant thee. – Come, neighbour Mugs, we'll call up
the gentlemen. They will along with company, for they          44
have great charge.                          *Exeunt [Carriers].*


*Enter* Chamberlain.


GADSHILL    What ho, chamberlain!


35–6 **I . . . that** i.e. I am not such a fool; proverbial (Dent, T518)

38 **Ay . . . tell** i.e. What time is it? Don't *you* know? (The Second Carrier is as wary as his friend and is evasive here, reluctant to give Gadshill any information.)

42 **Time . . . candle** i.e. some time tonight (another evasion)

43 **warrant** assure
**neighbour Mugs** The First Carrier is here named; *neighbour* is a polite honorific.

44–5 **They . . . charge** They wish to travel with us because they have valuable baggage.

45.1 Most editions place the Chamberlain's entrance after Gadshill's call (46), though QF place it before, and indeed in all the quartos it is in front of and on the same line as the Carriers' exit. Often

entrances are placed by the compositor where there is room on the page (see p. 128), but Gadshill's line is short and leaves plenty of space to fit it in. Dessen (71–2) notes that, played as the early texts indicate, 'Gadshill could be looking at the two figures exiting through one stage door while the Chamberlain (seen only by the spectators) appears through the other and sneaks up behind him (thereby giving more punch to the Chamberlain's first line – "at hand, quoth pickpurse").'

46 **chamberlain** a servant at an inn. Chamberlains were often assumed to be complicit with robbers; cf. Harrison, 398: 'Certes, I believe not that a chapman or traveller in England is robbed by the way without the knowledge of some of them.'

35 by God, soft] soft I pray ye *F*    36 i'faith] *om. F*    37 SD] *Folg²* pray thee] prethee *Q3–F*
38 'Lend . . . lantern'] *Folg²*; lend . . . lanterne *QF*    39 quoth he] quoth-a *F*    45 SD *Carriers*] *Rowe*

CHAMBERLAIN    'At hand', quoth Pickpurse.

GADSHILL    That's even as fair as ' "At hand", quoth the
chamberlain,' for thou variest no more from picking of
purses than giving direction doth from labouring: thou        50
layest the plot how.

CHAMBERLAIN    Good morrow, Master Gadshill. It holds
current that I told you yesternight. There's a franklin
in the Weald of Kent hath brought three hundred
marks with him in gold. I heard him tell it to one of his        55
company last night at supper – a kind of auditor, one
that hath abundance of charge too, God knows what.
They are up already, and call for eggs and butter. They
will away presently.

GADSHILL    Sirrah, if they meet not with Saint Nicholas's        60
clerks, I'll give thee this neck.

CHAMBERLAIN    No, I'll none of it; I pray thee keep that
for the hangman, for I know thou worshippest Saint
Nicholas as truly as a man of falsehood may.

GADSHILL    What talkest thou to me of the hangman?        65
If I hang, I'll make a fat pair of gallows; for, if I hang,

---

47 **At hand** I'm ready; proverbial (Dent, H65)

49–51 **thou ... how** you are as little different from a thief as the supervisor is from the labourer; you arrange how the work is done

51 **layest the plot** plan

52–3 **holds current that** is still true what

53 **franklin** small landowner, freeholder

54 **Weald of Kent** wooded plain in the county of Kent
**hath** who has

54–5 **three ... gold** £200 in gold; a mark was not a coin but a conventional unit of value, equal to two-thirds of a pound.

56 **auditor** treasury official, accountant

57 **abundance of charge** a large quantity of baggage

58 **eggs and butter** breakfast; see 1.2.20

59 **presently** immediately

60–1 **Saint Nicholas's clerks** thieves, highwaymen; cf. *Martin's Month's Minde*: 'like the Saint Nicholas Clarkes on Salsburie plaine ... [they] stept out before vs in the high waie, and bidde vs stand' (sig, B1ʳ⁻ᵛ; cited Ard¹).

61 **give ... neck** let you hang me

66 **fat ... gallows** two fat prisoners destined for the gallows; Gadshill must have been played by a fat actor in Shakespeare's company.

---

47 'At hand,'] *this edn;* At hand *QF*    48–9 ' "At hand" ... chamberlain'] *Ard² subst.;* at hand ... Chamberlaine *QF*    54 Weald] *Singer;* wild *Q0;* wilde *Q1–5 F*    62 pray thee] prythee *F*

old Sir John hangs with me, and thou knowest he is no
starveling. Tut, there are other Trojans that thou
dreamest not of, the which for sport sake are content to
do the profession some grace, that would, if matters     70
should be looked into, for their own credit sake make all
whole. I am joined with no foot-landrakers, no long-
staff sixpenny strikers, none of these mad mustachio
purple-hued maltworms, but with nobility and
tranquillity, burgomasters and great oneyers, such as     75
can hold in, such as will strike sooner than speak, and
speak sooner than drink, and drink sooner than pray –

68 **starveling** emaciated person (*OED
   sb.* a)
   **Trojans** convivial fellows (*OED* 2); cf.
   *Kemp's Nine Days' Wonder* (1600): 'a
   kinde good fellow, a true Troyan' (sig.
   C2$^r$; Chettle & Kemp, 19).
69 **the which** who
69, 71 **sake** see 1.2.147n.
70 **profession** i.e. of robbing; for the tendentious use of *profession*, cf. *vocation*
   at 1.2.100.
71–2 **make all whole** fix things up
72 **foot-landrakers** vagabonds; *rake* =
   wander (*OED v.*$^2$ 1)
72–3 **long-staff . . . strikers** thieves
   armed with long staves, stealing small
   sums from travellers
73–4 **mad . . . maltworms** purple-faced
   drunkards with fierce-looking mous-
   taches; cf. *2H4* 2.4.322: 'his face is
   Lucifer's privy-kitchen, where he doth
   nothing but roast malt-worms'.
74–5 **nobility and tranquillity** high-
   born nobles living in ease and tranquillity (*tranquillity* is Gadshill's made-up
   social category)
75 **burgomasters** town councillors,
   aldermen
   **great oneyers** The meaning is uncertain, but probably it is merely, as

Johnson suggested, a cant variation of
'great ones', with the '-yers' serving as
a derivative substantive as in 'law-yers'.
Cf. Selden's *Table-Talk*: 'So you mind
a Lawyer in the Temple that gets little
for the present; but he is fitting himself
to be in time of those Great Ones that
do get' (Selden, 142; cited Ard$^1$). The
phrase, however, has been much discussed and often ingeniously emended:
e.g. 'one-eyers' (Pope, 1728); 'money-
ers' (i.e. officials of the mint,
Theobald), 'owners' (Hanmer), 'myn-
heers' (i.e. gentlemen, Capell), 'onyers'
(i.e. public accountants, Malone),
'oyeas' (Davison), 'younkers' (West),
'oyezers' (i.e. court officials, Jowett,
*TxC*), 'honeyers' (Cam$^2$); however, the
fact that Q1 is content to follow Q0's
'Oneyres' is itself an argument against
emendation here, suggesting the form
was thought to be intelligible.
76 **hold in** hold their ground (or hold
   their tongue)
76–7 **strike . . . pray** a rhetorical device
   called by Puttenham the 'marching figure' or 'clyming figure', which picks
   up on the last term of each phrase to
   move the idea forward, e.g. 'Peace
   makes plentie, plentie makes pride, /

67 knowest] knowes *Q5*   he is] hee's *F*   68 Trojans] *(*Troyans*)*   72 foot-landrakers] *Q4;* footland
rakers *Q0–3;* foot-land rakers *Q5;* Foot-land-Rakers *F*   75 oneyers] *(*Oneyres*), Q2–F⁻*   76 in,] *F;*
in *Q*

and yet, zounds, I lie, for they pray continually to their
saint the commonwealth, or, rather, not pray to her but
prey on her, for they ride up and down on her and make          80
her their boots.

CHAMBERLAIN    What, the commonwealth their boots?
Will she hold out water in foul way?

GADSHILL    She will, she will; justice hath liquored her.
We steal as in a castle, cocksure. We have the receipt of        85
fern-seed; we walk invisible.

CHAMBERLAIN    Nay, by my faith, I think you are more
beholden to the night than to fern-seed for your
walking invisible.

GADSHILL    Give me thy hand; thou shalt have a share in         90

Pride breeds quarrel, and quarrell brings warre' (Puttenham, sig. A[a]1ʳ).

79 **commonwealth** i.e. nation. The literal sense of the term, i.e. 'wealth held communally', was often discussed; social reformers pointed to it as the ideal of social organization, others denied that any such radical redistribution of wealth was desirable for the 'commonweal', i.e. the community's well-being.

80 **prey** on the shift from *pray*, 79, to *prey* is the rhetorical figure Puttenham calls '*atanaclasis*' or 'the Rebound', which 'playeth with one word written all alyke but carrying divers sences', and for which he gives as an example: 'To pray for you euer I cannot refuse, / To pray vpon you I should much abuse' (Puttenham, sig. A[a]1ʳ). The pun on *pray–prey* is common, and the idea of the commonwealth being exploited by the wealthy was (and remains) a theme of social reform: cf. More, *Utopia*: 'I can perceaue nothing but a certein conspiracy of riche men procuringe theire owne commodities under the

name and title of the commen wealth' (More, 163).

81 **boots** source of plunder; cf. *2H6* 4.1.13: 'make boot of this'; the Chamberlain puns on the more familiar meaning of 'boots' in the next line.

83 **hold . . . way** let you stay dry on a muddy road

84 **liquored** greased (to make waterproof; cf. *MW* 4.5.92: 'liquor fishermen's boots'), but also literally, made drunk

85 **as . . . castle** in complete safety (Dent, C122.1)
   **cocksure** with complete confidence

85–6 **receipt of fern-seed** formula using fern-seed, which, according to folk belief, if gathered on 23 June (St John's Eve), could be used to make a potion allowing the user to be invisible, probably a projection of the fact Gerard notes in his *Herbal* (1597): 'The Ferne is one of those plants which have their seede on the back of the leaf, so small as to escape the sighte'; cf. Jonson, *New Inn*, 1.6.16–18: 'I had / No med'cine, sir, to goe inuisible: / No Ferne-seed in my pocket' (Jonson, 6.418).

78 zounds] *om. F* to] vnto *F*    79 pray] to pray *F*    80 prey] (pray), *Q5*    87 by my faith] *om. F*
think] thinke rather, *F*    88 beholden] *Pope;* beholding *QF*    fern-seed] the Fernseed *F*    90–1] *F*
*lines* hand. / purpose, / man /

our purchase, as I am a true man.

CHAMBERLAIN    Nay, rather let me have it as you are a
false thief.

GADSHILL    Go to. *Homo* is a common name to all men.
Bid the ostler bring my gelding out of the stable.    95
Farewell, you muddy knave.    [*Exeunt.*]

**2.2**    *Enter* PRINCE, POINS, PETO [*and* BARDOLL].

POINS    Come, shelter, shelter! I have removed Falstaff's
horse, and he frets like a gummed velvet.

PRINCE    Stand close! [*Poins, Peto and Bardoll hide.*]

*Enter* FALSTAFF.

FALSTAFF    Poins! Poins, and be hanged! Poins!

PRINCE    Peace, ye fat-kidneyed rascal! What a brawling    5
dost thou keep!

---

91 **purchase** plunder, booty

94 *Homo . . .* **men** well-known phrase
from Lily and Colet's *Short Introduction
of Grammar*, where it is used to illus-
trate the definition of the 'Noun
Substantive' (Lyly & Colet, 7); Nashe
quotes the phrase in a marginal note in
*Piers Penniless* (Nashe, 1.187–8):
*'Newgate, a common name for al prisons,
as 'Homo' is a common name for a man or
a woman'.* Here Gadshill's point as he
replies to the Chamberlain is that he is
*a true man* (i.e. truly a man, if not an
honest one), as he claimed in 91, since
*homo* (Latin, man) applies to all men,
even a *false thief*, 93.

96 **muddy** muddled, dull-witted

2.2 The action takes place as the characters move along the road near Gad's
Hill, the place set for the robbery

(1.2.119).

0.1 *\*and* BARDOLL Bardoll is not named
in the entry directions of QF, but Q's
'*&c.*' obviously admits other characters, and he and Peto are with Falstaff
for the robbery; Falstaff calls to him
and Peto at 20.

1 **shelter** hide yourself

2 **he** i.e. Falstaff
**frets . . . velvet** fusses (*frets*) like
cheap velvet stiffened with resin
(which easily *frets* or frays); proverbial
(Dent, T8)

3 **Stand close** hide (*close* = concealed)

5 **fat-kidneyed rascal** large-bellied
scoundrel (but *rascal* also refers to a
young or underweight deer, the first of
a number of references to Falstaff as a
deer; see Berry, 133–8)

6 **keep** make

---

91 purchase] purpose *F*    95 my] the *F*    96 you] ye *Q2–F*    SD] *F*    **2.2**.0.1 PETO *and* BARDOLL]
*Oxf¹ subst.; and Peto, &c. Q; and Peto F*    3 SD] *Dyce subst.*

---

FALSTAFF   Where's Poins, Hal?

PRINCE   He is walked up to the top of the hill. I'll go seek
him. [*Hides with the others.*]

FALSTAFF   I am accursed to rob in that thief's company.      10
The rascal hath removed my horse and tied him I know
not where. If I travel but four foot by the square further
afoot, I shall break my wind. Well, I doubt not but to
die a fair death for all this, if I scape hanging for killing
that rogue. I have forsworn his company hourly any      15
time this two-and-twenty years, and yet I am bewitched
with the rogue's company. If the rascal have not given
me medicines to make me love him, I'll be hanged. It
could not be else: I have drunk medicines. Poins! Hal!
A plague upon you both! Bardoll! Peto! I'll starve ere      20
I'll rob a foot further. An 'twere not as good a deed as
drink to turn true man and to leave these rogues, I am
the veriest varlet that ever chewed with a tooth. Eight
yards of uneven ground is threescore and ten miles

10–19 I . . . medicines Falstaff's protests
here must literally be directed at Poins,
since he says he has 'forsworn his company hourly any time this two-and-
twenty years', 15–16, and the Prince is
still a teenager (historically Hal would
be about sixteen at the time of the
action); nonetheless, the language
seems more to describe the relationship with Hal, and audiences tend to
hear it this way.
11 The . . . horse The hiding of a fat
man's horse was an obvious enough
practical joke; cf. Nashe's *Piers Penniless*
(1592): 'The *Roman* Censors, if they
lighted vpon fat corpulent man, they
straight tooke away his horsse, and constrained him to goe a foot: . . . If we had
such horse-takers amongst vs, . . . surfit-

swolne Churles, who now ride on their
foot-cloathes might be constrained to
carrie their flesh . . . on foote . . . and the
price of veluet and cloath would fall
with their belies' (Nashe, 1.201).
12 by the square exactly (*square* = mea-
suring tool)
13 break my wind get out of breath (but
also plays on the meaning 'fart')
I doubt . . . but I expect
14 fair honourable
for[1] in spite of
16 yet still
17 with by
19 medicines potions
20 starve die (*OED v.* 4a)
21–2 as . . . drink See 2.1.29n.
22 turn true man reform
23 veriest varlet worst scoundrel

7 Where's] What *Q2–F*   9 SD] *Dyce subst.*   10 thief's] Theefe *F*   12 square] *(*squire*), Q8
(*squaire*)   16 two-and-twenty] *(*xxii.*), Q5 (*22.*), F* years] yeare *Q2–F*   21 I'll] I *F*   21–2 as
drink] as to drinke *F*

afoot with me, and the stony-hearted villains know it          25
well enough. A plague upon it when thieves cannot be
true one to another! (*They whistle.*) Whew! [*Prince,
Poins, Bardoll and Peto come forward.*] A plague upon
you all! Give me my horse, you rogues; give me my
horse and be hanged!          30

PRINCE    Peace, ye fat-guts. Lie down, lay thine ear close to
the ground and list if thou canst hear the tread of
travellers.

FALSTAFF    Have you any levers to lift me up again being
down? 'Sblood, I'll not bear my own flesh so far afoot          35
again for all the coin in thy father's exchequer. What a
plague mean ye to colt me thus?

PRINCE    Thou liest: thou art not colted; thou art uncolted.

FALSTAFF    I prithee, good Prince Hal, help me to my
horse, good king's son.          40

PRINCE    Out, ye rogue; shall I be your ostler?

FALSTAFF    Hang thyself in thine own heir-apparent
garters! If I be ta'en, I'll peach for this. An I have not
ballads made on you all and sung to filthy tunes, let a

---

26–7 **when . . . another** Falstaff invokes
   the traditional notion of honour
   among thieves (Dent, T121A).
27 **Whew!** probably an expression of
   alarm (in response to the whistle,
   which startles him); in some productions, however, it represents Falstaff's
   feeble effort to return the whistle.
32 **list** listen
36 **exchequer** treasury
37 **colt** cheat
38 **uncolted** unhorsed
39 **good Prince Hal** Q has 'good prince,
   Hal', perhaps suggesting that these are
   two separate vocatives (a thought that
   gains some support from the perhaps
   surprising fact that *Prince Hal* does not

appear anywhere else in the play), but
the parallel with *good king's son* in the
next line suggests that this is the correct reading.
42–3 **Hang . . . garters** i.e. go hang yourself in your own garters, a proverbial
   saying (Dent, G42); but Falstaff's joke
   also involves knowing that Hal, the *heir
   apparent*, belonged to the Order of the
   Garter, the highest order of English
   knighthood.
43 **peach** turn informer (*OED v.* 2)
   **An** if
44 **ballads . . . all** ballads written about
   you. Ballads were written on various
   topical subjects, printed on single
   sheets (broadsides) and peddled in the

---

26 upon it] vpon't *F*    27–8 SD] *Dyce subst. after 31 SP and opp. 49*    32 canst] can *Q2–F*
35 'Sblood] *(zbloud); om. F*    my] mine *Q1–F*    41 ye] you *Q2–F*    42 Hang] Go hang *Q3–F*
43 An] *(And), T. Johnson*

cup of sack be my poison. When a jest is so forward,      45
and afoot too! I hate it.

*Enter* GADSHILL.

GADSHILL   Stand!

FALSTAFF   So I do, against my will.

POINS   O, 'tis our setter; I know his voice, Bardoll. – What
news?                                                                           50

GADSHILL   Case ye, case ye; on with your vizards!
There's money of the King's coming down the hill; 'tis
going to the King's exchequer.

FALSTAFF   You lie, ye rogue; 'tis going to the King's
tavern.                                                                        55

GADSHILL   There's enough to make us all –

FALSTAFF   To be hanged.

PRINCE   Sirs, you four shall front them in the narrow lane;
Ned Poins and I will walk lower. If they scape from
your encounter, then they light on us.                          60

PETO   How many be there of them?

GADSHILL   Some eight or ten.

FALSTAFF   Zounds, will they not rob us?

PRINCE   What, a coward, Sir John Paunch?

streets; they could be commissioned to lampoon an enemy, as in Jonson, *Bartholomew Fair*: 'and thou wrong'st mee . . . I'll finde a friend shall right me, and make a ballad of thee' (2.2.15–16, Jonson, 6.41).

**filthy** low, mean, vile

45 **forward** presumptuous, bold; well along

46 **afoot** underway (but also joking reference to his own horseless condition)

49 **setter** one who arranges or 'sets up' a robbery (*OED sb.*[1] 7a); Dekker defines

'Setter' as 'the party that fetcheth in the Gull' (*The Bellman of London*, Grosart, 3.130–1).

I . . . **voice** Presumably Gadshill enters masked.

51 SP *QF give the speech to Bardoll, but the request for information must be directed at the newly entered Gadshill, who is the 'setter' for the robbery.

51 **Case ye** put on your masks

56 **make us all** make our fortunes

58 **front** confront

59 **lower** further down

45 When a] when *Q2–5*   51 SP] *Johnson; Bar. QF*   54 ye] you *Q3–F*   58 Sirs, you] You *Q3–F*
59 Poins] *om. F*   61 How] but how *Q3–8, F*   be there] be they *Q2–6; be F*   63 Zounds] *om. F*

FALSTAFF   Indeed I am not John of Gaunt, your        65
    grandfather, but yet no coward, Hal.

PRINCE   Well, we leave that to the proof.

POINS   Sirrah Jack, thy horse stands behind the hedge.
    When thou needest him, there thou shalt find him.
    Farewell, and stand fast.                            70

FALSTAFF   Now cannot I strike him, if I should be hanged.

PRINCE *[aside to Poins]*   Ned, where are our disguises?

POINS *[aside to the Prince]*   Here, hard by. Stand close.

                          *[Exeunt Prince and Poins.]*

FALSTAFF   Now, my masters, happy man be his dole, say I.
    Every man to his business.                           75

*Enter the* Travellers.

1 TRAVELLER   Come, neighbour, the boy shall lead our
    horses down the hill. We'll walk afoot awhile and ease
    our legs.

---

65–6 Falstaff responds to Hal's gibe in the previous line by accepting the charge that he is fat *(Sir John Paunch* rather than *John of Gaunt)* but denying he is a coward. *Gaunt* is a form of Ghent, a city in Flanders where he was born, but Falstaff puns on its adjectival sense, 'extremely thin and haggard', as Gaunt himself does in *R2*: 'Old Gaunt indeed, and gaunt in being old' (2.1.74). Here, as GWW notes, is an example of the symbolic contrast between fatness and leanness, between those who feed on the state to make themselves fat and those who become lean through their sacrifices for the state.

67 **to the proof** to be tested

73 SD2 *No exit is indicated in QF, and it is possible Poins and Hal merely hide somewhere onstage. At 89, QF do have the two of them *Enter*, so this edition, following Malone and most others, indicates this as an exit. Nonetheless, the audience is asked to imagine them as nearby, since Hal reports that he has seen the ensuing action (2.4.246–7).

74 **happy . . . dole** may luck be with us; proverbial (Dent, M158), literally meaning 'may one's fate be that of a happy man'
    **dole** that which is dealt out or allotted

75 **Every . . . business** i.e. get ready to go about your business; like the proverbial 'Every man as his business lies' (Dent, M104)

77–8 **ease our legs** Oxf emends this to 'ease their legs', a plausible reading but based on the assumption that only the horses' legs would be tired. Travellers, however, might well be delighted at the opportunity to stretch their own legs

---

65 your] our *Q5u*   67 Well, we] Well, weele *Q3–5;* Wee'l *F*   72 SD] *Collier*   73 SD1] *Dyce² subst.*
SD2] *Malone subst.*   74 say I] say *Q5*   75.1 *the*] om. *F*   76 SP] *Capell subst.; Trauel. QF*

195

THIEVES    Stand!

2 TRAVELLER    Jesus bless us!                                              80

FALSTAFF    Strike! Down with them! Cut the villains'
throats! Ah, whoreson caterpillars, bacon-fed knaves!
They hate us youth. Down with them! Fleece them!

1 TRAVELLER    O, we are undone, both we and ours for
ever!                                                                      85

FALSTAFF    Hang ye, gorbellied knaves, are ye undone?
No, ye fat chuffs; I would your store were here. On,
bacons, on! What, ye knaves? Young men must live. You
are grand-jurors, are ye? We'll jure ye, faith. *Here they*
*rob them and bind them.*                                       *Exeunt.*

*Enter the* PRINCE *and* POINS.

PRINCE    The thieves have bound the true men; now could       90
thou and I rob the thieves, and go merrily to London,
it would be argument for a week, laughter for a month,

after riding for some time. The line
itself is a way of making dramatically
plausible their entrance on foot rather
than, as would be logical but theatri-
cally undesirable, on horseback.
82 **whoreson caterpillars** vile parasites
**bacon-fed knaves** over-fed scoundrels
84 **undone** ruined
86 **gorbellied** potbellied; cf. Cotgrave,
*bast*: 'Swagbellied, gorbellied, full
paunched'. The irony of Falstaff abus-
ing the travellers for being fat inevitably
draws a laugh in performance.
87 **chuffs** rich misers; cf. Florio: '*Averone*:
a chuff, a niggard, a great couetous
man'.
**store** possessions
88 **bacons** fat men
89 **grand-jurors** men of substance; only

wealthy property-owners were eligible
to serve on grand juries.
**jure ye** a reflexive, sarcastic response;
i.e. I'll show you who are jurors.
89 SD2 *Exeunt* The travellers presumably have had only their hands bound
and so are able to be led off by the
thieves. The stage is here then possibly
cleared, and the reappearance of the
Prince and Poins has plausibly been
understood by some editors (e.g. Oxf[1])
to mark a new scene. The action, however, is continuous, and the two clearly
know what has gone on (see note at 73
SD2); therefore this edition does not
introduce a new scene here, accepting
the traditional arrangement first established in F.
92 **argument** topic of conversation

79 Stand] Stay *Q5–F*    80 SP] *Dyce² subst.; Trauel. QF*    Jesus] Iesu *F*    82 Ah, whoreson] *Rowe;* a
horeson *QF*    84 SP] *Capell subst.; Tra. QF*    86 are ye] are you *F*    89 ye, faith] yee yfaith *Q3–F*
SD2 *Exeunt.*] *om. Q4–F*

and a good jest for ever.

POINS   Stand close. I hear them coming. [*They conceal themselves.*]

*Enter the* Thieves *again.*

FALSTAFF   Come, my masters, let us share, and then to        95
horse before day. An the Prince and Poins be not two
arrant cowards, there's no equity stirring. There's no
more valour in that Poins than in a wild duck. *As they
are sharing, the Prince and Poins set upon them.*

PRINCE   Your money!

POINS   Villains!                                                       100

*They all run away, and Falstaff, after a blow or two,
runs away too, leaving the booty behind them.*

PRINCE

Got with much ease. Now merrily to horse.
The thieves are all scattered and possessed with fear
So strongly that they dare not meet each other.
Each takes his fellow for an officer.
Away, good Ned. Falstaff sweats to death                       105
And lards the lean earth as he walks along.

---

95–6 **to horse** i.e. we'll ride off
97 **arrant** thoroughgoing, utter
   **no equity stirring** no truth in the world
101–7 *printed as prose in QF, but, following Pope, most editors have, as here, relined, allowing Hal to return to verse at the end of the scene (as, for example, in 1.2). Q0's lineation, followed by Q1, may well be a function of the need to crowd the text on to what is a very full page (sig. C4ᵛ; see p. 126).
102 i.e. each is now so nervous that he

thinks his fellow thieves are officers of the law; proverbial: 'The thief does fear each bush an officer' (Dent, T112).
105 **sweats to death** The image, while obviously appropriate for the corpulent Falstaff, may have additional relevance for the character when still thought of as Oldcastle, as the historical Oldcastle was martyred by burning (see Fig. 6).
106 **lards** drips fat, bastes; cf. Dekker, *The Wonderful Year*: 'out of the house he wallowed presently, being followed

---

94 SD] *Dyce subst.* 94.1 *the] om. F* 98 more] moe *F* SD] *as Dyce; opp.* 99 *Q; after 100 F*
100.1–2] *as Dyce; opp.* 99–100 *Q; They all run away, leauing the booty behind them. F* 101–7] *as Pope;
prose QF* 102 are all] are *Q2–F* scattered] scattred *F* 105 sweats] sweares *Q3–5*

Were't not for laughing, I should pity him.

POINS    How the fat rogue roared!                                    *Exeunt.*

**2.3**           *Enter* HOTSPUR *alone, reading a letter.*

HOTSPUR    *But for mine own part, my lord, I could be well
contented to be there, in respect of the love I bear your house.*
He could be contented; why is he not then? In the
respect of the love he bears our house! He shows in this
he loves his own barn better than he loves our house.         5
Let me see some more. *The purpose you undertake is
dangerous* – Why, that's certain: 'tis dangerous to take a
cold, to sleep, to drink; but I tell you, my lord fool, out
of this nettle, danger, we pluck this flower, safety. *The
purpose you undertake is dangerous, the friends you have*    10
*named uncertain, the time itself unsorted, and your whole*

with two or three dozens of napkins to
drie vp the larde, that ran so fast
downe his heeles' (Grosart, 1.140).

108  **fat rogue roared** Only Q0 has *fat*, its
presence arguing for it being the first
of the 1598 quartos (see p. 108). The
Q0 fragment, however, ends with this
line.

**2.3** This scene, with no precedent in the
historical sources, is set at Hotspur's
estate (historically Warkworth Castle
in Northumberland, which was first
identified as the scene's location by
Capell, though it is nowhere mentioned in the play). The text, from this
point on, is based on Q1; see p. 108.

0.1  *letter* It is nowhere indicated from
whom the letter comes, though its subject is obvious enough from Hotspur's
reading. In the posthumously published *Chronicle of John Hardyng*
(1543), Hardyng writes in the headnote
that he had seen various letters sent to
Percy 'in the castell of Werkeworth,

when I was constable of it vnder my
lord, Sir Robert Vmfreuile' (Hardyng,
sig. C1ᵛ), though Shakespeare is
unlikely to have consulted Hardyng's
*Chronicle* or known about the letters.

2    *there* i.e. where the rebels are assem-
bling (historically this would have been
somewhere near Shrewsbury)
*in respect of* for the sake of
*house* family

5    **barn** Hotspur plays here by taking
*house*, 2, in its literal sense.

7    **take** catch

8–9  **out . . . safety** i.e. as a flower can be
picked if one is willing to face the
stinging nettles (or to grasp it firmly
enough to prevent their sting), so can
safety be found by facing danger
bravely; cf. the proverbial 'Danger and
delight grow both upon the same stalk'
(Tilley, D28) or 'Danger is the best
remedy for danger' (Dent, D30).

11  *uncertain* unreliable
*unsorted* unsuitable

108  fat] *om. Q1–F*    2.3.0.1 *alone*] *solus Q*    1 SP] *Capell; om. QF*    3–4 the respect] respect *F*

*plot too light for the counterpoise of so great an opposition.*
Say you so; say you so? I say unto you again you are a
shallow, cowardly hind, and you lie. What a lack-brain
is this! By the Lord, our plot is a good plot as ever was          15
laid, our friends true and constant; a good plot, good
friends, and full of expectation; an excellent plot, very
good friends. What a frosty-spirited rogue is this! Why,
my lord of York commends the plot and the general
course of the action. Zounds, an I were now by this              20
rascal, I could brain him with his lady's fan. Is there not
my father, my uncle and myself, Lord Edmund
Mortimer, my lord of York and Owen Glendower? Is
there not, besides, the Douglas? Have I not all their
letters to meet me in arms by the ninth of the next              25
month, and are they not some of them set forward
already? What a pagan rascal is this! An infidel! Ha, you
shall see now, in very sincerity of fear and cold heart
will he to the King and lay open all our proceedings! O,
I could divide myself and go to buffets for moving such          30
a dish of skim-milk with so honourable an action! Hang
him! Let him tell the King. We are prepared; I will set
forward tonight.

12 *plot too light* conspiracy too weak
    *for . . . of* to counterbalance, to com-
    pete with
14 **hind** coward (literally a female deer,
    hence timid)
    **lack-brain** idiot
17 **expectation** promise
19, 23 **my . . . York** i.e. Archbishop of
    York, Richard Scrope, who appears in
    4.4
20 **an** if
    **by** close to

24 **the Douglas** i.e. Archibald, Earl of
    Douglas; for *the*, see 1.3.258n.
27 **pagan** unbelieving (the same idea that
    generates *An infidel* later in the line)
28 **in . . . of** truly motivated by
30 **I . . . buffets** i.e. I am furious with
    myself (*go to buffets* = come to blows)
    **moving** tempting
31 **dish of skim-milk** i.e. insubstantial,
    unworthy person (*skim-milk* = milk
    with the cream skimmed off; the
    *OED*'s earliest citation)

15 By the Lord] I protest *F*    a good] as good a *F*    16 friends] friende *Q4–F*    20 Zounds] By this
hand *F*    an] *(*and*)*, Capell; if *F*    27 this! An] *F (*this? An*)*; this, an *Q1*; this, and *Q2–5*    29 proceedings!] *(*proceedings?*)*; proceedings. *Q2–F*    31 skim-milk] skim'd Milk *F*    32 King. We] *Pope;*
king, we *Q;* King we *F*    33 forward] forwards *F*

*Enter his* LADY.

How now, Kate? I must leave you within these two
hours.                                                        35

LADY PERCY

O my good lord, why are you thus alone?
For what offence have I this fortnight been
A banished woman from my Harry's bed?
Tell me, sweet lord, what is't that takes from thee
Thy stomach, pleasure and thy golden sleep?                  40
Why dost thou bend thine eyes upon the earth
And start so often when thou sitt'st alone?
Why hast thou lost the fresh blood in thy cheeks
And given my treasures and my rights of thee
To thick-eyed musing and curst melancholy?                   45
In thy faint slumbers I by thee have watched
And heard thee murmur tales of iron wars,
Speak terms of manage to thy bounding steed,

34 **Kate** The actual name of Hotspur's
wife was Elizabeth (Holinshed calls
her Elianor), the older sister of the
Mortimer who married Glendower's
daughter; see List of Roles, 9n., and
1.3.80 (see also Maguire).
39 **sweet lord** In many productions, Kate
and Hotspur embrace here; in any
case, her genuine concern is obvious
(cf. the similar scene between Portia
and Brutus in *JC* 2.1.233–308, where
Portia urges Brutus to share with her
his 'cause of grief', 2.1.255).
**thee** Kate shifts to the intimate pronoun here and through the rest of the
speech after her *you*, 36 (answering his
*you*, 35). Elizabethan usage does not
divide the two forms of the second-
person pronoun neatly into formal and

familiar functions, but the shifts
between them can be emotionally
expressive; cf. Abbott, 231.
40 **stomach** appetite
**golden** precious; cf. *R3* 4.1.83: 'the
golden dew of sleep'
44 **my treasures . . . rights** the intimacy
that is both my joy and right
45 **thick-eyed musing** heavy-eyed (from
lack of sleep) meditation; some editors
gloss *thick-eyed* as 'dull of sight', but
this seems not to characterize Lady
Percy's concern.
**curst** bad-tempered (*OED* cursed 4)
46 **faint slumbers** restless sleep
**watched** stayed awake
47 **iron** cruel
48 **Speak . . . manage** give commands

46 thy] my *Q4–F*   thee have] thee *Q4–5*   47 thee] *(the), Q2–F;* the murmur *Q1*

Cry 'Courage! To the field!' And thou hast talked
Of sallies and retires, of trenches, tents,                    50
Of palisadoes, frontiers, parapets,
Of basilisks, of cannon, culverin,
Of prisoners' ransom, and of soldiers slain,
And all the currents of a heady fight.
Thy spirit within thee hath been so at war,                    55
And thus hath so bestirred thee in thy sleep,
That beads of sweat have stood upon thy brow
Like bubbles in a late-disturbed stream,
And in thy face strange motions have appeared
Such as we see when men restrain their breath                    60

49–54 **And . . . fight**. Military terms had become an increasingly fashionable rhetoric. An epigram by John Davies describes a soldier recently returned from 'Friesland', similarly enchanted with the exotic vocabularies of warfare: 'He talkes of counterscarfes, and casomates, / Of parapets, curteynes and pallizadois, / Of flankers, ravelings, gabions he prates, / And of false brayes, and sallies and scaladoes' (Davies, 139).
50 **sallies and retires** advances and retreats
51 **palisadoes** barriers of fixed stakes used to defend a military position
   **frontiers** ramparts, outer fortifications
   **parapets** earthwork defensive walls
52 **basilisks, cannon, culverin** three sizes of cannon from largest to smallest: *basilisk*, taking its name from a mythical beast whose breath (or look) was fatal, was, according to Harrison (236), the largest of the guns, weighing about 9,000 lb and able to fire a 60 lb ball; *cannon*, often the generic name for such artillery pieces but specifically a

gun weighing about 7,000 lb; *culverin*, from the French *couleuvre*, adder, a smaller-bore but extremely long-barrelled gun, with the greatest range of any of these pieces (about 2,500 paces, and the use of which during the Armada battle in 1588 helped determine the English victory).
53 **prisoners' ransom** as in Q; Capell, and others, plausibly suggest 'prisoners ransomed', making the phrase grammatically parallel to *soldiers slain*, though, as it is at least as likely that Hotspur is thinking about the ransom as about the prisoners, there is no reason to emend Q.
54 **currents** movements, flow (though possibly a contraction of 'occurrents', as *Ham* 5.2.357: 'th'occurrents more and less / Which have solicited')
   **heady** violent
58 **late-disturbed** late-disturbèd: recently stirred up
59 **motions** expressions, grimaces (though 'emotions' is certainly suggested)
60 **restrain** hold, control

49 'Courage . . . field!'] *Ard²;* courage . . . field. *QF*   50 of trenches, tents] *(of trenches tents), Q2;* trenches, tents *Q4–F*   54 currents] current *Q4–F*   57 beads] beds *Q2–F*   have] hath *Q4–F*

On some great sudden hest. O, what portents are these?
Some heavy business hath my lord in hand,
And I must know it, else he loves me not.

HOTSPUR

What ho!

[*Enter* Servant.]

Is Gilliams with the packet gone?

SERVANT    He is, my lord, an hour ago.                              65

HOTSPUR

Hath Butler brought those horses from the sheriff?

SERVANT    One horse, my lord, he brought even now.

HOTSPUR

What horse? Roan? A crop-ear, is it not?

SERVANT

It is, my lord.

HOTSPUR              That Roan shall be my throne.

Well, I will back him straight. O, Esperance!                        70

Bid Butler lead him forth into the park.        [*Exit Servant.*]

LADY PERCY

But hear you, my lord.

---

61 **hest** undertaking, *OED* 3; (rather than
'command' or 'behest', as often in
Shakespeare, e.g. *Tem* 1.2.274)
62 **heavy** serious
64 **packet** packet of letters, dispatch
67 **even** just
68 **Roan** apparently the horse's name here
(cf. *Cut*, as the horse's name in 2.1.5),
obviously derived from the colour of its
coat, the dark, prevailing colour (usually red when unspecified) muted by the
presence of grey or white hairs. It is
possible that Q3's 'a roane' is correct,
as it adds a tenth syllable; but the line is
in any case metrically rough, and if the

intended structure were to modify the
kind of horse rather than the particular
one, 'a crop-eared roan' would be more
the natural phrasing.
**crop-ear** with the upper part of the
ears cut
70–85 ***Well . . . true*** QF print this as
prose; see t.n. It seems correct, however, that after the servant's interruption Hotspur and Kate would return to
verse. See p. 75.
70 **back** mount
**Esperance!** the Percy family motto:
*Esperance ma Comforte* ('In hope is my
strength')

---

61 hest] haste *Q2–3;* hast *Q4–F* 64.1] *Capell; after 63 Dering* 65 ago] agone *F* 68 Roan] A roan
*Q3–F* 69–71 That . . . park] *as Pope; prose QF* 70 O] *om. Q5–F* 71 SD] *Dering, Hanmer*

HOTSPUR                    What sayst thou, my lady?

LADY PERCY

What is it carries you away?

HOTSPUR                    Why, my horse,

My love, my horse.

LADY PERCY          Out, you mad-headed ape!

A weasel hath not such a deal of spleen                    75

As you are tossed with. In faith,

I'll know your business, Harry, that I will.

I fear my brother Mortimer doth stir

About his title and hath sent for you

To line his enterprise; but if you go –                    80

HOTSPUR

So far afoot? I shall be weary, love.

LADY PERCY

Come, come, you paraquito, answer me

Directly unto this question that I ask.

---

73 **carries you away** makes you so wild; transports you beyond reason; Kate uses the marked *you* here in opposition to Hotspur's *thou*, 72, and doesn't return to *thou* until 84. The contrast between the two second-person forms marks the shifts in emotional distance between them in this exchange, here her *you* expressing her frustration.

**Why, my horse** Hotspur deflects her question by interpreting her phrase literally, his characteristic mode of joking (cf. 79–80).

75 **weasel** Weasels were proverbially quarrelsome (Dent, W211.1); cf. *Cym* 3.4.159: 'as quarrellous as the weasel'.

**spleen** irritability, from the organ which was thought to be the source of a person's bad temper and impulsiveness; cf. 5.2.19, where Hotspur is said

to be 'governed by a spleen'.

76 **tossed with** troubled by

78 **my brother Mortimer** See List of Roles, 10n.

78–9 **stir . . . title** is taking action to claim his rightful crown

80 **line** support, strengthen; cf. *Mac* 1.3.112–13: 'line the rebel / With hidden help'.

**enterprise** project, undertaking

81 **So . . . weary** Cf. the *uncolted* Falstaff in 2.2.11–38.

82 **paraquito** little parrot (affectionate in tone, but the charge is that he is not conversing but responding reflexively). Also see 2.4.96–7, where Hal, immediately before turning to his mimicry of Hotspur, says of Francis that he has 'fewer words than a parrot'.

83 **Directly** to the point

73–4 Why . . . horse] *as Malone; one line QF*   74–80 Out . . . go] *as Capell; prose QF*   76 faith] sooth *F*   82–5] *as Pope; prose QF*   83 ask] shall aske *Q2–F*

In faith, I'll break thy little finger, Harry,
An if thou wilt not tell me all things true.                    85

HOTSPUR

Away, away, you trifler! Love? I love thee not;
I care not for thee, Kate. This is no world
To play with mammets and to tilt with lips.
We must have bloody noses and cracked crowns,
And pass them current, too – God s' me, my horse! –      90
What sayst thou, Kate? What wouldst thou have with me?

LADY PERCY

Do you not love me? Do you not indeed?
Well, do not, then, for since you love me not
I will not love myself. Do you not love me?
Nay, tell me if you speak in jest or no.                        95

HOTSPUR

Come, wilt thou see me ride?
And when I am a-horseback, I will swear
I love thee infinitely. But hark you, Kate.
I must not have you henceforth question me
Whither I go, nor reason whereabout.                          100
Whither I must, I must, and, to conclude,
This evening must I leave you, gentle Kate.

---

84 **break** pull or pinch (some business is
demanded; Kate often catches
Hotspur by the finger as he is putting
on his boots or coat, putting him at her
mercy; her use of *thy little finger* marks
the tone as playful and intimate)

88 **mammets** dolls, puppets; though
possibly playing on the Latin *mamma*,
meaning 'breasts', which, given the
following phrase, is a more consistent
thought.
**tilt with lips** exchange kisses (*tilt* =

joust)

89 **cracked crowns** battered heads (but,
in addition, the injury to Henry's royalty that the rebels intend); see also
following note.

90 **pass them current** pass them on to
others (though playing on the monetary sense of *crowns* that will *pass . . .
current*; i.e. circulate)
**God s' me** a familiar oath, i.e. God
save me

100 **reason whereabout** enquire why

84 In faith] Indeede *F*   85 An] *(and), Theobald; om. F*   me all things] me *F*   92 you . . . you] ye .
. . ye *F*   95 you speak] thou speak'st *F*   100, 101 Whither] Whether *F*   102 you] thee *F*

I know you wise but yet no farther wise
Than Harry Percy's wife. Constant you are
But yet a woman; and for secrecy                    105
No lady closer, for I well believe
Thou wilt not utter what thou dost not know.
And so far will I trust thee, gentle Kate.

LADY PERCY    How! So far?

HOTSPUR

Not an inch further. But hark you, Kate,            110
Whither I go, thither shall you go too.
Today will I set forth, tomorrow you.
Will this content you, Kate?

LADY PERCY                    It must, of force.    *Exeunt.*


2.4                    *Enter* PRINCE.

PRINCE    Ned, prithee come out of that fat room and lend
    me thy hand to laugh a little.


103–7 Cf. *JC* 2.1.290–301, where Portia
makes the same claim to share her
'husband's secrets', 301, by turning
the language that Hotspur uses here to
her own advantage; e.g. 'I grant I am a
woman: but withal / A woman that
Lord Brutus took to wife', 291–2.
106 **closer** more close-mouthed
107 **Thou . . . know** similar to the
proverbial expression, 'A woman conceals what she knows not' (Dent,
W649)
111 **Whither . . . too** The language
comes from Ruth's unwillingness to
leave Naomi in Ruth, 1.16: 'Whither
thou goest, I will go also.'
113 **of force** of necessity
2.4 The action takes place in a tavern. In

1.2.123–4, 182, the Prince and Poins
make an appointment to meet in
Eastcheap the night following the robbery. Often editions specify the tavern
as the Boar's Head, a tavern in
Eastcheap in the sixteenth century; it is,
however, nowhere named by Shakespeare; nonetheless Gayton in 1654
differentiated Oldcastle and Falstaff:
'Sir John of famous memory; not he of
the Boares-head in Eastcheap' (Gayton,
277). In *Famous Victories*, 1.74, the
drinking scenes take place in the 'old
tavern in Eastcheap'.
1    **fat** full of stale air, stuffy (*OED a.* 7c),
    though perhaps *fat* = vat (*OED*, fat,
    *sb.*[1] 2)
1–2 **lend . . . hand** help me

103 farther] further *F*    106 well] wil *Q4*; will *Q5–F*    108 far will] farewill *Q5*; farre wilt *F*
2.4.0.1] *Dyce; Enter Prince and Poines QF*

[*Enter* POINS.]

POINS    Where hast been, Hal?

PRINCE    With three or four loggerheads, amongst three or
fourscore hogsheads. I have sounded the very bass      5
string of humility. Sirrah, I am sworn brother to a leash
of drawers and can call them all by their Christian
names, as Tom, Dick and Francis. They take it already,
upon their salvation, that, though I be but Prince of
Wales, yet I am the king of courtesy, and tell me flatly I      10
am no proud jack, like Falstaff, but a Corinthian, a lad
of mettle, a good boy – by the Lord, so they call me –
and when I am King of England I shall command all the
good lads in Eastcheap. They call drinking deep 'dyeing

4    **loggerheads** blockheads (refers to the
drawers who have taken the Prince
down to the cellar, an experience
reserved for favoured customers); the
Prince's contempt for his new *sworn*
brothers, 6, is apparent as he jokes
with Poins at their expense.
5    **fourscore** eighty (*score* = twenty)
     **hogsheads** wine casks
5–6 **sounded . . . humility** I have
behaved with as much humility as is
possible
6    **sworn brother** intimate friend
     **leash** set of three (usually used of ani-
mals tied together, *OED sb.* 2)
7    **drawers** tapsters, bartenders
7–8 **call . . . names** i.e. he has become
quite familiar with the drawers, as
Dekker advises in his *Gull's Horn-
Book*: 'grow most inwardly acquainted
with the drawers, to learne their
names, as *Jack*, and *Will*, and *Tom*'
(Grosart, 2.260; cited Ard²).
8    **Tom . . . Francis** perhaps an inten-
tional variation on the now conventional phrase for men taken at random,

'any Tom, Dick, and Harry', though
*OED* has no citation for the particular
form of this phrase before 1815;
*Francis* for the expected 'Harry'
would, however, have some point, as
Hal replaces his own given name with
the name of the helpless drawer whom
he teases.
11    **proud jack** pompous knave
     **Corinthian** good fellow (like *Trojans*,
2.1.68); here derived from the putatively riotous behaviour of inhabitants
of Corinth (a characterization derived
mainly from Paul's First Letter to the
Corinthians, upbraiding them for for-
nication and drunkenness)
11–12 **lad of mettle** worthy lad (Dent,
M908.1)
14–15 **'dyeing scarlet'** presumably because *drinking deep* reddens the face
and leaves the eyes bloodshot; the
phrase is apparently proverbial (cf.
Dent, D659.1); Wilson (Cam¹) suggests that the meaning has to do with
the fact that urine, especially from
heavy drinkers, was used to fix scarlet

2.1] *Dyce*    4 three] 3. *F*    5 bass] *(*base*)*    7 them all] them *F*    7–8 Christian names] *Q5;* christen
names *Q1–4;* names *F*    9 salvation] confidence *F*    10 and tell] telling *F*    11 no] not *Q4–5*    jack]
*(*lacke*)*    14–15 'dyeing scarlet'] *Ard²;* dying scarlet *QF*

scarlet', and, when you breathe in your watering, they     15
cry 'Hem!' and bid you 'Play it off!' To conclude, I am
so good a proficient in one quarter of an hour that I can
drink with any tinker in his own language during my
life. I tell thee, Ned, thou hast lost much honour that
thou wert not with me in this action. But, sweet Ned –     20
to sweeten which name of Ned I give thee this
pennyworth of sugar, clapped even now into my hand
by an underskinker, one that never spake other English
in his life than 'Eight shillings and sixpence', and 'You
are welcome', with this shrill addition, 'Anon, anon, sir!     25
Score a pint of bastard in the Half-moon!' or so. But,
Ned, to drive away the time till Falstaff come,
I prithee, do thou stand in some by-room, while

dye (cf. Davison's suggestion about *watering* in the following note).

15 **breathe . . . watering** pause while drinking. Davison, however, argues that *watering* 'is surely urinating', holding that the word is not used to apply to drinking; but cf. Dekker, *The Wonderful Year*: 'mine Hosts house [i.e. tavern] being the auncient watring place where he did vse to cast Anchor' (Grosart, 1.142); and Dryden, *The Wild Gallant*: 'I see thou long'st to be at thy mornings watering' (1.1.108; Dryden, 8.11).

16 **Hem** throat-clearing sound, meaning 'get to it' or 'drink up'; cf. *2H4*: 'our watchword was "Hem, boys!"' (3.2.217–18).
**Play it off** finish it up

18 **drink . . . language** i.e. can be an amiable drinking mate with people of any social class; tinkers were menders of pots, with a reputation for drinking heavily; cf. Thomas Overbury, *Characters* (1615), who says you always

find the tinker 'where the best ale is' (Overbury, G8ᵛ). The Prince's ability to speak the various idiolects of the nation will be one of his strengths as a ruler in *H5*.

20 **action** encounter (jokingly)

22 **pennyworth of sugar** small quantity of sugar sold in taverns for those who wished to sweeten sack; cf. 3.3.158.

23 **underskinker** waiter, or busboy in US idiom (skink = serve or pour wine)

25 **Anon, anon, sir** I'm coming, sir (the call of a waiter in response to an impatient customer)

26 **Score** add to the bill, tally
**bastard** sweet wine from Spain, the name coming either because it was 'oftentimes adulterated and falsified with honey' or because it had 'neither manifest sweetnesse nor manifest astriction' (*Country*, 642, 645)
**Half-moon** a room in the tavern, as is *Pomegranate*, 36

28 **by-room** side room (first use in *OED*)

15 they] then they *F*   16 'Hem!'] *Ard²;* hem, *QF*   'Play it off!'] *Ard²;* play it off. *QF*   24 'Eight . . . sixpence'] *Ard²;* eight . . . sixe pence *QF*   24–5 'You are welcome'] *Ard²;* you are welcome *QF*
25–6 'Anon . . . Half-moon!'] *Ard²;* anon . . . halfe moone, *QF*   27 the time] time *Q4–F*

I question my puny drawer to what end he gave me the
sugar, and do thou never leave calling 'Francis!', that          30
his tale to me may be nothing but 'Anon'. Step aside,
and I'll show thee a precedent.                          [*Exit Poins.*]

POINS [*within*]  Francis!
PRINCE  Thou art perfect.
POINS [*within*]  Francis!                                         35

*Enter* Drawer [FRANCIS].

FRANCIS  Anon, anon, sir! – Look down into the Pomegranate,
    Ralph!
PRINCE  Come hither, Francis.
FRANCIS  My lord?
PRINCE  How long hast thou to serve, Francis?                     40
FRANCIS  Forsooth, five years, and as much as to –
POINS [*within*]  Francis!
FRANCIS  Anon, anon, sir!
PRINCE  Five year! By'r Lady, a long lease for the clinking
    of pewter. But, Francis, darest thou be so valiant as to      45
    play the coward with thy indenture, and show it a fair
    pair of heels, and run from it?

---

29 **puny** inexperienced (*OED a.* 1); cf.
   Middleton: 'like a punie-Barber, (new
   come to the trade)' (*Blurt*, sig. G3ʳ).
30 **leave** stop
31 **nothing but 'Anon'** Cf. Heywood,
   *The Fair Maid of the West* (1602?), Part
   1, 3.3.98, where an ambitious drawer
   says: 'The first line of my part was
   "Anon, anon, sir"' (Heywood, *Fair
   Maid*, 1.54).
32 **precedent** an example worth remembering
36 **Pomegranate** a room in the tavern

40 **to serve** still left in your apprentice-
   ship (the usual term was seven years)
41 **as . . . to –** the first of several times
   that Francis is interrupted before he
   can finish his thought; cf. 49.
44 **By'r Lady** mild oath, by Our Lady
   **lease** contract
44–5 **long . . . pewter** long apprentice-
   ship to learn to be a tapster
46 **indenture** formal articles of appren-
   ticeship
46–7 **show . . . heels** leave it behind;
   proverbial (Dent, P31)

30 do thou] doe *Q4–F*  'Francis!'] *Ard²*; Frances *QF*    31 'Anon'] *Ard²*; anon *QF*    32 precedent] *F*
(President), *Pope*; present *Q*   SD] *Theobald subst.*    33, 35 SD] *Dyce*   35 SP] *Q4–F*; *Prin. Q1–3*
35.1 FRANCIS] *Rowe subst.*   36 Pomegranate] (Pomgarnet)   42 SD] *Capell*   44 year] yeeres *Q3–F*

FRANCIS   O Lord, sir, I'll be sworn upon all the books in
   England, I could find in my heart –

POINS [*within*]   Francis!                                      50

FRANCIS   Anon, sir!

PRINCE   How old art thou, Francis?

FRANCIS   Let me see; about Michaelmas next I shall be –

POINS [*within*]   Francis!

FRANCIS   Anon, sir! [*to the Prince*]   Pray, stay a little,      55
   my lord.

PRINCE   Nay, but hark you, Francis. For the sugar thou
   gavest me, 'twas a pennyworth, was't not?

FRANCIS   O Lord, I would it had been two!

PRINCE   I will give thee for it a thousand pound. Ask me      60
   when thou wilt, and thou shalt have it.

POINS [*within*]   Francis!

FRANCIS   Anon, anon.

PRINCE   'Anon', Francis? No, Francis. But tomorrow,
   Francis; or, Francis, o'Thursday; or, indeed, Francis,      65
   when thou wilt. But Francis –

FRANCIS   My lord?

PRINCE   Wilt thou rob this leathern-jerkin, crystal-

---

48, 71 **O Lord, sir** a phrase no less of an
empty cliché than anon, anon; cf. *AW*
2.2.40–55, where the Clown demonstrates that 'O Lord, sir' can serve as
an answer to all questions.

48 **be . . . books** swear upon all the bibles
(i.e. not just the single bible upon
which one placed one's hand to inten-
sify the promise to tell the truth)

49 **I . . . heart** Francis seems, as Dover
Wilson suggested (Cam[1]), to take Hal's
interest in his willingness to break his
indenture as a sign that he might be
offered a position in the Prince's

household, a hope repeatedly interrupted by Poins's calls.

53 **Michaelmas** 29 September (the
Feast of St Michael)

55 **stay a little** wait a moment. This edition assumes Francis says this to the
Prince, hoping that Hal will complete
the offer Francis imagines is forthcom-
ing, although it is possible Francis is
merely trying to get Poins to wait a
moment while he deals with an insistent customer.

68 **rob** i.e. run away from, rob your master of your service

---

48 all the] all *Q4–5*   50 SD] *Capell*   51 Anon] Anon, anon *F*   54 SD] *Capell*   55 SD] *this edn*
Pray] pray you *Q2–F*   59 Lord] Lord sir *F*   62 SD] *Capell*   64 'Anon'] *this edn;* Anon *QF*
65 o'Thursday] *(*a Thursday*), Cam;* on thursday *Q3–F*

button, not-pated, agate-ring, puke-stocking, caddis-
garter, smooth-tongue, Spanish-pouch?                    70

FRANCIS    O Lord, sir, who do you mean?

PRINCE    Why, then, your brown bastard is your only
drink! For look you, Francis, your white canvas doublet
will sully. In Barbary, sir, it cannot come to so much.

FRANCIS    What, sir?                                   75

POINS [*within*]    Francis!

PRINCE    Away, you rogue! Dost thou not hear them call?
*Here they both call him. The Drawer stands amazed,*
*not knowing which way to go.*

*Enter* Vintner.

68–70 **this . . . Spanish-pouch** i.e. the
innkeeper; the Prince identifies him in
terms of his conventional dress and
accoutrement, which presumably he
wears when he enters at 77.1.

68 **leathern-jerkin** a close-fitting leather
jacket; cf. Marston's *The Dutch
Courtesan*, where 'thy spanish leather
jerkin' (sig. A3ʳ) is used to identify the
vintner.

68–9 **crystal-button** fashionable button
made of quartz; Ard² quotes Stow,
*Annals* (1631): 'many young Citizens
and others began to weare Christall
buttons upon their doublets, coats and
Ierkins' (Stow, 4M3ʳ).

69 **not-pated** short-haired (*OED* not *a.*
†1)
    **agate-ring** ring set with carved agate
stone
    **puke-stocking** wearing dark, woollen
stockings

69–70 **caddis-garter** gartered with
coarse cloth tape (instead of silk)

70 **Spanish-pouch** pouch made of
Spanish leather

72–4 **Why . . . much** Hal's lines seem
intended mainly as nonsense to befud-

dle the drawer, but whatever sense can
be taken from them appears to be
designed to reconcile Francis to the
life he has in the tavern; it is a secular
version of 1 Corinthians, 7.20: 'Let
every man abide in the same vocation
wherein he was called'; cf. 1.2.100.
Perhaps for Hal the joke has meaning
because he as heir to the throne is also
called to a vocation to which he has
trouble reconciling himself.

72 **brown bastard** sweet Spanish wine
(sweeter than the white bastard; see
26n.)

72–3 **your only drink** i.e. the best of all
drinks

73–4 **your . . . sully** i.e. if you leave, you
will not achieve much

73 **doublet** close-fitting jacket

74 **In . . . much** i.e. even if you go to
Barbary (North Africa), you won't
have any more than you have now; *it* =
sugar (Barbary was the place from
which most sugar was imported); the
Prince is saying that in Barbary one
would never get the £1,000 the Prince
has just offered for the *pennyworth*, 58.

77 SD *amazed* confused, dumbfounded

74 In Barbary] Barbary *Q4u*    76 SD] *Capell*    77 thou not] thou *F*

VINTNER   What, standest thou still and hear'st such a
    calling? Look to the guests within.        [*Exit Francis.*]
    My lord, old Sir John with half a dozen more are at the        80
    door. Shall I let them in?
PRINCE   Let them alone awhile and then open the door.

                                        [*Exit Vintner.*]
    Poins!


                    *Enter* POINS.

POINS   Anon, anon, sir!
PRINCE   Sirrah, Falstaff and the rest of the thieves are at        85
    the door. Shall we be merry?
POINS   As merry as crickets, my lad. But hark ye, what
    cunning match have you made with this jest of the
    drawer? Come, what's the issue?
PRINCE   I am now of all humours that have showed        90
    themselves humours since the old days of Goodman
    Adam to the pupil age of this present twelve o'clock at
    midnight.

---

87 **As . . . crickets** proverbial comparison
(Dent, C825)
88 **cunning match** clever contest
89 **what's the issue** what comes of this,
what's the point; Poins's question
seems appropriate: what is the point of
tormenting Francis? See 72–4 and
note; and p. 47.
90–3 i.e. I am now experienced with all
the temperaments that anyone has had
from the beginning of time; perhaps
this suggests no more than 'now I've
seen it all', but cf. Cooke, *Greene's Tu
Quoque*: 'I will fit myself to all
humours: I will game with a gamester,
drink with a drunkard, be civil with a
citizen, fight with a swaggerer, and

drab with a whore-master' (1.3.136–8).
As an answer to Poins's question,
*what's the issue?* (89), Hal's reply is not
very satisfying, except in that it may
indicate that the Prince understands
that to govern effectively he requires
knowledge of the people he would
rule; cf. *2H4* 4.4.68–9: 'The Prince but
studies his companions / Like a
strange tongue.'
90 **humours** dispositions, moods
91–2 **old . . . Adam** i.e. when Adam was
alive in Eden ('Goodman' was a polite
honorific for one not of noble birth; cf.
'Goodman Verges', *MA* 3.5.9).
92 **pupil age** youthful present

---

79 SD] *Johnson subst.*   82 SD] *Theobald*   83.1] *F; opp. 84 Q*   92, 94 o'clock] *(a clocke), Theobald*

[*Enter* FRANCIS.]

What's o'clock, Francis?                                              94

FRANCIS    Anon, anon, sir.                                    [*Exit.*]

PRINCE    That ever this fellow should have fewer words
than a parrot, and yet the son of a woman! His industry
is upstairs and downstairs, his eloquence the parcel of a
reckoning. I am not yet of Percy's mind, the Hotspur of
the North, he that kills me some six or seven dozen of     100
Scots at a breakfast, washes his hands, and says to his
wife, 'Fie upon this quiet life! I want work.' 'O my
sweet Harry', says she, 'how many hast thou killed
today?' 'Give my roan horse a drench', says he, and
answers, 'Some fourteen', an hour after, 'a trifle, a      105

---

96 **fewer words** The limited and predictable vocabulary of drawers had
become a stage joke; cf. 31n.
97 **yet** still be
97–8 **His . . . downstairs** his activity
consists of running up and down
stairs; cf. Heywood, *The Fair Maid of
the West*, Part 2, 5.3.15–16: 'shall I do
nothing but run up stairs and down
stairs with "Anon, anon, Sir"?'
(Heywood, *Fair Maid*, 2.185).
98–9 **parcel . . . reckoning** item on a tavern bill (*OED* parcel *sb.* †3)
99 **I . . . mind** i.e. I do not see the world
as Hotspur does. Humphreys (Ard²)
says that 'This change of subject is
surprising', but it seems to follow from
Hal's exuberant sense that he is *of all
humours*, 90, as he shifts from the
single-minded Francis to the no less
single-minded Hotspur. Both are
referred to as parrots: Francis at 97
and Hotspur by Kate at 2.3.82.
100 **kills me** kills (*me* here is an obsolete

form similar to the classical ethical
dative, where 'me' functions mainly to
draw attention to the speaker, usually
by making the remark sound colloquial;
cf. Abbott, 220; Hal uses it in his parody of Hotspur, and indeed Hotspur
does use the form, as at 3.1.97, 4.3.85.
102–6 **Fie . . . trifle** The Prince skilfully
satirizes Hotspur's style, exaggerating
his offhand hyper-masculinity. The
interruption in 104 to address his
groom and the delay (*an hour after*) in
completing his answer to 'Kate' catch
the exact qualities Hotspur exhibits in
the previous scene. The parody has
extended in the theatre as far as having
Michael Warre's Hal, at London's
New Theatre in 1945, imitate the distinctive hesitation of Laurence
Olivier's Hotspur with words beginning with 'w': 'I w-w-want w-w-work'
(McMillin, 27); see 1.3.56n.
104 **drench** a draught of medicine (*OED*
3)

---

93.1] *Malone subst.* 95 SD] *Collier* 102 'Fie . . . work.'] *Ard²;* fie . . . worke. *QF* 102–3 'O . . .
Harry,'] *Ard²;* O . . . Harry *QF* 103–4 'how . . . today?'] *Ard²;* how . . . to day? *QF* 104 'Give . . .
drench,'] *Ard²;* Giue . . . drench *QF* 105 'Some fourteen'] *Ard²;* some foureteene *QF* 105–6 'a . .
. trifle'] *Ard²;* a . . . trifle *QF*

trifle'. I prithee, call in Falstaff. I'll play Percy, and that
damned brawn shall play Dame Mortimer his wife.
'Rivo!' says the drunkard. Call in Ribs; call in Tallow.

*Enter* FALSTAFF[, BARDOLL, PETO *and* GADSHILL,
*followed by* FRANCIS *carrying wine*].

POINS    Welcome, Jack. Where hast thou been?
FALSTAFF    A plague of all cowards, I say, and a vengeance    110
too. Marry and amen! – Give me a cup of sack, boy. –
Ere I lead this life long, I'll sew netherstocks and mend
them, and foot them too. A plague of all cowards. – Give
me a cup of sack, rogue. – Is there no virtue extant?
[*Francis hands Falstaff a cup and*] *he drinketh.*
PRINCE    Didst thou never see Titan kiss a dish of butter    115
(pitiful-hearted Titan) that melted at the sweet tale of

---

**106–7 I'll . . . wife** Hal, not content
merely with his mimicry of Hotspur,
now suggests that he and Falstaff
should play Hotspur and Kate, anticipating the *play extempore*, 271, in
which he and Falstaff will alternate in
the roles of King and Prince.

**107 brawn** i.e. Falstaff (*brawn* = boar
meat)

**108 Rivo!** obviously a drinking cry, like
'bottoms up!', but the exact meaning
and source are unknown; perhaps it
derives from the Spanish, *arriba*, i.e.
up; cf. Marston, *What You Will*
(1607): 'If thou art sad at others fate /
Rivo Drinke deepe; give care the mate'
(sig. C3ᵛ).
**Ribs . . . Tallow** Both refer to Falstaff,
*Ribs* as fatty meat on bones (or possibly
ironically, as emaciated with ribs showing?), *Tallow* as the dripping fat.

**110 of** on (cf. Abbott, 175)

**111 Marry and amen** i.e. it should be so
(as if following a prayer)

**112–13 Ere . . . too** Before I live any
longer I'll stitch, darn and even
remake the feet of my stockings (since
he has been forced to walk a great distance). In some productions, he has
just sat down, taken off a boot, and is
rubbing his foot.

**114 virtue extant** bravery surviving

**115–17 Didst . . . sun?** The Prince's
comparison here is obscure, and various editors have suggested emendations; Warburton's bracketing of
*pitiful-hearted Titan* allows sense to be
made of the lines: presumably the red-
faced Falstaff's loving embrace of his
sack is imagined as a *kiss* like the sun's
(Titan's) which melts the dish of butter, just as the sack melts away down
Falstaff's throat. In another sense, the
Prince may be Titan, or the sun, who
makes Falstaff, the *butter* (cf. 4.2.60),
sweat (cf. 2.2.105).

**116 pitiful-hearted** tender
**sweet tale** blandishments

---

108 'Rivo!'] *Oxf¹; Riuo QF*    108.1 BARDOLL . . . GADSHILL] *Theobald subst.*    108.2 *followed . . .*
*wine*] *Dyce*    113 them . . . them] them *F*    114 SD *Francis . . . and*] *this edn    he drinketh*] *om. Q5–F*

the sun? If thou didst, then behold that compound.

FALSTAFF [*to Francis*]   You rogue, here's lime in this sack
too. – There is nothing but roguery to be found in
villainous man, yet a coward is worse than a cup of sack      120
with lime in it. A villainous coward! Go thy ways, old
Jack; die when thou wilt. If manhood, good manhood,
be not forgot upon the face of the earth, then am I a
shotten herring. There lives not three good men
unhanged in England and one of them is fat and grows      125
old, God help the while. A bad world, I say. I would I
were a weaver; I could sing psalms or anything. A
plague of all cowards, I say still.

PRINCE   How now, woolsack, what mutter you?

FALSTAFF   A king's son! If I do not beat thee out of thy      130
kingdom with a dagger of lath and drive all thy subjects

117 **compound** mixture; i.e. Falstaff and
sack, or Falstaff in his sweat (or perhaps Falstaff and the Prince; cf.
115–17n.)

118 **lime** calcium oxide added to wines to
preserve them; *OED* cites Hawkins,
*Voyage into the South Sea* (1622), on
'Spanish sacks . . . which (for conser-
vation) are mingled with lime in its
making'.

119–20 **There . . . man** The sentence is
quoted in *Palladis Tamia* (1598): 'in
these declining and corrupt times,
where there is nothing but rogery in
villanous man' (Meres, sig. OO1ʳ). This
is perhaps the earliest extant quotation
from the play, although the thought
may be proverbial (cf. Dent, F34:
'There is no faith (trust, honesty) in
man', but he gives no example earlier
than this).

121 **Go thy ways** i.e. goodbye; you've
had it (*ways* = way)

124 **shotten herring** a herring that has
spawned; i.e. thin and weak

126 **the while** these present times; cf. *KJ*
4.2.100: 'bad world the while!'

126–7 **I would . . . anything** Many
weavers were refugee Dutch Cal-
vinists, whose religious service and
own pious practices involved psalm
singing; cf. Davenant, *The Wits* (1636):
'more devout / Than a weaver of
Banbury, that hopes / T''entice Heaven
by singing' (1.1.84–6; Davenant,
2.124). In 1784, Thomas Davies noted
that 'It is a common expression, in this
day in Scotland, to say 'psalm-singing
weavers' (Davies, *DM*, 1.235). F prints
'I could sing all manner of songs', a
particularly scrupulous bit of expurgation in accordance with the 1606 Act
against blasphemy on stage.

129 **woolsack** large bale of wool (the particular image of Falstaff's bulk suggested by the mention of a weaver)

131 **dagger of lath** wooden dagger carried by comic Vice in the morality
plays; cf. *TN* 4.2.123–5: 'Like to the
old Vice . . . with dagger of lath'.

117 sun] *Q3–F (*sunne*); sonnes Q1–2*   118 SD] *Folg²*   120 than] *(*then*); the Q5u*   121 lime in it]
in't *Fu;* lime *Fc*   127 psalms or anything] all manner of songs *F*

afore thee like a flock of wild geese, I'll never wear hair
on my face more. You, Prince of Wales!

PRINCE   Why, you whoreson round man, what's the
matter?                                                                                           135

FALSTAFF   Are not you a coward? Answer me to that. And
Poins there?

POINS   Zounds, ye fat paunch, an ye call me coward, by
the Lord, I'll stab thee.

FALSTAFF   I call thee coward? I'll see thee damned ere I      140
call thee coward, but I would give a thousand pound I
could run as fast as thou canst. You are straight enough
in the shoulders; you care not who sees your back. Call
you that backing of your friends? A plague upon such
backing! Give me them that will face me. – Give me a      145
cup of sack; I am a rogue if I drunk today.

PRINCE   O villain, thy lips are scarce wiped since thou
drunkest last.

FALSTAFF   All is one for that. (*He drinketh.*) A plague of
all cowards, still say I.                                                                 150

PRINCE   What's the matter?

FALSTAFF   What's the matter? There be four of us here
have ta'en a thousand pound this day morning.

PRINCE   Where is it, Jack? Where is it?

FALSTAFF   Where is it? Taken from us it is. A hundred      155
upon poor four of us.

---

134 **whoreson** a common term of contempt where the literal meaning is
largely irrelevant (like 'son-of-a-bitch'
today)

138 **an ye** if you

149 **All . . . that** i.e. it makes no difference

153 **a thousand pound** Falstaff's characteristic hyperbole; only 300 marks
(i.e. 200 pounds) were taken (cf.
2.1.54–5; 2.4.507).

**this day morning** this morning

156 **poor** merely

---

136 not you] you not *Q2–F*   138 SP] *Prin. Q5–F*   Zounds, ye fat] Ye fatch *F*   138–9 by the Lord]
*om. F*   141 thee coward] the Coward *F*   149 All is] All's *Q3–F*   152 There . . . here] here be foure
of vs *Q3–F*   153 this day] this *Q3–F*

PRINCE　What, a hundred, man?

FALSTAFF　I am a rogue if I were not at half-sword with a
　　dozen of them, two hours together. I have scaped by
　　miracle. I am eight times thrust through the doublet,　160
　　four through the hose, my buckler cut through and
　　through, my sword hacked like a handsaw. *Ecce signum*!
　　I never dealt better since I was a man. All would not do.
　　A plague of all cowards! [*Indicates Gadshill, Peto and
　　Bardoll.*] Let them speak. If they speak more or less　165
　　than truth, they are villains and the sons of darkness.

PRINCE　Speak, sirs, how was it?

BARDOLL　We four set upon some dozen –

FALSTAFF [*to the Prince*]　Sixteen at least, my lord.

BARDOLL　And bound them.　　　　　　　　　　　　　170

PETO　No, no, they were not bound.

FALSTAFF　You rogue, they were bound, every man of

---

158 **if I were not** The subjunctive is not
　required here, but Elizabethan English
　often used it where the meaning is 'if it
　were true that I was not' (cf. Abbott,
　301); similarly at 3.3.156.
　　**at half-sword** in close combat (*OED*
　2a)

160 **doublet** tunic

161 **hose** long breeches
　　**buckler** small shield with a projecting
　pike (see 1.3.228n.)

162 **hacked . . . handsaw** i.e. with its
　edge so notched from the fierce fight-
　ing that it now looks almost serrated
　like a saw
　　*Ecce signum* behold the proof; prover-
　bial (Dent, S443); the origin of the
　phrase is unknown; perhaps it is
　derived from '*Ecce lignum crucis*'
　(Behold the wood of the cross) in the
　Good Friday service. Falstaff holds up

or otherwise indicates his *hacked* sword
as he delivers the line.

163 **dealt** i.e. fought
　　**All . . . do** whatever I did, it wasn't
　enough

166 **sons of darkness** plays on a familiar
　biblical text, 1 Thessalonians, 5.5: 'Ye
　are all children of the light . . . we are
　not of the night nether of darkenes.'

167 SP *Q gives the line to Gadshill; F
　and Dering assign it to the Prince,
　which most editions follow, as the line
　must be delivered by someone who was
　not present and has the commanding
　tone appropriate only to Hal.

168 SP *Q assigns this line, and the
　speeches at 170 and 174, to '*Ross*.' (for
　Rossill or Russell, the original name
　Shakespeare gave the character). F
　assigns them to Gadshill, and some
　editions follow (e.g., Oxf[1]). See p. 117.

---

164–5 SD] *Folg[2] subst.*　167 SP] *F, Dering; Gad. Q*　168, 170, 174 SP] *Dering, Collier MS; Ross. Q;
Gad. F*　169 SD] *Oxf*　171 SP] *Bard. Dering*

them, or I am a Jew else, an 'Ebrew Jew.

BARDOLL    As we were sharing, some six or seven fresh
men set upon us.                                                                          175

FALSTAFF    And unbound the rest, and then come in the
other.

PRINCE    What, fought you with them all?

FALSTAFF    All? I know not what you call all, but if I
fought not with fifty of them, I am a bunch of radish.      180
If there were not two- or three-and-fifty upon poor old
Jack, then am I no two-legged creature.

PRINCE    Pray God you have not murdered some of them.

FALSTAFF    Nay, that's past praying for. I have peppered
two of them. Two I am sure I have paid, two rogues in      185
buckram suits. I tell thee what, Hal, if I tell thee a lie,
spit in my face, call me horse. Thou knowest my old
ward. Here I lay, and thus I bore my point. Four rogues
in buckram let drive at me.

PRINCE    What, four? Thou saidst but two even now.          190

FALSTAFF    Four, Hal; I told thee four.

POINS    Ay, ay, he said four.

173 **a Jew else** i.e. otherwise not to be
trusted; 'Jew' is regularly used as a term
of opprobrium in the sixteenth century,
though perhaps here specifically as a
function of Falstaff thinking of 'Jew'
as usurer (*OED sb.* 2), a meaning possibly suggested by the reiteration of
*bound*, 170–2, producing its commercial sense of 'under contractual obligation', as in *MV* 1.3.4–5: 'Antonio shall
be bound'.
    **an 'Ebrew Jew** an authentic Jew; an
intensification of the previous phrase
174 **sharing** dividing up the spoils
    **fresh** new
177 **other** others
182 **two-legged creature** refers to the

classical definition of man as a feather-
less biped
184 **peppered** trounced
185 **paid** killed
186 **buckram suits** clothing made of
coarse linen (at 1.2.170–1 Poins says he
has *cases of buckram* to disguise their
*noted outward garments*)
187 **call me horse** insult me (cf. 182 and
note)
188 **ward** defensive position
    **Here . . . point** i.e. this is how I stood,
and this is how I held my sword. (*Here*
and *thus* are implicit SDs for Falstaff
here as he mimes his putative action.)
189 **let drive** attacked, struck out

173 an] and *Q2–4*    174 six or seven] *(*6. or 7.*)*, F    178, 179 you] ye *Q2–F*    183 SP] *Poines. Q5–F*
God] Heauen *F*    188 ward] word *Q5–F*    190 What, four?] *Q2–F;* What foure? *Q1*

FALSTAFF  These four came all afront and mainly thrust
at me. I made me no more ado, but took all their seven
points in my target, thus.                                          195

PRINCE  Seven? Why, there were but four even now.

FALSTAFF  In buckram?

POINS  Ay, four in buckram suits.

FALSTAFF  Seven, by these hilts, or I am a villain else.

PRINCE [*to Poins*]  Prithee, let him alone. We shall have          200
more anon.

FALSTAFF  Dost thou hear me, Hal?

PRINCE  Ay, and mark thee too, Jack.

FALSTAFF  Do so, for it is worth the listening to. These
nine in buckram that I told thee of –                               205

PRINCE  So, two more already.

FALSTAFF  Their points being broken –

POINS  Down fell their hose.

FALSTAFF  Began to give me ground, but I followed me
close, came in foot and hand, and, with a thought, seven            210
of the eleven I paid.

PRINCE  O monstrous! Eleven buckram men grown out of
two!

---

193 **afront** abreast
   **mainly** vigorously
194 **made . . . ado** delayed no longer
195 **points** sword points
   **target** shield
196 **even now** a moment ago
199 **by these hilts** by this sword; Falstaff
   swears on the cross formed by his
   sword's grip and cross-guard, as in
   *Ham* 1.5.154. The plural *hilts* is a
   result of the pommel, handle and
   guard that make up the hilt; cf. *H5*
   2.0.9: 'hides a sword from hilts unto
   the point'.
200 SD *Many editions mark this as an
   aside spoken out of Falstaff's hearing,

though nothing in QF so marks it. Hal
seems at least as likely to wish Falstaff
to hear his scepticism as to share the
joke only privately with Poins.
203 **mark** pay attention to
207 **points** sword points (as at 195)
208 **Down . . . hose** Poins mockingly
   takes *points* as the tagged laces used for
   attaching the hose to the doublet; cf.
   *TN* 1.5.22–5, where Maria also plays
   on the meaning of 'points' as 'laces'.
209 **followed me** followed (*me* is the colloquial usage similar to the Latin ethical dative, as at 2.4.100)
210 **with a thought** as quick as thought

194 made me] made *Q3–F*   200 SD] *White subst.*   203 too, Jack] *Q2–F;* to iacke *Q1*   208 their]
his *Q2–F*

FALSTAFF  But, as the devil would have it, three
    misbegotten knaves in Kendal green came at my back   215
    and let drive at me, for it was so dark, Hal, that thou
    couldst not see thy hand.

PRINCE  These lies are like their father that begets them,
    gross as a mountain, open, palpable. Why, thou clay-
    brained guts, thou knotty-pated fool, thou whoreson   220
    obscene greasy tallow-catch.

FALSTAFF  What, art thou mad? Art thou mad? Is not the
    truth the truth?

PRINCE  Why, how couldst thou know these men in
    Kendal green when it was so dark thou couldst not see   225
    thy hand? Come, tell us your reason. What sayst thou
    to this?

POINS  Come, your reason, Jack, your reason.

FALSTAFF  What, upon compulsion? Zounds, an I were
    at the strappado, or all the racks in the world, I would   230

---

215 **Kendal green** green, coarse wool fabric made in Kendal (in modern Cumbria), which, as Fynes Moryson reports, was 'famous for the making of woolen cloth' (4.160)

219–20 **clay-brained** dull-witted

220 **knotty-pated** thick-headed; however, at 69, Hal uses the epithet *not-pated* (i.e. with cropped hair) to describe the vintner, and it is possible that Hal in fact intends this word, rather than what in essence repeats *clay-brained* immediately before. Certainly on stage *knotty-pated* could be heard as either word, and 'notty-pated' would fit with the set of images identifying Falstaff as a Puritan (see pp. 61–2), as cropped hair was commonly taken as an identifying sign of the godly (giving rise to the term 'Roundhead' later in the seventeenth century).

221 **tallow-catch** lump of fat; many edi-

tors emend to 'tallow-keech', but it is unnecessary. The image is presumably of the hardened fat that had accumulated beneath roasting meat.

222–3 **Is . . . truth?** a proverbial expression; cf. *AW* 4.3.154, 'a truth's a truth', and Dent, T581.

229 **an** if

230 **strappado** a torture device; Blount defines 'Strappado' as 'a punishment most commonly of Souldiers for some offence; which is hanging them by the arms drawn backward, and being so bound they are drawn up on high, and let down again with a violent swing, which (if used with rigor) unjoynts their back and arms'.

**racks** instruments of torture consisting of a frame with rollers on each end to which were attached a victim's hands and feet, which then could be painfully stretched in opposite direc-

---

218 their] the *Q2–F*   229 Zounds] No *F*   an] *(and), Cam; om. F*   I were] were I *F*

not tell you on compulsion. Give you a reason on
compulsion? If reasons were as plentiful as
blackberries, I would give no man a reason upon
compulsion, I.

PRINCE    I'll be no longer guilty of this sin. This sanguine      235
coward, this bed-presser, this horse-back-breaker, this
huge hill of flesh –

FALSTAFF    'Sblood, you starveling, you eel-skin, you
dried neat's tongue, you bull's pizzle, you stock-fish! O,
for breath to utter what is like thee! You tailor's yard,      240
you sheath, you bow-case, you vile standing tuck –

tions; Thomas defines the Latin *fidicu-
lae* as 'A torment or rack with cordes
and stringes to make men confesse'.
232–3 **reasons . . . blackberries** The
particular simile is suggested by the
fact that *reasons* would have been pronounced something like 'raisins'; cf.
*AYL* 2.7.98–102, where Jaques puns
on 'reason/raison' as he takes fruit
from the table after Orlando has pro-
hibited it.
235 **sanguine** literally, red-faced, ruddy;
but also hopeful; in the last sense, *sanguine coward* is something of an oxy-
moron, as the Prince seemingly enjoys
pointing out.
236 **bed-presser** i.e. one whose weight
will flatten a bed
238 **'Sblood** By God's blood; a mild oath
238–41 **you**[1] **. . . tuck** Falstaff's string of
epithets mocking Hal's thinness return
Hal's set of epithets mocking Falstaff's great size, 219–21, and indeed
on stage are often delivered by mocking the rhythms of Hal's delivery of
his list.
238  **starveling** one who is extremely thin
from lack of food
*eel-skin** Hanmer's emendation of
Q1–2's 'elsskin', which fits well with
the set of slender objects that are

named, and is a term used by
Shakespeare in *2H4* 3.2.319–21, where
Falstaff says that Shallow is so thin that
'you might have thrust him and all his
apparel into an eelskin'; see also Field,
*Weathercock*, in an apparent echo of
*1H4*: 'that little, old, dri'de Neats
tongue, that Eele-skin' (sig. C1ᵛ).
Nonetheless, 'elfskin', the reading of
Q3–5 and F ('Elfe-skin'), is not impossible, and the image is used by
Shakespeare in *MND* 2.1.255–6: 'the
snake throws her enamell'd skin, /
Weed wide enough to wrap a fairy in',
though, as GWW points out, an elf is
not a fairy. The droll, *The Bouncing
Knight, or the Robbers Robbed*, prints
'Elf-skin' (*Wits*, sig. C3ᵛ; see p. 81).
239 **neat's tongue** cow or ox tongue
**bull's pizzle** dried bull's penis, used
sometimes as a whiplash
**stock-fish** dried cod
240 **yard** yardstick
241 **sheath** case for a knife or sword,
closely conforming to the shape of the
weapon
**bow-case** leather carrier for an
archer's bows
**vile standing tuck** useless rapier;
*standing* is usually glossed as 'upright',
but none of the other images of thin

232 plentiful] plentie *Q2–F*   238 'Sblood] *(Zbloud); Away F*   eel-skin] *Hanmer;* elsskin *Q1–2;* elf-
skin *Q3–5;* Elfe-skin *F*

PRINCE   Well, breathe awhile and then to it again, and
when thou hast tired thyself in base comparisons, hear
me speak but this.

POINS   Mark, Jack.                                                      245

PRINCE   We two saw you four set on four, and bound
them, and were masters of their wealth. Mark now how
a plain tale shall put you down. Then did we two set on
you four, and, with a word, outfaced you from your
prize, and have it, yea, and can show it you here in the        250
house. And, Falstaff, you carried your guts away as
nimbly, with as quick dexterity, and roared for mercy,
and still run and roared, as ever I heard bull-calf. What
a slave art thou to hack thy sword as thou hast done and
then say it was in fight! What trick, what device, what         255
starting-hole canst thou now find out to hide thee from
this open and apparent shame?

POINS   Come, let's hear, Jack. What trick hast thou now?

FALSTAFF   By the Lord, I knew ye as well as he that made
ye. Why, hear you, my masters: was it for me to kill the        260
heir apparent? Should I turn upon the true prince?

objects makes its orientation an issue; *standing* seems rather here to mean 'rigid' (*OED* II †8), referring to the blade's loss of resilience, which would minimize its usefulness; cf. Chapman, *May Day*, where Quin says: 'Here's a blade Boy; it was the old Dukes first predecessors', and one boy then worries: 'me thinks it stands a little' (4.1.22–6; Chapman, 358).

242 **to it** i.e. get back to it, restart
243 **base comparisons** Cf. *TC* 1.3.194: 'To match us in comparisons with dirt'.
247 **masters** possessors
249 **with a word** by a single shout
    **outfaced** frightened
250 **prize** plunder (*OED sb.* 3)

253 **still run** went on running
254 **hack** i.e. put notches in it so it looks as if it has been used in a fight
256 **starting-hole** hiding place
257 **open . . . shame** undeniable and manifest disgrace; Falstaff's reaction to the speech should be as interesting to an audience as is Hal's exposure of the fat knight: Samuel Phelps, for example, one of the great nineteenth-century Falstaffs, grew ever more apprehensive as Hal went on, but 'feigned indignation' as the accusations mounted; his 'uneasy chuckle develop[ed] into a roar of laughter as he regained his effrontery, and he cried, "By the Lord, . . . "' (Towse, 50).

242 to it] to't *F*   243 tired] tried *Q5*   244 this] thus *Q4–F*   250 you here] you *F*   253 run] ranne *F*   roared] roare *Q2–5;* roar'd *F*   259 By the Lord] *om. F*   260 you] ye *F*

Why, thou knowest I am as valiant as Hercules, but
beware instinct. The lion will not touch the true prince;
instinct is a great matter. I was now a coward on instinct.
I shall think the better of myself, and thee, during my　　265
life – I for a valiant lion and thou for a true prince. But,
by the Lord, lads, I am glad you have the money.
[*Calls.*] Hostess, clap to the doors. Watch tonight; pray
tomorrow. – Gallants, lads, boys, hearts of gold, all the
titles of good fellowship come to you! What, shall we be　　270
merry? Shall we have a play extempore?

PRINCE　Content, and the argument shall be thy running
away.

FALSTAFF　Ah, no more of that, Hal, an thou lovest me.

*Enter* HOSTESS.

HOSTESS　O Jesu, my lord the Prince!　　　　　　　275

PRINCE　How now, my lady the hostess; what sayst thou to
me?

HOSTESS　Marry, my lord, there is a nobleman of the
court at door would speak with you. He says he comes
from your father.　　　　　　　　　　　　　　　280

PRINCE　Give him as much as will make him a royal man

---

263 **beware** pay heed to
　　**The**[1] . . . **prince** a familiar piece of
　　folklore, that a lion will recognize roy-
　　alty and refuse to attack; cf. Fletcher,
　　*The Mad Lover*, 4.5.55–8, where a
　　'*Numidian* Lyon' is used to test the
　　birthright of the Princess: 'If she be
　　sprung from royal bloode, the Lyon/
　　He'l do ye reverence, else . . . he'l teare
　　her all to pieces' (Bowers, 5.44).
268 **clap to** shut
268–9 **Watch . . . tomorrow** Have fun
　　tonight (*Watch* = stay awake); leave
　　prayers until tomorrow

269 **hearts of gold** a colloquial phrase
　　for 'good-natured fellows'; cf. *H5*
　　4.1.44: 'The King's a bawcock and a
　　heart of gold'.
271 **play extempore** improvised drama
272 **Content** I am content
　　**argument** plot, story
281 **make . . . man** Hal jokes that the
　　*nobleman*, 278, who has come from the
　　court should be made a *royal man* by giv-
　　ing him the difference between a 'noble',
　　a coin worth 6s. 8d, and a 'royal', a coin
　　worth ten shillings; see 522n.

264 now] *om. Q2–F*　267 by the Lord] *om. F*　268 SD] *Oxf*　270 titles of good] good Titles of *F*
275 O Jesu] *om. F*　278 lord] *(Lo.), Q2; (L..), F*

and send him back again to my mother.

FALSTAFF    What manner of man is he?

HOSTESS    An old man.

FALSTAFF    What doth Gravity out of his bed at    285
midnight? Shall I give him his answer?

PRINCE    Prithee do, Jack.

FALSTAFF    Faith, and I'll send him packing.    *Exit.*

PRINCE    Now, sirs: [*to Gadshill*] by'r Lady, you fought
fair; so did you, Peto; so did you, Bardoll. You are lions    290
too; you ran away upon instinct. You will not touch the
true prince, no, fie!

BARDOLL    Faith, I ran when I saw others run.

PRINCE    Faith, tell me now in earnest, how came Falstaff's
sword so hacked?    295

PETO    Why, he hacked it with his dagger, and said he
would swear truth out of England but he would make
you believe it was done in fight, and persuaded us to do
the like.

BARDOLL    Yea, and to tickle our noses with speargrass to    300

---

**282 send . . . mother** i.e. having now
made him a *royal man* (i.e. a king,
though see previous note) now send
him back to his wife. The easy reversal
of *from your father*, 280, to *to my moth-*
*er* is obvious enough, but this is the
only mention of Hal's mother in the
play. Hal's mother, Mary Bohun, was
the first wife of Henry IV; after her
death, however, the king married Joan
of Navarre, daughter of Charles the
Bad, and perhaps it is of his step-
mother that Hal is thinking here,
though the witticism is surely the
main point.

**283 manner** kind

**285 Gravity** Falstaff refers to the noble-

man who has come from the King
with a personification of his aged
respectability.

**297 swear . . . England** i.e. lie with such
conviction that the truth would be
unrecognizable in England
**but** unless

**300 speargrass** a coarse, sharp-edged
grass (couch grass); cf. Gerard, *Herbal*:
'Couch grasse hath long leaves like
unto the small Reede, sharpe at the
point, cutting like a knife at the edges'
(Gerard, 21). In *Famous Victories*,
Derick confesses: 'Every day I went
into the field, I would take a straw and
thrust it into my nose, and make my
nose bleed' (19.15–17).

---

285 Gravity] *(grauitie), F*    289 SD] *Folg²*    by'r Lady] *(birlady), Pope; om. F*    290–1 lions too;]
*(lions to); lions, to Q1u*    294 Faith] *om. F*    300 SP] *Car. Q2–5*

make them bleed, and then to beslubber our garments
with it and swear it was the blood of true men. I did
that I did not this seven year before: I blushed to hear
his monstrous devices.

PRINCE    O villain, thou stolest a cup of sack eighteen years    305
ago, and wert taken with the manner, and ever since
thou hast blushed extempore. Thou hadst fire and
sword on thy side, and yet thou ran'st away. What
instinct hadst thou for it?

BARDOLL    My lord, do you see these meteors? Do you    310
behold these exhalations?

PRINCE    I do.

BARDOLL    What think you they portend?

PRINCE    Hot livers and cold purses.

BARDOLL    Choler, my lord, if rightly taken.    315

PRINCE    No, if rightly taken, halter.

*Enter* FALSTAFF.

Here comes lean Jack; here comes bare-bone. How now,
my sweet creature of bombast? How long is't ago, Jack,

301 **beslubber** smear
303 **that** something
   **blushed** The joke is that Bardoll's face
   is so red from his drinking that no
   blush could ever be seen (as Hal notes
   at 307)
304 **monstrous devices** outrageous lies
306 **taken . . . manner** caught red-handed;
   cf. Minsheu, 'Mainour': 'taken with
   the manner, that is, having the thing
   stolen with him'.
307 **extempore** spontaneously
307–8 **fire and sword** i.e. great firepower
   (but the continued joke is that, instead
   of the familiar meaning of the phrase,
   Bardoll had the *fire* in his face along
   with his sword by his side)
310 **these meteors** i.e. the eruptions on

Bardoll's nose (like the *exhalations* in
the next line)
313 **portend** predict
314 **Hot . . . purses** i.e. drunkenness and
   poverty
315 **Choler** anger
   **rightly taken** correctly understood
316 **rightly taken** lawfully arrested
   **halter** noose or 'collar', responding to
   *Choler*, 315
317 **lean Jack** an obvious sarcasm about
   Falstaff's size, but a 'jack' is also 'a soldier's quilted jacket' (*OED sb.*² 1b)
318 **bombast** untreated cotton used for
   stuffing quilts and jackets, picking up
   on the punning use of *Jack* in the
   previous line; cf. the similar play at
   4.2.48 and in *Oth* 1.1.12–13: 'bombast

303 year] yeeres *Q4–F*    316.1] *F; after 315 Q*

since thou sawest thine own knee?

FALSTAFF    My own knee? When I was about thy years,    320
Hal, I was not an eagle's talon in the waist; I could have
crept into any alderman's thumb-ring. A plague of
sighing and grief, it blows a man up like a bladder.
There's villainous news abroad. Here was Sir John
Bracy from your father; you must to the court in the    325
morning. That same mad fellow of the north, Percy,
and he of Wales that gave Amaimon the bastinado and
made Lucifer cuckold, and swore the devil his true
liegeman upon the cross of a Welsh hook – what a
plague call you him?    330

circumstance, / Horribly stuffed with
epithets of war'. Elizabethan military
writers, like Garrard, objected specifically to the wearing of 'great bumbast-
ed and bolstered hose', as it hindered
movement (sig. B3ʳ⁻ᵛ).
321 **not an** as thin as an
322 **alderman's thumb-ring** a seal-ring
often worn on the thumb by wealthy citizens (an *alderman* was a municipal
administrative officer); cf. Brome,
*Northern*, where 'A good man i'th' city is
... one that ... wears ... a thombe-Ring
with his Grandsires sheep-mark, or
Grannams butter-print on't' (sig. D2ʳ).
323 **bladder** any membraneous organ in
an animal's body that serves as a recep-
tacle for fluid; inflatable, these were
sometimes removed and prepared for
use as floats (cf. *H8* 3.2.259) or wind-
bags in instruments.
324–5 **Sir John Bracy** Neither a Bracy
nor a Braby (as in Q4–8 and F) is
mentioned by Holinshed or other
chronicle accounts of this reign.
Shakespeare might, however, be
recalling a John Brace (d. 1431), an
influential Worcestershire gentleman
who served as alnager and sheriff and
several times represented Droitwich

and Doverdale in Parliament. In 1403,
Brace was commissioned to muster
men in Worcestershire to fight against
Glendower. He also served as the
executor for Sir John Russell, the
name originally given to Bardoll (see
List of Roles 19n.).
326 **mad . . . Percy** i.e. Hotspur
327 **he of Wales** i.e. Owen Glendower
**gave . . . bastinado** cudgelled
Amaimon (the name of a devil, mentioned in *MW* 2.2.281: 'Amaimon
sounds well', and in Reginald Scot,
*Discovery of Witchcraft* (1584), where
'Amaymon' is one of the 'principall
divils', Scot, sig. LL2ʳ). Cf. Bullokar,
'*Bastinado*: a staff, a cudgell', which
perhaps also permits a pun on *Wales*,
327, as 'beats upon'.
328 **made Lucifer cuckold** seduced the
devil's wife
328–9 **swore . . . liegeman** caused the
devil to swear to be his loyal servant
329 **Welsh hook** pike or halberd with
inverted hook below the point (and not
in the shape of a cross)
329–30 **what a plague** i.e. what (*a plague*
is an colloquial intensifier, as in 'what
the devil')

321 talon] *(talent), Q7 (*tallon)    325 Bracy] Braby *Q4–F*    to] go to *Q5–F*    326 That] The *Q5–F*
327 Amaimon] Amamon *QF*

POINS  Owen Glendower.

FALSTAFF  Owen, Owen, the same; and his son-in-law
Mortimer, and old Northumberland, and that sprightly
Scot of Scots Douglas, that runs a-horseback up a hill
perpendicular –                                                            335

PRINCE  He that rides at high speed and with his pistol
kills a sparrow flying.

FALSTAFF  You have hit it.

PRINCE  So did he never the sparrow.

FALSTAFF  Well, that rascal hath good mettle in him;          340
he will not run.

PRINCE  Why, what a rascal art thou, then, to praise him
so for running!

FALSTAFF  A-horseback, ye cuckoo, but afoot he will not
budge a foot.                                                              345

PRINCE  Yes, Jack, upon instinct.

FALSTAFF  I grant ye, upon instinct. Well, he is there too,
and one Murdoch, and a thousand blue-caps more.
Worcester is stolen away tonight. Thy father's beard is
turned white with the news. You may buy land now as      350

331 *Owen Glendower Q reads 'O
Glendower'. It is possible that the Q
reading is correct, the 'O' functioning
as an interjection, and some editions
(e.g. Cam²) follow this. Dering, however, reads 'Owen Glendower', taking Q's
'O' as an abbreviation, and, since Poins
speaks in response to Falstaff's 'what a
plague call you him?', 329–30, the full
name seems the more likely reading
here, especially as Falstaff then replies,
'Owen, Owen, the same', 332.
334 Scot of Scots i.e. the best of the
Scots
336 pistol Pistols, as Samuel Johnson
noted, 'were not known in the age of

Henry. They were, in our author's
time, eminently used by Scots.'
338 hit it got it exactly right
340 mettle courage (also plays on
'metal', which will not easily *run*, or
melt; Q's spelling is 'mettall')
343 Why . . . running i.e. why praise him
for *running* (as at 334) if he *will not run*,
341?
344 ye cuckoo you simpleton
afoot i.e. fighting on foot
348 blue-caps Scottish soldiers (from
the blue woollen cap commonly worn
in Scotland)
349 is stolen away i.e. has left London

331 Owen] *Dering, Thirlby MS;* O *QF*     333 that] the *Q3–F*     sprightly] sprightie *Q3;* sprighty *Q4;*
sprighly *Q5*     336 his] a *Q3–F*     340 mettle] *(mettall)*     344 afoot] *(a foote), Q2*     348 Murdoch]
*(Mordacke), F (*Mordake*)*     349 tonight] by night *Q5–F*

cheap as stinking mackerel.

PRINCE    Why then, it is like if there come a hot June and this civil buffeting hold, we shall buy maidenheads as they buy hobnails: by the hundreds.

FALSTAFF    By the mass, lad, thou sayst true; it is like we    355
shall have good trading that way. But tell me, Hal, art not thou horrible afeard? Thou being heir apparent, could the world pick thee out three such enemies again as that fiend Douglas, that spirit Percy and that devil Glendower? Art thou not horribly afraid? Doth not thy    360
blood thrill at it?

PRINCE    Not a whit, i'faith. I lack some of thy 'instinct'.

FALSTAFF    Well, thou wilt be horribly chid tomorrow when thou comest to thy father. If thou love me, practise an answer.    365

PRINCE    Do thou stand for my father and examine me upon the particulars of my life.

---

352 **like** likely
352–4 **if . . . hundreds** i.e. if the weather is hot and the fighting continues,
one will be able to buy women's virtue
as cheap as shoe studs; Hal turns
Falstaff's *mackerel*, 351, into *maidenheads* by punning on the meaning of
'maiden' as 'fish' (*OED sb.* †8), probably because *mackerel* itself carries a
sexual connotation (*OED* 2).
353 **civil buffeting** civil war
    **hold** continues
355 **By the mass** See 2.1.16n.
356 **trading** commerce (with a sexual
overtone)
356–61 **But . . . it** At Stratford-upon-
Avon in 1975 there was a long pause
after Falstaff's speech, as the 'games
turn[ed] serious' (*The Times*, 25 April
1975), though this is perhaps a more

tendentious interpretation than the
text asks for here.
359 **spirit** fiend
361 **thrill** shudder with fear, prickle
362 **'instinct'** Hal mocks Falstaff's earlier claim that he was 'a coward on
instinct', 264; if Falstaff's questions at
356–61 indeed caused Hal any worry,
his joke here marks his regained self-
assurance.
363 **chid** scolded, rebuked
366–468 **Do . . . will** The *play extempore*,
271, has its origins in a few lines from
*Famous Victories* (4.95–9), where
Derick says: "Faith, John, I tell thee
what; thou shalt be my Lord Chief
Justice and thou sit in the chair; and
I'll be the young prince.'
366 **stand for** play the part of (as at 421)
367 **particulars** facts, incidents

352 Why . . . is] Then tis *Q3–F*    June] sun *Q4–F*    357 horrible] horribly *Q3*    360 thou not] not
thou *Q3–F*    horribly] horrible *Q4–F*    362 i'faith] *om. F*    'instinct'] *this edn;* instinct *QF*    363
horribly] *(*horriblie*), Q2;* horrible *Q4–F*    364 love] doe loue *Q3–F*

FALSTAFF   Shall I? Content. This chair shall be my state,
    this dagger my sceptre and this cushion my crown.

PRINCE   Thy state is taken for a joint-stool, thy golden          370
    sceptre for a leaden dagger and thy precious rich crown
    for a pitiful bald crown.

FALSTAFF   Well, an the fire of grace be not quite out of
    thee, now shalt thou be moved. Give me a cup of sack
    to make my eyes look red, that it may be thought I have     375
    wept, for I must speak in passion, and I will do it in
    King Cambyses' vein.

PRINCE   Well, here is my leg.

FALSTAFF   And here is my speech. Stand aside, nobility.

HOSTESS   O Jesu, this is excellent sport, i'faith.              380

FALSTAFF

Weep not, sweet Queen, for trickling tears are vain.

---

368 **Content** I am agreed, all right
    **state** throne
370 **taken for** understood to be (*OED*
    take 48b)
    **joint-stool** stool made by a joiner; cf.
    Cotgrave's definition for *Selle*: 'any ill-
    favoured, ordinary, or country stool, of
    a cheaper sort than the joined or
    buffet-stool'. There is a particular pro-
    priety in having a *joint-stool* serve as
    the throne in a play where political
    power is always less a function of indi-
    vidual charisma than of joining
    disparate interests into a common
    commitment; cf. Hotspur's claim that
    'all our joints are whole' (4.1.83).
371 **leaden dagger** a dagger of soft metal
    of little use as a weapon; cf. *LLL*
    5.2.480–1 'There's an eye / Wounds
    like a leaden sword.' The dagger used
    by the actors might well have been
    such a leaden dagger.
372 **crown** head
373 **an . . . grace** if the effects of divine

grace; cf. 1.2.16–17, where Falstaff
denies that Hal will accept grace.
374 **moved** stirred emotionally
376 **in passion** with great feeling
377 **King Cambyses' vein** ranting style;
    Cambyses was a stage tyrant in
    Thomas Preston's *Lamentable Tragedy
    . . . of Cambises, King of Persia* (1569);
    cf. George Villiers, *Rehearsal*: 'strut-
    ting Heroes, with a grim-fac'd train /
    Shall brave the Gods in King
    Cambyses vein' (Prologue, 9–10).
378 **here . . . leg** I make my bow
379 **Stand aside, nobility** Falstaff pre-
    sumably motions to the tavern crowd
    to clear the playing space.
381 Falstaff parodies the high tragic style,
    still in *King Cambyses' vein*. Editors
    have noted a number of analogues,
    though interestingly not to the archaic
    work of Preston and his contemporaries
    (see 377n.) but to Shakespeare's near
    contemporaries: e.g. Greene, *Alphonsus*,
    1,825: 'Then, daintie damsell, stint

---

370 joint-stool] *Rowe;* ioynd stoole *Q1–4, F;* ioynd Stole *Q5*   373 an] *(and), T. Johnson*   375 my]
mine *Q3–F*   377 vein] *(vaine)*   380 O Jesu] *om. F*

HOSTESS     O the father, how he holds his countenance!

FALSTAFF

For God's sake, lords, convey my tristful Queen,
For tears do stop the floodgates of her eyes.

HOSTESS     O Jesu, he doth it as like one of these harlotry     385
players as ever I see!

FALSTAFF     Peace, good pint-pot; peace, good tickle-brain.
– Harry, I do not only marvel where thou spendest thy
time but also how thou art accompanied. For though
the camomile, the more it is trodden on the faster it     390
grows, so youth, the more it is wasted the sooner it
wears. That thou art my son I have partly thy mother's

these trickling teares' (cited Oxf¹). The
Hostess's tears, however, are of laughter.
382 **O the father** The hostess is seemingly delighted by Falstaff's role-
playing (cf. 366: 'stand for my father'),
though it is not impossible that the
reading should be as in many editions
'O the Father', a mild oath. The fact
that the Folio text, which in general
has thoroughly expurgated oaths (see
p. 113), includes this (and even prints
'Father' rather than Q's 'father') suggests that it was understood as a reference to Falstaff rather than to God.
    **holds his countenance** keeps a
straight face
383 **convey** escort; presumably the
Hostess is led to a seat to watch the
developing playlet, though it is not
impossible, as Sisson suggested (2.32),
that Bardoll leads her offstage here. No
exits are provided for either of them in
QF, though exits for both are necessary, since Q specifies their entrances
at 468 and 472 respectively (see 467n.
on staging).
    **tristful** sorrowful (*tristful* is another
self-consciously poetic word); Q and F
all have 'trustfull'; this reading comes

from Dering (see pp. 349–50) and
seems almost certainly correct. It is
used in F *Ham* 3.4.50: 'With tristful
visage'.
385 **as like** as much like
385–6 **harlotry players** scurvy actors.
The Hostess says admiringly that
Falstaff is every bit as good as any of
those worthless professional players, the
joke for the audience of Shakespeare's
play lying in part in the fact that all of
this is enacted by such *harlotry players*.
387 **pint-pot . . . tickle-brain** Mom-
entarily back out of character, Falstaff
addresses the Hostess with familiar
tavern terms.
    **tickle-brain** strong liquor; cf. Daven-
port: 'The Drawers call it Tickle-
braine' (sig. E1ᵛ).
390–2 **camomile . . . wears** a proverbial
simile (Dent, C34); cf. Lyly's *Euphues*:
'Though the Camomill, the more it is
trodden and pressed downe, the more
it spreadeth, yet the violet the oftner it
is handled and touched, the sooner it
withereth and decayeth' (Lyly, 1.196).
Camomile is a creeping plant with
white flowers that spreads easily by
sending out runners.

383 tristful] *Dering, Rowe;* trustfull *QF*     385 Jesu] rare *F*     390 on] *om. Q5–F*     391 so] yet *Q3–F*
392 That] *om. Q3–F*

word, partly my own opinion, but chiefly a villainous
trick of thine eye and a foolish hanging of thy nether lip
that doth warrant me. If then thou be son to me – here     395
lies the point – why, being son to me, art thou so
pointed at? Shall the blessed sun of heaven prove a
micher and eat blackberries? A question not to be
asked. Shall the son of England prove a thief and take
purses? A question to be asked. There is a thing, Harry,     400
which thou hast often heard of, and it is known to many
in our land by the name of pitch. This pitch, as ancient
writers do report, doth defile; so doth the company
thou keepest. For, Harry, now I do not speak to thee in
drink but in tears, not in pleasure but in passion, not in     405
words only but in woes also. And yet there is a virtuous
man whom I have often noted in thy company, but I
know not his name.

PRINCE   What manner of man, an it like your majesty?
FALSTAFF   A goodly, portly man, i'faith, and a corpulent;     410
of a cheerful look, a pleasing eye and a most noble
carriage; and, as I think, his age some fifty, or, by'r

---

394 **trick** manner, gesture
  **foolish . . . lip** a hanging lower lip
  was considered a mark of wantonness;
  cf. Brome, *Queen's*: 'the hanging of
  the nether lip / Which the best
  Phisiognomists tell us / Shews women
  apt to lust, and strong incontinence'
  (sig. C2ᵛ).
397 **pointed at** mocked
  **blessed . . . heaven** i.e. the true prince
  (drawing on the traditional imagery of
  the sun for royalty, with the familiar
  play on *son*, 396)
398 **micher** truant (who might go off to
  *eat blackberries*)
402–3 **as . . . defile** The reference is to
  Ecclesiasticus, 13.1: 'Who so toucheth

pytch shalbe defyled withall' (and also
quoted by Lyly in both *Euphues to
Philautus* and *Letters Writ to Euphues*
(Lyly, 1.250, 320). Cf. *MA* 3.3.57:
'they that touch pitch will be defiled.'
405 **in passion** with sincere emotion
409 **an it like** if it please
410 **goodly, portly** handsome, dignified
  **corpulent** full-bodied, solid (though
  all three adjectives in the line carry an
  unmistakable sense of 'fat', to the
  delight of those watching his performance)
412 **carriage** bearing
412–13 **fifty . . . threescore** In productions, Falstaff's claim to be *fifty* often
  occasions howls of laughter from his

393 own] *om. Q3–F*   394 thy] the *Q4*   396 lies] lieth *Q3–F*   397 sun] *(sunne); sonne Q2–F*   404
Harry, now] Harrie now, *Q1u*   409 an] *(and); T. Johnson*   412–13 by'r Lady] *(birlady), F4*

Lady, inclining to threescore. And now I remember me:
his name is Falstaff. If that man should be lewdly given,
he deceiveth me, for, Harry, I see virtue in his looks. If,     415
then, the tree may be known by the fruit, as the fruit by
the tree, then peremptorily I speak it: there is virtue in
that Falstaff. Him keep with; the rest banish. And tell
me now, thou naughty varlet, tell me, where hast thou
been this month?                                                420

PRINCE   Dost thou speak like a king? Do thou stand for
me, and I'll play my father.

FALSTAFF   Depose me? If thou dost it half so gravely, so
majestically both in word and matter, hang me up by
the heels for a rabbit sucker or a poulter's hare.              425

PRINCE   Well, here I am set.

FALSTAFF   And here I stand. – Judge, my masters.

PRINCE   Now, Harry, whence come you?

FALSTAFF   My noble lord, from Eastcheap.

PRINCE   The complaints I hear of thee are grievous.          430

FALSTAFF   'Sblood, my lord, they are false. – Nay, I'll

friends, and he grudgingly corrects
himself (sometimes the correction
itself is greeted with continued disbe-
lieving delight).
414 **lewdly given** inclined to wickedness
415–17 **If . . . tree**   a proverbial saying
meaning that one knows only the quality of something by its results; based
on Luke, 6.44: 'Every tree is known by
its fruit' (cf. Dent, T497)
417 **peremptorily** decisively, conclu-
sively
418 **keep** stay
419 **naughty varlet** mischievous boy
(seemingly this strikes a nerve, since it
is here that Hal insists on trading roles
and playing his father)
423 **Depose** potentially a dangerous word
for Falstaff to speak even in jest to the

son of the king who deposed Richard
II to obtain the crown
**dost it** i.e. play the King
425 **rabbit sucker** baby rabbit (not yet
weaned)
**poulter's hare** dead hare displayed
for sale by a poulterer
426 **set** seated (on the mock throne; cf.
Falstaff's *here I stand*, 427)
427 **Judge, my masters** Falstaff asks the
assembled friends in the tavern to
judge if Hal can play the part of the
King *half so gravely* as he himself has
just done.
430 **grievous** serious, heinous
431–2 **Nay . . . prince** Falstaff comes out
of character, saying that he will be very
amusing (*tickle ye*) in the role of the
Prince.

415 deceiveth] deceiues *Q3–F*   431 'Sblood] *(Zbloud); Yfaith F*

tickle ye for a young prince, i'faith.

PRINCE Swearest thou, ungracious boy? Henceforth ne'er
look on me. Thou art violently carried away from grace.
There is a devil haunts thee in the likeness of an old fat     435
man; a tun of man is thy companion. Why dost thou
converse with that trunk of humours, that bolting-
hutch of beastliness, that swollen parcel of dropsies,
that huge bombard of sack, that stuffed cloak-bag of
guts, that roasted Manningtree ox with the pudding in     440
his belly, that reverend Vice, that grey Iniquity, that
father Ruffian, that Vanity in years? Wherein is he
good, but to taste sack and drink it? Wherein neat and

433 **ungracious** not only 'ungenerous'
but, more literally, 'without grace',
'profane' (see 434)
436 **tun** large wine cask (which perhaps
allows *fat* earlier in the line to pun on
its similar meaning, i.e. vat), but also
playing on 'ton' = 2000 lb
437 **converse** associate
**trunk of humours** container of diseases; *trunk* = container or chest (par-
alleling other containers like *tun*, 436,
and *bolting-hutch*, 437–8) as well as an
anatomical sense of the body without
its head and limbs; *humours*, here, are
the bodily fluids thought to determine
character.
437–8 **bolting-hutch** trough used to col-
lect sifted flour
438 **dropsies** disease that bloated the
body
439 **bombard** leather vessel for holding
wine
**cloak-bag** suitcase
440 **Manningtree ox** Essex town with a
well-known fair and cattle market,
probably not unlike the 'festival'
described by Fletcher and Rowley in
*The Fair Maid of the Inn*, which would

'provide a great and spacious English
Oxe and roste him whole, with a pudding in's belly' (4.2.173–4; Bowers,
10.619). Manningtree was also known
for performances of morality plays; cf.
Dekker's reference to 'the old Morralls
at *Manningtree*' (Grosart, 2.73), which
may have suggested the images at
439–40.
**pudding** stuffing
441–2 **reverend . . . years** The *Vice* was
the figure in the medieval morality
plays that sought to corrupt the innocent hero and whose particular threat
was usually indicated by his name. Here
there are four such personifications of
evil (capitalized in F), with the modifier
in each case (e.g. *reverend* = worthy of
respect) pointing to the incongruity of
Falstaff's age and actions.
441 **grey Iniquity** grey-haired sinfulness
(cf. *R3* 3.1.82: 'the formal Vice,
Iniquity')
442 **father Ruffian** elderly swaggerer
(but *Ruffian* may mean fiend or devil;
see *OED* ruffin)
**Vanity in years** aged pride
443–4 **neat and cleanly** delicate and deft

432 i'faith] *(*I faith*); om. F*    441 reverend Vice] *F;* reuerent vice *Q*

cleanly, but to carve a capon and eat it? Wherein
cunning, but in craft? Wherein crafty, but in villainy?        445
Wherein villainous, but in all things? Wherein worthy,
but in nothing?

FALSTAFF    I would your grace would take me with you.
Whom means your grace?

PRINCE    That villainous, abominable misleader of youth,        450
Falstaff, that old white-bearded Satan.

FALSTAFF    My lord, the man I know.

PRINCE    I know thou dost.

FALSTAFF    But to say I know more harm in him than in
myself were to say more than I know. That he is old, the        455
more the pity; his white hairs do witness it. But that he
is, saving your reverence, a whoremaster, that I utterly
deny. If sack and sugar be a fault, God help the wicked.
If to be old and merry be a sin, then many an old host
that I know is damned. If to be fat be to be hated, then        460
Pharaoh's lean kine are to be loved. No, my good lord,
banish Peto, banish Bardoll, banish Poins, but for sweet
Jack Falstaff, kind Jack Falstaff, true Jack Falstaff,
valiant Jack Falstaff, and therefore more valiant being

445  **cunning** skilful
  **craft** deceit, fraud
  **crafty** clever, ingenious
448  **take . . . you** explain your meaning
450–1  **misleader . . . Satan** Hal intensifies the criticism: no longer described
  as a morality play Vice-figure, Falstaff
  becomes here Satan himself.
452  **man** Falstaff emphasizes *man*; i.e.
  the man I know, but not this strange
  description of him.
457  **saving your reverence** an apolo-
  getic tag phrase used to introduce a
  disagreement or impropriety, usually
  spoken by a social inferior (cf. Dent,
  R93)

  **whoremaster** i.e. a villain, an evil-doer
458  **sack and sugar** See 1.2.108n.
459  **host** innkeeper
461  **Pharaoh's lean kine** a reference to
  Pharaoh's dream in Genesis, 41.1–31,
  in which seven emaciated *kine* (cattle
  or oxen) devour seven fat kine; Joseph
  interprets this as an indication that
  seven years of scarcity will follow
  seven years of plenty.
463–5  **sweet . . . . Falstaff** an interesting
  echo of Nashe, *Have with You*: 'curte-
  ous Dicke, comicall Dicke, liuely
  Dicke, louely Dicke, learned Dicke,
  olde *Dicke of Lichfield*' (Nashe, 3.5–6;
  cited by Evans)

458  God] Heauen *F*    461  lean] *Q2–F;* lane *Q1*

233

as he is old Jack Falstaff, banish not him thy Harry's     465
company, banish not him thy Harry's company. Banish
plump Jack and banish all the world.
      [*Loud knocking within. Exeunt Bardoll and Hostess.*]
PRINCE    I do; I will.


*Enter* BARDOLL *running.*

BARDOLL    O my lord, my lord, the sheriff with a most
      monstrous watch is at the door.                    470
FALSTAFF    Out, ye rogue! Play out the play. I have much
      to say in the behalf of that Falstaff.

---

467 SD *No direction exists in QF here,
but Bardoll and the Hostess must exit
somewhere in order to re-enter at 468
and 472 respectively. They could leave
earlier (perhaps at 386), but it is unlikely they would willingly leave the play-
acting. Many editions have proposed
the knocking of the Sheriff as the
impetus for their departure, though
usually one line later, after Hal's
response. This, however, creates the
awkwardness of an exit and an immediate re-entrance for Bardoll, with no
lines being spoken. This edition suggests that the Sheriff knocks just as
Falstaff finishes, Bardoll and the
Hostess respond to it, and Hal speaks
his final line more intimately to Falstaff
than the traditional arrangement allows.
468 **I do; I will** The sentence structure, as
GWW notes, is 'masterful': the first
clause is present and is all play; the second is future and is all serious. Though
the words can be spoken lightheartedly
(as in 1945 at the New Theatre, where
Michael Warre's Hal spoke them as he
playfully threw the cushion that served
as his crown at Falstaff), most recent
productions have Hal delivering this

line so that we sense the inevitability
of Falstaff's eventual rejection.
Sometimes Hal is clearly aware of what
this will cost him, as in 1955 at the Old
Vic, when Robert Hardy's Hal spoke
the second clause 'gently but with an
unshakeable resolution' and then 'with
tears in his eyes, caught the fat old rascal to him in a sudden hot embrace'
(Wood & Clark, 160); less sentimental-
ly, Alan Howard, at Stratford-upon-
Avon in 1975, gave the line 'a chilling
authority that stops the old knight dead
in his tracks' (*Guardian*, 25 April
1975). Although the line seems in most
modern productions central to the
understanding of the play, in the eighteenth and nineteenth centuries it was,
along with the rest of the *play extempore* (271), inevitably cut in performance. See p. 85.
469–70 **most monstrous** unusually large
470 **watch** group of citizens functioning
as watchmen
471 **Play . . . play** Falstaff is irritated at
the interruption, both enjoying the
sport and eager to continue his defence
of *that Falstaff.*

467 SD] *Steevens subst. after 468*    469 most] most most *F*    471 ye] you *Q2–F*

*Enter the* HOSTESS.

HOSTESS   O Jesu, my lord, my lord!

PRINCE   Hey, hey! The devil rides upon a fiddlestick.
What's the matter.                                                    475

HOSTESS   The sheriff and all the watch are at the door.
They are come to search the house. Shall I let them in?

FALSTAFF   Dost thou hear, Hal? Never call a true piece of
gold a counterfeit. Thou art essentially made without
seeming so.                                                          480

PRINCE   And thou a natural coward without instinct.

FALSTAFF   I deny your major. If you will deny the sheriff,
so; if not, let him enter. If I become not a cart as well as

---

474 **The . . . fiddlestick** i.e. something
important must be up; proverbial
(Dent, D263); cf. Heywood & Brome,
sig. F4ʳ: 'does the devil ride o' your fid-
dlesticks?'

478–9 **Never . . . counterfeit** an odd
remark, following the announcement
of the Sheriff's presence, but suggested perhaps by a play on *sheriff* and
'shroff', an expert retained to detect
counterfeit coin (noted by West, 545)

479–80 **Thou . . . so** i.e. you are true and
loyal even if your recent behaviour
doesn't show it (although *essentially
made* allows a significant ambiguity:
either 'made with a true essence', or 'in
fact constructed, made up'. The ambiguity here crystallizes the play's complex exploration of the nature and
source of value (see pp. 63–9). In F3–4
*made* is 'mad', a reading some editors,
e.g. Malone, Dover Wilson (Cam¹),
have adopted, meaning that Hal is
*essentially* (i.e. according to his
essence) the madcap prodigal (cf.
1.2.135) rather than a responsible
prince (who might turn Falstaff over
to the Sheriff), but the QF1–2 text
demands no emendation.

481 **And . . . instinct** The Prince parallels the structure of Falstaff's last sentence: you (i.e. Falstaff) are essentially
a coward and didn't run away in 2.2
because you recognized the Prince.

482 **deny your major** reject your logic;
*major* = major premise, the first term
in a syllogism. The syllogism presumably is: (a) major premise: all men who
run away are cowards; (b) minor
premise: Falstaff ran away; (c) conclusion: Falstaff is a coward. Falstaff
denies the *major premise*, in suggesting
that one might run away for various
reasons other than cowardice. Many
editors have also proposed a quibble on
'major' and 'mayor', assuming, with
Kittredge, that '*major* was almost or
quite identical in pronunciation with
*mayor*', but this seems unlikely;
although they could be spelled the
same way (e.g. F's '*Maior*' could represent either word), their pronunciations
would be so different as to make an
intended quibble impossible to recognize in the theatre.
**deny the sheriff** not allow the sheriff
to enter

483 **so** well and good

483–4 **If . . . man** 'if I am not as
impressive in the hangman's cart as

---

473 Jesu] *om.* F   474 SP] *Fal. Q4–F*   482 major] *(Maior), F (Maior)*

another man, a plague on my bringing up. I hope I shall
as soon be strangled with a halter as another.                              485

PRINCE    Go hide thee behind the arras. – The rest walk up
above. Now, my masters, for a true face and good
conscience.

FALSTAFF    Both which I have had, but their date is out;
and therefore I'll hide me. [*Hides behind the arras.*]        490
                                              [*Exeunt all but the Prince and Peto.*]

PRINCE    Call in the sheriff.

*Enter* Sheriff *and the* Carrier.

Now, master sheriff, what is your will with me?

SHERIFF

First, pardon me, my lord. A hue and cry
Hath followed certain men unto this house.

PRINCE    What men?                                                          495

SHERIFF

One of them is well known, my gracious lord,

the next man' (Falstaff is denying
that he is afraid and promising that
he will conduct himself bravely as he
is taken to the gallows, no doubt
delivering an impressive speech of
repentance)

484 **bringing up** upbringing (though
with a joke on being brought *up* or
summoned to the court for sentencing,
and perhaps led *up* the ladder to the
gallows)

485 **as . . . another** as willingly be hanged
as any other man (*as soon* also suggests
'as quickly', since his great weight
would ensure a quick death by hanging, as Wilson notes in Cam[1])

486 **arras** tapestry (originally from Arras,
in Picardy), usually hung somewhat
away from the wall to ensure it did not

mildew from the damp and, thus, permitting Falstaff's concealment; the
word may also suggests 'haras', an
enclosure used for breeding horses,
which is possibly what generates the
next phrase: 'snorting like a horse'
(noted by West, 552).

486–7 **walk up above** go upstairs (*above*
is a common stage direction indicating
the use of a gallery above the discovery
space, but here the characters, once
they exit, are not visible in the theatre)

489 **date is out** lease has expired, time
for that is past; proverbial (Dent,
D42.1)

493 **hue and cry** horns and voices raised
as a felon was pursued by citizens, but
the phrase comes to mean the group of
citizens themselves

490 SD1] *Oxf[1]* SD2 *Exeunt*] *Rowe*; *Exit. F*; *om. Q* all . . . *Peto*] *Johnson subst.*    492 Now]
*Theobald*; *Prin.* Now *QF*    493–4] *as Pope; prose QF*    496–7] *as Pope; prose QF*

A gross, fat man.

CARRIER    As fat as butter.

PRINCE

The man, I do assure you, is not here,

For I myself at this time have employed him.                    500

And, sheriff, I will engage my word to thee

That I will by tomorrow dinner-time

Send him to answer thee or any man

For anything he shall be charged withal.

And so let me entreat you leave the house.                      505

SHERIFF

I will, my lord. There are two gentlemen

Have in this robbery lost three hundred marks.

PRINCE

It may be so. If he have robbed these men,

He shall be answerable. And so, farewell.

SHERIFF    Good night, my noble lord.                          510

PRINCE

I think it is good morrow, is it not?

SHERIFF

Indeed, my lord, I think it be two o'clock.

*Exit [with Carrier].*

499 **not here** The Prince equivocates, but
what he says is literally true: Falstaff is
not in the exact space in which the
Prince is standing (and perhaps Hal
gestures to emphasize *here*) but behind
the arras. J. P. Kemble cut 499–500
from his acting edition, no doubt
because the equivocation seemed unbecoming to the Prince; cf. Steevens's
regret that Shakespeare allows Hal 'to
have recourse to absolute falsehood,
and that too uttered under the sanction
of so strong an assurance' (Steevens).
Nonetheless, he does *engage* himself
(501) for Falstaff's appearance.

501 **engage** pledge
502 **dinner-time** i.e. midday
503 **answer thee** appear before you
504 **withal** with
505 **entreat** The Prince's verb might
indicate the Prince's courtesy toward
the Sheriff, but might also be delivered
with sarcasm as he tries to ensure his
quick exit.
507 **three hundred marks** Cf. 2.1.54–5.
509 **answerable** held responsible
511 **morrow** morning
512 **be** is; Abbott (298) says that '*Be*
expresses more doubt than *is* after a
verb of thinking.'

507 three hundred] *(300.), F*    510 Good] *Q3–F;* God *Q1–2*    511 good] *Q3–F;* god *Q1–2*
512 SD *with Carrier*] *Hanmer subst.*

237

PRINCE    This oily rascal is known as well as Paul's. Go call
 him forth.

PETO  [*Pulls back the arras.*]    Falstaff! Fast asleep behind  515
 the arras and snorting like a horse.

PRINCE    Hark how hard he fetches breath. Search his
 pockets. (*Peto searcheth his pocket and findeth certain
 papers.*) What hast thou found?

PETO    Nothing but papers, my lord.        520

PRINCE    Let's see what they be. Read them.

PETO  [*Reads.*]

| | |
|---|---|
| *Item: a capon* | *2s. 2d.* |
| *Item: sauce* | *4d.* |
| *Item: sack, two gallons* | *5s. 8d.* |
| *Item: anchovies and sack after supper* | *2s. 6d.* 525 |
| *Item: bread* | *ob.* |

PRINCE    O monstrous! But one halfpennyworth of bread
 to this intolerable deal of sack! What there is else keep
 close; we'll read it at more advantage. There let him

---

513  **oily rascal** shifty scoundrel (*OED* 3,
using this example); *rascal* also means a
lean deer; see 2.2.5n.
 **Paul's** St. Paul's cathedral, the most
conspicuous and best-known building
in Elizabethan London, destroyed in
the fire of 1666
517  **fetches breath** snores
518–19 SD In some productions, Peto
closes the curtain immediately after
searching Falstaff's pocket or searches
with one hand while holding the curtain open with the other. The singular
*pocket* of the SD after the *pockets*, 518,
of the dialogue seems a theatrical
adjustment to speed the stage business.
522  *Item* used to introduce articles in a
list; from Latin for 'likewise'
 *2s. 2d.* 2 shillings and 2 pence (the
abbreviations of shilling and pence

actually are abbreviations of Latin
words: 's.' is an abbreviation of *sester-
tius* and 'd.' of *denarius*, both small silver coins of ancient Rome). In the
English monetary system before it was
officially decimalized on 15 February
1971, 20 shillings made up a pound
and there were 12 pence to the shilling.
525  *anchovies* small, salted fish often used
to provoke thirst (like salted nuts today);
cf. Bullokar, who says they are 'used by
gallants to draw downe drinke'.
526  *ob.* abbreviation of *obolus*, a small silver coin of ancient Greece, which came
to mean any small coin, esp. a halfpenny
527  **halfpennyworth** pronounced hay-
pennyworth
528  **intolerable deal** excessive quantity
529  **close** secret
 **more advantage** a more suitable time

---

515 SD] *Collier³ subst.* 518 SD *Peto*] *Capell; He QF* *pocket*] *pockets Q4–F* 519 What] *Hanmer;
Pr.* What *QF* 521 they be] be they: *Q4–F* 522 SP] *F; om. Q* SD] *Capell* 527 SP] *F; om. Q*

sleep till day. I'll to the court in the morning. We must          530
all to the wars, and thy place shall be honourable. I'll
procure this fat rogue a charge of foot, and I know his
death will be a march of twelvescore. The money shall
be paid back again with advantage. Be with me betimes
in the morning, and so good morrow, Peto.                         535

PETO   Good morrow, good my lord.

*[The Prince closes the arras, and] exeunt.*

**3.1**   *Enter* HOTSPUR, WORCESTER, Lord MORTIMER
          *[and]* Owen GLENDOWER.

MORTIMER

These promises are fair, the parties sure,
And our induction full of prosperous hope.

HOTSPUR   Lord Mortimer and cousin Glendower, will you

---

530  **day** daylight
532  **charge of foot** command of an
     infantry unit
533  **twelvescore** i.e. 240 yards
     **The money** i.e. the money that was
     robbed from the travellers at Gad's
     Hill
534  **advantage** interest
     **betimes** early
536 SD *There is no direction in QF for
     the arras to be drawn, but the scene
     ends with Falstaff still asleep, and the
     actor must be allowed to leave the stage
     (probably through a stage door over
     which the arras is hanging; though see
     518–19n.). It isn't obvious who draws
     the curtain, but the action seems more
     pointed if it is Hal rather than Peto. In
     a modern theatre, where act changes
     are often marked with blackouts, the
     action is not necessary.
3.1  Shakespeare gives no location for this
     scene, but a meeting of Glendower,
     Mortimer and Hotspur, according

to Holinshed, did take place 'in the
house of the archdeacon of Bangor'
(Holinshed, 3.521) in northern Wales; cf.
3.1.70: 'the Archdeacon hath divided it'.
1  **promises are fair** offers of support
   bode well
   **sure** reliable
2  **induction** beginning (also a technical
   term for the preparatory scene for a
   play, as in *TS*)
   **prosperous hope** hopes of success
3–11  *\*Lord . . . of* Q prints this as prose;
   F sets 3–9 as verse, though perhaps
   only to use up space (see p. 126).
   Hotspur's anxious speech (3–5) seems
   metrically too uncertain to be confidently rendered as verse, but in
   Glendower's lines beginning at 7 the
   iambic pattern clearly returns as he
   tries to calm Hotspur.
3  **cousin** a more general term of relatedness than in its modern usage;
   Glendower is Hotspur's brother-in-
   law's father-in-law.

---

533  march] *match Q4–F*   536 SD *The . . . and] this edn*   3.1.0.1 *and] Rowe*   3–5 Lord . . . map!]
*F lines Glendower, / downe? / it, / Mappe. /*

    sit down? And uncle Worcester – A plague upon it, I
    have forgot the map!                                                    5
GLENDOWER   No, here it is. Sit, cousin Percy.
    Sit, good cousin Hotspur, for by that name,
    As oft as Lancaster doth speak of you,
    His cheek looks pale, and with a rising sigh
    He wisheth you in heaven.
HOTSPUR                And you in hell                     10
    As oft as he hears Owen Glendower spoke of.
GLENDOWER
    I cannot blame him. At my nativity
    The front of heaven was full of fiery shapes,
    Of burning cressets; and at my birth

---

**4–6 I . . . is** A map must be physically present (one of two required by Shakespeare; the other in *KL* 1.1.36), but, since it isn't clear exactly what gesture accompanies Glendower's *here it is*, no SD is provided. Perhaps he pulls it out from a pouch he wears or merely indicates that it is inside his jacket; perhaps he spots it rolled up somewhere on Hotspur's person and pulls it out, which would be particularly effective if Hotspur had been anxiously patting his jacket as he searched for it; perhaps the map is already unrolled upon a table and Glendower merely points to it, which would make more obvious the irony of Hotspur characteristically forgetting the very thing that so much exercises him here.

**8 Lancaster** i.e. Henry IV, who held title to the Duchy of Lancaster from his father, John of Gaunt, who had succeeded to it through his wife's right. Henry, when he returned to England from his exile in France, protested that he had come not to take the crown but only to claim his inheritance: cf. *R2*

2.3.113: 'I come for Lancaster.' Glendower's reference to Henry by his ducal rather than his royal title not only is disrespectful (cf. 62, where Glendower calls the King *Bolingbroke*) but also reflects Glendower's support of Mortimer's title to the throne. On the Duchy of Lancaster, see Dutton.

**9 rising sigh** passionate groan; cf. Nathaniel Lee, *Caesar Borgia* (1680): 'though trembling thus from head to foot, / I will be calm, press down the rising sighs, / And stifle all the swellings in my heart' (Lee, 35).

**12 At my nativity** Holinshed writes, 'Strange wonders happened (as men reported) at the natiuitie of this man, for the same night he was borne, all his fathers horsses in the stable were found to stand in bloud vp to the bellies' (3.521).

**13 front** face (and at 37)

**14 cressets** i.e. stars (literally torches in small iron baskets set on poles for light); cf. Cotgrave, '*Falot*': 'a cresset light (such as they use in playhouses) . . . put into small cages of iron'.

---

6–10 No . . . heaven.] *as Staunton; prose Q; F lines* is: / Hotspurre: / you, / sigh, / Heauen. /
9 cheek looks] Cheekes looke *F*   sigh] sight *Q2–4*   10–11 And . . . of.] *as Collier; prose QF*

The frame and huge foundation of the earth                    15
Shaked like a coward.

HOTSPUR   Why, so it would have done at the same season
   if your mother's cat had but kittened, though yourself
   had never been born.

GLENDOWER
   I say the earth did shake when I was born.                  20

HOTSPUR
   And I say the earth was not of my mind,
   If you suppose as fearing you it shook.

GLENDOWER
   The heavens were all on fire; the earth did tremble.

HOTSPUR
   O, then the earth shook to see the heavens on fire
   And not in fear of your nativity.                           25
   Diseased nature oftentimes breaks forth
   In strange eruptions. Oft the teeming earth
   Is with a kind of colic pinched and vexed
   By the imprisoning of unruly wind
   Within her womb, which for enlargement striving           30
   Shakes the old beldam earth and topples down

17 **season** time
22 **as fearing you** because it feared you
26 **Diseased** diseasèd: disturbed, disordered; as well as sick
27–32 **Oft . . . towers** In *VA* 1,046–7, Shakespeare invokes the same explanation for earthquakes: 'As when the wind imprison'd in the ground. / Struggling for passage, earth's foundation shakes'. This was the current state of Renaissance scientific understanding; cf. David Person's account: 'dry and cold exhalations . . . enclosed within the bowels and concavities of the earth (for nature hath no vacuity) and there converted into winds, doe struggle and strive as it were, to burst up through this earth to attaine to its right place, which is upwards, and that is the cause of this trembling and motion of the earth which we call Earthquakes' (*Varieties*, sig. F8$^{r-v}$).
27 **eruptions** outbreaks
   **teeming** fertile, fruitful
28 **colic** an irritation of the stomach producing painful spasms
30 **womb** belly
   **for enlargement striving** seeking for release
31 **beldam** grandmother (or old lady)

15 and huge] and *Q2–F*   24] *F lines* shooke / fire, /   27 eruptions.] *F (*eruptions;*)*; eruptions, *Q* Oft] of *Q4*; and *Q5–F*   31 topples] tombles *F*

241

> Steeples and moss-grown towers. At your birth
> Our grandam earth, having this distemperature,
> In passion shook.

GLENDOWER Cousin, of many men

> I do not bear these crossings. Give me leave                    35
> To tell you once again that at my birth
> The front of heaven was full of fiery shapes,
> The goats ran from the mountains, and the herds
> Were strangely clamorous to the frighted fields.
> These signs have marked me extraordinary,                       40
> And all the courses of my life do show
> I am not in the roll of common men.
> Where is he living, clipped in with the sea
> That chides the banks of England, Scotland, Wales,
> Which calls me pupil or hath read to me?                        45
> And bring him out that is but woman's son
> Can trace me in the tedious ways of art
> And hold me pace in deep experiments.

HOTSPUR

> I think there's no man speaks better Welsh.

---

33 **grandam earth** grandmother earth;
cf. Dekker, *The Raven's Almanac*
(Grosart, 4.205): 'our aged Grandam
(the earth)'.
**distemperature** disorder

34 **passion** distress, suffering
**of** from

35 **bear these crossings** tolerate these
affronts or contradictions

39 **frighted fields** fields pervaded by
fear; cf. Milton, *Paradise Lost*, 2.993–5:
'such a numerous host / Fled not in
silence through the frighted deep'
(*OED* ¶b gives Milton as the earliest
example of this usage).

40 **extraordinary** All six syllables are
required by the metre, as at 3.2.78.

41 **all the courses** the entire progress

42 **roll** list

43 **clipped in with** surrounded by

44 **chides** contends with, beats against

45 who can claim to be my teacher (*read
to* = instructed, tutored)

46 and show me any mere mortal

47 **Can trace** who can follow
**tedious . . . art** demanding proceedings of magic

48 **hold me pace** keep up with me
**deep experiments** abstruse investi-
gations

49 **speaks better Welsh** There is some
obvious insult here, but it isn't clear
whether the phrase means 'utters more
nonsense' or 'brags more outrageously'.
Oxf emends *speaks* to 'speaketh' to
standardize the metre; Pope, for the

35 crossings] crossing *Q3–4*   43 he] the *Q4–F*   44 Wales] and Wales *Q5–F*

I'll to dinner.                                                                    50

MORTIMER

Peace, cousin Percy; you will make him mad.

GLENDOWER

I can call spirits from the vasty deep.

HOTSPUR

Why, so can I, or so can any man,

But will they come when you do call for them?

GLENDOWER

Why, I can teach you, cousin, to command the devil.          55

HOTSPUR

And I can teach thee, coz, to shame the devil:

By telling truth. 'Tell truth, and shame the devil.'

If thou have power to raise him, bring him hither,

And I'll be sworn I have power to shame him hence.

O, while you live, 'tell truth and shame the devil'.          60

MORTIMER

Come, come, no more of this unprofitable chat.

GLENDOWER

Three times hath Henry Bolingbroke made head

Against my power; thrice from the banks of Wye

And sandy-bottomed Severn have I sent him

---

same end, changed Q's 'theres' at the
beginning of the line to 'there is'. The
fact that there are multiple ways of
emending the line to produce regular
blank verse may itself argue against
the practice of editorial regularization.
52 **call** summon up
   **vasty** immense; a poetical form of
   'vast'; cf. *H5* 2.2.123: 'vasty Tartar'.
54 Hotspur interprets Glendower's *call*
   (52) to mean 'call to'; cf. Nashe,
   *Unfortunate Traveller* (1594): 'heauens
   will not alwayes come to witnes when
   they are cald' (Nashe, 2.259; cited

Cam[1]). The question, assumed by
Hotspur and most readers to be purely
rhetorical, receives an answer, however, at 226–8.
57, 60 **Tell . . . devil** proverbial (Dent,
   T566)
62–5 **Three . . . back** in 1400, 1403 and
   1405 (though this last action happened
   after the events the play represents)
62 **made head** took military action
63 **power** army, forces
   **Wye** a river on the Welsh–English borders; see Fig. 21.
64 **Severn** See 1.3.98n. and Fig. 21.

55 you] thee *Q5–F*    56 coz] *(coose); coosen Q5;* Cousin *F*    57 'Tell . . . devil.'] *this edn;* Tel . . .
deuil: *Q; Tell . . . Deuill. F*    60 'tell . . . devil'] *this edn;* tel . . . deuil *QF*    64 sent] hent *Q4–F*

Bootless home and weather-beaten back.                              65
HOTSPUR

Home without boots, and in foul weather too!

How scapes he agues, in the devil's name?
GLENDOWER

Come, here is the map. Shall we divide our right

According to our threefold order ta'en?
MORTIMER

The Archdeacon hath divided it                                     70

Into three limits very equally:

England, from Trent and Severn hitherto,

By south and east is to my part assigned;

All westward, Wales beyond the Severn shore

And all the fertile land within that bound,                        75

To Owen Glendower; – and, dear coz, to you

The remnant northward lying off from Trent.

And our indentures tripartite are drawn,

65 **Bootless** unsuccessful
   **weather-beaten** defeated by the weather; cf. Holinshed, who says Glendower was successful because '(as was thought) through art magike, he caused such foule weather of winds, tempests, raine snow, and haile to be raised, for the annoiance of the kings armie' (3.520).
66 **without boots** Hotspur literalizes the image, as is characteristic of his verbal play (see 2.3.73).
67 **agues** fevers
68 **right** legitimate claim
69 **threefold order ta'en** three-party agreement
70 **Archdeacon** anonymous character, nowhere else mentioned in the play, but derived from Holinshed's account of the meeting of the rebels at the home of the Archdeacon of Bangor;

see 3.1n.
71 **limits** portions
72 **hitherto** to this point (Mortimer presumably calls attention to the boundaries on the map)
72–7 According to Holinshed, 'all England from Seuerne and Trent, south and eastward, was assigned to the earle of March: all Wales, & the lands beyond Seuerne westward, were appointed to Owen Glendouer: and all the remnant from Trent northward to the lord Persie' (3.521).
77 **off from Trent** with the river Trent as the southern boundary (see Fig. 21)
78 **indentures tripartite** three-party contract; Holinshed says that Mortimer, Glendower and Hotspur 'diuided the realme amongst them, causing a tripartite indenture to be made and sealed', but a marginal note

66] *F lines* Bootes, / too, /    68] *F lines* Mappe: / Right, /    here is] heere's *F*    map.] *Oxf¹*; map, *Q;* Mappe: *F*

244

Which, being sealed interchangeably –
A business that this night may execute – 80
Tomorrow, cousin Percy, you and I
And my good lord of Worcester will set forth
To meet your father and the Scottish power,
As is appointed us, at Shrewsbury.
My father Glendower is not ready yet, 85
Nor shall we need his help these fourteen days.
[*to Glendower*] Within that space you may have drawn
    together
Your tenants, friends and neighbouring gentlemen.

GLENDOWER

A shorter time shall send me to you, lords;
And in my conduct shall your ladies come, 90
From whom you now must steal and take no leave,
For there will be a world of water shed
Upon the parting of your wives and you.

HOTSPUR

Methinks my moiety, north from Burton here,
In quantity equals not one of yours. 95
See how this river comes me cranking in
And cuts me from the best of all my land

there points to the irony: 'a diuision of that which they had not' (Holinshed, 3.521). A Scottish reader about 1630 notes in his copy of the 1623 folio: 'The Kingdome shared in the Imagination of the conspirators' (Yamada, 115).
    **drawn** drafted, drawn up
79 **sealed interchangeably** sealèd (so each party has a copy with a seal and signature from the other two)
80 **this . . . execute** may be completed tonight
84 **is appointed** has been agreed by
    **Shrewsbury**, town in Shropshire on the Severn near the Welsh border (see

Fig. 21); pronounced 'Shròse-bry' (although local pronunciation today is as often 'Shroos-bry')
85 **father** father-in-law
90 **in my conduct** escorted by me
92 **world of water** i.e. many tears; *world* = a great quantity (*OED* IIc)
94 **moiety** share, portion (not 'half')
    **Burton** Burton-upon-Trent, a town on the Trent, about 25 miles north-east of Leicester; see Fig. 21.
96 **comes . . . in** bends into my part (*me* = to my cost; see Abbott, 220)
97 **best . . . land** The Trent, which flows approximately in a 'V' shape, turns north-east near Burton-upon-Trent

87 SD] *Capell*

A huge half-moon, a monstrous scantle, out.
I'll have the current in this place dammed up,
And here the smug and silver Trent shall run                    100
In a new channel fair and evenly.
It shall not wind with such a deep indent
To rob me of so rich a bottom here.

GLENDOWER

Not wind? It shall; it must. You see it doth.

MORTIMER

Yea, but mark how he bears his course and runs me up       105
With like advantage on the other side,
Gelding the opposed continent as much
As on the other side it takes from you.

towards the Humber, and so, according to the proposed division, would deprive Hotspur of Lincolnshire and part of Nottinghamshire; see Fig. 21. Walter (138) argues that the episode might have a topical resonance, referring to a land dispute between the Earl of Shrewsbury and the Stanhope family over an oxbow at Shelford-on-Trent, and which Shrewsbury pre-empted by having a channel dug to change the flow of the river.

98 **scantle** small piece; the Folio reads 'Cantle' (i.e. a segment cut off some larger whole), and most editions follow this, but all the quartos print 'scantle' (i.e. a small piece), and, while this might merely be the result of the final 's' in *monstrous* somehow being carried over to the next word, it is, significantly, what Sir John Suckling remembers of the text in a letter where he talks about going to see the river, 'about the uneven running of which, my friend Mr *William Shakespeare* makes *Henry Hotspur* quarrel so highly with his

Fellow-Rebels; and for his sake I have been somewhat curious to consider the scantlet of ground' (Suckling, 1.144). Q's 'monstruous scantle' is, as Humphreys says, 'a virtual contradiction in terms' (Ard², lxxiv), but such illogic is in fact characteristic of Hotspur when he becomes angry.

100 **smug** smooth
101 **fair and evenly** in a direct line (cf. *trim and neatly*, 1.3.33)
102 **indent** indentation
103 **bottom** river valley
105 **Yea ... up** The line is hypermetrical, but the initial *Yea, but* can be considered an exclamatory addition to emphasize Mortimer's effort to placate Hotspur.
107 **Gelding ... much** cutting as large a piece out of the opposite bank; Mortimer here echoes Hotspur's idiom, perhaps as a conscious strategy, trying to reason with him, and the verb continues the horse image prevalent in the play; see 1.1.60, 63n.
**opposed** opposèd

98 scantle] Cantle *F*   99 dammed] *(damnd), Rowe (damm'd)*   104 wind?] *Q2–F;* wind *Q1*
105–8] *as Pope; prose Q; F lines* course, / side, / much, / you. /

WORCESTER

    Yea, but a little charge will trench him here,

    And on this north side win this cape of land,                    110

    And then he runs straight and even.

HOTSPUR

    I'll have it so; a little charge will do it.

GLENDOWER

    I'll not have it altered.

HOTSPUR                    Will not you?

GLENDOWER

    No, nor you shall not.

HOTSPUR                    Who shall say me nay?

GLENDOWER    Why, that will I.                    115

HOTSPUR    Let me not understand you, then: speak it in
    Welsh.

GLENDOWER

    I can speak English, lord, as well as you,

    For I was trained up in the English court,

    Where, being but young, I framed to the harp                    120

    Many an English ditty lovely well

    And gave the tongue a helpful ornament –

109 **charge** expense
    **trench him** divert it by means of a
    trench (*OED v.* 4a); the river is
    referred to by the masculine pronoun
    (again at 111).
110 **this cape** this spur of land; Worcester
    is obviously pointing at the map.
115 The short prose line, following the
    two previous shared lines of verse con-
    frontation, allows for a strained silence
    before Hotspur tries to defuse it with a
    tactless joke.
116–17 **speak . . . Welsh** i.e. I'll be sure
    not to understand it
119 **I . . . court** Cf. Holinshed, who says
    that Glendower first 'set to studie the

lawes of the realme, and became an
vtter barrister, or an apprentise of the
lawe, . . . and serued King Richard at
Flint castell . . . though other haue written that he serued this king Henrie the
fourth, before he came to atteine the
crowne, in roome of an espquier'
(3.518).
120 **framed to** composed for (framèd)
121 **ditty** lyrics of a song
122 **gave . . . ornament** perhaps means
that he made the English language
more beautiful by speaking it with his
Welsh lilt, or, more likely, that he
enriched the language with his literary
achievement

A virtue that was never seen in you.

HOTSPUR

    Marry, and I am glad of it, with all my heart.

    I had rather be a kitten and cry 'mew'             125

    Than one of these same metre ballad-mongers.

    I had rather hear a brazen can'stick turned

    Or a dry wheel grate on the axle-tree,

    And that would set my teeth nothing on edge,

    Nothing so much as mincing poetry.            130

    'Tis like the forced gait of a shuffling nag.

GLENDOWER    Come, you shall have Trent turned.

HOTSPUR

    I do not care. I'll give thrice so much land

    To any well-deserving friend;

    But, in the way of bargain, mark ye me,       135

    I'll cavil on the ninth part of a hair.

    Are the indentures drawn? Shall we be gone?

GLENDOWER

    The moon shines fair. You may away by night.

---

124 Hotspur is delighted that he has no skill in poetry, which he views as a courtly affectation unbecoming to a true soldier.

126 **metre ballad-mongers** peddlers of jangling ballads; cf. William Webbe, *A Discourse of English Poetry*, 'the vncountable rabble of ryming Ballet Makers' (Smith, 1.246).

127 **brazen can'stick turned** brass candlestick formed on a lathe (which produced a sharp grating noise as the metal was worked)

128 **dry** unlubricated
    **axle-tree** axle

129 **nothing** not at all

130 **mincing** affected, self-consciously dainty; cf. Vaughan, sig. Y4$^r$: 'Sundry times haue I beene conuersant with such, as blasphemed Poetry, by calling it mincing and lying Poetry.'

131 **forced . . . nag** awkward stride of a hobbled horse; Hotspur ironically makes use of a striking metaphor to express his dislike of poetry, which presents the opposite of Gabriel Harvey's definition of good verse as being like 'a good horse, that trippeth not once in a iourney' (Smith, 1.96) and the metre of the line is itself mimetic of the action.

132 Glendower picks up Hotspur's earlier use of *turned*, 127, as he returns the conversation to the proposed division of the land.

136 **cavil on** argue over

125 'mew'] *Ard²;* mew *QF*   126 metre] *(miter), F (Meeter)*   ballad-mongers] *(ballet mongers), F (Ballad-mongers)*   127 can'stick] *(cansticke);* Candlestick *F*   129 on] *(an), Q3*

I'll haste the writer, and withal
Break with your wives of your departure hence.                140
I am afraid my daughter will run mad,
So much she doteth on her Mortimer.                *Exit.*

MORTIMER

Fie, cousin Percy, how you cross my father!

HOTSPUR

I cannot choose. Sometime he angers me
With telling me of the moldwarp and the ant,                145
Of the dreamer Merlin and his prophecies,
And of a dragon and a finless fish,
A clip-winged griffin and a moulten raven,
A couching lion and a ramping cat,
And such a deal of skimble-skamble stuff                150
As puts me from my faith. I tell you what:

---

139 **haste the writer** make the scrivener (who is drawing up the clean copy of the indentures) hurry
**withal** also, at the same time
140 **Break with** break the news to
143 **cross** antagonize
144 **choose** help it
**Sometime** occasionally
145–50 **moldwarp . . . stuff** Hotspur impatiently lists examples of what he feels is the pretentious nonsense that Glendower speaks. A Scottish reader about 1630 notes here in his copy of the 1623 Folio: 'Tediousnesse of Incredible talk' (Yamada, 115). The language here is drawn from Holinshed's account of the division of the map, which was drawn in accordance with 'a vaine prophesie, as though king henrie was the moldwarpe, curssed of Gods owne mouth, and they three were the dragon, the lion, and the woolfe, which should diuide this realme betweene them' (3.521).

145 **moldwarp . . . ant** i.e. one of Glendower's numerous prophecies and maxims; *moldwarp* = mole (and refers to Henry IV; see previous note)
146 **dreamer Merlin** wizard at King Arthur's court in the legendary history of Britain, whose putative prophecies were often invoked and circulated in the sixteenth century at times of political crisis (see Dobin, 20–45)
148 **griffin** a mythical beast, half lion, half eagle
**moulten** having moulted (archaic past participle of 'moult' = shed)
149 **couching** lying down (an anglicized version of the heraldic term 'couchant')
**ramping** rearing (an anglicized version of the heraldic term 'rampant')
150 **skimble-skamble stuff** ridiculous talk
151 **puts . . . faith** makes me reject my religion (not literal, but more like the modern 'drives me crazy')

138] *F lines* faire, / Night:/

He held me last night at least nine hours
In reckoning up the several devils' names
That were his lackeys. I cried, 'Hum!' and 'Well, go to',
But marked him not a word. O, he is as tedious          155
As a tired horse, a railing wife,
Worse than a smoky house. I had rather live
With cheese and garlic in a windmill, far,
Than feed on cates and have him talk to me
In any summer-house in Christendom.          160

MORTIMER

In faith, he is a worthy gentleman,
Exceedingly well read and profited
In strange concealments, valiant as a lion,
And wondrous affable, and as bountiful
As mines of India. Shall I tell you, cousin?          165
He holds your temper in a high respect
And curbs himself even of his natural scope
When you come cross his humour; faith, he does.

153 **several** various
154 **lackeys** attendants
155 **marked ... word** paid him no attention
156–7 **railing . . . house** proverbially two of man's worst afflictions: 'A smoking house and a chiding wife make man run out of doors' (Dent, H781); cf. *AW* 2.3.290–1: 'Wars is no strife / To the dark house and the detested wife.'
158 i.e. poorly and uncomfortably; cheese and onions were proverbially the food of the poor (cf. Heywood, *Captives*, 4.1.485, where 'the poore' are said to fill their bellies 'with cheese and onions'); and windmills were notoriously noisy and unsteady (cf.

Jonson, *Epicoene*, 5.3.61–3, Jonson, 5.258: 'My very house turnes round with the tumult! I dwell in a windmill!').
159 **cates** delicacies
160 **summer-house** a rich man's country residence
162–3 **profited ... concealments** proficient in occult arts
165 **mines of India** commonplace image of great wealth (confusing India and the new colonies in the West Indies, which were thought to have great quantities of gold)
166 **temper** temperament, character
167 **curbs . . . scope** restrains his most instinctive reactions
168 **come ... humour** i.e. provoke him

154] *F lines* Lacqueyes: / too, / 'Hum!'] *Ard²*; hum, *QF* 'Well, go to'] *Ard²*; wel go to *QF* 161 is] was *Q3–F* 162 Exceedingly] Exceeding *Q3–F* 163–5] *F lines* Concealements: / affable, / India. / Cousin, / 168 come] doe *F*

I warrant you, that man is not alive
Might so have tempted him as you have done                    170
Without the taste of danger and reproof.
But do not use it oft, let me entreat you.
WORCESTER [*to Hotspur*]
In faith, my lord, you are too wilful-blame
And, since your coming hither, have done enough
To put him quite besides his patience.                    175
You must needs learn, lord, to amend this fault.
Though sometimes it show greatness, courage, blood
(And that's the dearest grace it renders you),
Yet oftentimes it doth present harsh rage,
Defect of manners, want of government,                    180
Pride, haughtiness, opinion and disdain,
The least of which haunting a nobleman
Loseth men's hearts and leaves behind a stain
Upon the beauty of all parts besides,
Beguiling them of commendation.                    185
HOTSPUR
Well I am schooled. Good manners be your speed.

---

170 **tempted** provoked
171 **danger and reproof** dangerous rebuke
172 **use it oft** make a habit of it (i.e. this provocative behaviour)
173 **wilful-blame** culpable for excessive wilfulness (*OED* blame *v.* 6)
175 **besides his patience** beyond the bounds of his self-control
176 **must needs** have to
177 **show** testifies to, reveals
   **blood** spirit
178 **dearest grace** best advantage
   **renders** offers, supplies
179 **present** indicate
180 **want of government** lack of self-control
181 **opinion** conceit, arrogance (*OED* 4†c)

182 **haunting** appearing in
184 **parts besides** other qualities or accomplishments
185 cheating them of their deserved praise
186 **Well . . . schooled** I am well instructed; many editions read 'Well, I am schooled' (as in F), a more heavy-handed sarcasm, but Q has no punctuation after 'Well'.
   **Good . . . speed** may your good manners bring you success (in battle). In the eighteenth and nineteenth centuries, the scene often ended here, as in Betterton's 1700 version (Q9), not only keeping the focus on the political action but also avoiding the need for Welsh speakers and an actress who can sing.

173 SD] *Folg²*    175 besides] beside *Q2*

251

*Enter* GLENDOWER *with the* LADIES [PERCY *and* MORTIMER].

Here come our wives, and let us take our leave.
[*Lady Mortimer speaks to Mortimer in Welsh.*]
MORTIMER

This is the deadly spite that angers me:
My wife can speak no English, I no Welsh.
GLENDOWER

My daughter weeps; she'll not part with you.                    190
She'll be a soldier, too; she'll to the wars.
MORTIMER

Good father, tell her that she and my aunt Percy
Shall follow in your conduct speedily.
*Glendower speaks to her in Welsh, and she answers him
in the same.*
GLENDOWER

She is desperate here – a peevish, self-willed harlotry,
One that no persuasion can do good upon.                        195
*The Lady speaks in Welsh.*

---

187 **and** Unlike modern English grammar, sixteenth-century usage permitted a conjunction to join an affirmation
and a command; cf. 5.4.33.
188 **deadly spite** terrible problem
192 **my aunt Percy** At 2.3.78, Lady Percy
refers to *my brother Mortimer*, and historically the Edmund Mortimer who
married Glendower's daughter was her
brother (but not the designated heir to
the throne); see List of Roles, 9–10n.
193 **in your conduct** along with you
193 SD See Fig. 20 for a page of the
prompt copy from the 1964 RSC production, directed by John Barton and
Peter Hall, which provides a sample of
the Welsh that must be spoken.
Shakespeare's own company must have

had at least two actors who either were
Welsh or could passably speak the language. Welsh was increasingly heard on
the Elizabethan and Jacobean stage, e.g.
in Dekker, *Patient Grissel* and
Middleton, *A Chaste Maid in
Cheapside.*
194 **desperate here** miserable because of
what they are talking about (i.e. his
departure)
**peevish . . . harlotry** bad-tempered,
headstrong hussy; cf. *RJ* 4.2.14, 'a
peevish self-will'd harlotry it is',
though Glendower's usage is far more
affectionate than Capulet's.
195 **do good upon** have any positive
influence on

186.1]; *after* 187 *QF* PERCY *and* MORTIMER] *Dyce subst.*    187 SD] *Oxf* our] your *Q3–F*    SD]
194–5] *as Pope; Q lines* here, / doe / vpon. /; *F lines* heere: / Harlotry, / vpon. /

MORTIMER

I understand thy looks. That pretty Welsh,
Which thou pourest down from these swelling heavens,
I am too perfect in, and but for shame
In such a parley should I answer thee.
*The Lady [speaks] again in Welsh.*

MORTIMER

I understand thy kisses, and thou mine, 200
And that's a feeling disputation;
But I will never be a truant, love,
Till I have learnt thy language, for thy tongue
Makes Welsh as sweet as ditties highly penned,
Sung by a fair queen in a summer's bower 205
With ravishing division to her lute.

GLENDOWER

Nay, if you melt, then will she run mad.
*The Lady speaks again in Welsh.*

MORTIMER

O, I am ignorance itself in this!

GLENDOWER

She bids you on the wanton rushes lay you down
And rest your gentle head upon her lap, 210

---

196 **pretty Welsh** i.e. her tears (perhaps a pun on Welsh and 'wash')
197 **swelling heavens** i.e. eyes brimming with tears
198 **I . . . in** I understand only too well
199 **parley** language, discourse
201 **feeling disputation** i.e. heartfelt conversation without the use of words; *feeling* suggests both 'in sympathy' and 'through touch'; cf. Marlowe, *Hero and Leander*: 'These lovers parled by the touch of hands' (Marlowe, 1.193).
202 **be a truant** cease trying
204 **highly penned** written in lofty style

206 **ravishing division** delightful variations (*division* is a technical term in musicology referring to an elaboration of a musical phrase by dividing a simple succession of long notes into an intricate run of short ones, *OED* †7)
207 **you melt** you give way to your feelings (*you* is stressed, as is *she* later in the line)
208 **this** i.e. the Welsh language
209 **wanton rushes** lush covering of reeds (on the floor, as there would have been in the theatre itself)

---

199 SD *speaks*] *Malone*  204 sweet] sweets *Q5*  207 you] thou *Q4–F*  209] *F lines* you, / downe, /

253

And she will sing the song that pleaseth you,
And on your eyelids crown the god of sleep,
Charming your blood with pleasing heaviness,
Making such difference 'twixt wake and sleep
As is the difference betwixt day and night          215
The hour before the heavenly harnessed team
Begins his golden progress in the east.

MORTIMER
With all my heart, I'll sit and hear her sing.
By that time will our book, I think, be drawn.

GLENDOWER
Do so, and those musicians that shall play to you          220
Hang in the air a thousand leagues from hence,
And straight they shall be here. Sit and attend.

HOTSPUR
Come, Kate; thou art perfect in lying down.
Come, quick, quick, that I may lay my head in thy lap.          224

LADY PERCY    Go, ye giddy goose!          *The music plays.*

HOTSPUR
Now I perceive the devil understands Welsh,
And 'tis no marvel he is so humorous.

---

212 **crown . . . sleep** give sleep dominion
213 **heaviness** drowsiness
216 **heavenly harnessed team** i.e. sun
(from the classical image of the horse-
drawn chariot driven by the sun-god,
Helios)
217 **progress** journey, but particularly
the official travel of royalty (*OED n.* 2),
emphasizing the sun's dignity
219 **book** documents of agreement, cf.
78–9
  **drawn** drawn up in a final, clean copy
221 i.e. are spirits (*leagues* = units of distance, each about three miles)
222 **straight** immediately
223–5 **perfect . . . goose** The good-
natured sexual play compares interest-

ingly with the similar but far more
disturbing scene in *Ham* 3.2.113–23.
226 In response to the music, Hotspur
jokingly admits that Glendower seemingly has successfully called musicians
'a thousand leagues from hence', 221,
as GWW observes. Hotspur gibes that
he is not surprised to discover that
Welsh can be used to call satanic spirits, though he is presumably aware, as
is the audience of the play, that the
musicians in the theatre company are
most likely sitting behind a curtain in
the music gallery and so might indeed
be said to 'Hang in the air', 221.
227 i.e. no wonder the devil is so capri-
cious (since he can speak Welsh)

---

211 song] sung *Q4*    214 'twixt] betwixt *Q4–F*    220] *F lines* so: / you, /    221 hence] thence *Q4–F*

By'r Lady, he is a good musician.

LADY PERCY

Then should you be nothing but musical,

For you are altogether governed by humours.                    230

Lie still, ye thief, and hear the lady sing in Welsh.

HOTSPUR    I had rather hear Lady, my brach, howl in Irish.

LADY PERCY    Wouldst thou have thy head broken?

HOTSPUR    No.

LADY PERCY    Then be still.                    235

HOTSPUR    Neither; 'tis a woman's fault.

LADY PERCY    Now God help thee!

HOTSPUR    To the Welsh lady's bed.

LADY PERCY    What's that?

HOTSPUR    Peace; she sings. (*Here the Lady sings a Welsh*    240
*song.*) Come, Kate, I'll have your song too.

LADY PERCY    Not mine, in good sooth.

HOTSPUR    Not yours, in good sooth!

Heart, you swear like a comfit-maker's wife:

---

228 **By'r Lady** i.e. by Our Lady
230 **humours** whims
232 **Lady, my brach** my hound, Lady
(the dog's name); Johannes Caisus, *Of*
*English Dogs* (1576), defines 'Brach' as
what 'we Englishmen call bytches,
belonging to the hunting kinde of
dogges' (sig. C1ʳ).

    **howl in Irish** reflexive answer to *sing*
*in Welsh*, 231, with particular sense of
a grating, unpleasant sound; cf. *AYL*
5.2.109–10: ''tis like the howling of
Irish wolves against the moon'.

233 **Wouldst . . . broken** Kate obviously
playfully attacks Hotspur in some
manner, as in the 1986 English
Shakespeare production in which
Jennie Stoller's Kate wrestled with
Jonathan Pryce's Hotspur as part of

their 'engagingly frank and physical'
relationship (McMillin, 45).
235 **still** silent
236 i.e. I won't do that either; women are
silent.
242 **sooth** truth
244–8 **you . . . Finsbury** Hotspur
expresses his aristocratic contempt for
what he takes as Kate's bourgeois prim-
ness of speech, suggesting that she is
behaving like an unsophisticated citizen's wife who has travelled no further
from her home in London than
Finsbury Fields, half a mile away.
(Hotspur reveals a surprising knowledge of the habits of London citizen-
ry.)
244 **comfit-maker's**    confectioner's
(*comfits* = crystallized fruit)

228 he is] hee's *F*    229 should] would *Q4–F*    233 thou have] haue *Q3–F*    243–6] *as F; prose Q*
244 Heart, you] You *F*

'Not you, in good sooth,' and 'As true as I live!'                                                  245
And 'As God shall mend me!' and 'As sure as day!'
And givest such sarcenet surety for thy oaths
As if thou never walk'st further than Finsbury.
Swear me, Kate, like a lady as thou art,
A good mouth-filling oath, and leave 'in sooth'                                               250
And such protest of pepper gingerbread
To velvet-guards and Sunday citizens.
Come, sing.

LADY PERCY    I will not sing.

HOTSPUR    'Tis the next way to turn tailor or be redbreast          255
teacher. An the indentures be drawn, I'll away within
these two hours; and so come in when ye will.                              *Exit.*

GLENDOWER

Come, come, Lord Mortimer. You are as slow
As hot Lord Percy is on fire to go.

---

246 **mend** amend
247 **sarcenet surety** weak assurance; *sarcenet* = light silk used as lining
248 **Finsbury** Finsbury Fields north of London, used recreationally by citizens on Sundays and holidays (cf. *Sunday citizens*, 252)
249 **Swear me** swear for me
251 **protest . . . gingerbread** mealy-mouthed phrases (*pepper gingerbread* was a bread in which pepper was added for some of the required ginger in the usual recipe, producing a coarser and somewhat milder-tasting bread); Hotspur's image here suggests he is still thinking about the comfit-maker.
252 **velvet-guards . . . citizens** citizens in their Sunday best; *velvet-guards* = those who have trimmed their clothes

in velvet, like the aldermen's wives Moryson describes, who at 'publike meetings' would wear 'a close gowne of skarlet with gards of blacke velvet' (Moryson, 4.234).
255–6 **'Tis . . . teacher** Hotspur jokingly responds to Kate's refusal to sing by saying that it is probably for the best, since, if she did sing, she might end up as a tailor or as a teacher of birds.
255 **next** quickest
**tailor** Tailors were held to be enthusiastic singers; cf. Beaumont, *Knight of Burning Pestle*, 2.2.437–8: 'never trust a Tailor that does not sing at his worke' (Bowers, 1.42).
256 **An** if
**away** depart

245 'Not . . . sooth,'] *Ard²;* not . . . sooth, *Q;* not . . . south; *F*    'As . . . live!'] *Ard²;* as . . . liue, *Q;* as . . . liue; *F*    246 'As . . . me!'] *Ard²;* as . . . me, *Q;* as . . . me; *F*    'As . . . day!'] *Ard²;* as . . . day: *QF* 250 'in sooth'] *Ard²;* in sooth *QF*    256 An] *(*And*), T. Johnson*    259 hot] *F;* Hot. *Q1–3;* Hort, *Q4;* Hot *Q5*

By this our book is drawn. We'll but seal                    260
And then to horse immediately.

MORTIMER                    With all my heart.    *Exeunt.*

3.2            *Enter* KING, PRINCE *of* Wales *and others.*

KING

Lords, give us leave; the Prince of Wales and I must
    have
Some private conference. But be near at hand,
For we shall presently have need of you.    *Exeunt Lords.*
– I know not whether God will have it so
For some displeasing service I have done,                    5
That, in His secret doom, out of my blood
He'll breed revengement and a scourge for me;
But thou dost in thy passages of life
Make me believe that thou art only marked

---

260 **book** agreement (i.e. the indentures, 256)
   **drawn** drawn up
   **but** just
3.2 As is usual, nowhere in the scene does Shakespeare make the setting explicit, but the action clearly takes place at court. Earlier Hal has stated that he will go 'to the court in the morning' (2.4.530). Holinshed identifies this scene's historical encounter as taking place in the royal court at Westminster.
1 **give us leave** a formal request to be left alone
2 **But . . . hand** Does the King fear some attack from his son? Holinshed reports the rumours that reached the King's ears that his 'sonne would presume to vusrpe the crowne' and wished him harm (Holinshed, 3.539; cf. 22–5). Or is he merely alerting the

Prince that he has other business and doesn't have much time to devote to him?
3 SD The Lords have just entered at the beginning of the scene and now must depart; seemingly the time-consuming double action is designed to highlight the intimate father–son discussion that will follow. The same double action occurs at the beginning of *Per* 1.2.
6 **secret doom** inscrutable judgement
   **out . . . blood** from my own offspring
7 **revengement** retribution
   **scourge** human agent of divine punishment
8 **passages of life** behaviour, way of living
9–11 **marked . . . mistreadings** selected by God to punish me for my transgressions

**3.2**.1–2] Q lines I, / hand, / ; *F lines* leaue: / I, / conference: / hand, /    4 God] Heauen *F*    8 thy] the *Q2–5*

For the hot vengeance and the rod of heaven          10
To punish my mistreadings. Tell me else,
Could such inordinate and low desires,
Such poor, such bare, such lewd, such mean attempts,
Such barren pleasures, rude society
As thou art matched withal and grafted to,          15
Accompany the greatness of thy blood
And hold their level with thy princely heart?

PRINCE

So please your majesty, I would I could
Quit all offences with as clear excuse
As well as I am doubtless I can purge          20
Myself of many I am charged withal.
Yet such extenuation let me beg
As, in reproof of many tales devised
(Which oft the ear of greatness needs must hear),
By smiling pickthanks and base newsmongers,          25
I may for some things true, wherein my youth
Hath faulty wandered and irregular,
Find pardon on my true submission.

10 **rod** instrument of punishment
11 **mistreadings** transgressions
   **else** how else, otherwise
12 **inordinate and low** inappropriate and base (*inordinate* would also carry the sense of 'out of control')
13 **bare** wretched, paltry (but also, as at 1.3.108, 'undisguised')
   **lewd** base, vulgar
   **attempts** undertakings, escapades
14 **rude society** vulgar companions
15 **matched withal** associated with
   **grafted to** committed to (though the botanical metaphor, which refers to a process by which a shoot of one plant is inserted into another allowing the two to grow together, notably intensifies the previous phrase, suggesting, at least to the King, how fully Hal has accepted his prodigal, tavern life as his authentic existence)

17 **hold . . . with** satisfy, seem adequate to
19 **Quit** acquit myself, prove my innocence
20 **doubtless** confident
21 **withal** with
22-8 i.e. let me find forgiveness, not for the many bad acts that court gossip falsely attributes to me, but for the bad things I have actually done, which I am willing to acknowledge
22 **extenuation** mitigation
23 **reproof** disproof
25 **pickthanks** sycophantic informers; cf. Holinshed: 'Thus were the father and sonne reconciled, betwixt whom the said pickthanks had sowne diuision' (3.539).
   **newsmongers** tale-bearers, gossips
27 **irregular** lawlessly
28 **true submission** honest acknowledgement of faults

KING

> God pardon thee! Yet let me wonder, Harry,
> At thy affections, which do hold a wing                30
> Quite from the flight of all thy ancestors.
> Thy place in Council thou hast rudely lost,
> Which by thy younger brother is supplied,
> And art almost an alien to the hearts
> Of all the court and princes of my blood.              35
> The hope and expectation of thy time
> Is ruined, and the soul of every man
> Prophetically do forethink thy fall.
> Had I so lavish of my presence been,
> So common-hackneyed in the eyes of men,                40
> So stale and cheap to vulgar company,
> Opinion, that did help me to the crown,
> Had still kept loyal to possession

30 **affections** inclinations, feelings
  **hold a wing** fly
31 **from** different from, contrary to
32–3 The king refers to the Prince's
  expulsion from the Privy Council and
  replacement there by his younger
  brother; here no specific reason is
  given, though the story of Hal's
  removal for striking the Lord Chief
  Justice was well known from many
  sources, but perhaps most popularly
  from scene 4 of *Famous Victories*, and
  is referred to in *2H4* 1.2.193–5: 'For
  the box of the ear that the Prince gave
  you, he gave it like a rude prince, and
  you took it like a sensible lord.'
32 **rudely** boorishly
33 **supplied** fulfilled
34 **alien** stranger
36 **of thy time** for your life; cf. *Oth*
  1.1.159: 'what's to come of my
  despised time'.
38 **do forethink** does anticipate; Rowe,

followed by many editors, corrected
the grammar to 'does', but, while *every
man*, 37, is singular, it logically suggests plurality, and sixteenth-century
usage often followed such nouns with a
plural verb form.
40 **common-hackneyed** cheap and vulgar (*hackney* = horse available for hire)
42 **Opinion** public opinion; usually used
  by Elizabethan writers negatively, as in
  'Satire VI' in Guilpin's *Skialetheia*
  (1598), where 'Opinion' is called 'the
  hisse of Geese, the peoples noyse, / The
  tongue of humours, and phantasticke
  voyce / Of hair-brain'd Apprehension'
  (Guilpin, sig. E1ʳ; cited Ardˡ)
43 **Had . . . possession** would have
  retained their allegiance to the posses-
  sor of the crown (i.e. Richard II); 'the
  emotional counterstress' of *loyal*, however, suggests, as Mahood, 35, notes,
  'that Henry cannot free himself from
  the usurper's burden of guilt'.

29] *F lines* thee: / *Harry,* /

And left me in reputeless banishment,
A fellow of no mark nor likelihood.                                    45
By being seldom seen, I could not stir
But, like a comet, I was wondered at,
That men would tell their children 'This is he!'
Others would say, 'Where? Which is Bolingbroke?'
And then I stole all courtesy from heaven                              50
And dressed myself in such humility
That I did pluck allegiance from men's hearts,
Loud shouts and salutations from their mouths,
Even in the presence of the crowned King.
Thus did I keep my person fresh and new,                               55
My presence like a robe pontifical,
Ne'er seen but wondered at; and so my state,
Seldom but sumptuous, showed like a feast

---

45 **mark** eminence
**likelihood** promise of success
47 **comet** an extraordinary celestial phe-
nomenon (but almost always thought
to be an omen of ill fortune)
50 **I . . . heaven** i.e. I took on a manner of
almost godlike graciousness. A similar
expression appears in Massinger, *The
Great Duke of Florence*, where it is said
that the gracious Prince Giovanni
'Stole courtesie from heaven' (2.3.153;
Massinger, 3.135), though it is possible
Massinger is remembering Shakespeare's words rather than using a commonplace phrase.
51 **dressed myself in** behaved with; cf.
Bacon, *Advancement of Learning*,
'Behaviour seemeth to me as a
Garment of the Mind' (Bacon, 158),
which reveals the logic of
Shakespeare's image. Henry's language
in 50–2 reveals his own awareness of

the illegitimacy of his possession of the
crown.
54 **crowned** crownèd
56 **pontifical** belonging to a bishop
57 **Ne'er . . . at** was never seen without
wonder; the exact terms of the King's
awareness that political power rests
upon the desire of his subjects are
strikingly anticipated by the Prince's
soliloquy in 1.2.185–93, where the
Prince promises to 'imitate the sun', so
that when he pleases 'again to be himself . . . he may be more wondered at'.
The King's fears here that his son does
not understand political power are
obviously unfounded. See Kastan,
*SAT*, 137–40.
**but** except
**state** formal appearance in public
58 **Seldom** i.e. seldom seen; for this
adjectival use, cf. *Son* 52.4: 'the fine
point of seldom pleasure'.

---

48 'This is he!'] *Ard²*; this is he: *QF*    49 'Where? . . . Bolingbroke?'] *Ard²*; where, . . . Bullingbrooke? *QF*    54 the presence] presence *Q2*    55 did I] I did *Q5–F*

And won by rareness such solemnity.

The skipping King, he ambled up and down               60

With shallow jesters and rash bavin wits,

Soon kindled and soon burnt; carded his state,

Mingled his royalty with cap'ring fools,

Had his great name profaned with their scorns,

And gave his countenance against his name            65

To laugh at gibing boys and stand the push

Of every beardless vain comparative;

Grew a companion to the common streets,

Enfeoffed himself to popularity,

That, being daily swallowed by men's eyes,           70

They surfeited with honey and began

To loathe the taste of sweetness, whereof a little

More than a little is by much too much.

So, when he had occasion to be seen,

He was but as the cuckoo is in June,                 75

---

59 **won . . . solemnity** earned great respect through its rarity (*solemnity* = grandeur, dignity, *OED* 4)

60 **skipping** frivolous
**up and down** here and there, around (*OED adv.* 3a)

61 **rash bavin** meretricious, superficial; *rash* = quick acting; *bavin* = bundle of brushwood or kindling, which lights easily but quickly burns up; cf. the proverb: 'the bavin burns bright but it is but a blaze' (Dent, B107).

62 **carded his state** contaminated or debased his dignity (*card* = weaken by mixing); the phrase is effectively glossed in his following line. Cf. Greene, *Quip*: 'you card your beare (if you see your guest begin to be drunke) half small and half strong' (sig. G1ʳ; cited Ard¹).

64 **profaned** profanèd
**profaned with** desecrated by

65 **countenance** authority

**against his name** to the dishonour of his reputation

66 **gibing** mocking
**stand the push** expose himself to the mockery; cf. *TC* 2.2.137–8: 'To stand the push and enmity of those / This quarrel would excite'.

67 **comparative** one who mocks another with derisive comparisons; cf. 1.2.77

68 **Grew** became

69 became dependent on public opinion
**Enfeoffed** committed; from the relationship of a feof-holder's grant of land on the condition of loyalty to a superior lord

70 **That** so that

72–3 **a . . . too much** proverbial?

75–6 **as . . . regarded** i.e. by June no one pays the cuckoo any attention, although when it first appears each year it is welcomed as a sign of the return of spring (proverbial, cf. Dent, C894)

---

59 won] *(wan), F (wonne)*   63 cap'ring] *(capring); carping Q2–F*   71–2] *as T. Johnson; QF line* loath / little /

Heard, not regarded; seen, but with such eyes
As, sick and blunted with community,
Afford no extraordinary gaze
Such as is bent on sun-like majesty
When it shines seldom in admiring eyes,                    80
But rather drowsed and hung their eyelids down,
Slept in his face, and rendered such aspect
As cloudy men use to their adversaries,
Being with his presence glutted, gorged and full.
And in that very line, Harry, standest thou,               85
For thou hast lost thy princely privilege
With vile participation. Not an eye
But is a-weary of thy common sight,
Save mine, which hath desired to see thee more,
Which now doth that I would not have it do,                90
Make blind itself with foolish tenderness.

PRINCE
I shall hereafter, my thrice-gracious lord,

---

77 **blunted with** weakened by
   **community** what is common or
   familiar (*OED* 5a)
78 **Afford** provide, bestow (*OED* 5)
80 **admiring** wondering
81 **drowsed** became drowsy, lost interest
   **hung . . . down** The image is of the
   eyelids as curtains, as in *Tem* 1.2.409,
   where Prospero orders Miranda: 'The
   fringed curtains of thine eye advance'.
82 **face** presence
   **such aspect** the sort of expression,
   such a look
83 **cloudy** sullen (the image is saved from
   cliché by its relation to *sun-like
   majesty*, 79)
84 **glutted** filled to excess, surfeited; cf.
   North 'to preuent that the people
   should not be glutted with seeing him
   too oft . . . [Pericles] neither came
   much abroade among them but

reserued himself . . . for matters of
great importance' (sig. P1ᵛ; cited
Ardⁱ).
85 **line** category, class (and not the line of
   descent from which his behaviour has
   seemingly alienated him)
87 **vile participation** mixing with the
   vulgar; cf. *2H4* 5.1.69: 'the participation of society'.
90 **that** what
91 i.e. filling my eyes with tears; cf.
   Holinshed, 3.539, where he reports of
   the reconciliation (which took place in
   1410, seven years later than Shakespeare
   locates it): 'the king mooued herewith . . .
   imbracing the prince kissed him and
   with shedding teares confessed in deed
   he had him partlie in susupicion,
   though now (as he perceiued) not with
   iust cause'.

83 to] to doe to *Q3–F*

Be more myself.

KING            For all the world,

As thou art to this hour was Richard then,

When I from France set foot at Ravenspur,     95

And even as I was then is Percy now.

Now by my sceptre, and my soul to boot,

He hath more worthy interest to the state

Than thou, the shadow of succession;

For, of no right, nor colour like to right,     100

He doth fill fields with harness in the realm,

Turns head against the lion's armed jaws,

And, being no more in debt to years than thou,

Leads ancient lords and reverend bishops on

To bloody battles and to bruising arms.     105

What never-dying honour hath he got

Against renowned Douglas, whose high deeds,

Whose hot incursions and great name in arms,

Holds from all soldiers chief majority

And military title capital     110

---

93 **Be more myself** behave as my birth and position suggest I should; cf. the King's similar claim at 1.3.5; the phrasing is proverbial (Dent, O64.1).
**For . . . world** i.e. exactly; with the half-line, Henry reclaims the scene from Hal's promise to amend, revealing how little the King credits it as he shifts the focus to the seemingly more worthy Hotspur.

94 **to this hour** up to now

98 **more . . . state** a more valid claim to the kingdom; for *interest* as 'title', cf. *KJ* 5.2.89: 'interest to this land'.

99 **shadow of succession** i.e. a poor imitation of a successor (since your legal claim is not supported by merit)

100 **colour like to** semblance of

101 **harness** armour

102 **Turns head** leads an army (and, given the rest of the line, perhaps draws some meaning from the expression 'to put one's head in the lion's mouth')
**armed** armèd

103 **no . . . thou** no older than you are; see 1.1.86–8.

105 **bruising arms** injurious weapons (or, metonymically, deeds of arms)

107 **renowned** renownèd
**whose** refers to Hotspur, not Douglas

108 **hot incursions** fierce assaults

109–10 **chief . . . capital** the reputation for martial pre-eminence

---

107 renowned] *(renowmed)*, *Q4*    109 soldiers] souldier *Q3*

Through all the kingdoms that acknowledge Christ.
Thrice hath this Hotspur, Mars in swaddling-clothes,
This infant warrior, in his enterprises
Discomfited great Douglas; ta'en him once,
Enlarged him, and made a friend of him,                        115
To fill the mouth of deep defiance up
And shake the peace and safety of our throne.
And what say you to this? Percy, Northumberland,
The Archbishop's grace of York, Douglas, Mortimer,
Capitulate against us and are up.                              120
But wherefore do I tell these news to thee?
Why, Harry, do I tell thee of my foes,
Which art my nearest and dearest enemy?
Thou that art like enough, through vassal fear,
Base inclination and the start of spleen,                      125
To fight against me under Percy's pay,
To dog his heels and curtsy at his frowns,
To show how much thou art degenerate.

PRINCE

Do not think so. You shall not find it so;
And God forgive them that so much have swayed                  130

---

112–14 **Thrice . . . Douglas** Hotspur and
his forces fought three times with
Douglas's Scottish troops: at Otterburn
in 1385, at Nesbit in June 1402 and at
Humbleton in September 1402.

112 **Mars in swaddling-clothes** an
infant Mars (further emphasis upon
Hotspur's ahistorical youth; see 103n.)

114 **ta'en him** once on one occasion captured him (an event nowhere mentioned in the chronicle sources)

115 **Enlarged** enlargèd: freed

116 to complete the number of those
opposing us

120 **Capitulate** have formed a league
(*OED v.* 2)
**up** in arms, in open rebellion

121 **these news** For 'news' as a plural
noun, see *2H4* 4.4.102: 'these good
news'.

123 **nearest and dearest** a familiar doublet generated by the rhyme; *dearest*
here means both 'most beloved' and
'direst' (*OED* dear *a.*[2] 2).

124 **like** likely
**vassal** here means 'base' or 'reprehen-
sible', generalizing the social slur (*vassal* = serf or servant) to a moral quality

125 **Base inclination** a tendency to
ignoble behaviour
**start of spleen** fit of bad temper

126 **under Percy's pay** on the side of the
Percys

112 this] the *Q5–F*    swaddling] *(*swathling*)*; swathing *Q4–F*    130 God] Heauen *F*

Your majesty's good thoughts away from me.
I will redeem all this on Percy's head
And in the closing of some glorious day
Be bold to tell you that I am your son,
When I will wear a garment all of blood                                    135
And stain my favours in a bloody mask,
Which washed away shall scour my shame with it.
And that shall be the day, whene'er it lights,
That this same child of honour and renown,
This gallant Hotspur, this all-praised knight,                             140
And your unthought-of Harry chance to meet.
For every honour sitting on his helm,
Would they were multitudes, and on my head
My shames redoubled, for the time will come
That I shall make this northern youth exchange                             145
His glorious deeds for my indignities.
Percy is but my factor, good my lord,
To engross up glorious deeds on my behalf;
And I will call him to so strict account
That he shall render every glory up,                                       150

132 **redeem** atone for (but also 'make [Percy] pay'); the complex image of redemption in the play, as it shifts among commercial, social and spiritual meanings, begins at 1.2.198–207.
133 **closing . . . day** triumphant end of some battle (and not a temporal reference to the end of a beautiful day)
134 **I . . . son** i.e. worthy of you and my birth (though, for an account of just how much Hal emerges as Henry's son in the sense of replicating his father's pragmatic values, see p. 32)
136 **favours** features (but also chivalric ornamentation worn as pledges or

rewards)
**bloody mask** covering of blood
138 **lights** dawns
140 **all-praised** praised for everything and by everyone
**praised** praisèd
141 **unthought-of** ignored, disregarded (obviously in contrast to *all-praised* in the previous line)
146 **indignities** dishonours, humiliations (*OED* indignity †2)
147 **factor** buyer, agent
148 **engross up** accumulate, buy up
150 **render . . . up** give back every honour

142 sitting] fitting *Q3–F*    148 up] my *Q3–5*

Yea, even the slightest worship of his time,
Or I will tear the reckoning from his heart.
This, in the name of God, I promise here,
The which, if He be pleased I shall perform,
I do beseech your majesty may salve                           155
The long-grown wounds of my intemperance.
If not, the end of life cancels all bonds,
And I will die a hundred thousand deaths
Ere break the smallest parcel of this vow.

KING

A hundred thousand rebels die in this.                        160
Thou shalt have charge and sovereign trust herein.

*Enter* BLOUNT.

How now, good Blount? Thy looks are full of speed.

BLOUNT

So hath the business that I come to speak of.
Lord Mortimer of Scotland hath sent word

151 **worship . . . time** honour he has
gained in his lifetime
152 **reckoning** accounting (with an allusion to 'the day of reckoning')
   **from his heart** i.e. by his death
154 **if . . . pleased** God willing that
   **shall** may
156 **intemperance** lack of self-control;
some editors print F's 'intemperature',
meaning both 'intemperance' and a
distempered condition of the body, but
this seems at best a sophistication and
possibly a compositorial error, perhaps
recalling *distemperature* at 3.1.33.
157 **bonds** promises
159 **parcel** part, portion
161 **charge** command
   **sovereign trust** royal responsibility
161 SD That Blount would enter unbid-

den, in spite of the King's desire for a
*private conference*, 2, with his son, suggests the urgency of the message he
carries.
162 **are . . . speed** convey great urgency
163 i.e. not just my *looks* are urgent, but
so is the matter that I come to discuss
164 **Lord . . . Scotland** Shakespeare, following Holinshed's 'the earle of
March, a Scotishman' (3.521), seemingly assumed from the title that this
must be one of the Mortimer family,
but the Scottish earl was actually
George Dunbar, who in fact defected
to Henry, who then successfully 'used
the counsell & advise of the erle of
March in the obteining of this victorie'
(Holinshed, 2.255).

153 God] Heauen *F*   154 He . . . perform] I performe, and doe suruiue *F*   156 intemperance]
intemperature *F*   157 bonds] (bands), *Rowe*   158 thousand] thousands *Q4*   161.1] *F; after 162 Q*

That Douglas and the English rebels met                165
The eleventh of this month at Shrewsbury.
A mighty and a fearful head they are,
If promises be kept on every hand,
As ever offered foul play in a state.

KING

The Earl of Westmorland set forth today,                170
With him my son, Lord John of Lancaster,
For this advertisement is five days old.
On Wednesday next, Harry, you shall set forward.
On Thursday we ourselves will march.
Our meeting is Bridgnorth, and, Harry, you                175
Shall march through Gloucestershire, by which
    account,
Our business valued, some twelve days hence
Our general forces at Bridgnorth shall meet.
Our hands are full of business. Let's away.                179
Advantage feeds him fat while men delay.    *Exeunt.*

**3.3**                *Enter* FALSTAFF *and* BARDOLL.

FALSTAFF    Bardoll, am I not fallen away vilely since this

---

167 **head** army
169 **foul play** rebellion
172 **advertisement** information (main accent on second syllable)
173 **shall** must
174–9 Wilson (Cam¹) suggests that the repetitions of *march*, *Bridgnorth* and *business* in these six lines point to the existence of 'two textual strata' imperfectly revised, and suggests that *by . . . hence*, 176–7, 'was intended to be deleted'. Nonetheless, in performance, the repetitions can work to reveal the strain that slips from Henry's rhetorical control.

175 **Bridgnorth** a town on the Severn in Shropshire, about 20 miles south-east of Shrewsbury; see Fig. 21.
176 **Gloucestershire** (pronounced Gloster-shir)
    **account** calculation
177 **Our business valued** considering what we have to do
    **valued** valuèd
180 **Advantage . . . fat** The opportunity is lost (grows fat and sluggish through inactivity).
3.3 The action takes place in the same London tavern in which 2.4 is set.
1 **fallen away vilely** terribly shrunk

173 you shall] thou shalt *Q3–F*    174–6] *T. Johnson*; *Q lines* meeting / march / account / ; *F lines* march. / march / account, /

267

*King Henry IV, Part One*

last action? Do I not bate? Do I not dwindle? Why, my
skin hangs about me like an old lady's loose gown. I am
withered like an old apple-john. Well, I'll repent, and
that suddenly, while I am in some liking. I shall be out          5
of heart shortly, and then I shall have no strength to
repent. An I have not forgotten what the inside of a
church is made of, I am a peppercorn, a brewer's horse.
The inside of a church! Company, villainous company,
hath been the spoil of me.                                        10

BARDOLL   Sir John, you are so fretful you cannot live
long.

FALSTAFF   Why, there is it. Come, sing me a bawdy song;
make me merry. I was as virtuously given as a
gentleman need to be. Virtuous enough: swore little;             15
diced not above seven times – a week; went to a bawdy-

(GWW notes that this scene begins
with Falstaff's insistence on his
shrinking size, contrasting with the
last line of the previous scene where
*Advantage* is lost by being allowed to
grow *fat*)
2   **last action** i.e. the robbery on Gad's
Hill
    **bate** grow thin
4   **apple-john** variety of apple, 'whose
wither'd rind, entrench'd By many a
furrow, aptly represents Decrepid
age', according to Phillips's *Cider*
(1708; cited *OED*); cf. *2H4* 2.4.2–7,
where Falstaff's dislike of the fruit is
explained by an account of a time
when Hal put a dish with five 'apple-
johns' in front of Falstaff, and then
left, saying: 'I will now take my leave of
these six, dry, round, old, withered
knights.'
5   **suddenly** immediately
    **in some liking** in the mood; but also
overweight (Cotgrave: '*Grasselet . . .*
Fattish, fattie, somewhat fat, in pretie
good liking'). There is the further play

here and in the next line for those who
know the full story of Falstaff and Hal
that, although the fat knight is now in
the Prince's *liking*, he will eventually
be *out of heart*, 5–6.
5–6   **out of heart** without such inclination; but also, out of condition (and see
previous note)
6   **strength** of both purpose and body
7   **An** if
8   **peppercorn** dried berry of the pepper
plant; i.e. very small and shrivelled
    **brewer's horse** a tired, worn-out nag;
brewers' horses were proverbial for
being on their last legs; cf. Dekker, *If
This be not a Good Play the Devil is in it*
(1611): 'as noble-men vse their great
horses, when they are past seruice: sell
'em to brewers and make 'em drey-
horses' (3.1.10–11; Dekker, 3.162).
11   **fretful** anxious (but also, worn away);
cf. 2.2.2: 'frets like a gummed velvet'.
13   **there is it** that's it, what can I do
about it?
16   **\*times – a week** a pause after *times* (as
after *once* and *borrowed*), as Falstaff

3.3.7 An] *(And), T. Johnson*   16 times –] *Staunton;* times *QF*

house not above once in a quarter – of an hour; paid
money that I borrowed – three or four times; lived well
and in good compass. And now I live out of all order,
out of all compass.                                               20

BARDOLL  Why, you are so fat, Sir John, that you must
needs be out of all compass, out of all reasonable
compass, Sir John.

FALSTAFF  Do thou amend thy face, and I'll amend my
life. Thou art our admiral, thou bearest the lantern in    25
the poop, but 'tis in the nose of thee. Thou art the
Knight of the Burning Lamp.

BARDOLL  Why, Sir John, my face does you no harm.

FALSTAFF  No, I'll be sworn, I make as good use of it as
many a man doth of a death's head, or a *memento mori*.    30
I never see thy face but I think upon hell-fire and Dives
that lived in purple: for there he is in his robes,
burning, burning. If thou wert any way given to virtue,
I would swear by thy face; my oath should be 'By this

immediately undercuts his apparent
claim of moderate behaviour; the
punctuation was first adopted by
Hanmer.

19 **good compass** moderation

20 **out . . . compass** with no self-control;
cf. Cotgrave: '*Desordonné*: Disorderly
. . . unbridled, out of all good compass'; Bardoll in 22 plays on the phrase
to refer to Falstaff's great size.

25 **admiral** i.e. admiral's flagship; the
flagship, first of the fleet, would carry
a lantern in its stern (*poop*, 26) to guide
the other ships; cf. *AC* 3.10.2–3: 'The
Egyptian admiral . . . fly and turn the
rudder.' Dekker uses the same image
in *The Wonderful Year* (1603) describ-
ing the carbuncles on the tavern-
keeper's nose, joking that someone in
'an East-Indian voyage' offered to pay

him 'to haue stoode a nightes in the
Poope of their Admirall, onely to saue
the charges of candles' (Grosart, 1.139).

27 **Knight . . . Lamp** parody of titles
assumed by knights-errant in chivalric
romances; the title of Beaumont and
Fletcher's *Knight of the Burning Pestle*
(1607) is a similar mock.

30 **death's-head . . . *mori*** a ring with a
skull as a symbol of mortality (Latin
*memento mori* comes to signify a
reminder of death)

31–2 **Dives . . . purple** uncharitable rich
man in the parable of Lazarus (Luke,
16.19–31, unnamed in English transla-
tions, but Dives in the Vulgate; Latin
*dives* = rich) who goes to hell for
allowing the beggar Lazarus to starve

34–5 ***By . . . angel*** plays on Exodus, 3.2:
'the angel of the Lord appeared unto

17 quarter –] *Hanmer*; quarter *QF*   18 borrowed –] *Hanmer*; borrowed *Q;* borrowed, *F*   20 all
compass] compasse *Q5–F*   24 my] thy *F*   34–5 'By . . . that is . . . angel'] *this edn*; by . . . that . . .
Angell *Q1–2*; By . . . thats . . . Angel *Q3–5*; *By this Fire F*   37 son] Sunne *Q5–F*

fire that is God's angel.' But thou art altogether given   35
over and wert indeed, but for the light in thy face, the
son of utter darkness. When thou rann'st up Gad's Hill
in the night to catch my horse, if I did not think thou
hadst been an *ignis fatuus*, or a ball of wildfire, there's
no purchase in money. O, thou art a perpetual triumph,   40
an everlasting bonfire-light! Thou hast saved me a
thousand marks in links and torches walking with thee
in the night betwixt tavern and tavern, but the sack that
thou hast drunk me would have bought me lights as
good cheap at the dearest chandler's in Europe. I have   45

him in a flame of fire'; cf. *Misogonus* (1565): 'by this fier that bournez thats Gods aungell I sweare a great oth' (3.1.240). F omits 'that is God's angel', seemingly in response to the 1606 Act against blasphemy on stage. Most editions emend Q's defective 'that' to 'that is', but, as Q characteristically resists contractions, this edition does the same (see pp. 110–111).

35–6 **given over** committed (to wickedness)

36 **wert** would be
    **light . . . face** i.e. the red nose and carbuncles about which Falstaff has been teasing Bardoll

37 **son . . . darkness** person of complete wickedness; in Q5–8 and F *son* is 'sunne', suggesting the play on *light* in 36; on 'son of utter darkness'; see 2.4.166n.; 'utter darkness' appears in Matthew, 8.12, and elsewhere in English Bibles before the King James translation in 1611 changed it to 'outer darkness'.

39 *ignis fatuus* phosphorescent marsh gas, usually known as will-o'-the-wisp
    **ball of wildfire** a form of firework; cf. Dekker, *If This be not a Good Play*: 'you shall see . . . a thousand Balles / Of wilde-Fire, flying round about the

Aire', with the SD: '*Fire-workes on Lines*' (2.1.190–2; Dekker, 3.150); Bevington (Oxf[1]), however, says plausibly that the phrase may merely be a clarification of *ignis fatuus*, but notes that *OED* has no citation of this meaning before 1663.

40 **purchase** value
   **triumph** pageant, festival (referring particularly to the torches that were used)

41 **everlasting bonfire-light** In *Mac* 2.3.19, the Porter's reference to the 'ever-lasting bonfire' suggests that this would be heard as an allusion to hell-fire.

42 **links** torches (London had no street lighting until the late seventeenth century, though during the evening hours many areas would be lit by householders' and shopkeepers' torches; Falstaff must then be referring to their late-night drinking activities.)

43–5 **but . . . Europe** 'For what I have paid for the sack you have drunk I could have lights from the most expensive chandler in Europe'

44 **drunk me** drunk at my expense

44–5 **as good cheap** at as good a price

45 **chandler's** candle-maker's

38 thou] that thou *Q3–F*   45 at] *as Q5–F*

maintained that salamander of yours with fire any time
this two-and-thirty years, God reward me for it.

BARDOLL     'Sblood, I would my face were in your belly!

FALSTAFF     God-a-mercy! So should I be sure to be heartburned.                                                      50

*Enter* HOSTESS.

How now, Dame Partlet the hen, have you enquired yet
who picked my pocket?

HOSTESS     Why, Sir John, what do you think, Sir John?
Do you think I keep thieves in my house? I have
searched, I have enquired, so has my husband, man by     55
man, boy by boy, servant by servant. The tithe of a hair
was never lost in my house before.

FALSTAFF     Ye lie, hostess: Bardoll was shaved and lost
many a hair, and I'll be sworn my pocket was picked.
Go to, you are a woman, go.                                  60

---

46 **salamander** small lizard supposed to
live in fire, but here another gibe at
Bardoll's nose
48 **I . . . belly** a proverbial expression of
irritation (Dent, B299), not unlike the
modern 'stuff it'
49–50 **be heartburned** have indigestion;
Falstaff plays on the literal sense of
Bardoll's proverbial phrase, continuing
the extended jest about Bardoll's red
face.
51 **Dame Partlet** traditional name for a
hen, as in Chaucer's *Nun's Priest's
Tale*; *partlet* = ruff, and was applied to
the hen because of the conspicuous
ruff of feathers at its neck. The
application to women may be a back-
formation from this fact, referring to
the ruff worn by many women.

56 *****tithe** tenth part; it is possible, as
some have suggested, that QF's 'tight'
should be retained as a joke marking
the Hostess's mispronunciation, but it
is hard to see how this would be heard
on the stage.
58 **shaved** Falstaff uses the literal fact of
Bardoll's having his beard shaved to
reject the Hostess's claim that not a
'tithe of a hair' had been lost in the
inn, but *shaved* might also refer to
heads shaved to rid them of lice, or
made bald from venereal disease, or
even 'robbed' (*OED* 7).
60 **you . . . woman** a common insult; i.e.
you are merely a woman (cf. Dent,
W637.1); the Hostess recognizes the
insult, but her response in 61–2 is
comically inadequate.

47 God] Heauen *F*   48 'Sblood] *(*Zbloud*)*; *om. F*   49 God-a-mercy] *om. F*   50.1] *F; after*
enquird *51 Q1–2; after 52 Q3–5*   56 tithe] *Theobald;* tight *QF*

HOSTESS   Who, I? No, I defy thee. God's light, I was
never called so in mine own house before.

FALSTAFF   Go to, I know you well enough.

HOSTESS   No, Sir John, you do not know me, Sir John; I
know you, Sir John. You owe me money, Sir John, and          65
now you pick a quarrel to beguile me of it. I bought you
a dozen of shirts to your back.

FALSTAFF   Dowlas, filthy dowlas. I have given them away
to bakers' wives; they have made bolters of them.

HOSTESS   Now, as I am a true woman, holland of eight          70
shillings an ell. You owe money here besides, Sir John,
for your diet, and by-drinkings, and money lent you:
four-and-twenty pound.

FALSTAFF   [*Points to Bardoll.*]   He had his part of it.
Let him pay.          75

HOSTESS   He? Alas, he is poor; he hath nothing.

FALSTAFF   How? Poor? Look upon his face. What call you
rich? Let them coin his nose; let them coin his cheeks.
I'll not pay a denier. What, will you make a younker of

---

61 **God's light** a mild oath, by God's
light
66 **beguile me of** trick me out of
67 **to your back** for you to wear
68 **Dowlas** coarse linen (from Doulas in
Brittany)
69 **bolters** canvas sieves for sifting flour
70 **holland** fine linen (originally from
Holland)
70–1 **of . . . ell** The Hostess claims that
the shirt was of costly material; cf.
Stubbes, sig. D8': 'Their Shirtes,
which all in a manner doe weare (for if
the Nobilitie or gentrie onely did
weare them, it were somedeal more
tollerable) are eyther of Camericke,

Holland, Lawne, or els of the finst
cloth that maye bee got'.
71 **ell** a unit of measurement equal to 45
inches
72 **by-drinkings** drinks between meals
74 **part** share
77–8 **What . . . rich?** i.e. 'if that's not
rich, I don't know what is', a response
to the Hostess's claim that Bardoll is
*poor* (76)
79 **denier** French copper coin; cf.
Cotgrave: '*Denier*: a penny, a deneere; a
small copper coin valued at the tenth
part of an English pennie'.
**younker** novice, dupe (from the
Dutch *jong* and *heer*, young gentleman)

---

61 No, I] I *Q5–F*   God's light] *om. F*   70 as] at *Q5*   70–1 eight shillings] *(viii s.), F*   73 four-
and-twenty] *(xxiiii.), F*   pound] pounds *F*   74 SD] *Folg² subst.*

me? Shall I not take mine ease in mine inn, but I shall          80
have my pocket picked? I have lost a seal ring of my
grandfather's worth forty mark.

HOSTESS [*to Bardoll*]   O Jesu, I have heard the Prince tell
him, I know not how oft, that that ring was copper!

FALSTAFF   How? The Prince is a jack, a sneak-up.          85
'Sblood, an he were here I would cudgel him like a dog
if he would say so.

*Enter the* PRINCE [*with* PETO] *marching, and* FALSTAFF *meets
him, playing upon his truncheon like a fife.*

How now, lad? Is the wind in that door, i'faith? Must we
all march?

---

80 **take . . . inn** proverbial expression
implying something like 'a man's inn is
like his own house'; cf. Dent, E42.

81 **seal ring** finger ring with an engraved
seal or signet, which could be used to
stamp wax with an authenticating
mark

82 **forty mark** i.e. 26 pounds, 13 shillings
and 4 pence (a mark was not a coin but
a unit of value equal to two-thirds of a
pound); see 2.4.522n.

85 **jack** knave
**sneak-up** sneaky person; 'Sneakup' is
a character in Brome's *City Wit* (1653);
some editions have replaced Q1's
'sneakup' with 'sneak-cup', the reading of Q3–5 and F, supposing that the
second 'e' in Q1 was a misreading and
inventing for the nonce word some
meaning like 'one who steals cups from
taverns or who drinks from other tav-
ern-goers' cups', or, as Kittredge, 'one
who "sneaks drinks" – does not drink
glass for glass with friends'. The context makes clear that the Q1 reading is
correct.

87.1 \**with* PETO The addition to the
direction of QF is necessary because
Peto, although he does not speak in the
scene, is addressed by the Prince at
196.

87.2 *playing . . . fife*. At 86, Falstaff
threatens to *cudgel* the Prince, presumably with the appropriate gesture;
when the Prince suddenly enters,
Falstaff quickly shifts his action, usually drawing a laugh from the audience. In Gildon's *Measure for Measure;
Or, Beauty's Best Advocate* (1700),
Shakespeare's ghost recalls how
Falstaff did 'his Truncheon weild',
though in some productions, e.g.
Charles Kemble's in 1824, Hal carries
the truncheon, based upon the ambiguity of the pronouns in the SD
(Sprague, *Actors*, 87–8).
*truncheon* cudgel (a symbol of
Falstaff's new command)
*fife* small shrill transverse flute used
for military music

88 **Is . . . door** is that what's up

---

83 SD] *Folg²*   O Jesu] *om.* F   85 sneak-up] *(sneakup); sneak-cup Q3–F*   86 'Sblood] *(Zbloud);
om.* F   an] *(and), Boswell-Malone; and if* F   87.1 *with* PETO] *Theobald subst.*   87.2 upon] *on Q3–F*
88 How] *Dyce; Falst.* How *QF*   i'faith] *om.* F

BARDOLL     Yea, two and two, Newgate fashion.          90
HOSTESS     My lord, I pray you hear me.
PRINCE     What sayst thou, Mistress Quickly? How doth
     thy husband? I love him well; he is an honest man.
HOSTESS     Good my lord, hear me.
FALSTAFF     Prithee, let her alone and list to me.          95
PRINCE     What sayst thou, Jack?
FALSTAFF     The other night I fell asleep here, behind the
     arras, and had my pocket picked. This house is turned
     bawdy-house: they pick pockets.
PRINCE     What didst thou lose, Jack?          100
FALSTAFF     Wilt thou believe me, Hal? Three or four
     bonds of forty pound apiece and a seal ring of my
     grandfather's.
PRINCE     A trifle, some eightpenny matter.
HOSTESS     So I told him, my lord, and I said I heard your          105
     grace say so. And, my lord, he speaks most vilely of
     you, like a foul-mouthed man as he is, and said he
     would cudgel you.
PRINCE     What? He did not.
HOSTESS     There's neither faith, truth nor womanhood in          110
     me else.
FALSTAFF     There's no more faith in thee than in a stewed
     prune, nor no more truth in thee than in a drawn fox,

---

90 **Newgate fashion** two-by-two, like
shackled prisoners on their way to
Newgate prison; cf. Dekker, *Satiro-
mastix*: 'we'll walke arme in arme as
tho we were leading one another to
Newgate' (3.1.235–6; Dekker, 1.343;
cited by Kittredge).
104 **eightpenny matter** trivial thing
112–13 **stewed prune** i.e. bawd (*stews* =
brothels); cf. Dekker, *2 Honest Whore*:
'two dishes of stew'd prunes, a Bawde
and a Pander' (4.3.36; Dekker, 2.197)

113 **drawn fox** a lure, or train, drawn
over the ground to attract a fox; cf.
Turberville, *The Book of Hunting*,
where the recipe is given for such a
lure (bacon skin marinated in the 'gob-
bits' of the fox's kidney and 'gutte')
and the assurance that 'if there be a
foxe neare to any place where the
trayne is drawne, he will follow it'
(Turberville, sig. M5ᵛ-6ʳ). Some editors, however, plausibly gloss this as a
fox that has been *drawn* from its cover

---

92 doth] doeth *Q2–3;* dow *Q5;* does *F*     112 in a] a *Q2–F*

and, for womanhood, Maid Marian may be the
deputy's wife of the ward to thee. Go, you thing, go!          115

HOSTESS   Say, what thing, what thing?

FALSTAFF   What thing? Why, a thing to thank God on.

HOSTESS   I am no thing to thank God on. I would thou
shouldst know it. I am an honest man's wife, and, setting
thy knighthood aside, thou art a knave to call me so.          120

FALSTAFF   Setting thy womanhood aside, thou art a beast
to say otherwise.

HOSTESS   Say, what beast, thou knave thou.

FALSTAFF   What beast? Why, an otter.

PRINCE   An otter, Sir John? Why an otter?          125

FALSTAFF   Why? She's neither fish nor flesh; a man
knows not where to have her.

HOSTESS   Thou art an unjust man in saying so. Thou or
any man knows where to have me, thou knave thou.

PRINCE   Thou sayst true, hostess, and he slanders thee          130

and exercising cunning to avoid being
caught.

114 **Maid Marian** clownish character
from the morris dance, usually played
by a boy; cf. Coles: 'Maid-Marrian (or
Morion) a boy Dressed in Maids
apparel, to dance the morisco'; boys, of
course, played female parts on
Shakespeare's stage, so there is some
irony in this image being used as a sign
of deceit.

115 **deputy's . . . ward** wife of the
deputy of the ward, i.e. respectable
woman
**to** compared to
**you thing** a term of contempt, implying unworthiness to be deemed a person; cf. *WT* 2.1.82: 'O thou thing'.

117 **on** for

119–20 **setting . . . aside** ignoring my
respect for your title

124–6 **otter . . . flesh** The otter, an
aquatic mammal with webbed feet and
fin-like legs, seems generically
ambiguous; its nature, as Walton says
in *The Compleat Angler*, 'hath been
debated among many great clerks, and
they seem to differ about it; yet most
agree his tail is fish' (Walton, sig. D5ʳ).

127 **where . . . her** in which category (*fish*
or *flesh*) to place her (with the obvious
sexual meaning as well)

129 **any . . . me** The Hostess's outraged
innocence, insisting that all men do
indeed know how to categorize her,
reproduces the sexual joke at her own
expense.

115 thing] nothing *F*   117, 118 God] heauen *F*   118 no thing] *Q5–F;* nothing *Q1–4*   128 art an]
art *F*

most grossly.

HOSTESS    So he doth you, my lord, and said this other day
you owed him a thousand pound.

PRINCE    Sirrah, do I owe you a thousand pound?

FALSTAFF    A thousand pound, Hal? A million. Thy love    135
is worth a million. Thou owest me thy love.

HOSTESS    Nay, my lord, he called you 'jack' and said he
would cudgel you.

FALSTAFF    Did I, Bardoll?

BARDOLL    Indeed, Sir John, you said so.    140

FALSTAFF    Yea, if he said my ring was copper.

PRINCE    I say 'tis copper. Darest thou be as good as thy
word now?

FALSTAFF    Why, Hal, thou knowest as thou art but man I
dare, but, as thou art prince, I fear thee as I fear the    145
roaring of the lion's whelp.

PRINCE    And why not as the lion?

FALSTAFF    The King himself is to be feared as the lion.
Dost thou think I'll fear thee as I fear thy father? Nay,
an I do, I pray God my girdle break.    150

PRINCE    O, if it should, how would thy guts fall about thy
knees! But, sirrah, there's no room for faith, truth nor
honesty in this bosom of thine; it is all filled up with
guts and midriff. Charge an honest woman with
picking thy pocket? Why, thou whoreson, impudent,    155
embossed rascal, if there were anything in thy pocket
but tavern reckonings, memorandums of bawdy-

146 **whelp** cub
148 **The . . . lion** Proverbs 19.12: 'The
Kings wrath is like the roaring of a
lyon.'
150 **pray . . . break** the breaking of one's
girdle (belt) was considered an omen of

bad luck; the phrase is a common
asseveration (cf. Dent, G116.1).
156 **embossed rascal** swollen knave (but
also *embossed* = foaming at the mouth;
*rascal* = young or underweight deer;
see 2.2.5)

133 owed] *(ought), F4 (*ow'd)    137 'jack'] *this edn;* iacke *Q1;* Iacke *Q2–F*    144 man] a man *Q3–F*
145 prince] a Prince *F*    150 an] *(and), Capell;* if *F*    I pray God] let *F*

houses and one poor pennyworth of sugar-candy to
make thee long-winded, if thy pocket were enriched
with any other injuries but these, I am a villain. And yet     160
you will stand to it; you will not pocket up wrong.
Art thou not ashamed?

FALSTAFF   Dost thou hear, Hal? Thou knowest in the
state of innocency Adam fell, and what should poor
Jack Falstaff do in the days of villainy? Thou seest I     165
have more flesh than another man and therefore more
frailty. You confess, then, you picked my pocket?

PRINCE   It appears so by the story.

FALSTAFF   Hostess, I forgive thee. Go make ready
breakfast, love thy husband, look to thy servants,     170
cherish thy guests. Thou shalt find me tractable to any
honest reason; thou seest I am pacified still. Nay,
prithee, be gone.                                        *Exit Hostess.*

159 **long-winded** capable of extended
physical exertion
160 **injuries** i.e. objects whose loss you
call injuries
161 **stand to it** persist in your story
**pocket up wrong** tamely accept the
rebuke (with *pocket* playing on the
earlier use at 159)
163–5 **Thou . . . villainy** i.e. you know
that Adam fell even while living in the
innocence of Eden, so what chance
does Falstaff have living in our fallen
world
165–7 **I . . . frailty** Falstaff plays with the
biblical notion, 'the flesh is frail'
(Psalms, 39.4; Matthew, 26.41, Bishops' Bible; and proverbial, Dent,
F363), arguing that, since he has *more
flesh* than other men, it stands to reason he would have *more frailty*.
Perhaps the immediate source is

Foxe's *Acts and Monuments* (1583),
where Henry Pendleton tries to cheer
up Laurence Saunders about the dangers they face as Protestants in Queen
Mary's England: 'there is a great deale
more cause in me to be afeard then in
you, for as much as you see I cary a
greater masse of flesh upon my backe
then you do, and being so laden with a
heavier lumpe of this vile carkase
ought therfor of nature to bee more
frayle then you' (1499).
168 **by the story** i.e. by the accurate catalogue of the contents of your pocket
171 **tractable** agreeable
172 **pacified still** always easily appeased;
Hanmer printed 'pacify'd—still?',
seemingly trying to indicate something
like 'are you still lingering?' and perhaps recording a stage tradition of the
line's delivery.

169–73] *F lines* thee: / Husband, / Guests: / reason: / still. / gone. /    171 guests] *(ghesse), Q2
(ghests), F*

Now, Hal, to the news at court: for the robbery, lad, how
is that answered?                                          175

PRINCE   O, my sweet beef, I must still be good angel to
thee. The money is paid back again.

FALSTAFF   O, I do not like that paying back; 'tis a double
labour.

PRINCE   I am good friends with my father and may do      180
anything.

FALSTAFF   Rob me the exchequer the first thing thou
dost, and do it with unwashed hands too.

BARDOLL   Do, my lord.

PRINCE   I have procured thee, Jack, a charge of foot.     185

FALSTAFF   I would it had been of horse. Where shall I
find one that can steal well? O, for a fine thief of the age
of two-and-twenty or thereabouts. I am heinously
unprovided. Well, God be thanked for these rebels;
they offend none but the virtuous. I laud them; I praise   190
them.

---

175 **answered** *TN* 3.3.33–4: 'It might
have since been answer'd in repaying /
What we took from them.'

176 **sweet beef** Perhaps *sweet* is only an
unspecific, affectionate adjective (*OED*
8b), but, given the consistency with
which Falstaff is mocked by identifying him with specific cuts and types of
meat, *sweet beef* may mean fresh,
unsalted meat.
　**still** always
　**good angel** protector, but an *angel* is
also a coin; Hal tells Falstaff that the
stolen money has been *paid back*, 177.

178–9 **double labour** (in taking it in the
first place and then giving it back)

182 **Rob me** rob (*me* functions as the ethical dative, as at 2.4.100)

183 **with unwashed hands** at once, i.e.

without waiting to wash your hands;
proverbial (Dent, H125)

185 **charge of foot** command of an
infantry unit (as at 2.4.532); in the theatre, Hal's continued complicity with
Falstaff can be measured by whether
Hal announces this warmly or puni-
tively.

186 **of horse** i.e. a cavalry unit

187 **one** i.e. a man to serve him

187–8 **fine . . . twenty** (a momentary fantasy of a skilful thief who will get him
a horse)

188–9 **heinously unprovided** terribly
ill-equipped

189–90 **God . . . virtuous** i.e. the war
provides opportunities to thrive for all
but *the virtuous*

---

174 court: for] *Theobald;* court for *QF*   176–7] *F lines* Beefe: / thee. / againe. /   187–8 the age of]
of *F*   188 two-and-twenty] *(xxii.), F*   thereabouts] ther about *Q4–5;* thereabout *F*

PRINCE   Bardoll.

BARDOLL   My lord?

PRINCE

Go bear this letter to Lord John of Lancaster –

To my brother John; this to my lord of Westmorland.     195

                                                     *[Exit Bardoll.]*

Go, Peto, to horse, to horse, for thou and I

Have thirty miles to ride yet ere dinner time.     *[Exit Peto.]*

Jack, meet me tomorrow in the Temple hall

At two o'clock in the afternoon.

There shalt thou know thy charge and there receive     200

Money and order for their furniture.

The land is burning, Percy stands on high,

And either we or they must lower lie.

FALSTAFF

Rare words! Brave world!     *[Calls.]*

                            Hostess, my breakfast, come!     204

O, I could wish this tavern were my drum!     *[Exeunt.]*

---

196 **Peto** Here Peto is about to set off with the Prince on a thirty-mile ride; at 4.2.9 he appears with Falstaff. To resolve the seeming contradiction, some editors have substituted another name for Peto here, usually 'Poins' (and indeed an abbreviated form of the name might easily confuse a compositor). Nonetheless, although by 4.2 Hal's own plans have obviously changed (or been forgotten by Shakespeare), the emendation seems editorially inappropriate, correcting Shakespeare, rather than trying merely to recover what he wrote.

198 **the Temple hall** hall in the Inner or Middle Temple, two of the London Inns of Court

200 **thy charge** your regiment

201 **furniture** equipment

202–3 The Prince concludes with a rousing couplet expressing his new-found commitment, which might be expected to end the scene.

202 **burning** not literally on fire, but 'on the verge of destruction'
**stands on high** has risen up

204–5 **Rare . . . drum** Falstaff's uncharacteristic couplet trumps Hal's noble sentiment spoken immediately before. The Prince is eager for battle; Falstaff thinks of his breakfast and voices his ignoble desire to remain in the tavern (*I could wish . . . drum*; i.e. I wish I could enlist my soldiers here).

195 SD] *Dyce*   196 to horse, to horse] to horse *Q3–F*   197 to ride yet] yet to ride *Q5*   SD] *Cam¹; Exit Pointz. / Dyce*   203 we or they] they or we *Q4–5;* they, or we *F*   204 SD] *Oxf*   205 SD] *Q2–5; Exeunt omnes. F*

**4.1** [*Enter* HOTSPUR, WORCESTER *and* DOUGLAS.]

HOTSPUR

    Well said, my noble Scot. If speaking truth
    In this fine age were not thought flattery,
    Such attribution should the Douglas have
    As not a soldier of this season's stamp
    Should go so general current through the world.    5
    By God, I cannot flatter. I do defy
    The tongues of soothers, but a braver place
    In my heart's love hath no man than yourself.
    Nay, task me to my word; approve me, lord.

DOUGLAS

    Thou art the king of honour.    10
    No man so potent breathes upon the ground
    But I will beard him.

HOTSPUR               Do so, and 'tis well.

*Enter* [Messenger] *with letters.*

    What letters hast thou there? [*to Douglas*] I can but
        thank you.

MESSENGER    These letters come from your father.

HOTSPUR

    Letters from him? Why comes he not himself?    15

---

4.1 The action takes place in the rebel camp, near Shrewsbury.
2 **fine** refined
3 **attribution** praise, credit
4 **this season's stamp** this year's coinage
5 **go . . . current** be so widely recognized (completing the coinage image from the previous line; *go . . . current* = be put into circulation)

6 **defy** despise
7 **soothers** flatterers
  **braver** finer, better
9 **task . . . word** test my assertion
  **approve** prove, test
11 **so potent** however powerful
12 **beard** challenge, defy (literally, contemptuously pull by the beard)
13 **but** only

4.1.0.1] *Q2–F subst.* HOTSPUR] *Harrie Hotspurre F* 1+ SP] *Q2–F (Hot.); Per. to 90 Q1*
2 thought] though *Q5u* 6 God] heauen *F* I do] I *Q2–F* 12.1] *Malone subst.; Enter one with letters after* him. *Q; Enter a Messenger. after* him. *F* 12–13 Do . . . you.] *as Capell; Q1–2, F line* him. /
there? / you. /; *prose Q3–5* 13 hast thou] hast *F* SD] *Folg²* 15–16] *F lines* him? / himselfe? /
Lord, / sicke. /

MESSENGER

He cannot come, my lord. He is grievous sick.

HOTSPUR

Zounds, how has he the leisure to be sick

In such a jostling time? Who leads his power?

Under whose government come they along?

MESSENGER

His letters bears his mind, not I, my lord.                20

WORCESTER

I prithee, tell me: doth he keep his bed?

MESSENGER

He did, my lord, four days ere I set forth;

And at the time of my departure thence

He was much feared by his physicians.

WORCESTER

I would the state of time had first been whole          25

Ere he by sickness had been visited.

His health was never better worth than now.

---

16 **grievous sick** Holinshed reports that 'The earle of Northumberland himself was not with them, but being sicke, had promised vpon his amendement to repair vnto them (as some write) with all conuenient speed', but this news reaches the rebels well before the eve of the battle (3.522). In *2H4* Induction 37, Rumour says that Northumberland 'lies crafty-sick', even the verb casting doubt upon the reality of his illness.

18 **jostling** unquiet
**power** army

19 **government** command

20 **bears his mind** reveal his thoughts; the singular verb after a plural subject, as in Q1–6 and F, has led many, following Q7, to correct the grammar to 'bear', but Shakespeare occasionally gives plural subjects singular verbs, especially when, as here (where the received *letters* are one communication), the noun may be understood as logically, if not grammatically, singular. ***my lord** Q1–2 printed 'my mind', and later quartos and F emended to 'his mind' (or 'minde'), trying to make sense of the line. Capell first suggested 'my lord', and this has been accepted by most modern editors; the Messenger uses the phrase two other times (16, 22).

21 **doth . . . bed?** is he bedridden?

24 **feared** feared for

25 **state of time** present situation
**whole** healthy

27 **better worth** more valuable

17 Zounds, how] How? *F*   sick] sicke now, *F*   18 jostling] *(*iustling*)*   20 I, my lord] *Capell;* I my mind *Q1–2;* I his mind *Q3–F*   24 physicians] *(*Phisitions*);* Phisition *Q4–5;* Physician *F*

HOTSPUR

Sick now? Droop now? This sickness doth infect
The very life-blood of our enterprise.
'Tis catching hither, even to our camp.                    30
He writes me here that inward sickness –
And that his friends by deputation could not
So soon be drawn; nor did he think it meet
To lay so dangerous and dear a trust
On any soul removed but on his own.                        35
Yet doth he give us bold advertisement
That with our small conjunction we should on
To see how fortune is disposed to us,
For, as he writes, 'there is no quailing now,
Because the King is certainly possessed                    40
Of all our purposes'. What say you to it?

WORCESTER

Your father's sickness is a maim to us.

HOTSPUR

A perilous gash, a very limb lopped off.
And yet, in faith, it is not. His present want

---

30 **'Tis catching hither** it will infect us
here
31 **sickness** – Many editors have viewed
the unfinished line in QF as defective
and have suggested various comple-
tions, like Capell's 'holds him'; but the
quick change of subject away from
what he has just read of his father's
*sickness* seems psychologically true and
dramatically effective, as Hotspur
shifts attention from what might be
seen as his father's betrayal to an
account of his father's thoughtfulness.
32 **deputation** through others acting for
him
33 **drawn** assembled, involved; cf. *KJ*

4.2.118: 'That such an a army could be
drawn in France'.
**meet** appropriate
34 **dear** demanding, important
35 **soul removed** person not directly
concerned
**but . . . own** except on himself
36 **bold advertisement** confident advice
37 **conjunction** assembly of forces
39 **quailing** losing courage; cf. Cotgrave,
'*Flestisseure*', which has as definitions
'quailing', 'failing' 'drooping' and
'falling away'.
40 **possessed** informed
42 **maim** crippling injury
44 **present want** absence now

---

31 sickness –] *Rowe;* sicknesse, *QF;* Sickness holds him *Capell;* sickness [ ] *Ard²* 32–3] *as Capell;*
*QF line* deputation / meet / 39–41 'there . . . purposes.'] *this edn;* there . . . purposes, *Q;* there
. . . purposes. *F*

Seems more than we shall find it. Were it good          45
To set the exact wealth of all our states
All at one cast, to set so rich a main
On the nice hazard of one doubtful hour?
It were not good, for therein should we read
The very bottom and the soul of hope,          50
The very list, the very utmost bound
Of all our fortunes.

DOUGLAS                    Faith, and so we should,
Where now remains a sweet reversion:
We may boldly spend upon the hope of what is to
     come in.
A comfort of retirement lives in this.          55

HOTSPUR

A rendezvous, a home to fly unto,
If that the devil and mischance look big
Upon the maidenhead of our affairs.

WORCESTER

But yet I would your father had been here.
The quality and hair of our attempt          60
Brooks no division. It will be thought

---

45 **find it** discover it to be in fact
46–7 **set . . . cast** gamble everything on a single throw of the dice
47 **main** The primary meaning here is 'stake in a game of chance', but it also means 'army'.
48 **nice hazard** finely balanced chance (but, like *main* in the previous line, *hazard* carries the particular sense of 'a wager' – the two quibbles effectively revealing Hotspur's attitude about battle)
50 **very bottom** whole extent
51 **very list** absolute limit
   **bound** boundary
53 whereas now we have the comfort of something to fall back upon

**reversion** expected inheritance
55 **retirement** something to fall back on
56 **rendezvous** retreat, refuge (*OED sb.* †3)
57 i.e. if things look as if they are going wrong
   **big** menacingly; cf. Heywood, *Wise-Woman*, 'Ile goe, although the Devill and mischance looke bigge' (sig. H1ʳ; cited Ard¹).
58 **maidenhead** first trial, beginning
59 **would** wish
60 **quality and hair** nature (*quality* and *hair* mean roughly the same thing; *hair* = peculiar quality, *OED sb.* 6)
61 **Brooks no division** permits no disunity

45–6] *F lines* it. / states /     54] *F lines* hope / in: /     is] *F*; tis *Q*     60 hair] *(*haire*); heaire Q4; heire Q5–F*

By some that know not why he is away
That wisdom, loyalty and mere dislike
Of our proceedings kept the Earl from hence;
And think how such an apprehension                    65
May turn the tide of fearful faction
And breed a kind of question in our cause.
For, well you know, we of the off'ring side
Must keep aloof from strict arbitrement
And stop all sight-holes, every loop from whence      70
The eye of reason may pry in upon us.
This absence of your father's draws a curtain
That shows the ignorant a kind of fear
Before not dreamt of.
HOTSPUR                        You strain too far.
I rather of his absence make this use:                75
It lends a lustre and more great opinion,
A larger dare to our great enterprise,
Than if the Earl were here; for men must think
If we without his help can make a head
To push against a kingdom, with his help            80
We shall o'erturn it topsy-turvy down.
Yet all goes well; yet all our joints are whole.

---

63 **mere** absolute, downright
65 **apprehension** thought, imagination
   (*OED* 10)
66 **fearful faction** alliance causing fear
   (*OED* fearful 1); it is possible that *fearful* has its more common meaning of
   'timid', but in 72–4 it is clear that
   Worcester does not think that his supporters are afraid but worries, rather,
   that the news of Northumberland's
   sickness might make them so.
67 **breed . . . question** raise doubts
   **in our cause** among our followers

68 **off'ring side** party taking the offen-
   sive
69 **strict arbitrement** careful scrutiny,
   impartial adjudication
70 **loop** opening to look through; loop-
   hole
72 **draws** draws aside, opens
76 **opinion** prestige, reputation
77 **dare** boldness, risk
79 **make a head** raise an army
81 **o'erturn . . . down** i.e. topple it completely
82 **joints** limbs

72 father's] *(fathers)*; Father *Q5–F*   77 our] your *Q3–F*   80 a] the *Q5–F*   81 shall o'erturn] shall
or turne *Q3;* shall, or turne *Q4–5*

DOUGLAS

As heart can think. There is not such a word
Spoke of in Scotland as this term of fear.

*Enter* Sir Richard VERNON.

HOTSPUR

My cousin Vernon! Welcome, by my soul.                    85

VERNON

Pray God my news be worth a welcome, lord.
The Earl of Westmorland, seven thousand strong,
Is marching hitherwards; with him Prince John.

HOTSPUR

No harm. What more?

VERNON                              And, further, I have learned
The King himself in person is set forth,                   90
Or hitherwards intended speedily,
With strong and mighty preparation.

HOTSPUR

He shall be welcome too. Where is his son,
The nimble-footed madcap Prince of Wales,
And his comrades that daffed the world aside               95
And bid it pass?

VERNON                      All furnished, all in arms,

83 **As . . . think** i.e. as can be wished;
proverbial: cf. Dent, H300.1.
89 **No harm** i.e. that's no problem
91 **intended speedily** will soon be ready
to march
92 **preparation** army in battle array
94 **nimble-footed** Hotspur's sarcasm
seemingly picks up the Prince's reputation for athleticism; cf. Holinshed:
'In strength and nimblenesse of bodie
from his youth few to him comparable,
for wrestling, leaping, and running, no
man well able to compare' (3.583).

95 **daffed** tossed
96 **bid it pass** i.e. without any concern
for it; similar to other expressions of
indifference; cf. *TS* Induction 5: 'let
the world slide' and the proverbial, 'let
the world wag' (Dent, W879).
96–102 **All . . . bulls** Many emendations
have been proposed in this passage, and
many editors believe a line is somewhere
missing, some suggesting it has dropped
out after 98 (e.g. Malone), some after 99
(e.g. Douce, 269). What is clear is that
Vernon's speech expresses his wonder at

83–4] *F lines* thinke: / Scotland, / Feare. /    84 as] at *Q5–F*    term] *(tearme); deame *Q5;* Dreame
*F*    84.1 Richard] *(Ri:), Q5 (Rih.), F*    88 with him] with *Q2–F*    90 is] hath *Q3–F*

All plumed like ostriches, that with the wind
Bated like eagles having lately bathed,
Glittering in golden coats like images,
As full of spirit as the month of May                    100
And gorgeous as the sun at midsummer,
Wanton as youthful goats, wild as young bulls.
I saw young Harry with his beaver on,
His cuisses on his thighs, gallantly armed,
Rise from the ground like feathered Mercury,             105
And vaulted with such ease into his seat
As if an angel dropped down from the clouds
To turn and wind a fiery Pegasus

the appearance of Hal and the assembled forces, and the disjunctive syntax may therefore voice his own breathless effort to find the appropriate terms for what he has seen, one simile tumbling over the next. It is evocative rather than strictly logical, as Edmund Burke realized in 1770, using the speech as an example of a certain kind of excitement where the 'mind is so dazzled as to make it impossible to attend to the exact coherence and agreement of the allusions, which we should require on every other occasion' (Burke, 72).

97 **ostriches** Q's spelling, 'estridges', can also refer to goshawks, but the image here with its emphasis on plumage suggests the more obvious meaning, especially as three ostrich feathers make up the emblem of the Prince of Wales.

98 **Bated** beat their wings impatiently (*OED* bate *v.*[1] 2)
**eagles . . . bathed** As many editors have noted, a similar image appears in Spenser's *Faerie Queene*, where the Red Cross Knight is said to appear for battle as an 'Eagle, fresh out of the ocean wave' (1.11.34).

99 **coats** sleeveless surcoats with richly embroidered heraldic arms, worn over armour; cf. Chaucer, *House of Fame*: 'a

vesture, / Which that men clepe a cote-armure, / Embrowded wonderliche riche' (Chaucer, 3.1325–7).
**images** gilded statues

100 **spirit** vigour (*OED* III 13)

102 **Wanton** exuberant

103 **beaver on** face mask of helmet down (i.e. ready to fight); cf. Bullokar, '*Beaver*': 'In armour it signifieth that part of the helmet which may bee lifted vp, to take breth the more freely.'

104 **cuisses** thigh armour (presumably Q's spelling 'cushes' approximates to the Elizabethan pronunciation); cf. 5.4.127, where Falstaff stabs the dead Hotspur in the thigh.

105 **feathered Mercury** messenger of the Roman gods, with his feathered sandals

106 **vaulted . . . seat** jumped as easily into the saddle (no small feat, fully armoured); cf. *H5* 5.2.136–7: 'If I could win a lady at leapfrog, or by vaulting into my saddle with my armour on my back'.

108 **wind** wheel about
**fiery** spirited (but also referring to the belief that Pegasus breathed fire from his nostrils)
**Pegasus** winged horse in Greek mythology

98 Bated] *(Baited)*, *Q5 (Bayted)*    107 dropped] *Q2–F*; drop *Q1*

And witch the world with noble horsemanship.

HOTSPUR

No more, no more. Worse than the sun in March                    110
This praise doth nourish agues. Let them come!
They come like sacrifices in their trim,
And to the fire-eyed maid of smoky war
All hot and bleeding will we offer them.
The mailed Mars shall on his altar sit                    115
Up to the ears in blood. I am on fire
To hear this rich reprisal is so nigh,
And yet not ours! Come, let me taste my horse,
Who is to bear me like a thunderbolt
Against the bosom of the Prince of Wales.                    120
Harry to Harry shall, hot horse to horse,
Meet and ne'er part till one drop down a corpse.
O, that Glendower were come.

VERNON                    There is more news.

I learned in Worcester, as I rode along,
He cannot draw his power this fourteen days.                    125

---

109 **witch** bewitch
110–11 **Worse . . . agues** i.e. this glowing
account makes me shudder more than
the sun does in March (alluding to the
belief that the spring sun nurtured
fevers; cf. Overbury: 'The March
Sunne breedes agues' sig. M3ʳ; cited
Ardⁱ).
112 **sacrifices . . . trim** sacrificial beasts
readied for the ceremony
113 **the fire-eyed maid** i.e. Bellona,
goddess of war
114 **offer** offer up as sacrifice
115 **mailed** mailèd
**mailed Mars** Mars, the god of war, in
armour
**altar** place of sacrifice (i.e. the battlefield)

116 **on fire** impatient
117 **reprisal** prize
**nigh** near
118 **yet** still
**taste** test (*OED v.* 2)
124 **Worcester** a town (pronounced
Wòo-ster) about 50 miles south-east of
Shrewsbury; see Fig. 21
125 He cannot gather his forces for two
weeks; cf. 3.1.86. Shakespeare here follows Daniel, who says that the King's
'swift approche and vnexpected speed'
in arriving at Shrewsbury 'dasht' the
rebels' hopes of aid from Glendower
(S. Daniel, 4.36); Holinshed, however,
says that Welsh troops were present at
the battle, but he does not mention
Glendower (Holinshed, 3.522).

---

110] *F lines* more, / March: / 115 altar] *Q4–F;* altars *Q1–3* 118 taste] take *Q3–F* 121 Harry
shall, hot] *(*Harry shal hot*), Johnson;* Harry, shall hot *Q2;* Harry, shall not *Q3–F* 122 ne'er] *Q2–F*
*(*ne're*);* neare *Q1* corpse] *(*coarse*)* 125 cannot] *Q5c–F;* can *Q1–Q5u*

DOUGLAS

That's the worst tidings that I hear of yet.

WORCESTER

Ay, by my faith, that bears a frosty sound.

HOTSPUR

What may the King's whole battle reach unto?

VERNON

To thirty thousand.

HOTSPUR                         Forty let it be.

My father and Glendower being both away,            130

The powers of us may serve so great a day.

Come, let us take a muster speedily.

Doomsday is near. Die all; die merrily.

DOUGLAS

Talk not of dying; I am out of fear                       134

Of death or death's hand for this one half year.      *Exeunt.*

**4.2**                         *Enter* FALSTAFF [*and*] BARDOLL.

FALSTAFF   Bardoll, get thee before to Coventry. Fill me a

bottle of sack. Our soldiers shall march through. We'll

---

126 **yet** to this point
127 **bears . . . sound** is discouraging
128 What is the total number of the King's forces?
129 **thirty thousand** Holinshed says that the forces opposing the King numbered 'about fourteene thousand chosen men' (3.523), but he does not give the size of the King's forces. Hall says that 'on bothe partes were aboue fourty thousand men assembled' (sig. D1$^r$).
131 **powers of us** forces we have
   **serve** suffice
132 **take a muster** assemble and review

our forces
133 **Die . . . merrily** i.e. if we must die, let's do it cheerfully; cf. Holinshed's account that Hotspur exhorted his troops saying, 'better it is to die in battell for the commonwealths cause, than through cowardlike feare to prolong life' (3.522); it is interesting that Shakespeare removes Hotspur's political concern from the buoyant embrace of his fate.
134 **out of** free from
**4.2** The action takes place on a road near Coventry.
2 **march through** continue on

126 yet] *Q5–F;* it *Q1–4*   133 merrily] *(merely)* *Q2–F*   135 SD] *Exeunt Omnes. F*   **4.2.0.1** *and*] *Q2–F*

to Sutton Coldfield tonight.

BARDOLL   Will you give me money, captain?

FALSTAFF   Lay out, lay out.                                                        5

BARDOLL   This bottle makes an angel.

FALSTAFF   An if it do, take it for thy labour; an if it make
twenty, take them all. I'll answer the coinage. Bid my
lieutenant Peto meet me at town's end.                              9

BARDOLL   I will, captain. Farewell.                                   *Exit.*

FALSTAFF   If I be not ashamed of my soldiers, I am a
soused gurnet. I have misused the King's press

---

3   *Sutton Coldfield** a town in Warwickshire about 20 miles north-east of Coventry; the second word was probably pronounced 'Co-fil'. Q2 reads 'cophill' (though the other quartos and F have 'cop-hill', the hyphen required to divide the word at the end of the line) suggesting the pronunciation.

4–8   **Will . . . coinage** Bardoll presumably gives *this bottle* to Falstaff, who characteristically avoids paying, giving the lie to his claim at 3.3.43–5 about how much he has spent on Bardoll's drink.

4   **captain** Bardoll's term of rank efficiently establishes Falstaff in his new military role (probably also involving some change to his costume).

5   **Lay out** pay out of your own funds

6   **makes** brings the cost to
   **angel** An *angel* was a gold coin varying in value from 6s. 8d. to 10s. The name of the coin came from the picture stamped on one side of the archangel Michael slaying the dragon.

8   **answer the coinage** guarantee their worth

12   **soused gurnet** pickled fish

12–47   **I . . . hedge** The entire speech highlights well-known abuses in the Elizabethan recruiting system. Falstaff selects men who are well off and permits them to buy their way out of service, leaving him with only old and weak men to fight. By Shakespeare's time the practice was already an old one. Next to a marginal note, 'a great abuse in choise of souldiers', Holinshed writes of Richard, Earl of Arundel, who in 1387 'vsed all diligence, and spared for no costs', to choose the fittest soldiers, 'not following the euill example of others in times past, which receiued tag and rag to fill vp their numbers, whom they hired for small wages, and reserued the residue to their pursses' (Holinshed, 3.454). At the end of the eighteenth century, John Henderson's Falstaff reportedly drew 'bursts of laughter' with his account of the unsuitable men he pressed (Siddons, 1.124–5); modern audiences are far less likely to ignore or condone Falstaff's self-serving cynicism.

12   **press** power of conscription

---

3 Coldfield] *Johnson;* cop-hill *QF*   7 An] *(*And*), Hanmer*   an] *(*and*), Hanmer*   12 soused] *(*souct*), F (*sowc't*)*

damnably. I have got, in exchange of a hundred and
fifty soldiers, three hundred and odd pounds. I press
me none but good householders, yeomen's sons;          15
inquire me out contracted bachelors, such as had been
asked twice on the banns, such a commodity of warm
slaves as had as lief hear the devil as a drum, such as
fear the report of a caliver worse than a struck fowl or
a hurt wild duck. I pressed me none but such toasts-      20
and-butter, with hearts in their bellies no bigger than
pins' heads, and they have bought out their services;
and now my whole charge consists of ensigns,
corporals, lieutenants, gentlemen of companies – slaves
as ragged as Lazarus in the painted cloth where the      25
glutton's dogs licked his sores – and such as indeed

14–15 **press me none** conscript no one
  other than
15 **good** of substantial means, well-to-do
16 **inquire** seek
  **contracted** engaged to be married
17 **asked . . . banns** i.e. on the verge of
  their wedding (*banns* were public
  announcements of an intended marriage read in church on three successive Sundays)
  **commodity** stock, supply; Falstaff
  speaks of men as merchandise for
  profit.
17–18 **warm slaves** well-to do knaves
  (*warm* = well-to-do, comfortably off,
  *OED a.* 8, but also, especially in regard
  to betrothed men, sexually eager)
18 **lief** soon, happily
19 **caliver** small musket (which became
  prominent only in Elizabeth's reign)
  **struck fowl** wounded game bird; it is
  possible, however, that *fowl* is the compositor's misreading of 'sorrel' (i.e.
  deer), as Dr Johnson proposed, since
  *hurt wild duck* in the next line merely
  repeats this first image to no obvious
  end.

20 **wild duck** an image of cowardice at
  2.2.97–8: 'There's no more valour in
  that Poins than in a wild duck.'
20–1 **toasts-and-butter** contemptuous
  term for pampered citizens; cf.
  Moryson: 'all within the sound of Bow-
  Bell, are in reproch called Cocknies,
  and eaters of buttered tostes' (3.463;
  cited by Malone).
22 **bought . . . services** paid me bribes to
  be released from service
23 **charge** command, unit
  **ensigns** standard-bearers
24 **gentlemen of companies** gentlemen
  soldiers not holding formal rank
  **slaves** rogues
25–6 **Lazarus . . . sores** The story of
  Lazarus is told in Luke, 16.19–21 (and
  is earlier referred to at 3.3.31–2); biblical scenes were often displayed on
  tapestries or, in a cheaper form, on
  painted cloth; cf. Lupton: 'In these
  [ale]houses you shall see the History of
  *Iudeth, Susanna, Daniel* in the Lyons
  Den, or *Diues & Lazarus* painted vpon
  the Wall' (sig. I^r).

13–14 a . . . fifty] *(150.), F*  14 three hundred] *(300.), F*  19 fowl] *(foule); foole Q4–F*
23 ensigns] *(Ancients)*

were never soldiers, but discarded unjust servingmen,
younger sons to younger brothers, revolted tapsters and
ostlers trade-fallen – the cankers of a calm world and a
long peace, ten times more dishonourable-ragged than    30
an old feazed ensign. And such have I to fill up the
rooms of them as have bought out their services that
you would think that I had a hundred and fifty tattered
prodigals lately come from swine-keeping, from eating
draff and husks. A mad fellow met me on the way and    35
told me I had unloaded all the gibbets and pressed the
dead bodies. No eye hath seen such scarecrows. I'll not
march through Coventry with them, that's flat. Nay,
and the villains march wide betwixt the legs as if they
had gyves on, for indeed I had the most of them out of    40
prison. There's not a shirt and a half in all my company,
and the half-shirt is two napkins tacked together and

27 **discarded unjust servingmen** servants fired for dishonesty
28 **younger sons . . . brothers** i.e. those
   having no prospects of inheritance
   **revolted tapsters** runaway apprentice
   barmen (as Francis contemplates
   becoming, provoked by the Prince in
   2.4)
29 **ostlers trade-fallen** unemployed
   horse-grooms
29–30 **cankers . . . peace** the social parasites that thrive in peacetime; cf.
   Nashe, *Piers Penniless* (1592), 'all the
   canker-womes that breed on the rust of
   piece' (Nashe, 1.213; cited Cam[1]).
31 **feazed ensign** tattered flag
   **such** men of such kind
32 **them** as those who
34 **prodigals** The story of the prodigal
   son, who lives so extravagantly that he
   is finally reduced to feeding pigs, is in
   Luke, 15.11–31, 35.
35 **draff and husks** pig swill and corn-

husks, recalling Luke, 15.16 (the use of
*husks* points to Shakespeare's familiarity with the Geneva Bible; in the
Bishops' Bible the word is 'cods')
36 **gibbets** gallows
   **pressed** conscripted
38 **flat** certain
39–40 **march . . . on** walk awkwardly as if
   in leg-irons (*gyves* = leg-shackles)
40–1 **out of prison** perhaps a topical reference; in 1596, prisoners were apparently freed from London prisons to
   provide soldiers for the Earl of Essex's
   expedition to Cadiz (see Cam[1]).
41 **There's . . . company** i.e. they are all
   poorly dressed and outfitted
42 **napkins tacked together** handker-
   chiefs knotted to make a halter top; cf.
   *The Duchess of Malfi*, 1.1.36–8: 'I wore
   two towels instead of a shirt, with a
   knot in the shoulder, after the fashion
   of a Roman mantle' (Webster, 2.38).

29–30 a long] long *Q5–F*   31 old feazed] *(*olde fazd*)*; old-fac'd *F*   ensign] *(*ancient*)*   32 as] that
*F*   33 tattered] *F3 (*tatter'd*)*; tottered *QF*

291

thrown over the shoulders like a herald's coat without
sleeves; and the shirt, to say the truth, stolen from my
host at Saint Albans or the red-nose innkeeper of          45
Daventry. But that's all one; they'll find linen enough
on every hedge.

*Enter the* PRINCE *[and the]* Lord of WESTMORLAND.

PRINCE    How now, blown Jack? How now, quilt?
FALSTAFF    What, Hal? How now, mad wag? What a devil
    dost thou in Warwickshire? – My good lord of     50
    Westmorland, I cry you mercy. I thought your honour
    had already been at Shrewsbury.
WESTMORLAND    Faith, Sir John, 'tis more than time that
    I were there – and you too – but my powers are there
    already. The King, I can tell you, looks for us all.     55
    We must away all night.

---

**43–4 herald's . . . sleeves** a sleeveless
garment, known as a tabard, with open
sides and often decorated with a coat
of arms
**45 host at Saint Albans** innkeeper in St
Albans, a town about 25 miles north-
west of London on the road to Coventry
**46 Daventry** a Northamptonshire town
about 40 miles north-west of St
Albans (and some 15 miles south-east
of Coventry). Q6–8's 'Daintry' represents its pronunciation; cf. *3H6* 5.1.6:
'at Daintry, with a puissant troop'.
**that's all one** no matter
**46–7 linen . . . hedge** laundry placed out
on hedges to dry and whiten in the
sun; cf. *WT* 4.3.5: 'The white sheet
bleaching on the hedge'.
**48 blown** swollen (but also out of breath)
**Jack** not merely Falstaff's name but

also a quilted leather jacket
**quilt** picking up the secondary meaning of Jack
**49–52 What . . . Shrewsbury** Falstaff's
comments, first wondering about what
the Prince is doing in Warwickshire
(pronounced Wŏ-rick-shir) and then
expressing some surprise that
Westmorland is not yet at Shrewsbury,
seem to be efforts to suggest to them
his own vigorous commitment.
**51 cry you mercy** beg your pardon
**55 looks for** expects
**56 away all night** travel all night; F's
'away all to night' (i.e. all leave tonight)
might, however, be correct; the Quarto
reading could have come from the Q
compositor missing 'to', perhaps influenced by 'us all' at the end of the previous clause.

45 at] of *Q5–F*   47.1 *and the*] *Q2–F*   55 can tell] can *Q5u*̂   56 night] to Night *F*

FALSTAFF    Tut, never fear me. I am as vigilant as a cat to
steal cream.

PRINCE    I think to steal cream indeed, for thy theft hath
already made thee butter. But tell me, Jack, whose          60
fellows are these that come after?

FALSTAFF    Mine, Hal, mine.

PRINCE    I did never see such pitiful rascals.

FALSTAFF    Tut, tut, good enough to toss; food for
powder, food for powder. They'll fill a pit as well as      65
better. Tush, man, mortal men, mortal men.

WESTMORLAND    Ay, but Sir John, methinks they are
exceeding poor and bare, too beggarly.

FALSTAFF    Faith, for their poverty, I know not where they
had that, and for their bareness I am sure they never       70
learned that of me.

PRINCE    No, I'll be sworn, unless you call three fingers in
the ribs bare. But, sirrah, make haste. Percy is already
in the field.                                          *Exit.*

FALSTAFF    What, is the King encamped?                      75

WESTMORLAND    He is, Sir John. I fear we shall stay too
long.

---

57 **never fear me** don't worry about me
57–8 **vigilant . . . cream** i.e. ready to go;
proverbial (Dent, C167)
60 **butter** i.e. fat; cf. 2.4.498.
61 **come after** i.e. follow you
64 **toss** impale on the end of a pike; cf.
*3H6* 1.1.251: 'The soldiers should have
tossed me on their pikes.'
64–5 **food for powder** cannon fodder,
bodies to be thrown into battle with little hope they will survive
65 **pit** mass grave
68 **bare** poorly clothed, ragged
**beggarly** impoverished

70–1 **bareness . . . me** Falstaff chooses
to interpret Westmorland's *bare* (68) as
bare-boned, and admits that they
could not have learned that from him.
72–3 **three . . . ribs** three fingers' thick-
ness of fat around the ribs; a 'finger'
was a conventional measure equal to ¾
inch.
74 **in the field** at the battlefield
75 **encamped** i.e. already at the battlefield
76 **stay** delay

57 me] tell me *Q5*   66 better] a better *Q2*   72 in] on *Q3–F*   74 SD] *om. F*

293

FALSTAFF

Well, to the latter end of a fray and the beginning of a
     feast

Fits a dull fighter and a keen guest.                    *Exeunt.*


**4.3** *Enter* HOTSPUR, WORCESTER, DOUGLAS [*and*] VERNON.

HOTSPUR

We'll fight with him tonight.

WORCESTER                    It may not be.

DOUGLAS

You give him then advantage.

VERNON                    Not a whit.

HOTSPUR

Why say you so? Looks he not for supply?

VERNON

So do we.

HOTSPUR          His is certain; ours is doubtful.

WORCESTER

Good cousin, be advised. Stir not tonight.          5

VERNON [*to Hotspur*]

Do not, my lord.

---

78–9 **Well . . . guest** The end of a fight
and the beginning of a feast are the
best times for one who is more fond of
food and drink than battle; proverbial
(Dent, C547). Falstaff ends the scene
with a doggerel couplet with the
approximate rhyme of *feast/guest.*

79 SD Many editions, following Capell,
have Westmorland exit after 77, leaving
Falstaff alone on stage to speak his final
couplet, though there is no indication
of this in QF. Mack (Signet) comments: 'Falstaff's last speech sounds as
if Westmoreland had departed, and
Falstaff winks at the audience.' It is,
however, as interesting and revealing if

Falstaff says this directly to
Westmorland or at least is aware that
Westmorland is present to hear it,
though it may well be an exit couplet
spoken out of Westmorland's hearing
as they exit separately.

4.3 The action takes place in the rebel
camp near Shrewsbury.

1–6 **We'll . . . well** The anxiety among
the rebel leaders is made clear by the
staccato movement of the verse; the
four speakers blurt out twelve short
sentences in six lines.

1 **him** i.e. the King

2 **then** i.e. if you wait until morning

3 **supply** reinforcements

---

4.3.0.1 DOUGLAS *and*] *Q2–F; Doug: Q1*   6 SD] *Folg²*

DOUGLAS              You do not counsel well.
  You speak it out of fear and cold heart.
VERNON
  Do me no slander, Douglas. By my life
  (And I dare well maintain it with my life),
  If well-respected honour bid me on,                    10
  I hold as little counsel with weak fear
  As you, my lord, or any Scot that this day lives.
  Let it be seen tomorrow in the battle
  Which of us fears.
DOUGLAS              Yea, or tonight.
VERNON                              Content.
HOTSPUR   Tonight, say I.                                 15
VERNON
  Come, come, it may not be. I wonder much,
  Being men of such great leading as you are,
  That you foresee not what impediments
  Drag back our expedition. Certain horse
  Of my cousin Vernon's are not yet come up.             20
  Your uncle Worcester's horse came but today,
  And now their pride and mettle is asleep,
  Their courage with hard labour tame and dull,
  That not a horse is half the half of himself.
HOTSPUR
  So are the horses of the enemy                         25

10 **well-respected** well-considered,
thoughtful (as opposed to the fervid
commitment to honour displayed by
Hotspur)
  **bid me on** inspires me
11 **hold . . . with** am as little moved by
17 **leading** military experience, leadership

19 **Drag back** inhibit, slow down
  **expedition** enterprise (with suggestion of haste)
  **Certain horse** cavalry (as in 21)
20 **come up** arrived
21 **horse** cavalry horses
24 that no horse has even a quarter of its
usual strength

13 Let it] Let *Q2–4*   13–14 Let . . . fears] *as F; one line Q*   14 SP DOUGLAS] *om. Q3–4*   16–17]
*as T. Johnson; QF line* be. / are, /   21 horse] *Q5–F*; horses *Q1–4*   22 mettle] *(mettall)*

In general journey-bated and brought low.
The better part of ours are full of rest.

WORCESTER

The number of the King exceedeth ours.
For God's sake, cousin, stay till all come in.

*The trumpet sounds a parley.*

*Enter* Sir Walter BLOUNT.

BLOUNT

I come with gracious offers from the King,                    30
If you vouchsafe me hearing and respect.

HOTSPUR

Welcome, Sir Walter Blount; and would to God
You were of our determination.
Some of us love you well, and even those some
Envy your great deservings and good name                    35
Because you are not of our quality
But stand against us like an enemy.

BLOUNT

And God defend but still I should stand so,
So long as out of limit and true rule
You stand against anointed majesty.                         40
But to my charge: the King hath sent to know

26 **journey-bated** wearied by the long march
28 **number** i.e. the number of cavalry
29 SD *parley* off-stage trumpet call announcing the approach of an envoy
29.1 The offer of pardon that Blount carries here was historically delivered to 'the abbat of Shrewesburie, and one of the clerkes of the priuie seale' (Holinshed, 3.523).
31 **vouchsafe** grant, permit

**respect** attention
33 **determination** mind, point of view
34 **even** precisely
35 **Envy** begrudge
36 **quality** party (*OED* 5)
38 **defend but still** ensure that always (*defend* = forbid; *but* = but that)
39 **out . . . rule** outside the bounds of natural order and good government
41 **charge** task

28 ours] *F;* our *Q1–5*   32–3] *F lines Blunt:* / determination. /   38 God] Heauen *F*   41] *F lines* Charge. / know /

The nature of your griefs and whereupon
You conjure from the breast of civil peace
Such bold hostility, teaching his duteous land
Audacious cruelty. If that the King　　　　　　　45
Have any way your good deserts forgot,
Which he confesseth to be manifold,
He bids you name your griefs, and with all speed
You shall have your desires with interest
And pardon absolute for yourself and these　　　50
Herein misled by your suggestion.

HOTSPUR

The King is kind, and well we know the King
Knows at what time to promise, when to pay.
My father and my uncle and myself
Did give him that same royalty he wears;　　　　55
And when he was not six-and-twenty strong,
Sick in the world's regard, wretched and low,
A poor unminded outlaw sneaking home,
My father gave him welcome to the shore;
And when he heard him swear and vow to God　60
He came but to be Duke of Lancaster,
To sue his livery and beg his peace

---

42 **griefs** grievances (*OED* grief 2b)
　　**whereupon** on what grounds
43 **conjure** call forth
44 **teaching** demonstrating to
49 **desires with interest** what you want
　　and more
51 **suggestion** urging, instigation
53 **what . . . pay** perhaps has a proverbial
　　basis in Dent, P602: 'Great promise,
　　small performance'; on the language of
　　debt, see pp. 67–9.
56 **six-and-twenty** Holinshed says that
　　Bolingbroke returned with 'not past
　　three score persons' (3.498).
57 **Sick . . . regard** weak and inconse-

quential in so far as anyone cared
58 **unminded** unnoticed, disregarded
61 When Henry returned in 1399 from
　　exile in France, he insisted that he was
　　returning only to claim his ducal rights
　　by inheritance from his father; cf.
　　5.1.41–5 and *R2* 2.3.113: 'as I come, I
　　come for Lancaster'.
62 **sue his livery** bring suit for his ducal
　　inheritance; upon the death of John of
　　Gaunt, the Duchy of Lancaster tech-
　　nically reverted to the King, but
　　Bolingbroke as eldest son did have the
　　right to sue for possession, needing to
　　prove himself only of legal age and

52] *F lines* kinde: / King /　54 and my] my *Q3–F*　61 be] the *Q4–Q5u*

With tears of innocency and terms of zeal,
My father, in kind heart and pity moved,
Swore him assistance and performed it too.                      65
Now when the lords and barons of the realm
Perceived Northumberland did lean to him,
The more and less came in with cap and knee,
Met him in boroughs, cities, villages,
Attended him on bridges, stood in lanes,                        70
Laid gifts before him, proffered him their oaths,
Gave him their heirs as pages, followed him
Even at the heels in golden multitudes.
He presently, as greatness knows itself,
Steps me a little higher than his vow                           75
Made to my father while his blood was poor
Upon the naked shore at Ravenspur,
And now forsooth takes on him to reform
Some certain edicts and some strait decrees
That lie too heavy on the commonwealth,                         80

willing to do homage to the King; cf. *R2* 2.1.201–5, where York warns Richard about the danger in refusing Henry the right to 'sue / His livery'.

**beg his peace** reconcile himself with the King

63 **terms of zeal** assurances of loyalty

67 **did lean to** favoured

68 **more and less** nobles and commoners
**with . . . knee** with cap in hand and knee bowed (in respect)

70 **Attended** awaited
**lanes** facing rows

72 **\*heirs as pages** children as attendants, marking their fathers' loyalty to Bolingbroke (rather than as hostages to secure their commitment, as in Cam[1] and Oxf[1]); QF place a comma after 'heirs', making the line say that the fathers follow Bolingbroke as 'pages', a not impossible notion, especially if 'as

pages' is read as a simile, but strained enough as applied to 'the lords and barons of the realm', 66, that the emendation of the punctuation first suggested by Malone has been generally followed. Cf. Marmion, sig. B4[r]: 'Your rich men / Shall strive to put their sonnes to be his Pages', perhaps an echo, but certainly confirming Malone's conjecture.

73 **golden** an emotive word expressing their great happiness; cf. *2H4* 5.3.100, the 'golden joys' of the news of Henry V's accession.

74 **knows itself** feels its own power

76 **while . . . poor** i.e. when he was not yet King (and so, while his spirit still was humble)

77 **Ravenspur** See 1.3.245 and note.

79 **strait** strict

80 **lie . . . on** burden, oppress

70 Attended] Attend *Q4–5*   72 heirs as pages,] *F4 (*Heires, as Pages,*)*; heires, as Pages *QF*
80 lie] lay *Q5c–F*

Cries out upon abuses, seems to weep
Over his country's wrongs; and, by this face,
This seeming brow of justice, did he win
The hearts of all that he did angle for;
Proceeded further: cut me off the heads                    85
Of all the favourites that the absent King
In deputation left behind him here
When he was personal in the Irish war.

BLOUNT

    Tut, I came not to hear this.

HOTSPUR               Then to the point.

    In short time after, he deposed the King,                    90
Soon after that deprived him of his life,
And in the neck of that tasked the whole state;
To make that worse, suffered his kinsman March

---

82 **face** show of sympathy
85–6 **cut . . . favourites** In *R2* 3.1.29–35, Bolingbroke orders Northumberland to have Bushy and Green 'dispatched', following Holinshed's account of how Bolingbroke at Bristol captured 'William Scoope, earle of Wiltshire and tresuror of England, Sir Henrie Greene, and sir Iohn Bushie knights' and after a trial in which they were found guilty of treason 'for misgouerning the king and the realme, . . . had their heads smit off' (3.498). The *me* in 85 is a version of the ethical dative; see 2.4.100n.
87 **In deputation** as his deputies
88 **personal** himself, personally engaged
90 **deposed** Partisans debated whether Richard was *deposed* by Henry or had in fact abdicated his throne; Bolingbroke's supporters predictably argued that Richard had willingly resigned and named Henry as his heir.
91 **deprived . . . life** Bolingbroke's responsibility for Richard's death was similarly debated along partisan lines.

Clearly Henry wanted Richard dead; it is less clear that he took responsibility for ensuring it. Shakespeare in *R2* 5.4 dramatizes Piers of Exton's reaction to Henry's expressed desire to be 'rid . . . of this living fear' (5.4.2), and in 5.6.40, after Exton has murdered Richard, Henry expresses his ambivalence, admitting, 'I hate the murderer, love him murdered.' Holinshed reports Henry's wish for someone to 'deliuer me of him, whose life will be my death, and whose death will be the preseruall of my life' (Holinshed, 3.517) but similarly hedges about whether Henry suborned the deed.
92 **in . . . of** immediately after; cf. *Son* 131.10–11: 'A thousand groans . . . One on another's neck do witness bear.'
    **tasked** taxed (*OED v.* 1); among the stated grievances of the rebels was Henry's 'leuieng of taxes and tallages, contrarie to his promise' (Holinshed, 3.522).
93 **suffered** permitted
    **his kinsman March** i.e. Mortimer

82 country's] *Rowe;* Countrey *Q1–Q5u;* Countries *Q5c–F*

299

(Who is, if every owner were well placed,
Indeed his king) to be engaged in Wales,                                    95
There without ransom to lie forfeited;
Disgraced me in my happy victories,
Sought to entrap me by intelligence,
Rated mine uncle from the Council board,
In rage dismissed my father from the court,                                 100
Broke oath on oath, committed wrong on wrong,
And, in conclusion, drove us to seek out
This head of safety and withal to pry
Into his title, the which we find
Too indirect for long continuance.                                         105

BLOUNT

Shall I return this answer to the King?

HOTSPUR

Not so, Sir Walter. We'll withdraw awhile.
Go to the King, and let there be impawned
Some surety for a safe return again,
And in the morning early shall mine uncle                                   110
Bring him our purposes. And so farewell.

BLOUNT

I would you would accept of grace and love.

HOTSPUR

And maybe so we shall.

BLOUNT                              Pray God you do.              [*Exeunt.*]

---

94 **if . . . placed** if everyone in fact held
   the position to which he were entitled
95 **Indeed his king** in fact Henry's king;
   i.e. if Mortimer were on the throne as
   he should be by right, he would be
   king and Henry would be his subject.
   **engaged** held hostage
98 **intelligence** spies
99 **Rated** berated
103 **head of safety** army to protect us

**withal** in addition
105 **indirect** out of the direct line of
   inheritance (but also morally compromised)
108 **impawned** given as a pledge
109 **surety . . . return** collateral to guarantee Worcester's return; see 5.2.28.
113 **And . . . shall** Holinshed's account
   notes that, as a result of the ambas-
   sadors sent from the King, 'the lord

94 were well] were *Q5–F* 99 mine] my *Q5–F* 107] *F lines Walter. / while: /* 110 mine] my
*Q3–F* 111 purposes] porpose *Q4;* purpose *Q5–F* 113 And] And't *F* God] Heauen *F* SD] *F*

**4.4**     *Enter [the]* ARCHBISHOP *of* York *[and]* SIR MICHAEL.

ARCHBISHOP

Hie, good Sir Michael, bear this sealed brief
With winged haste to the Lord Marshal,
This to my cousin Scrope, and all the rest
To whom they are directed. If you knew
How much they do import, you would make haste.          5

SIR MICHAEL

My good lord, I guess their tenor.

ARCHBISHOP                              Like enough you do.

Tomorrow, good Sir Michael, is a day
Wherein the fortune of ten thousand men

Henrie Persie began to giue eare vnto the kings offers, & so sent with them his vncle the earle of Worcester, to declare vnto the king the causes of those troubles, and to require some effectuall reformation in the same' (3.523).

**4.4** The scene has no historical basis, but the action takes place away from the rebel camp of 4.3, presumably at the palace of the Archbishop of York. The scene has often been cut in performance.

0.1 SIR MICHAEL no known historical character (Q1 'Mighell'); *Sir* here seems most likely to be a courtesy title for a priest (cf. *Sir* Oliver Martext in *AYL*), perhaps the Archbishop's chaplain, rather than a knight.

1 **sealed** sealèd
    **brief** letter; Holinshed reports that the Percys, advised by the Archbishop, 'deuised certeine articles', which 'being shewed to diuerse noblemen, and other states of the realme, mooued them them to fauour their purpose' (3.521).

2 **winged** wingèd
    **Lord Marshal** Thomas Mowbray, Earl Marshall and third earl of Nottingham, and elder son of Thomas

Mowbray, Duke of Norfolk, banished in *R2* 1.3. He joined the rebellion and participated in the events portrayed in *2H4*; he surrendered at Gaultree Forest and was executed (see *2H4* 4.2).

3 **my cousin Scrope** It is not made clear to which Scrope this refers. The Scrope family was large with several extensive collateral branches (many of which seem to be involved in rebellions against their kings; see Kelly). Possibly Shakespeare is thinking of Sir Stephen Scrope, the younger brother of the Earl of Wiltshire, whose execution (along with Sir John Bushy's and Sir Henry Green's) Scrope reports to Aumerle in *R2* 3.2.141–2; or of Lord Scrope of Masham, who appears as one of the traitors in 2.1 of *H5* (but who was not the son of the Sir Stephen Scrope mentioned above, as many editions suggest, though confusingly also with a father named Stephen but from another branch of the family).

5 **How . . . import** how great is their importance

6 **tenor** intent; cf. Blount, 'Tenor': 'the content or substance of a matter'.

**4.4.0.1** *the*] F   *and*] *Q2–F*   MICHAEL] *(Mighell)*, *Q5 (Michell)*, *Q7*   4–5] F *lines* directed. / import, / haste. /

Must bide the touch; for, sir, at Shrewsbury,
As I am truly given to understand,                              10
The King with mighty and quick-raised power
Meets with Lord Harry. And I fear, Sir Michael,
What with the sickness of Northumberland,
Whose power was in the first proportion,
And what with Owen Glendower's absence thence,               15
Who with them was a rated sinew too,
And comes not in, o'erruled by prophecies,
I fear the power of Percy is too weak
To wage an instant trial with the King.

SIR MICHAEL

Why, my good lord, you need not fear;                         20
There is Douglas and Lord Mortimer –

ARCHBISHOP     No, Mortimer is not there.

SIR MICHAEL

But there is Murdoch, Vernon, Lord Harry Percy,
And there is my lord of Worcester, and a head
Of gallant warriors, noble gentlemen.                          25

ARCHBISHOP

And so there is; but yet the King hath drawn

---

9  **bide the touch** be put to the test (the image is of gold tested with a touchstone)

11  **quick-raised** quick-raisèd

12  **Meets with** confronts, encounters **Lord Harry** Hotspur

13  **sickness of Northumberland** See 4.1.16 and note.

14  whose army was of the greatest magnitude

16  **rated sinew** anticipated support (*sinew* = mainstay, *OED* 4)

17  **o'erruled by prophecies** a motive invented by Shakespeare and different from what Vernon says at 4.1.125–6 (see 125n.); Shakespeare shows the

Welsh reliance on prophecies in *R2* 2.4.8–12.

19  **instant trial** immediate combat

22  **Mortimer . . . there** Mortimer was historically not present at Shrewsbury, nor is he in the play; it is not obvious, then, why Sir Michael mentions his name only to have it here denied by the Archbishop in what is, as RP notes, an epic-style catalogue of warriors. Perhaps it is to remind the audience of his seduction by Glendower's daughter, which politically undercuts his claim to the crown and his place in the historical action (see pp. 74–5).

15 what with] what *Q3–5*   16 a rated sinew] rated sinew *Q4;* rated firmly *Q5–F*   24–5] *F lines* Worcester, / Warriors, / Gentlemen. /

The special head of all the land together:
The Prince of Wales, Lord John of Lancaster,
The noble Westmorland and warlike Blount,
And many more corrivals and dear men                    30
Of estimation and command in arms.

SIR MICHAEL

Doubt not, my lord, they shall be well opposed.

ARCHBISHOP

I hope no less, yet needful 'tis to fear;
And to prevent the worst, Sir Michael, speed.
For if Lord Percy thrive not, ere the King                    35
Dismiss his power he means to visit us,
For he hath heard of our confederacy,
And 'tis but wisdom to make strong against him.
Therefore make haste. I must go write again                    39
To other friends. And so farewell, Sir Michael.        *Exeunt.*

**5.1**            *Enter the* KING, PRINCE *of* Wales,
Lord John of LANCASTER,
Sir Walter BLOUNT [*and* ] FALSTAFF.

KING

How bloodily the sun begins to peer

---

27 **special head** noble warriors
30 **corrivals** partners
   **dear** honourable, worthy
31 **estimation** value
34 **speed** hurry
36 **means . . . us** Cf. 5.5.34–8, where Henry
   sends Lancaster and Westmorland 'To
   meet Northumberland and the prelate
   Scrope'.
37 **confederacy** united opposition
5.1 All of the fifth act is set on or near the
   battlefield at Shrewsbury. Elizabethan

staging practices, rarely specifying
precise locations and with unmarked
scene shifts, allow brilliantly for the
quick changes of focus that define the
course of the battle in this final act.
This first scene takes place where the
King has gathered his troops, as
Holinshed reports, 'lieng in campe
neere to Shrewesburie' (3.522).

0.2–3 *LANCASTER . . . BLOUNT QF
have Westmorland entering with the
King's party here, though at 5.2.28

---

30 more] *(mo), F3*   32 lord] *(Lo:), Q2 (L.), Q5*   they] he *Q4–F*   35 not,] *Q2–3, F;* not *Q1, Q4–5*
37 our] out *Q4*   5.1.0.2 LANCASTER, Sir] *Hanmer; Lancaster, Earle of Westmorland sir QF*   0.3 *and*]
*Q2–F*

Above yon bulky hill. The day looks pale
At his distemperature.
PRINCE                              The southern wind
Doth play the trumpet to his purposes,
And by his hollow whistling in the leaves                              5
Foretells a tempest and a blustering day.

KING

Then with the losers let it sympathize,
For nothing can seem foul to those that win.

*The trumpet sounds.*

*Enter* WORCESTER [*and* VERNON].

Hotspur identifies Westmorland as the *surety* that was asked for at 4.3.109. Therefore, most editors, following Hanmer, have removed him from the entry direction. Certainly in performance it would be odd for him to appear, though audiences might not notice the contradiction. Although the presence of Westmorland's name in the entry direction in QF indicates that the manuscript included it, the fact he has no lines assigned to him in the scene suggests that Shakespeare realized he could not be present but either he forgot to cancel the name from the SD or his cancellation was ignored by the compositor.

2  **bulky** looming; Humphreys (Ard²) refers to the representation of Wrekin Hill on Saxton's map of Shropshire (1577), which indeed looks *bulky*. Q2–5 and F print 'busky' i.e. bushy, wooded, which, though possible and often adopted, seems an unnecessary emendation and a less distinctive reading. *Bulky* is particularly appealing in a play where not only Falstaff but also the King grow 'portly', 2.4.410; 1.3.13 (and Falstaff is called a *huge hill of*

*flesh*, 2.4.237). The argument, sometimes made, that the apparent 'l' of Q1's 'bulky' is actually a long 's', seems untrue upon careful examination and is undermined by the fact that a long 's' before a 'k' was usually avoided in printing to prevent the possible contact of the kerns of each letter (and indeed some printer's cases had an 'sk' ligature to avoid this problem).

3  **his distemperature** its unhealthy appearance
4  **trumpet** trumpeter, herald
5  **hollow** thin
8  a version of the proverb 'He laughs that wins' (Dent, L93), though behind the meteorological meaning of *foul* (wet and windy) is a moral sense (unfair) that exposes the cynicism of the sentiment; cf. *Mac* 1.3.38: 'So foul and fair a day'.
8.1  *\*and* VERNON Vernon's entry here is not in any of the early texts, and he neither speaks nor is spoken to in the scene; nonetheless, his presence here is made clear with his report of the Prince's challenge of Hotspur (5.2.51–68) and most editions have accepted Theobald's emendation.

2 bulky] busky *Q2–F*    5 by his] by the *Q3;* by *Q4–5*    8.1 *and* VERNON] *Theobald subst.*

How now, my lord of Worcester? 'Tis not well
That you and I should meet upon such terms          10
As now we meet. You have deceived our trust
And made us doff our easy robes of peace
To crush our old limbs in ungentle steel.
This is not well, my lord; this is not well.
What say you to it? Will you again unknit           15
This churlish knot of all-abhorred war
And move in that obedient orb again
Where you did give a fair and natural light,
And be no more an exhaled meteor,
A prodigy of fear and a portent                     20
Of broached mischief to the unborn times?

WORCESTER

Hear me, my liege:
For mine own part I could be well content
To entertain the lag-end of my life
With quiet hours, for I protest                      25
I have not sought the day of this dislike.

KING

You have not sought it? How comes it, then?

FALSTAFF    Rebellion lay in his way, and he found it.

---

12 **doff** remove (the King and the nobility with him are presumably already in
their armour)
13 **our old limbs** In fact, Henry was only
thirty-six at the time of the battle, but
the play, from the beginning, makes
him seem tired and old (cf. 1.1.1).
16 **all-abhorred** all-abhorrèd
17 **obedient orb** natural path of loyalty
that should determine your actions
19 **exhaled meteor** See 1.1.10n. and cf.
*RJ* 3.5.13: 'It is some meteor that the
sun exhales.'
20 **prodigy of fear** terrifying portent

21 **broached** broachèd: already begun
(*broach* = tap a cask)
24 **entertain** occupy, fill
**lag-end** closing years
25 The metrics of the line seemingly
demand a strong medial pause after
*hours*.
26 **day . . . dislike** time of dissension
28 Falstaff exposes the hollowness of
Worcester's *protest*, 25, that he has not
*sought*, 26, the encounter with the
King, by invoking the familiar defence
of a thief that he merely found the
goods with which he has been caught.

25 I] I do *F*

PRINCE [*to Falstaff*]     Peace, chewet, peace.
WORCESTER [*to the King*]

It pleased your majesty to turn your looks             30
Of favour from myself and all our house;
And yet I must remember you, my lord,
We were the first and dearest of your friends.
For you my staff of office did I break
In Richard's time, and posted day and night        35
To meet you on the way and kiss your hand
When yet you were in place and in account
Nothing so strong and fortunate as I.
It was myself, my brother and his son
That brought you home and boldly did outdare     40
The dangers of the time. You swore to us –
And you did swear that oath at Doncaster –
That you did nothing purpose 'gainst the state,
Nor claim no further than your new-fall'n right,
The seat of Gaunt, dukedom of Lancaster.         45

29 **chewet** jackdaw, or other crow-like bird (figuratively, a chatterer)
32 **remember** remind
33 another reminder to Henry that the Percys had helped him achieve the throne following his return from exile in France (and to the audience that Henry had once been himself a rebel as they are rebels now)
34–5 **For . . . time** Holinshed reports that Worcester, the 'lord steward of the kings house, . . . brake his white staffe, which is the representing signe and token of his office, and without delaie went to duke Henrie' (3.500); cf. *R2* 2.3.23–32.
35 **posted** rode

37 **account** general estimation
38 **Nothing so** in no way as
40 **brought** escorted
41–2 **You . . . Doncaster** Holinshed writes of Henry's promise 'at his coming into Doncaster, . . . where he sware vnto those lords, that he would demand no more, but that the lands that were to him descended by inheritance from his father, and in right of his wife' (3.498); cf. *R2* 2.3.147–9.
44 **new-fall'n right** recently inherited title (i.e. to the Duchy of Lancaster, for which Bolingbroke sued upon his father's death); see 4.3.62n.
45 **seat** estates

29 SD] *this edn*   30 SD] *Oxf*   40 outdare] outdate *Q2–5*   41 dangers] danger *Q5–F*
43 purpose] of purpose *Q5–F*

To this we swore our aid, but in short space
It rained down fortune show'ring on your head,
And such a flood of greatness fell on you –
What with our help, what with the absent King,
What with the injuries of a wanton time,                           50
The seeming sufferances that you had borne,
And the contrarious winds that held the King
So long in his unlucky Irish wars
That all in England did repute him dead –
And from this swarm of fair advantages                             55
You took occasion to be quickly wooed
To grip the general sway into your hand,
Forgot your oath to us at Doncaster
And, being fed by us, you used us so
As that ungentle gull, the cuckoo's bird,                          60
Useth the sparrow: did oppress our nest,
Grew by our feeding to so great a bulk
That even our love durst not come near your sight
For fear of swallowing. But with nimble wing
We were enforced for safety sake to fly                            65

49 **the absent King** the King's absence; Richard was then in Ireland, on his expedition to put down an Irish rebellion.
50 **injuries . . . time** abuses in a period of misgovernment
51 **sufferances** injustices
52 **contrarious** contrary
53 **unlucky** unsuccessful
56 **occasion** opportunity
56–7 **wooed . . . sway** persuaded to take control of the entire kingdom
58 See 42 and n.
60 **ungentle . . . bird** the aggressive nestling of the cuckoo (*gull, bird* = chick)

61 **Useth the sparrow** treats the sparrow (by letting the sparrow hatch the cuckoo's egg which has been laid in the sparrow's nest and subsequently care for the hatchling)
   **oppress** take over, tyrannize (*OED* 4)
62 **great a bulk** The cuckoo hatchling will eventually grow so large in comparison to the sparrow that it forces out the sparrow nestlings and may even destroy (by *swallowing*, 64) the foster parent.
63 **our love** i.e. we who loved you
64 **swallowing** being swallowed; cf. *TGV* 2.1.24: 'one that fears robbing', where 'robbing' means 'being robbed')

46 swore] sweare *Q5;* sware *F*   50 of a] of *Q5–F*   53 his] the *Q5–F*   57 grip] *(*gripe*)*

Out of your sight and raise this present head
Whereby we stand opposed by such means
As you yourself have forged against yourself
By unkind usage, dangerous countenance
And violation of all faith and troth                                      70
Sworn to us in your younger enterprise.

KING

These things indeed you have articulate,
Proclaimed at market crosses, read in churches,
To face the garment of rebellion
With some fine colour that may please the eye                             75
Of fickle changelings and poor discontents,
Which gape and rub the elbow at the news
Of hurly-burly innovation;
And never yet did insurrection want
Such water colours to impaint his cause,                                  80
Nor moody beggars starving for a time

66 **head** army
67 **opposed** opposèd
   **opposed . . . means** provoked to
   opposition by such actions
68 **against yourself** i.e. to be used
   against yourself
69 **unkind usage** unnatural (ungrateful
   as well as ungenerous) conduct
   **dangerous countenance** threatening
   behaviour
70 **faith and troth** promises and vows
71 **your younger enterprise** the outset
   of your undertaking
72 **articulate** set forth, articulated
74 **face** adorn, trim
75 **colour** (the *colour* of the facing but
   also, as the metaphor insists, pretence)
76 **changelings** turncoats
   **discontents** discontented persons
77 **rub the elbow** a gesture implying
   delight (hugging oneself with each
   elbow in the palm of the opposite
   hand); cf. *LLL* 5.2.109–10: 'One

rubbed his elbow thus, and fleered,
and swore / A better speech was never
spoke before.'
78 **hurly-burly innovation** tumultuous
   commotion; 'innovation' can mean rev-
   olution, though usually it is defined
   more generally, as by Cawdrey: 'making
   new, an alteration'. In either case, it
   usually has negative connotations; cf.
   Chettle, *Kind Heart's Dream* (1592):
   'lewd mates that long for innovation;
   and when they see advantage . . . make
   boote of clothes, hats, purses, or what
   ever they can lay hold on in a hurley
   burley' (Chettle & Kemp, 43; cited
   Ard[1]).
79 **want** lack
80 **water colours** i.e. thin excuses (the
   image is of the translucency of water
   colour as compared to oil-based paint)
81 **moody** sullen
   **starving** eager (but the literal meaning of the hunger of *beggars* has a

71 in your] in *F*   72 articulate] articulated *F*

Of pell-mell havoc and confusion.
PRINCE
   In both your armies there is many a soul
   Shall pay full dearly for this encounter
   If once they join in trial. Tell your nephew        85
   The Prince of Wales doth join with all the world
   In praise of Henry Percy. By my hopes,
   This present enterprise set off his head,
   I do not think a braver gentleman,
   More active-valiant or more valiant-young,       90
   More daring or more bold, is now alive
   To grace this latter age with noble deeds.
   For my part, I may speak it to my shame,
   I have a truant been to chivalry,
   And so I hear he doth account me too.       95
   Yet this before my father's majesty:
   I am content that he shall take the odds
   Of his great name and estimation,
   And will, to save the blood on either side,
   Try fortune with him in a single fight.       100

poignancy that flickers across the line before it is snuffed by the King's aristocratic contempt.)

82 **pell-mell havoc** chaotic fighting

83 **both your armies** i.e. the King's and the rebels' armies

85 **join in trial** come together in battle

87 **By my hopes** i.e. I swear by my hopes of salvation

88 **set . . . head** not counted against him

90 **active-valiant . . . valiant-young** Q reads ' actiue, valiant' and 'valiant yong', but the repeated 'valiant' and the *or* make it clear that these are intended as two compound adjectives (see Abbott, 2); the hyphens were

added by Theobald and have been followed by most editors; cf. 'young-wise, wise-valiant' in Sidney's *Astrophel and Stella*, sonnet 75.

92 **latter** present

98 **name and estimation** fame and high esteem

99–100 **to . . . fight** Hal's offer to fight Hotspur in single combat is not in any of the chronicle sources, but is taken by Shakespeare from a later episode involving King Henry. In 1404, the King expressed his willingness to fight the Duke of Orleans 'by singular combat betweene them two onelie, for avoiding of more effusion of Christian bloud'

83 your] our *F*   88 off] *(of), F*   90 active-valiant] *Theobald;* actiue, valiant *Q1–2, F;* actiue, more valiant *Q3–5*   valiant-young] *(valiant yong), Theobald*   100 in a] in *Q2–5*

KING

And, Prince of Wales, so dare we venture thee,
Albeit considerations infinite
Do make against it. – No, good Worcester, no.
We love our people well, even those we love
That are misled upon your cousin's part;                    105
And will they take the offer of our grace,
Both he and they and you, yea, every man
Shall be my friend again, and I'll be his.
So tell your cousin, and bring me word
What he will do. But, if he will not yield,                 110
Rebuke and dread correction wait on us,
And they shall do their office. So be gone.
We will not now be troubled with reply.
We offer fair; take it advisedly.

*Exeunt Worcester [and Vernon].*

PRINCE

It will not be accepted, on my life.                        115
The Douglas and the Hotspur both together

---

(Holinshed, 3.525). The transfer of the
offer to Hal is part of the process by
which Shakespeare marks the Prince's
emergence at Shrewsbury as a worthy
successor; see p. 5.
101 **venture thee** stake your life
102–3 **Albeit . . . it** although countless
factors weigh against it; Henry, however, does not articulate any of them,
no doubt because the major consideration is that he fears his son would lose.
105 **upon . . . part** through the influence
of your cousin (i.e. nephew) Hotspur
106 **grace** pardon
111 **Rebuke . . . correction** terrible punishment
**wait on us** are at our command

112 **office** duty
113 Henry obviously stops Worcester,
who was about to say something.
114 **fair** i.e. fair terms: cf. Holinshed 'the
king had condescended vnto all that
was resonable at his hands to be
required, and seemed to humble himselfe more than was meet for his estate'
(3.523).
**take it advisedly** consider it carefully
116 **the Hotspur** 'The' before the name
signals the clan head, as in *The
Douglas*; in applying this to Hotspur,
the Prince acknowledges his military
pre-eminence among the rebel forces,
though there may be a hint of mockery
in the usage.

114 SD *and Vernon] Theobald subst.*

Are confident against the world in arms.

KING

Hence, therefore, every leader to his charge,

For on their answer will we set on them;

And God befriend us as our cause is just!                    120

*Exeunt all but [the] Prince [and] Falstaff.*

FALSTAFF     Hal, if thou see me down in the battle and
bestride me, so; 'tis a point of friendship.

PRINCE     Nothing but a colossus can do thee that
friendship. Say thy prayers, and farewell.

FALSTAFF     I would 'twere bedtime, Hal, and all well.     125

PRINCE     Why, thou owest God a death.                    *[Exit.]*

FALSTAFF     'Tis not due yet. I would be loath to pay him
before his day. What need I be so forward with him that
calls not on me? Well, 'tis no matter; honour pricks me
on. Yea, but how if honour prick me off when I come     130

---

118 **charge** unit
119 **on their answer** i.e. after receiving
their refusal to submit
**set on** attack
122 **bestride me** stand over me to defend
me from further harm; cf. *CE*
5.1.192–3: 'When I bestrid thee in the
wars, and took / Deep scars to save thy
life'.
**so** so be it, well and good
123 **colossus** giant (the Colossus of
Rhodes was one of the seven wonders
of the ancient world, an enormous stat-
ue of the sun god standing at the
entrance of the harbour. Many believed
that ships sailed in between its open
legs; cf. *JC* 1.2.134–6, where Caesar is
seen as a 'colossus' and 'we petty men /
walk under his huge legs').
125 **I . . . . bedtime** Falstaff, with surprising poignancy, expresses his ner-

vousness about what awaits them on
the battlefield; the particular language
of his anxiety, the expressed desire to
be safely in bed, is prompted by Hal's
advice to *Say thy prayers*, 124.
126 **thou . . . death** a proverbial statement of the inevitability of death
(Dent, G237), owed to God in return
for Christ's death on the cross; with a
pun on 'debt', which was pronounced
similarly (see 1.3.185 and note)
128 **forward** eager
129 **calls . . . me** does not yet demand
repayment
129–31 **honour . . . on** honour spurs me
on, but what if honour marks me off
(cf. *JC* 4.1.1) the list of the living when
I go bravely forward; 'honour pricks
me on' was proverbial (cf. Dent,
*PLED*, H572.11). Toby Matthew anxiously wrote to Dudley Carleton on 20

---

120 SD *all but the] (manent), Cam; Manet F    and] F    121–4] as Pope; QF line* battel / friendship.
/ friendship, / farewell. /    126 God] heauen *F*    SD] *Hanmer*    130 Yea, but] But *F*    131 then?
Can] *Q2–3, F; then can Q1, Q4–5*

on? How then? Can honour set to a leg? No. Or an arm?
No. Or take away the grief of a wound? No. Honour
hath no skill in surgery, then? No. What is honour? A
word. What is in that word 'honour'? What is that
'honour'? Air. A trim reckoning. Who hath it? He that      135
died o'Wednesday. Doth he feel it? No. Doth he hear it?
No. 'Tis insensible then? Yea, to the dead. But will it
not live with the living? No. Why? Detraction will not
suffer it. Therefore I'll none of it. Honour is a mere      139
scutcheon. And so ends my catechism.                    *Exit.*

**5.2**    *Enter* WORCESTER [*and*] Sir Richard VERNON.

WORCESTER

O no, my nephew must not know, Sir Richard,

September 1598 about military actions in the Low Countries: 'Honour pricks them on, and the world thinks honour will quickly prick them off again' (*CSPD*). Though the wordplay might have occurred to Matthew independently of Shakespeare's usage, it seems likely that this is a very early quotation from the play.

131 **set to** reattach (*set* meaning fix in place to allow a bone to heal)

132 **grief** pain (*OED sb.* 5)

133–4 **What . . . word** Falstaff voices a kind of nominalism, the idea that essences do not exist in reality, an obvious counter to Hotspur's understanding of honour as something real that he can *pluck* from the moon or the bottom of the sea (1.3.200–7). Cf. Daniel, *A Pastoral* (1592): 'That Idle name of wind: / That Idoll of deceit, that empty sound / Call'd Honor' (11.42–4, S. Daniel, 1.260); also see pp. 69–72.

135 **trim reckoning** fine accounting (ironic)

137 **insensible** unable to be felt by the senses

138 **Detraction** slander

139 **suffer** allow

140 **scutcheon** decorative panels or shields with coats of arms to be displayed at funerals and later in churches as memorials to the dead (and thus particularly appropriate to *Honour*, which belongs only to him 'that died o'Wednesday', 135–6.
**catechism** a course of instruction carried on by set questions and answers (a staple of Catholic religious education), though technically this is an example of *antipophora*, the name of the rhetorical figure for reasoning with oneself (Puttenham, sigs Z3ᵛ–4ʳ).

5.2 The action takes place somewhere in the rebel camp.

134 in] *om. Q4–F*    word 'honour'?] *Folg²;* word honor? *Q1, Q3–4;* word? honor: *Q2;* word Honour? *Q5–F*    134–5 What is that 'honour'?] *Folg²;* what is that honour? *Q1–4; om. Q5–F*
137 'Tis] Is it *F*    will it] *Q2–F;* wil *Q1*    5.2.0.1 *and*] *Q2–F*

The liberal and kind offer of the King.
VERNON
    'Twere best he did.
WORCESTER                Then are we all undone.
    It is not possible, it cannot be
    The King should keep his word in loving us.          5
    He will suspect us still and find a time
    To punish this offence in other faults.
    Supposition all our lives shall be stuck full of eyes,
    For treason is but trusted like the fox,
    Who, never so tame, so cherished and locked up,          10
    Will have a wild trick of his ancestors.
    Look how we can, or sad or merrily,
    Interpretation will misquote our looks,

---

3   *undone ruined ('undone' is the read-
    ing of Q5 and has generally been
    accepted by modern editors, but
    Q1–4's 'vnder one' is not impossible,
    meaning 'united', but would demand
    that Worcester ignore Vernon's objec-
    tion to keeping from Hotspur the news
    of the King's offer)
6   suspect us still always be suspicious
    of us
7   in by punishing
8   Supposition an unconfirmed notion;
    Rowe emended this to 'Suspicion' and
    this has been plausibly followed by
    many editors, but the QF reading does
    not demand correction. It is intelligible,
    is used by Shakespeare elsewhere in this
    sense (cf. *AW* 4.3.293–4: 'to beguile the
    supposition of that lascivious young
    boy'), and it is consistent, as Cam¹
    observes, with Worcester's own willing-
    ness to engage in similar 'supposition'
    throughout the play; cf. 1.3.281, where
    Worcester confidently speculates about
    the King's motivations. It is worth not-

ing that, if the desire here to emend is
provoked by the line's uncertain metrics, 'Suspicion' still leaves the line
hypermetrical. RP suggests more radically for 7–8, '. . . faults supposed. / So
all . . .', which arguably has logical and
metrical advantages over both readings.
stuck . . . eyes i.e. always watching
over us (the image is perhaps based on
the legendary monster, Argus, with
one hundred eyes, some of which
never closed until Hermes charmed it
to sleep and killed it (the eyes were
then used to adorned the peacock's
tail), or on Ezekiel, 10.12, where the
four cherubim are described as 'full of
eyes round about'; Spenser's Envy is
'ypainted full of eyes' (*Faerie Queene*,
1.4.31)).
10  never so tame however tame he is
11  wild . . . ancestors inherited trait of
    savageness (*wild* = undomesticated)
12  or sad either seriously (*or . . . or =
    either . . . or)
13  misquote falsely report

3 undone] *Q5–F*; vnder one *Q1–4*   5 should] would *Q4–F*   7 other] others *Q5–F*   12 we] he
*Q4–F*   merrily] *(merely)*, *Q2* *(merily)*, *Q3*

And we shall feed like oxen at a stall,
The better cherished still the nearer death.                    15
My nephew's trespass may be well forgot;
It hath the excuse of youth and heat of blood,
And an adopted name of privilege:
A hare-brained hotspur governed by a spleen.
All his offences live upon my head                    20
And on his father's. We did train him on,
And, his corruption being ta'en from us,
We as the spring of all shall pay for all.
Therefore, good cousin, let not Harry know
In any case the offer of the King.                    25

VERNON

Deliver what you will; I'll say 'tis so.


*Enter* HOTSPUR [*and* DOUGLAS].


Here comes your cousin.

HOTSPUR                    My uncle is returned.

Deliver up my lord of Westmorland.

---

14 **shall** must
15 treated ever better the nearer they are
to being slaughtered
18 **adopted. . . . privilege** nickname (i.e.
Hotspur) that seemingly justifies his
actions
19 **hotspur** here a common noun for a
hothead
**governed . . . spleen** controlled by an
impetuous disposition
20 **live . . . head** are blamed on me
21 **train** lead, entice (*OED v.* II)
22 **ta'en** derived
23 **spring** source
26 **Deliver** report
26.1 *The wording and placement of the
entry direction is difficult to establish
with certainty. Q1 has '*Enter Percy*'

following 25; F has '*Enter Hotspurre*'
following cousin, 27 – and neither
marks the necessary entry for Douglas,
though he speaks at 31. Bevington
(Oxf[1]) plausibly follows Capell in
adding '[*with Soldiers*]', since at 75
Hotspur addresses *fellows, soldiers,
friends,* a group seemingly more inclu-
sive than the scene's indicated entries
would allow, though it is not obvious
that the additional personnel must
enter here. On the treatment of SDs in
this edition, see p. 128–30.
28 **Deliver . . . Westmorland** Westmorland has been held hostage by Percy as
'surety for a safe return' (4.3.109) of
Worcester and Vernon and is now to be
released; *deliver up* = release, hand over.

---

19 hare-] *F2;* hair- *QF*    22 being] beene *Q4;* benig *Q5*    26.1 *Enter* HOTSPUR] *F (after* Cosin. *27);*
*Enter Percy. after 25 Q1; Enter Hotspur after 25 Q2–5*    *and* DOUGLAS] *Rowe*    26–7 Deliver . . .
cousin.] *as F; one line Q1*

– Uncle, what news?

WORCESTER

The King will bid you battle presently.                    30

DOUGLAS

Defy him by the lord of Westmorland.

HOTSPUR

Lord Douglas, go you and tell him so.

DOUGLAS

Marry, and shall, and very willingly.          *Exit Douglas.*

WORCESTER

There is no seeming mercy in the King.

HOTSPUR

Did you beg any? God forbid!                                35

WORCESTER

I told him gently of our grievances,
Of his oath-breaking, which he mended thus:
By now forswearing that he is forsworn.
He calls us 'rebels', 'traitors', and will scourge
With haughty arms this hateful name in us.               40

---

29 **Uncle, what news** The short line allows an articulate pause before Worcester tells the lie that commits the rebels to battle.

30 **The ... presently** This is not what the King has said; cf. 5.1.104–8, where the King, in fact, offers the rebels pardon; *presently* = immediately. Worcester, here and again at 36–40, misreports his encounter with the King; cf. Holinshed, 'the earle of Worcester (vpon his returne to his nephue) made relation cleane contrarie to that the king had said', and the marginal note: 'The earle of Worcesters double dealing in wrong reporting the kings words' (3.523).

31 **Defy him by** send our defiance with

32 **Douglas** Many editors observe that Douglas could be pronounced here

with three syllables to achieve a regular iambic pentameter line; Shakespeare's metrics, however, are far more flexible than often allowed, and do not usually demand forced pronunciations; all that is needed is a pause after *Douglas*; see Appendix 2.

33 **Marry, and shall** indeed I will ('Marry' is a mild oath derived from the Virgin Mary; the tag phrase itself is proverbial; cf. Dent M699.1)

34 **no seeming** no sign of

36 **told him gently** Cf. 5.1.30–71 (does this qualify as *gently*?).

37 **mended** amended

38 **forswearing . . . forsworn** falsely swearing that he is innocent of having perjured himself

39 'rebels', 'traitors'] *this edn;* rebels, traitors *QF*

315

*Enter* DOUGLAS.

DOUGLAS

    Arm, gentlemen, to arms; for I have thrown

    A brave defiance in King Henry's teeth,

    And Westmorland, that was engaged, did bear it,

    Which cannot choose but bring him quickly on.

WORCESTER

    The Prince of Wales stepped forth before the King    45

    And, nephew, challenged you to single fight.

HOTSPUR

    O, would the quarrel lay upon our heads

    And that no man might draw short breath today

    But I and Harry Monmouth! Tell me, tell me,

    How showed his tasking? Seemed it in contempt?    50

VERNON

    No, by my soul. I never in my life

    Did hear a challenge urged more modestly,

    Unless a brother should a brother dare

    To gentle exercise and proof of arms.

    He gave you all the duties of a man,    55

    Trimmed up your praises with a princely tongue,

    Spoke your deservings like a chronicle,

    Making you ever better than his praise

---

42 **brave** proud
43 **engaged** held as a hostage
  **bear** carry
44 **Which** i.e. the rebels' *defiance*, 42
  **him** i.e. the King
49 **Monmouth** a surname for the Prince
  deriving from his birth at Monmouth
  in Wales
50 **How . . . tasking** how did he set forth
  the challenge. Only Q1 reads 'tasking';
  Q2 and all the subsequent quartos read
  'talking', but this seems an example of
  a more common word being substitut-

ed in the printing house for the less
familiar, though appropriate, one; cf.
*task* at 4.1.9.
52 **urged** proposed
54 **gentle exercise** noble action
  **proof** test, trial
55 **duties of** respect due to (*OED* duty 2)
56 **Trimmed up** adorned; cf. Thomas,
  '*Mangonizatus*: . . . trimmed vp to
  make it seeme the fayrer'.
57 **like a chronicle** i.e. as detailed and
  truthful as in a historical record
58 **ever** always

50 tasking] talking *Q2–F*

316

By still dispraising praise valued with you;
And, which became him like a prince indeed,                    60
He made a blushing cital of himself
And chid his truant youth with such a grace
As if he mastered there a double spirit
Of teaching and of learning instantly.
There did he pause. But let me tell the world,                    65
If he outlive the envy of this day,
England did never owe so sweet a hope
So much misconstrued in his wantonness.

HOTSPUR

Cousin, I think thou art enamoured
On his follies. Never did I hear                    70
Of any prince so wild a liberty.
But, be he as he will, yet once ere night
I will embrace him with a soldier's arm
That he shall shrink under my courtesy.
– Arm, arm with speed! And fellows, soldiers, friends,                    75
Better consider what you have to do
Than I, that have not well the gift of tongue,
Can lift your blood up with persuasion.

---

59 **still . . . you** always denying that the expressions of praise itself were comparable to your actual worth
61 **blushing cital** modest report ('cital' often had a legal sense of a formal reading of charges)
62 **chid** rebuked
63–4 **mastered . . . instantly** simultaneously possessed the twin gifts of teaching and learning (i.e. he was at once the responsible adult and the truant youth who was *chid*)
66 **envy** malice, hostility
67 **owe** own
68 **wantonness** dissolute behaviour
69 **enamoured** enamourèd
70 **On** of

71 **so . . . liberty** with so much irresponsible freedom; Capell emended *liberty* to 'libertine', which makes some obvious sense and is graphically possible, as Humphreys (Ard[2]) observes, if Shakespeare wrote 'libertie' (with the tilde standing in for the 'n'), but the emendation is unnecessary.
74 **shrink . . . courtesy** tremble at his reception (*courtesy* here is ironic, referring to the *embrace*, 73, of combat)
76–8 It is better that you should remind yourselves of the battle in prospect than rely on me, who lack any gift of eloquence (*persuasion*), to inspire you to 'lift your blood up'.

71 a] at *Q5–F*    75 fellows] fellow's *Q5–F*    77 Than] (Then); That *Q3–F*

317

*Enter a* Messenger.

1 MESSENGER   My lord, here are letters for you.

HOTSPUR   I cannot read them now.                                    80

– O gentlemen, the time of life is short;

To spend that shortness basely were too long

If life did ride upon a dial's point,

Still ending at the arrival of an hour.

An if we live, we live to tread on kings;                            85

If die, brave death when princes die with us.

Now, for our consciences, the arms are fair

When the intent of bearing them is just.

*Enter another* [Messenger].

2 MESSENGER

My lord, prepare; the King comes on apace.

HOTSPUR

I thank him that he cuts me from my tale,                            90

For I profess not talking; only this:

Let each man do his best. And here draw I

A sword whose temper I intend to stain

---

79–80 **here . . . now** Hotspur's unwillingness to take time to read what might have been important information is typical of his impetuous behaviour; there is no indication from whom these letters come; it seems unlikely that this is one of the letters sent from the Archbishop in 4.4.1–4, since those letters apparently are directed to potential partisans informing them of what the Percys have begun.

83 **If** even if

**dial's point** hand of an Elizabethan clock (clocks had only a single hand marking the hours; minute hands began to appear late in the seventeenth century). *Dial* must here mean 'clock face' rather than 'sundial', because the gnomon of a sundial does not move, while Hotspur imagines life riding on the *point* to the 'arrival of an hour', 84.

84 **Still** always

86 **brave** glorious

87 **for** as for

**fair** just, legitimate

93 **temper** brightness

---

79 SP] *Cam¹ subst.; Mes. QF*   85 An] *(And), Capell*   87 are] is *Q5–F*   88 of] for *Q5–F*
88.1 Messenger] *F*   89 SP] *Cam¹ subst.; Mes. QF*   92 draw I] I draw *F*   92–3] *as Pope; QF line*
sword, / staine /   93 whose] Whose worthy *F*

With the best blood that I can meet withal
In the adventure of this perilous day.                                    95
Now Esperance! Percy! And set on!
Sound all the lofty instruments of war,
And by that music let us all embrace,
For, heaven to earth, some of us never shall
A second time do such a courtesy.                                        100
　　　*Here they embrace.*　　　　　　*The trumpets sound.*
　　　　　　　　　　　　　　　　　　　　　　　[*Exeunt.*]


5[.3]　　　　　*The* KING *enters with his power*
　　　　[*and they pass over the stage*]. *Alarum to the battle.*
　　　　*Then enter* DOUGLAS *and* Sir Walter BLOUNT
　　　　　　[*wearing the King's colours*].

BLOUNT
What is thy name that in battle thus thou crossest me?


95 **adventure** hazardous enterprise
96 **Esperance!** motto or rallying cry of the Percy family; see 2.3.70. Holinshed writes: 'Then suddenlie blew the trumpets, the kings part crieng S. George upon them, the adversaries cried *Esperance Persie*, and so the two armies furiouslie joined' (3.523).
99 **heaven to earth** I'll wager heaven against earth; i.e. I am so sure I am right that I'll wager something valuable against something paltry (like 'dollars to doughnuts', in American slang).
100 **A second time** again
100 SD3 *Exeunt* Q has no exit direction to clear the stage and indeed places the *embrace* and the sounding trumpet in the same paragraph as the King's entry *with his power*, which marks the opening of the next scene here, as in most editions. Though Q is often imprecise with entry and exit directions, here the

absence seems purposeful, suggesting the action of the battle as continuous from scene 2 into scene 3, an instance of the fluid shifts of action on the battlefield possible on the Elizabethan stage.
5.3 The scene takes place on the battlefield at Shrewsbury; the scene division is not indicated in F (the source of all the play's other scene divisions, none of which is marked in Q). It was suggested first by Capell and has been generally followed since, as the rebels must leave the stage before or just as the King and his forces enter.
0.1 *power* army (the soldiers cross the stage to give a sense of the larger military action, but, though QF do not specify their exit, they must depart before or as Douglas and Blount enter) *Alarum* a trumpet call to arms
1 **What . . . name** Blount is not only enquiring about who has presumed to

100 SD1 *Here*] om. F　SD3 *Exeunt*] Rowe　5.3] Capell　0.3 *wearing . . . colours*] Cam¹ subst.

What honour dost thou seek upon my head?

DOUGLAS

Know then my name is Douglas,
And I do haunt thee in the battle thus
Because some tell me that thou art a king.                      5

BLOUNT

They tell thee true.

DOUGLAS

The Lord of Stafford dear today hath bought
Thy likeness, for instead of thee, King Harry,
This sword hath ended him. So shall it thee
Unless thou yield thee as my prisoner.                          10

BLOUNT

I was not born a yielder, thou proud Scot,
And thou shalt find a king that will revenge
Lord Stafford's death.    *They fight. Douglas kills Blount.*


*Then enter* HOTSPUR.


HOTSPUR

O Douglas, hadst thou fought at Humbleton thus,
I never had triumphed upon a Scot.                              15


attack the King (in whose colours Blount is dressed) but also determining whether or not the combatant be of name, i.e noble. (*What is*, at the beginning, provides an example of a place where an actor would presumably contract to produce a regular alexandrine line; see p. 127.)

**crossest me** cross my path

2  **upon my head** by fighting me

4  **haunt** follow

7  **Lord of Stafford** Edmund, Earl of Stafford; Holinshed says that he was 'that daie made by the king constable of the realme', but he does not indicate that he was one of the nobles dressed like the King on the battlefield, noting only that he was one of those killed defending the King's standard (3.523).

7–8  **dear . . . likeness** has paid heavily today for his resemblance to you.

10 my] a *Q5–F*   11 a yielder] *(*a yeelder*);* to yeeld *Q5–F*   proud] haughty *F*   Scot] *Sot Q5*   13 Lord] Lords *F*   13 SD–13.1] *Fight, Blunt is slaine, then enters Hotspur. F*   15 triumphed upon] triumpht ouer *Q3–5;* triumphed o're *F*

DOUGLAS

All's done; all's won. Here breathless lies the King.

HOTSPUR    Where?

DOUGLAS    Here.

HOTSPUR

This, Douglas? No. I know this face full well.

A gallant knight he was; his name was Blount,                    20

Semblably furnished like the King himself.

DOUGLAS [*to the fallen Blount*]

A fool go with thy soul, whither it goes!

A borrowed title hast thou bought too dear.

Why didst thou tell me that thou wert a king?

HOTSPUR

The King hath many marching in his coats.                    25

DOUGLAS

Now, by my sword, I will kill all his coats.

I'll murder all his wardrobe, piece by piece,

Until I meet the King.

HOTSPUR                         Up and away!

Our soldiers stand full fairly for the day.                    [*Exeunt.*]

---

16 **breathless** dead

21 **Semblably furnished like** similarly attired to; cf. Cotgrave, 'Pareillement': 'in a like manner, semblably, after the same fashion'. Daniel says that Henry's purpose in ordering some soldiers to dress like the King was 'To be less known, and yet known everywhere, / The more to animate his people's hearts' (S. Daniel, 4.51).

22 **A . . . with** may the name of 'fool' accompany; cf. *Promos and Cass.*: 'Go and a knave with thee' (sig. C1ᵛ; 2.4.15).

**whither** wherever

23 **too dear** at too great a cost (i.e. your life)

25 **many . . . coats** The King has instructed a number of soldiers to wear surcoats like his own (see 4.1.99n.); cf. Holinshed's account that Douglas 'slue Sir Walter Blount, and three other, apparreled in the kings sute and clothing, saieng: I maruell to see so many kings thus suddenlie arise one in the necke of an other' (3.523).

29 **stand . . . day** are on the verge of victory

---

16 won. Here] *Q2–3* (won: here*); won here, *Q1;* won, here *Q4–F*    22 SD] *Oxf* subst.    A fool] *Capell;* Ah foole, *Q;* Ah foole: *F*    29 SD] *F*

*Alarum. Enter* FALSTAFF *alone.*

FALSTAFF   Though I could scape shot-free at London,    30
I fear the shot here. Here's no scoring but upon the
pate. Soft, who are you? Sir Walter Blount. There's
honour for you. Here's no vanity. I am as hot as molten
lead and as heavy too. God keep lead out of me; I need
no more weight than mine own bowels. I have led my    35
ragamuffins where they are peppered; there's not three
of my hundred and fifty left alive, and they are for the
town's end to beg during life.

*Enter the* PRINCE.

But who comes here?

PRINCE

What, stands thou idle here? Lend me thy sword.    40
Many a noble man lies stark and stiff
Under the hoofs of vaunting enemies,
Whose deaths are yet unrevenged. I prithee,
Lend me thy sword.

FALSTAFF   O Hal, I prithee, give me leave to breathe    45

30 **shot-free** without paying ('scot-free' is the more common form)
31 **shot** bullets
   **scoring** Falstaff puns with the word to mean both keeping track of the tavern bill (cf. 2.4.26) and also wounding.
32 **pate** head
33 **Here's no vanity** i.e. once dead, there is no reason to worry any longer about hollow, worldly concerns; cf. 'all is vanity' (Ecclesiastes, 12.8) and 1.2.78–9: 'I prithee trouble me no more with vanity.'
35–6 **I . . . peppered** i.e. I have led my

pathetic troops into battle where they are cut down. John Smythe's *Certain Discourses* comments on those captains who send their troops into dangerous positions but 'hauing sure regard to theire owne safeties; as though they desired and hoped to haue more gaine and profite by the dead paies of their soldiers slaine' (Smythe, sig. ***2ʳ).
37–8 **for . . . end** fit only to beg at the outskirts of town
40 **stands** a recognizable form of the second person singular verb ending, like *gets* at 52; cf. Abbott, 340.

29.1 *Enter*] *and enter F   alone*] *(solus)*   34 God] heauen *F*   36 ragamuffins] *Capell*; rag of Muffins *QF*   37 hundred and fifty] *(150.)*, *Dering, Rowe*   they are] they *F*   38.1] *Malone; opp. 39 Q; after 39F*   40 stands] stand'st *Q2–F*   41 noble man] Nobleman *F*   lies] likes *F*   43 are yet] are *F*   I prithee] (I preethe); Prethy *F*   43–4 ] *as Dyce²; one line QF*

awhile. Turk Gregory never did such deeds in arms as
I have done this day. I have paid Percy; I have made him
sure.

PRINCE

He is indeed – and living to kill thee.

I prithee, lend me thy sword.                                                50

FALSTAFF    Nay, before God, Hal, if Percy be alive thou
gets not my sword. But take my pistol if thou wilt.

PRINCE

Give it me. What, is it in the case?

FALSTAFF    Ay, Hal. 'Tis hot; 'tis hot. There's that will
sack a city. *The Prince draws it out, and finds it to be a*          55
*bottle of sack.*

PRINCE

What, is it a time to jest and dally now?    *He throws the*
*bottle at him.*                                                          *Exit.*

FALSTAFF    Well, if Percy be alive, I'll pierce him. If he do
come in my way, so; if he do not, if I come in his

---

46 **Turk Gregory** a figure for unusual
cruelty and ferocity, derived from the
name of one of the medieval Popes
named Gregory, with *Turk* substituted
for 'Pope' as an intensifier; Gregory is
perhaps Pope Gregory VII (1023–85),
famous for asserting the temporal
power of the papacy and, to sixteenth-
century Protestants, for his hot temper
(or perhaps, anachronistically, it may
refer to Pope Gregory XIII (1572–85),
who, notoriously, had ordered a *Te
Deum* sung to celebrate the St
Bartholomew's Day massacre, and was
popularly viewed as one of the 'three
tyrants of the world'). Anti-Catholic
polemics often collapsed Turks and
Catholics into a single, demonized figure of what were seen as the two great

threats to the 'godly' kingdom; cf. John
Bale's sardonic joke in *The Pageant of
Popes* (1574), where he refers to Pope
Turban II (Bale sig. L6ᵛ).

47 **paid** settled his account (i.e. killed)

47–8 **made him sure** killed him (Hal in
49 takes the remark to mean 'found
him reliable')

53 **case** holster

54 **hot** Falstaff pretends that it is *hot* from
being fired.

55 **sack** ravage, plunder (but with the
obvious pun on the name of the drink)

57 **Percy . . . pierce** 'pierce' was pronounced near enough to the first syllable of 'Percy' to permit the wordplay;
cf. *R2* 5.3.125–6, where 'pierce' and
'rehearse' rhyme.

58 **so** well and good

---

51 before God] *om. F*    52 gets] getst *Q2–F*    55 SD] *The Prince drawes out a Bottle of Sacke. F*
56 SD] *Exit. Throwes it at him. F*    57 Well, if] If *Q5–F*

willingly, let him make a carbonado of me. I like not
such grinning honour as Sir Walter hath. Give me life,       60
which if I can save, so. If not, honour comes unlooked
for, and there's an end.                    [*Exit with Blount's body.*]

**5[.4]**              *Alarum. Excursions. Enter the* KING,
                 *the* PRINCE, Lord John of LANCASTER
                 [*and the*] Earl of WESTMORLAND.

KING

I prithee, Harry, withdraw thyself; thou bleed'st too
   much.
Lord John of Lancaster, go you with him.

LANCASTER

Not I, my lord, unless I did bleed too.

PRINCE

I beseech your majesty, make up,

---

59 **carbonado** meat scored with a knife
   to ready it for broiling
60 **grinning honour** the (insignificant)
   *honour* that survives *grinning* (from the
   rictus of the facial muscles) death
61–2 **honour . . . for** I shall win honour
   unsought
62 **there's an end** i.e. of both life and my
   speech
62 SD *Q indicates no exit for Falstaff
   here and has no provision for the
   removal of Blount's body. Falstaff
   must be off the stage as the action of
   5.4 begins, though it isn't obvious, as
   Oxf¹ and Cam² suggest, that Blount's
   body could not remain (although it
   would be tedious for an actor and he
   would have to leave the stage, in any
   case, some time before 5.5, as Hotspur
   does at 5.4.16–65).
5.4 The action of this scene is continuous
   with the last, and the *Excursions* of the

SD are designed to achieve this conti-
   nuity. F heads this '*Scena Tertia*', in
   the absence of a separate indication for
   the previous scene.
0.1 *Excursions* indicates various sword
   fights on the stage used to represent
   the ongoing battle
1–2 **Harry . . . you** Holinshed reports
   that the Prince 'was hurt in the face
   with an arrow' but would not leave the
   battlefield for fear it would discourage
   his soldiers (3.523). The King addresses
   the Prince intimately both by name
   and by the familiar pronoun, *thou*;
   John is addressed with full title and the
   more formal pronoun, *you*, the difference serving as one mark of the
   achieved reconciliation of the King
   with his eldest son.
4 **make up** move forward (on the battlefield), as at 57

---

62 SD] *Oxf; Exit. F*    **5.4**] *Capell; Scena Tertia. F*    0.3 *and the*] *F3; and Q2–F*    1 bleed'st] *Capell;*
bleedest *QF*    1–2] *prose Q2–F*

Lest your retirement do amaze your friends.                    5

KING

I will do so.

My lord of Westmorland, lead him to his tent.

WESTMORLAND

Come, my lord, I'll lead you to your tent.

PRINCE

Lead me, my lord? I do not need your help,

And God forbid a shallow scratch should drive                    10

The Prince of Wales from such a field as this,

Where stained nobility lies trodden on

And rebels' arms triumph in massacres!

LANCASTER

We breathe too long. Come, cousin Westmorland;

Our duty this way lies. For God's sake, come.                    15

                               [*Exeunt Lancaster and Westmorland.*]

PRINCE

By God, thou hast deceived me, Lancaster;

I did not think thee lord of such a spirit.

Before I loved thee as a brother, John,

But now I do respect thee as my soul.

---

5  **retirement** retreat
   **amaze** dismay, alarm (*OED* 3)
10  **shallow scratch** See 1–2n.;
Holinshed writes that, 'without regard
of his hurt, he continued with his men,
& neuer ceassed, either to fight where
the battell was most hot, or to incour-
age his men wher it seemed most need'
(3.523).
12  **stained** blood-stained (without inten-
tionally carrying the sense of disgraced)
14  **breathe** pause, rest (as at 46)
15  SD *QF have no direction for
Lancaster and Westmorland to exit,

though Lancaster's urgency suggests
they depart here rather than leave with
the Prince (and Q at 23 has a singular
*Exit* for him). The battlefield action is
throughout more or less continuous,
and their hurried exit would con-
tribute to the sense of the swirling battle. It is not impossible, however, that
all three exit together immediately
before Douglas enters, and the Prince's
lines in praise of Lancaster are actually spoken to him rather than, as here,
virtually as an aside.

19  **respect** regard

---

5 Lest your] Least you *F*   6–7] *as F; one line Q*   10 God] heauen *F*   15 God's] heauens *F*
SD] *Capell subst.*   16 God] heauen *F*

KING

    I saw him hold Lord Percy at the point        20
    With lustier maintenance than I did look for
    Of such an ungrown warrior.

PRINCE

    O, this boy lends mettle to us all!        *Exit.*

[*Enter* DOUGLAS.]

DOUGLAS

    Another king! They grow like Hydra's heads.
    I am the Douglas, fatal to all those        25
    That wear those colours on them. What art thou
    That counterfeit'st the person of a king?

KING

    The King himself, who, Douglas, grieves at heart
    So many of his shadows thou hast met
    And not the very King. I have two boys        30
    Seek Percy and thyself about the field,
    But seeing thou fall'st on me so luckily
    I will assay thee; and defend thyself.

---

20 **at the point** at sword's length
21 **lustier maintenance** more vigorous conduct
22 **ungrown warrior** At the time of the battle John was not yet fourteen years old.
24 **Hydra's heads** a reference to the Greek myth of the Lernean Hydra, who grew two new heads for every one that was cut off. Killing the Hydra was one of the legendary labours of Hercules. The image was commonplace (cf. Dent, H278); S.Daniel writes of 'New *Hidra's* of rebellion' (4.150).

26 **those colours** i.e. the King's coat of arms
27 **counterfeit'st** The issue of what makes a king is central to this play's politics; Hal and Falstaff take turns counterfeiting the King in 2.4, and arguably Henry IV, as a usurper, does no less; see pp. 63–4.
29 **shadows** i.e. those disguised as the King (*shadows* = appearances rather than the reality)
30 **very** true, actual
31 **Seek** who seek
33 **assay** test, try

23 mettle] *(*mettall*)*   23.1] *F*   33 and] so *F*

DOUGLAS

    I fear thou art another counterfeit,
    And yet, in faith, thou bearest thee like a king.      35
    But mine I am sure thou art, whoe'er thou be,
    And thus I win thee.   *They fight.*

    *The King being in danger, enter* PRINCE *of* Wales.

PRINCE

    Hold up thy head, vile Scot, or thou art like
    Never to hold it up again. The spirits
    Of valiant Shirley, Stafford, Blount are in my arms.    40
    It is the Prince of Wales that threatens thee,
    Who never promiseth but he means to pay.   *They fight.*
                                          *Douglas flieth.*

    Cheerly, my lord. How fares your grace?
    Sir Nicholas Gawsey hath for succour sent,
    And so hath Clifton. I'll to Clifton straight.    45

KING

    Stay and breathe awhile.
    Thou hast redeemed thy lost opinion
    And showed thou mak'st some tender of my life

---

35 **thou bearest thee** you conduct yourself
36 **mine** i.e. my victim
38–42 The scene of the Prince rescuing
   his father from Douglas is not in
   Holinshed, but Daniel does describe
   Hal lending 'present speedy aid / To
   thy endangered father nearly tired /
   Whom fierce encountring Douglas
   overlaid / That day had there his trou-
   blous life expired' (*Civil Wars*, 3.110).
38 **like** likely
40 **Shirley** Holinshed mentions Sir Hugh
   Shorlie as one of those slain at
   Shrewsbury (3.523); Shakespeare

makes no mention of him elsewhere
(and RP notes the metre would be regular should *Shirley* be dropped here).
42 **pay** fulfil the promise (on the play's
   reiterated language of debt and payment, see pp. 62–9)
43 **Cheerly** an exclamation of encouragement
44–5 **Sir . . . Clifton** Holinshed lists Sir
   Nicholas Gausell and Sir John Clifton
   among the dead at Shrewsbury
   (3.523). Neither is mentioned by
   Shakespeare except in this scene.
47 **opinion** reputation
48 **mak'st . . . of** have some regard for

---

35 bearest] bear'st *F*   37.1 PRINCE of Wales] *Prince F*   38 thy] they *F*

In this fair rescue thou hast brought to me.

PRINCE

O God, they did me too much injury                                      50
That ever said I hearkened for your death.
If it were so, I might have let alone
The insulting hand of Douglas over you,
Which would have been as speedy in your end
As all the poisonous potions in the world,                              55
And saved the treacherous labour of your son.

KING

Make up to Clifton; I'll to Sir Nicholas Gawsey.          *Exit.*

*Enter* HOTSPUR.

HOTSPUR

If I mistake not, thou art Harry Monmouth.

PRINCE

Thou speak'st as if I would deny my name.

HOTSPUR

My name is Harry Percy.

PRINCE                                    Why then, I see                60
A very valiant rebel of the name.
I am the Prince of Wales, and think not, Percy,
To share with me in glory any more.
Two stars keep not their motion in one sphere,
Nor can one England brook a double reign                                65

---

51 **hearkened for** eagerly awaited,
  desired
52–3 **have . . . you** i.e. not have prevent-
  ed the disdainful hand of Douglas,
  which was raised to slay you
64 a proverbial thought: 'Two suns cannot
  shine in one sphere' (Dent, S992)
65 **brook** endure (as at 73 and 77)

**a double reign** The idea of the political undesirability of a double reign
traces its origin at least as far back as
Suetonius' 'Life of Flavius Domin-
ianus': 'There is no good plurality in
lordship or in sovereignty' (Suetonius,
sig. Aa2$^r$).

50 God] heauen *F*   51 for] to *Q4–F*   57 Sir] *(S.), F*   SD] *Q5–F; Exit Ki: Q1–3; Exit K. Q4*
60–1] *as Rowe³; QF line* Percy. / name; /   61 the] that *Q3–F*

Of Harry Percy and the Prince of Wales.

HOTSPUR

Nor shall it, Harry, for the hour is come

To end the one of us, and would to God

Thy name in arms were now as great as mine.

PRINCE

I'll make it greater ere I part from thee,                    70

And all the budding honours on thy crest

I'll crop to make a garland for my head.

HOTSPUR

I can no longer brook thy vanities.    *They fight.*


*Enter* FALSTAFF.


FALSTAFF    Well said, Hal! To it, Hal! Nay, you shall find no

boy's play here, I can tell you.                              75


*Enter* DOUGLAS. *He fighteth with Falstaff,*
*who falls down as if he were dead.*


[*Exit Douglas.*]

*The Prince killeth Hotspur.*

HOTSPUR

O Harry, thou hast robbed me of my youth.

71 **budding ... crest** literally, the chivalric tokens gracing his helmet; figuratively, his noble reputation

72 **crop** harvest, pick

73 **vanities** vain boasts

74 **Well said** i.e. well done
**To it** go to it, keep it up

75 **boy's play** child's play; proverbial: cf. Dent, C324.

75.3 ***Exit Douglas*** QF do not indicate his exit here, but it seems impossible that he remains on stage. His presence would disrupt the double focus of the

scene: upon the long awaited confrontation of Hal and Hotspur and upon Falstaff's body.

75.4 *The ... Hotspur* Holinshed does not specify who killed Hotspur, noting only, after commenting on the King's great valour, that Hotspur was killed by some 'other on his part, incouraged by his doings' (3.523); earlier, however, in *The History of Scotland*, the text reads: 'the king got the victorie, and slue the lord Persie' (Holinshed, 2.254).

67 Nor] *F;* Now *Q*    68 God] heauen *F*    71 the] they *Q5*    73 SD] *Fight. F*    75.1 *fighteth] fights Q5–F*    75.2 *who] F; he Q*    75.3 *Exit Douglas] Capell*    75.4 *Hotspur] (Percy), F (Percie), Hanmer*

I better brook the loss of brittle life
Than those proud titles thou hast won of me.
They wound my thoughts worse than thy sword my
    flesh.
But thoughts, the slaves of life, and life, time's fool,       80
And time, that takes survey of all the world,
Must have a stop. O, I could prophesy,
But that the earthy and cold hand of death
Lies on my tongue. No, Percy, thou art dust
And food for –   [*He dies.*]                  85
PRINCE

For worms, brave Percy. Fare thee well, great heart.
Ill-weaved ambition, how much art thou shrunk!
When that this body did contain a spirit
A kingdom for it was too small a bound,
But now two paces of the vilest earth            90
Is room enough. This earth that bears thee dead

---

77 **brittle** fragile

80–2 **thoughts . . . stop** i.e. thoughts
(which are dependent upon life) and
life (which is subject to time) and even
time itself (which measures the life of
all mortal things) will come to an end

82 **prophesy** alludes to the idea that
dying persons had prophetic powers;
cf. *R2* 2.1.31, where the dying Gaunt
says, 'Methinks I am a prophet new
inspired'; and Dent, M514: 'Dying
men speak true.'

85 **food for** – Hotspur is unable to finish
his final sentence; Laurence Olivier's
Hotspur, in London at the New
Theatre in 1945, struggled, 'food for w-
w-', before he died; see 1.3.56n.
Olivier's particular choice for Hotspur's
slight stammer – on the 'w's – seemingly was decided by working backwards
from this line.

86 **worms** Hal finishes Hotspur's sentence, completing the familiar *memento
mori* idea: 'a man is nothing but
worm's meat' (Dent, M253).

87 **Ill-weav'd . . . shrunk** i.e. it is amaz-
ing how much your exorbitant ambi-
tion has now, like badly woven cloth,
shrivelled and *shrunk*

88 **this** i.e. Percy's
  **did . . . spirit** i.e. was alive

89 **bound** enclosure

91 ***thee dead** as in Q7–8, as opposed to
Q1–6 and F, which read 'the dead'.
Some editors have argued that the
Q1–6 reading does not need emenda-
tion, but 'This earth that bears the
dead' would refer only to the battle-
field at Shrewsbury, and the logic of
Hal's praise demands a wider canvas.
To say that there is no one of those still
alive on the battlefield who is more

---

79 thy] the *Q5–F*  80 thoughts, the slaves] *(*thoughts the slaues*)*; thought's the slaue *Q2–F*
83 earthy] earth *Q2–F*  and] and the *F*  85 for –] *F*; for. *Q1–2*; for *Q3–5*  SD] *Rowe*  86 Fare
thee well] Farewell *F*  91 thee dead] *Q7*; the dead *Q1–6, F*

Bears not alive so stout a gentleman.
If thou wert sensible of courtesy
I should not make so dear a show of zeal.
But let my favours hide thy mangled face,                    95
And even in thy behalf I'll thank myself
For doing these fair rites of tenderness.
Adieu, and take thy praise with thee to heaven.
Thy ignominy sleep with thee in the grave
But not remembered in thy epitaph.                           100
    *He spieth Falstaff on the ground.*
What, old acquaintance! Could not all this flesh
Keep in a little life? Poor Jack, farewell.
I could have better spared a better man.
O, I should have a heavy miss of thee
If I were much in love with vanity.                          105
Death hath not struck so fat a deer today,
Though many dearer in this bloody fray.
Embowelled will I see thee by and by;

noble than Hotspur is a far more
restrained compliment than to say, as I
take it Hal intends, that there is no one
on earth more noble than Hotspur was.
It would be easy enough for a compositor to read *thee* as 'the' (or indeed for
*thee* to have been spelled 'the' in the
copy; see 2.3.47 t.n.).
93 **sensible of** able to feel
94 **dear . . . zeal** heartfelt expression of
my respect
95 **favours** scarf or plumes worn on the
helmet
96 **in thy behalf** as your representative
97 **fair** deserved
99 **ignominy** i.e. whatever might engender shame
104–9 Recent productions have often
exploited the comedy of having Hal
aware that Falstaff is shamming, and

by having the Prince emphasize words
like *heavy*, 104, and *Embowelled*, 108,
inviting a response from the 'dead'
Falstaff perceptible to the audience, if
not to Hal. This has only questionable
textual warrant, as Hal has told John of
Lancaster that Falstaff was dead, 131,
though conceivably that could be, as
RP suggests, a tactic for Falstaff's later
discomfiture.
104 **have . . . thee** deeply miss you (with
the obvious pun on *heavy*)
106 **so . . . deer** Falstaff has been identified with deer throughout (see Berry,
133–8)
107 **dearer** more noble (but presumably
not more beloved) and of course playing on *deer* in the previous line
108 **Embowelled** disembowelled (to
ready the body for embalming)

94 dear] great *Q2–F*   97 rites] (rights), *Q2*   99 ignominy] ignomy *Q4–F*   100 SD] *om. F*
106 fat] faire *Q2–5*

Till then, in blood by noble Percy lie. *Exit.*
    *Falstaff riseth up.*

FALSTAFF    Embowelled? If thou embowel me today, I'll    110
give you leave to powder me, and eat me too, tomorrow.
'Sblood, 'twas time to counterfeit, or that hot
termagant Scot had paid me, scot and lot too.
Counterfeit? I lie; I am no counterfeit. To die is to be a
counterfeit, for he is but the counterfeit of a man who    115
hath not the life of a man. But to counterfeit dying
when a man thereby liveth is to be no counterfeit but
the true and perfect image of life indeed. The better
part of valour is discretion, in the which better part I
have saved my life. Zounds, I am afraid of this    120
gunpowder Percy, though he be dead. How if he should
counterfeit too and rise? By my faith, I am afraid he
would prove the better counterfeit. Therefore I'll make
him sure, yea, and I'll swear I killed him. Why may not

---

109 **in blood** i.e. in his own blood (but *in blood*, applied to deer being hunted, meant 'vigorous', a sense appropriate for Falstaff, who is merely pretending to be dead)

111 **powder** preserve in salt (but also embalm in brine, as one might a fallen warrior)

113 **termagant** savage (the word comes from an imaginary pagan deity, whose characteristic violent behaviour makes him an appropriate image for the fierce Scot)

    **had paid** would have killed

    **scot and lot** in full; proverbial (Dent, S159), but with the obvious play on *Scot* earlier in the line

117 **thereby liveth** survives by that means

118–19 **The . . . discretion** i.e. the most

important aspect of bravery is that it be directed by good judgement (otherwise it is mere foolhardiness), though Falstaff interprets the proverbial idea (cf. Dent, D354) to justify his cowardice; *part* means 'quality' not 'portion'.

119 **in** in the exercise of

121 **gunpowder Percy** referring to the explosive outbursts of the impetuous Hotspur, as much as to his prowess with arms

121–2 **How . . . rise** potentially a richly metadramatic moment, as Falstaff's anxious expression voices the reality of the actor playing (counterfeiting) Hotspur, who will, when the scene is over, *rise*

123–4 **make him sure** make his death absolutely certain

---

109 SD1 *om. Q4–5*   112 'Sblood] *(Zbloud); om. F*   114 I lie; I] *(I, lie I);* I *Q5–F*   120 Zounds] *om. F*   122 By my faith] *om. F*

he rise as well as I? Nothing confutes me but eyes, and      125
nobody sees me. [*Stabs the body.*] Therefore, sirrah,
with a new wound in your thigh, come you along with
me. *He takes up Hotspur on his back.*

*Enter* PRINCE [*and*] John of LANCASTER.

PRINCE

Come, brother John. Full bravely hast thou fleshed
Thy maiden sword.

LANCASTER                    But soft; whom have we here?      130
Did you not tell me this fat man was dead?

PRINCE

I did; I saw him dead,
Breathless and bleeding on the ground.
[*to Falstaff*] Art thou alive, or is it fantasy
That plays upon our eyesight? I prithee speak;      135
We will not trust our eyes without our ears.
Thou art not what thou seem'st.

FALSTAFF    No, that's certain: I am not a double man.

---

125 **Nothing . . . eyes** No one can refute
me but an eyewitness (though, of
course, the spectators are just such
eyewitnesses).

126 SD Falstaff's action of stabbing an
already dead foe recalls a famous
episode at the battle of Hastings where
'one of the souldiors when Harold was
slaine, did cut him the legge with a
sworde' and was then executed for the
dishonourable action (Stow, sig. I2ᵛ)

126 **sirrah** a demeaning term of address
normally of a superior to a social subordinate; Falstaff would never risk this
were he not certain Hotspur was dead.

127 **thigh** seemingly an odd place to aim
to kill a man, though the back of the

thigh would be one of the few exposed
places on an armoured soldier; Philip
Sidney's death in 1586 from a wound
in the thigh was well known, as Cam²
points out, though the wound came, as
Sir John Smythe noted, 'by not wearing his cuisses', a general tendency to
scorn armour which Smythe actively
opposed (Smythe, sig. B3ʳ).

129 **fleshed** initiated in bloodshed

130 **maiden** hitherto unused

138 **double man** a verbal and a visual joke
in response to Hal's amazement: Falstaff
denies that he is an apparition, a dead
man come back to life (hence *double*);
but also denies that he is the *double man*
he might seem to be as he carries

---

126 SD] *Malone subst. after* sirrah     127–8 with me] me *F*     128 SD *He takes up*] Takes *F*
128.1 *and*] Q2–F     129–30 Come . . . sword] *prose F*     130 whom] who Q5–F     132–7] *Delius; QF*
*line* dead, / aliue? / eiesight? / eies / seemst. /     134 SD] *Oxf*

[*He drops Hotspur's body.*] But, if I be not Jack Falstaff,
then am I a jack. There is Percy. If your father will do          140
me any honour, so; if not, let him kill the next Percy
himself. I look to be either earl or duke, I can assure
you.

PRINCE

Why, Percy I killed myself, and saw thee dead.

FALSTAFF    Didst thou? Lord, Lord, how this world is          145
given to lying! I grant you I was down and out of
breath, and so was he; but we rose both at an instant
and fought a long hour by Shrewsbury clock. If I may
be believed, so; if not, let them that should reward
valour bear the sin upon their own heads. I'll take it          150
upon my death I gave him this wound in the thigh. If
the man were alive and would deny it, zounds, I would
make him eat a piece of my sword.

LANCASTER

This is the strangest tale that ever I heard.

PRINCE

This is the strangest fellow, brother John.                        155

Hotspur on his back. In 1951, at
Stratford, Anthony Quayle removed
Michael Redgrave's Hotspur from the
stage by placing Redgrave's legs over his
shoulders and carrying him upside-
down, forming just such a double man.

139 SD *No stage direction is given in
the early texts for this action, and it is
possible Falstaff continues to carry
Hotspur on his back. This, however,
would be an exhausting feat, and also
makes it difficult to imagine the gesture that accompanies *There is Percy*,
140. In production, Falstaff inevitably
gets a laugh by gracelessly dumping
Hotspur to the stage, like Charles
Kemble, who 'convulsed the house'

with this final bit of 'roguery'
(*Theatrical Observer*, 3 May 1824). A
Charleston, South Carolina, reviewer
of 1787 observed the usefulness of
having 'a stump of a tree on which
*Falstaff* may rest the body of *Hotspur*,
during his conversation with the
Prince' (Sprague, *Actors*, 91).

140 **jack** knave
141, 149 **so** well and good
147 **at an instant** simultaneously
148 **long . . . clock** i.e. a long time in
combat (though it is not clear if this is
a reference to an actual *clock* in the
church tower or merely a metaphor for
the time of battle; cf.1.2.5–11)
150–1 **take . . . death** stake my life on it

139 SD] *Capell subst.*    145 this] the *Q5–F*    150–1 take it upon] take't on *F*    152 zounds] *om. F*
154 ever] e're *F*

[*to Falstaff* ] Come, bring your luggage nobly on your
    back.
For my part, if a lie may do thee grace
I'll gild it with the happiest terms I have.

*A retreat is sounded.*

The trumpet sounds retreat; the day is ours.
Come, brother, let us to the highest of the field          160
To see what friends are living, who are dead.          *Exeunt.*
FALSTAFF    I'll follow, as they say, for reward. He that
    rewards me, God reward him. If I do grow great,
    I'll grow less, for I'll purge and leave sack and live          164
    cleanly, as a nobleman should do.          *Exit [carrying the body].*

**5[.5]**    *The trumpets sound. Enter the* KING, PRINCE *of* Wales,
        Lord John *of* LANCASTER, Earl *of* WESTMORLAND,
            *with* WORCESTER *and* VERNON *prisoners.*

KING

Thus ever did rebellion find rebuke.
Ill-spirited Worcester, did not we send grace,

156 If indeed Falstaff has dropped
    Hotspur after 139, then he must pick
    him up again here to remove his body
    from the stage.
157 **lie . . . grace** this lie of yours will
    bring you credit
158 **gild** paint; support, corroborate
    **happiest** most favourable
160 **highest** highest vantage point
162 **as . . . reward** Humphreys (Ard²)
    relates this to the fact that hounds were
    rewarded with portions of the animal
    that has been killed; *as they say* would
    then refer to the hunter's jargon.
163–4 **If . . . less** If I become a powerful
    nobleman (cf. 142), I'll lose weight.
164 **purge** repent or purify myself,

though *purge* also has a medical sense
    of using a purgative to cause vomiting
    (which would enforce some weight
    loss)
5.5 The precise location is unspecified by
    Shakespeare, but the scene is imagined
    as taking place at the King's camp near
    the battlefield at Shrewsbury.
1 **find rebuke** meet defeat and punish-
    ment (though Henry's own *rebellion*
    against Richard II clearly did not)
2 **Ill-spirited** malicious, evil-minded
    (*spirited* perhaps pronounced with two
    syllables, sprìt-ed)
2–3 **grace . . . love** offer of pardon (see
    5.1.106–8); *grace* = promise of favour

156 SD] *Cam¹*    159 The] *F; Prin.* The *Q*    trumpet sounds] trumpets sound *Q4–F*    ours] *Q2–F;*
our *Q1*    160 let us] lets *Q4–F*    163 God] heauen *F*    great] great again *F*    165 nobleman] *Q4–F;*
noble man *Q1–3*    SD *carrying the body*] *Capell subst.*    5.5 *Capell; Scaena Quarta.* F    2 not we] we
not *F*

Pardon and terms of love to all of you?
And wouldst thou turn our offers contrary,
Misuse the tenor of thy kinsman's trust?                    5
Three knights upon our party slain today,
A noble earl and many a creature else
Had been alive this hour
If like a Christian thou hadst truly borne
Betwixt our armies true intelligence.                       10

WORCESTER

What I have done my safety urged me to;
And I embrace this fortune patiently,
Since not to be avoided it falls on me.

KING

Bear Worcester to the death and Vernon too.
Other offenders we will pause upon.                         15
                *[Exeunt Worcester and Vernon under guard.]*
How goes the field?

4   **thou** The King's use of the second person *thou* here to refer to Worcester, after using *all of you*, 3, to refer to the rebels in general, is a mark of Henry's anger and contempt.
    **turn . . . contrary** reverse the meaning of (not merely 'misreport'); see 5.2.30n.

5   exploit the nature (*tenor*) of Hotspur's trust in you; cf. Holinshed's report of Hotspur sending Worcester to Henry before 'to declare vnto the king the causes of those troubles, and to require some effectual reformation in the same', and Worcester's report on his return, where he 'made relation cleane contrarie to that the king had said' (3.523).

6–7 Holinshed reports that 'There were slaine vpon the kings part, beside the earle of Stafford, to the number of ten knights. . . . There died in all vpon the kings side sixteene hundred, and four

thousand were greeuioislie wounded'; two hundred knights on the rebel side were killed and in all 'about four thousand' (3.523).

6   **upon our party** on our side

7   **many . . . else** many other men

8   **Had** would have

10  **intelligence** information, report

11  **my safety** i.e. anxiety about my safety

12  **embrace** accept

14  **to the death** to execution; Holinshed writes: 'Vpon the mondaie folowing, the earle of Worcester, the baron of Kinderton, and sir Richard Vernon knights, were condemned and beheaded. The earles head was sent to London, there to be set on the bridge' (3.523–4).

15  **pause upon** postpone consideration of

16  **field** battle, i.e. events on the battlefield

15 SD *Exeunt*] Theobald; *Exit* F   *under guard*] Theobald subst.

PRINCE

The noble Scot, Lord Douglas, when he saw
The fortune of the day quite turned from him,
The noble Percy slain and all his men
Upon the foot of fear, fled with the rest;                                    20
And, falling from a hill, he was so bruised
That the pursuers took him. At my tent
The Douglas is, and I beseech your grace
I may dispose of him.

KING                                   With all my heart.

PRINCE

Then, brother John of Lancaster, to you                                       25
This honourable bounty shall belong.
Go to the Douglas and deliver him
Up to his pleasure, ransomless and free.
His valours shown upon our crests today
Have taught us how to cherish such high deeds                                  30
Even in the bosom of our adversaries.

LANCASTER

I thank your grace for this high courtesy,
Which I shall give away immediately.

KING

Then this remains, that we divide our power.
You, son John, and my cousin Westmorland,                                     35

---

20 **Upon. . . fear** i.e. in panicky flight
21 **falling . . . bruised** Cf. Holinshed: 'the earle of Dowglas, for hast, falling from the crag of an hie mountain, brake one of his cullions, and was taken' (3.523).
24 **dispose of him** have the disposal of him
26 **this honourable bounty** the honour of this magnanimous act
27–30 **deliver . . . deeds** Holinshed reports that, although Douglas was cap-

tured, he was 'for his valiantnesse, of the king freelie and franklie deliuered' (3.524). Again, in his account of the battle and its aftermath, Shakespeare makes Hal responsible for noble actions that historically were the actions of the King; see p. 5.
29 **crests** helmets
33 **give away** pass on, confer on (Douglas)
34 **power** forces

25–6] *as Pope; QF line* Lancaster, / belong. /     29 valours] valour *Q4–F*     30 Have] Hath *Q4–F*
32–3] om. *Q5–F*

Towards York shall bend you with your dearest speed
To meet Northumberland and the prelate Scrope,
Who, as we hear, are busily in arms.
Myself and you, son Harry, will towards Wales
To fight with Glendower and the Earl of March.                    40
Rebellion in this land shall lose his sway
Meeting the check of such another day;
And, since this business so fair is done,
Let us not leave till all our own be won.                    *Exeunt.*

36 **bend you** direct your course
   **dearest** utmost
37 **meet** engage in battle
38 **busily in arms** actively engaged in
   preparing for battle
39–40 Cf. Holinshed: 'The king hauing set
   a staie in things about Shrewesburie,
   went straight to Yorke' and only after
   'returning foorth of Yorkeshire, determined to go into Northwales, to chas-
   tise the persumptuous dooings of the
   vnrulie Welshmen' (3.524).
41 **his** its
42 if defeated in another battle such as
   today's
43–4 The play ends with a couplet, but,
   unlike most final couplets in
   Shakespeare's plays (e.g. *RJ*
   5.3.309–10: 'For never was a story of

more woe / Than this of Juliet and her
Romeo'), this one does not offer a
summary statement about the completed action. Clearly this forces attention on the still incomplete military
action. Although many editors see this
as explicitly anticipating a second part,
it may rather point to a generic difference between tragedy and history,
here asserting the necessary contin-
gency of any historical moment.
43 **this business** i.e. this battle
   **fair** successfully
44 **leave** leave off, cease
   **all . . . won** i.e. all that is rightfully
   ours be brought back under control
   (with a play on *won* and 'one'; cf.
   1.1.14–15 and p. 42)

36 bend you] *Q4–F;* bend, you *Q1–3*    41 lose] *(loose), Q2*    sway] way *Q5–F*

# APPENDIX 1

## THE SOURCES OF *1 HENRY IV*

Source study has been a staple of literary scholarship at least since the second century AD with Aulus Gellius' famous comparison of Caecilius and Menander, and of Shakespeare scholarship in particular at least since 1756, when Charlotte Lennox published her *Shakespeare Illustrated; or, the Novels and Histories on which the Plays of Shakespeare are Founded*. Collier's *Shakespeare's Library: A Collection of the Romances, Novels, Poems and Histories, Used by Shakespeare as the Foundation of his Dramas* (1853) continued what Lennox began, a project that has found its most magisterial modern form in Geoffrey Bullough's eight-volume *Narrative and Dramatic Sources of Shakespeare* (1957–75).

The assumptions and procedures of such scholarship are now seemingly so self-evident that, for example, there is no mention of 'source' or 'source study' in *Critical Terms for Literary Study* (Lentricchia & McLaughlin) or *The Columbia Dictionary of Modern Literary and Cultural Criticism* (Childers & Hentzi). Perhaps source study is not considered 'modern' enough for mention in these books; or perhaps it is that source study seems to be undemanding of comment or, worse, unworthy of it. Still, for all the theoretical neglect, editions of major texts inevitably include sections devoted to sources. Certainly many serious editions of Shakespeare, like the Arden series, have lengthy discussions devoted to the sources of the plays, and often reprint substantial sections of Plutarch or Holinshed or other texts that Shakespeare clearly read and transformed into drama.

Nonetheless, it is not so apparent what should be considered a source. Usually scholars consider a source to be the prior text on which the *story* is based, either in whole or in part; that is, the dependence upon an earlier text for plot, or sometimes character, is what marks that text as a source. Verbal dependency is less comfortably recognized, perhaps because what has come to be thought of as intertextuality – quotation, allusion, parody, etc. – seems part of the imaginative process rather than a precondition of it, as traditional understandings of 'source' seem to imply.

With regard to *1 Henry IV*, this has led scholars mainly to focus on Shakespeare's obvious dependency upon Holinshed and Samuel Daniel's *Civil Wars* (1595) for the historical material, and upon *The Famous Victories of Henry the Fifth* (published in 1598 but performed perhaps as early as the late 1580s) for the intermingling of historical and comic materials. Other substantive sources have also been plausibly suggested: Stow's *Chronicles of England* (1580) and his *Annals* (1592), as well as *The Mirror for Magistrates* (1559), especially the sections on Glendower (written by Thomas Phaer) and Henry Percy (by William Baldwin). But it is Holinshed, Samuel Daniel and *The Famous Victories* that serve as the essential sources for Shakespeare's play.

Shakespeare unquestionably had read the section on King Henry IV in the 1587 edition of Holinshed's *Chronicles* (3.509–42), drawing upon it for incidents, characterizations and even particular phrasings. Shakespeare's direct dependence upon Holinshed can be seen in the commentary notes in this edition, where relevant passages from the chronicles are reprinted when Shakespeare's play closely follows them. Shakespeare focuses on Holinshed's account of the Percy rebellion in 1402–3 (Holinshed 3.520–3), and, although it is not impossible that Shakespeare either recalled or indeed newly consulted Hall's *Union of the Two Noble Families* (1548), upon which Holinshed drew, nothing in the play demands that we recognize Hall as a source for Shakespeare.[1]

---

1   Though see W. Gordon Zeeveld, 'The influence of Hall on Shakespeare's historical plays', *ELH*, 3 (1936), 317–56.

Shakespeare's play restructures, through selection, omission and compression, the history found in Holinshed. *1 Henry IV* gives the narrative a shape only dimly perceivable in the chronicle, turning Holinshed's account of the troubled reign of King Henry into his own 'prodigal son' play. The major restructurings of the events as they are narrated in Holinshed are found in Shakespeare's transposition of the King's resolve to undertake a pilgrimage to the Holy Land to the beginning of Henry's reign (1.1.9–27) from its historical position near the end, where it is conceived of as a strategy to unite Christian Europe rather than, as in the play, to unify his own land torn by civil strife; and in the movement of the history's report of the reconciliation of the King and Prince Hal in 1412 to the period immediately before the battle at Shrewsbury in 1403 (3.2.1–160). Another significant change is, of course, the play's parallelism of Hal and Hotspur, achieved by making Hal somewhat older than historically he was and Hotspur considerably younger (Hotspur in fact being three years older than King Henry, rather than a contemporary of Hal), a structural change anticipated by Daniel (*Civil Wars*). Otherwise Shakespeare largely follows the order of events as they appear in Holinshed's account, though the playwright makes some consequential changes of emphasis, most notably the ahistorical dramatization of Hal's heroic behaviour at the battle at Shrewsbury and the de-emphasis of the King's actual military successes (see p. 5).

Although Holinshed, along with Daniel, provided the historical core of Shakespeare's play, the dramatic design in fact came from other sources. The story of the reformation of the prodigal prince was well enough known, circulating in manuscript even within the lifetime of Henry V (Walsingham, 2.290). The early chronicles reproduce the conversion story; Robert Fabyan, for example, talks about Hal's youthful attraction to 'ryottours and wylde disposed persons' but celebrates the fact that, upon his accession to the throne, 'sodaynly he became a newe man' (Fabyan, *Prima Pars Cronicarum* (1516), sig. XX5$^r$). But, although

Shakespeare would have found in Holinshed (or perhaps Stow's *Chronicles*) the bare bones of the story of the wild prince's reform, he found the focus of his play in the anonymous *Famous Victories of Henry the Fifth*.

*The Famous Victories* was published only in 1598 (having been entered in the Stationers' Register on 14 May 1594) and then in a text that is seemingly curtailed and corrupted from that which was played by the Queen's men. Although some critics have held that it is 'unlikely' that its 1,563 lines served as 'a direct source' for Shakespeare (Cam², 25), *1 Henry IV* indeed seems indebted to this precursor, which episodically traces the life of Henry V from his scapegrace youth to his conversion upon assuming the throne, to the great English victory at Agincourt and his marriage to the French princess. If Shakespeare is not much dependent upon the language of the earlier play, he does take from it the mingling of history and comedy that is his own play's major achievement, as well as its strong teleological emphasis upon the emergence of the Prince as a responsible leader from his dissolute youthful associations. The disorderly activity in the tavern (referred to but not dramatized in *Famous Victories*), the highway robbery, companions named Ned, Gadshill and Sir John ('Jockey') Oldcastle (though here with none of the outrageous wit or monstrous size of Shakespeare's renamed version) are all part of what the dramatist has taken from *Famous Victories* to establish the contrast between the seeming misrule promised by the Prince's early feckless behaviour and the capabilities that he eventually displays. If the Prince in *Famous Victories* gives too little evidence of his capacity for the transformation that comes to make his reformation completely plausible, Shakespeare's Hal arguably anticipates it too much to make the reformation entirely appealing, but the centrality of the Prince in the early play in its mingling of history and comedy is what determines the shape of Shakespeare's history, rather than Holinshed, in which the Prince plays a relatively minor role in the events the play covers and which of course narrates the history in a single mode.

The sources of the plot and characterization of *1 Henry IV* can, then, largely be found in Holinshed, Daniel's *Civil Wars* and *Famous Victories*. The tendency among scholars has been to overestimate Shakespeare's reading – that is, to turn Shakespeare into something more like themselves than he is likely to have been. Usually they are pleased to multiply the number of putative sources, seeing Shakespeare's reading as more extensive than it seems to have been (however unlikely, given the speed with which new plays were written for the company) and perhaps undervaluing how intensive was his reading of the relatively few books that clearly did serve as his sources.

Nevertheless, there is another group of texts that did serve as source material for Shakespeare, though in a manner that has made it difficult to know precisely how to talk about it. These are the texts that he did not consciously turn to in order to find plots, incidents or characters but which unquestionably left traces of his engagement with them upon the play. The heterogeneous and disconnected readings that have not usually found a place in the various genealogical accounts of the origins of *1 Henry IV* are nonetheless part of its genetic make-up. Biblical quotations, proverbial phrases and echoes of popular ballads (not least what Sidney calls the 'the old song of Percy and Douglas', referring to things like 'The Hunting of the Cheviot' and other ballads celebrating their military encounter; Sidney, *Prose*, 97) appear in the play and are noted in the commentary. All of these in some sense must be considered sources but differ from the borrowings from, for example, Holinshed in that Shakespeare seemingly did not have to open a book to find them; they are part of the imaginative and linguistic environment in which Shakespeare wrote.

Clearly a major contributor to this environment was Thomas Nashe. A number of scholars have noted the remarkable number of parallels in Shakespeare's play to Nashe's energetic prose. Wilson provided an appendix of 'Parallels from Nashe' (Cam[1], 191–6), and A. R. Humphreys's edition (Ard[2]) finds additional borrowings. The relationship seems unmistakable, but Wilson

343

admits he has 'no explanation to offer' for it (Cam[1], 191). Nonetheless, Nashe unquestionably seems to have stimulated Shakespeare linguistically.[1] A telling example can be found in Nashe's *Have with You to Saffron Walden*. Here Nashe mocks Gabriel Harvey by referring to Harvey's *Pierce His Supererogation* as 'an unconscionable vast gorbellied Volume' more 'cumbersome than a paire of Swissers omnipotent galeaze breeches' and insisting that Harvey must be 'ashamed of the incomprehensible copulencie therof' (Nashe, 3.35). Nashe's language seems to have provoked Shakespeare's 'gorbellied knaves' (2.2.86), 'omnipotent villain' (1.2.104–5) and 'incomprehensible lies' (1.2.176), and even Nashe's 'corpulencie' finds response in Shakespeare's description of Falstaff as 'a goodly, portly man, i'faith, and a corpulent' (2.4.410). Nashe's description of Harvey's having filled 'a whole cloke-bag full of condemnation' (Nashe, 3.97) similarly seems to have suggested Hal's description of Falstaff as 'that stuffed cloak-bag of guts' (2.4.439–40). Many other examples can be found in the notes to this and other editions. But it is not only around the character of Falstaff that Nashe's verbal influence can be felt. In *Piers Penniless*, Nashe speaks of those 'that stand most on their honour, have shut up their purses, and shifte us off with court holie bread: and on the other side, a number of hypocriticall *hot-spurres*' (Nashe, 1.161). The focus on honour, the Piers/Purse pun and even the nickname of Northumberland's hot-blooded son are constellated in the passage and seem somehow to have influenced Shakespeare. Nashe's exuberant language seems to be taken up by Shakespeare, not as a deliberate subtext but as an unconscious pre-text for the workings of his imagination. If this is not a source as source study usually understands the term, it is certainly a stimulus that must be acknowledged, especially as it anticipates and seemingly provokes some of the verbal ingenuity and energy for which Shakespeare has been so often praised.

1   See also J.J.M. Tobin, 'Nashe and *1 Henry IV*', n.s. *NQ*, 25 (1978), 129–31.

# APPENDIX 2

## A NOTE ON SHAKESPEARE'S METRICS

Iambic pentameter provides the dominant pattern of Shakespeare's verse. A line of ten syllables, every second stressed, creates the familiar rhythm: e.g. 'The hearts of all that he did angle for' (4.3.84). Shakespeare, however, often modifies the pattern, shifting the stresses and adding or subtracting syllables, and thus preventing the rhythm from becoming predictable and allowing poetic and thematic effects based upon the metrical variations to be heard against the norm. Shakespeare does not permit his blank verse to approximate 'the forced gait of a shuffling nag' (3.1.131), with an unvarying regularity limping across the line's meaning.

Nonetheless, Alexander Pope in his edition of 1723–5 notoriously 'repaired' the verse as he found it in the printed texts, assuming that almost every deviation from the rhythmical norm of the decasyllabic line pointed not to the playwright's deliberate artistry (or even to an unwitting lapse of attention) but to some sloppiness in the process of textual transmission, which allowed a word to be left out or the wrong word printed. Thus, in *1 Henry IV*, the King's caustic response to Worcester's claim that he had 'not sought the day of this dislike' – 'You have not sought it? How comes it, then?' (5.1.27) – is altered by Pope to 'You have not sought it, Sir? How comes it then'. A tenth syllable is dutifully provided, but there is no evidence that Shakespeare wrote the line in this way and a compelling dramatic logic to the line as it stands. The pause where one expects a stressed syllable is dramatically effective. 'We can imagine', writes George T. Wright, 'Henry stamping, snorting, sniffing, or turning on Worcester to mark the audible gap in the line' (Kastan, *Companion*, 267). And indeed there is precedent in the play for just such a pause. Earlier, when the King orders Worcester from the court – 'Worcester, get thee gone, for I do see / Danger and disobedience in thine eye' (1.3.15–16) – we hear the same rhythm. The first line has only nine syllables and the line is again 'completed' by a silence, here the ominous delay after 'gone'.

This line shows other variations, which further suggest how flexible Shakespeare's metrical practice can be. 'Worcester', of course, has only two syllables (pronounced 'wùh-ster'), but they reverse the expected iambic pattern of unstressed and stressed syllables; the stressed first syllable marking the King's fierce authority. The second line's metrics are no more regular and no less effective. The line seemingly has eleven syllables, unless 'disobedience' is pronounced with four (the last eliding the two final vowel sounds into something like '-yence'). 'Danger' again reverses the iambic norm, with a stressed followed by an unstressed syllable (a trochee), forcing it into prominence, and the last foot – 'thine eye' – demands a short pause after 'thine' to allow the first sound of 'eye' to be vocalized, the necessary hesitation itself adding to the menace of the King's words.

Clearly Shakespeare is not bound by the dominant rhythmical pattern he has established, and indeed part of his development as a theatre poet can be seen in the increasingly varied and complex metrical structuring of characters' thought. In the early plays, the verse line is generally both more rigidly iambic and more grammatically restrictive. It is characteristically endstopped with the line marking a complete grammatical unit: 'But soft, what light through yonder window breaks?' (*RJ* 2.2.1). Shakespeare's verse, however, grows more flexible, even conversational, in the later plays, as the logic of the sentence begins to overwhelm the logic of the verse line: e.g. 'And make the Douglas' son your only mean / For powers in Scotland, which for divers reasons / Which I shall send you written, be assured / Will easily be granted' (1.3.258–61).

Here the grammatical unit is not complete at the end of one line but carries across it, ending only in the middle of the next. Also the iambic norm, evident in the first line, is disrupted in the second, then re-established in the third.

There is, then, no reason either to assume or to desire metrical regularity (and our efforts to recognize or attain it are themselves compromised by how uncertain is our knowledge of the variations in early modern English pronunciation). Dramatic concerns trump metrical norms; individual speakers and specific social situations demand variations in the pentameter line. But if modern editors for the most part have repudiated the procrustean practice of Augustan editing, where not only syntax was rearranged but also words were both added and omitted to produce a regular five-stress iambic line, they still embrace many of the assumptions that were in play, although these now reveal themselves not in the text but in the notes. Consider 1.3.12–14:

WORCESTER
   And that same greatness too which our own hands
   Have holp to make so portly.
NORTHUMBERLAND
   My lord –

If, as many editors assume, lines 13 and 14 are a shared verse line, it has only nine syllables. Pope, therefore, characteristically changes Northumberland's vocative to 'My good lord' to provide the 'missing' syllable. Modern editors, of course, do not emend the text, but often tell us, as Humphreys does, that ' "portly" is trisyllabic' (Ard²), on the grounds that the 'r' was spoken so harshly that it produced an additional syllable. It does seem likely that Elizabethan 'r's were often sounded more aggressively than in modern practice, but the idea that an extra syllable can be heard in 'portly' seems to stem more from assumptions about Shakespeare's metrics than from any knowledge of his characteristic pronunciation. In truth we know all too little about

Elizabethan pronunciations with their regional variations for our assertions about how it affects versification to be other than circular. If it is a shared verse line, a pause after 'portly' will 'complete' the line without assuming the extra-syllabic, rolled 'r', and, if indeed the rolled 'r' is sounded, that also suggests that a temporal principle structures the line as much as a syllabic one; the extended 'r' in 'portly' draws out the time of the line (as would the pause after the word) to its expected length rather than adds a tenth syllable. Nonetheless, it is no less possible that, as this edition posits, the hypermetricality is itself the point clarifying the tensions of the scene. Worcester ends with an audibly incomplete line, emphasizing the strain of the encounter. Northumberland then tries to protect his angry kinsman, but is quickly cut off by the King. It is impossible to be completely confident about Shakespeare's intentions here, but the provocative uncertainties about the lineation and metrics should alert us to the fact that Shakespeare's versification not only allows a far more various set of rhythmical possibilities than a strict understanding of blank verse might suggest, but also demands to be understood as being rooted in dramatic necessities and based less upon syllable counts than upon an arrangement of stresses within an understood temporal norm, as is no doubt appropriate for a prosody that is to be spoken and heard in the theatre rather than read on the page.

# APPENDIX 3

## THE PLAY IN MANUSCRIPT

It is often stated that none of Shakespeare's dramatic writings survives in manuscript, although this is true only if we intend 'manuscript' to refer exclusively to a holograph manuscript (and then only if we ignore or reassign the 147 lines of 'Hand D' in the *Sir Thomas More* manuscript usually attributed to Shakespeare). But manuscripts of Shakespeare do exist. The Dering manuscript is perhaps the best known of these. A conflation of the two parts of *Henry IV* into a single play designed for an amateur performance, the Dering manuscript (see p. 80) was transcribed from a copy of Q5 of *1 Henry IV* (1613) and the second issue of the 1600 quarto of *2 Henry IV*. It was discovered in 1844 by the Reverend Lambert B. Larking in the library of the Dering estate at Surrendon Hall, near Pluckley, Kent. In 1897 the manuscript was purchased by Henry Clay Folger, and it now resides in the Folger Library in Washington, DC.

A small folio of fifty-five leaves, the manuscript was prepared by two different people. One was Edward Dering himself (1598–1644), a baronet with notable antiquarian and dramatic interests who would eventually assume a seat in the Long Parliament. He prepared the first page of the manuscript and then turned it over to a professional scribe, though Dering then corrected the scribal copy (Dering, vii). The conflation includes much more of *Part One* than of *Part Two*; only two scenes of the first play are entirely omitted (2.1 and 4.4) and only about one-quarter of the second play is present at all (806 of the play's 3,180 lines). Dering divided his play into acts and scenes, none of which is present in either of the quartos, omitted certain characters, reassigned a few speeches, revised and even added some speeches, provided a few additional stage directions and in general seems to have intelligently prepared a conflated version of the two plays that is both coherent and possible to act.

The manuscript's most substantial addition to Shakespeare's plays is the substitution of nine lines to replace 1.1.25–7 of *1 Henry IV*. 'And force proude Mahomett from Palestine' is the original manuscript's substitution, with a further addition also in Dering's hand: 'The high aspiring Cresant of the turke, / Wee'll plucke into a lower orbe, and then / Humbling her borrowed Pride to th' English lyon, / With labour and with honour wee'le fetch there / A sweating laurell from the glorius East / And plant new jemms on royall Englands crowne. / We'll pitch our honores att the sonnes uprise / and sell our selves or winn a glorious prize' (Dering, 4–5). These last eight lines are written on a torn scrap of paper attached to the first leaf of the manuscript, on the back of which appear three parallel columns, the first of which lists most of the characters in Fletcher's *The Spanish Curate* (the remainder presumably lost with the tear) and then two separate lists of friends and relatives of Dering as alternative casting suggestions. As *The Spanish Curate* was not licensed until 24 October 1622, we have an early limit to at least the revision of *Henry IV*, and its later limit of the summer of 1624 is apparently established by the presence in the cast lists of Francis Manouch, who at that time left the area and the service of the Wooten family (Sir Thomas Wooten also appearing in the cast lists) to join the household of Sir Edward Conway, then Secretary of State (Hemingway, 496–7). It is impossible to tell exactly when the conflation itself was begun, but, as its dependence upon the 1613 Q5 is clear from the appearance in the manuscript of two readings unique to that quarto, obviously it could not be any earlier than that date. *The Spanish Curate*'s amateur cast list also suggests that the *Henry IV* conflation was intended for a similar amateur performance.

But this is not the only early manuscript to include at least parts of the text of *1 Henry IV*. A manuscript of theological notes with a contemporary attribution to Thomas Harriot, now housed in the British Library and identified as Additional MS 64078, has on its verso leaves sixty-three lines of *1 Henry IV* (Kelliher, 145–78). If the Dering manuscript is more important as a document of social and theatrical history than as one of any textual authority, reminding us of a mode of amateur performance so often ignored, Additional MS 64078 also reminds us of cultural practices different from our own (and similarly lacks any textual authority). The transcriber has written out twenty-four extracts from the play drawn from 1.1, 1.3, 2.1, 3.1, 3.2 and 4.3. None is longer than nine lines. The extracts seem to be selected for inclusion in a commonplace book; marginal headings seek to classify the quotations: 'a valiant man taxed of feares' stands to the right of Vernon's 'I hold as little councell w$^{th}$ weake feare / as you' and 'lette it be seen tomorrow in the battayle' (*1H4* 4.3.11–12, 13). Speakers' names are omitted, and the speech is usually recast into indirect discourse to free the quotations from their specific contexts in the play; thus, for the play's 'And then I stole all courtesy from heaven / And dressed myself in such humility / That I did pluck allegiance from men's hearts, / Loud shouts and salutations from their mouths, / Even in the presence of the crowned King' (3.2.50–4), the copyist writes: 'he ['you' having been crossed out] must steal Curtesy / from Heavn, & dress hymself in / sutch humillity, as he may pluck / allegiance from mens harts euen in / the presence of the Queene.' Not only do the changes give the quotation a more general application (or perhaps a specific reference to Essex), but also the conscious or unconscious alteration of the final noun from Shakespeare's 'King' to 'Queene' seemingly allows the extracts to be dated no later than 24 March 1603, when Elizabeth died, to be succeeded by King James.

There is no way of knowing for certain how early the extracts were copied onto the verso leaves of the manuscript. One section of the theological observations on the recto side is dated, in a hand different from the compiler's, 1594. The play, however, was not available in print until 1598, and probably not on stage before the late summer of 1596. But, if we can then only date the extracts to some time between August 1596 and the end of March 1603, they still become the earliest-known manuscript extracts of any Shakespearean play. If they can tell us little about the play that was read or witnessed, they do tell us something important about how the play was engaged: less as an organic whole than as a repository of memorable phrases and ideas. Nonetheless, the extracts testify to the compiler's careful knowledge of and respect for the play. The extracts appear in the order in which they occur in *1 Henry IV*, which argues more than casual familiarity with the play; and, while the copyist regularly makes the kinds of generalizing alterations familiar in commonplace books, he also displays a concern for the correctness of the readings that further testifies to his knowledge of the play. Thus Henry's claim that 'Opinion, that did help me to the crown, / Had still kept loyal to possession' (3.2.42–3), if he had been prodigal with his appearances, appears in the extracts as: 'opinion w$^{ch}$ must & doth oft help [the word 'aid' having been erroneously written first and then crossed out] one to a crown will still keepe / loyall to possession.' Whether the lines were jotted down in the playhouse or recalled from previous readings, clearly the compiler sought to get them right, even as he reminds us that the popular stage could serve as a source of memorable phrases as much as memorable characters and plots.

One other manuscript merits mention here. In 1988 a single leaf came to light with its two sides filled with fifty-seven lines of blank verse in a late sixteenth- or early seventeenth-century hand. The manuscript now resides in the collection of Martin Schøyen (Oslo and London), where it is catalogued as MS 1627. The scene is a fragment of an unknown play consisting of a conversation between a tapster and two thieves. The section begins with the tapster telling the thieves of a lodger at his inn with '3 hundred marks' that he carries 'unto the kings exchequer'. The scene is clearly an analogue of the Gad's Hill robbery in *1 Henry IV*, where the Chamberlain tells Gadshill of the franklin staying at the inn and travelling with 'three hundred marks with him in gold'

(2.1.54–5), which Bardoll later adds is 'going to the King's exchequer' (2.2.53). Arthur Freeman, who is the only person to have carefully studied the manuscipt, concludes that the play is 'more likely to follow than precede Shakespeare's text', and speculates that it was for a play, perhaps an amateur performance in Oxford, written in 1600–20. While it seems most likely that the scene is derived, directly or indirectly, from Shakespeare's play, it is not impossible, as Freeman points out, that it is based upon a pre-Shakespearean version of *1 Henry IV*, or at least of the robbery scene, and might thus point to an unknown Shakespearean source (Freeman, 103).

# APPENDIX 4

## CASTING

It is impossible to know with certainty how many actors were used to perform the plays in Shakespeare's own time. Clearly the circumstances of performance would affect casting; playing at the Globe would almost certainly allow a larger cast than while on tour, when the company would presumably travel with a smaller company of players. In all circumstances, however, it appears that some roles were doubled. The Swiss visitor, Thomas Platter, reported seeing a performance of *Julius Caesar* at the Globe in 1599, in which the forty speaking roles were played by 'approximately fifteen actors' (Chambers, *Stage*, 2.364); but we do not know the principles that determined doubling. Did lead actors sometimes also play minor parts? Were speaking roles regularly cut or conflated to allow a smaller cast to play? Did boy actors only play female and adolescent male parts, or might they sometimes double a small adult role? How were the supernumerary parts distributed? How much time was necessary to permit a change of role? In the absence of certain information about casting practices, any suggestions must be speculative. The two scholars who have most searchingly explored the questions of casting on the Elizabethan stage, T. J. King and David Bradley, in fact reach different conclusions about how *1 Henry IV* would be played; King posits twenty-two actors (King, 254); Bradley, sixteen (Bradley, 234). The chart on p. 356, however, gives a possible way of playing *1 Henry IV* with thirteen actors (ten adults, three boys). The most problematic doubling here is in 5.4, where the actor playing Douglas appears also as John of Lancaster. He exits as Lancaster at line 15 and has only ten lines before he must re-enter as

Douglas, though presumably all that is involved is a change of cloak or tabard. The chart does not distribute the roles of servants, messengers, the Ostler and the travellers, as they are easily assumed by the company, and any assignment of these parts would be almost completely arbitrary.

# DOUBLING CHART

| Roles and scenes | T | 1.1 | 1.2 | 1.3 | 2.1 | 2.2 | 2.3 | 2.4 | 3.1 | 3.2 | 3.3 | 4.1 | 4.2 | 4.3 | 4.4 | 5.1 | 5.2 | 5.3 | 5.4 | 5.5 | Players |
|---|---|---|---|---|---|---|---|---|---|---|---|---|---|---|---|---|---|---|---|---|---|
| Prince | 10 | × | × | | | × | | × | | × | × | | × | | | × | | × | × | × | 1 |
| Falstaff | 8 | | × | | | × | | × | | | × | | × | | | × | | × | × | | 2 |
| Hotspur | 8 | | | × | | | × | | × | | | × | | × | | | × | × | × | | 3 |
| King | 7 | × | | × | | | | | | × | | | | | | × | | × | × | × | 4 |
| Worcester | 7 | | | × | | | | | × | | | × | | × | | × | × | | | × | 5 |
| Sheriff | 1 | | | | | | | × | | | | | | | | | | | | | 5 |
| Blount | 5 | × | | | | | | | | × | | | | × | | × | | × | | | 6 |
| Glendower | 1 | | | | | | | | × | | | | | | | | | | | | 6 |
| Gadshill | 3 | | | | × | × | | × | | | | | | | | | | | | | 6 |
| Douglas | 5 | | | | | | | | | | | × | | × | | | × | × | × | | 7 |
| Lancaster | 4 | × | | | | | | | | | | | | | | × | | | × | × | 7 |
| 1 Carrier | 2 | | | | × | | | × | | | | | | | | | | | | | 7 |
| Lady Percy | 2 | | | | | | × | | × | | | | | | | | | | | | 8 |
| Francis | 1 | | | | | | | × | | | | | | | | | | | | | 8 |
| Vernon | 5 | | | | | | | | | | | × | | × | | × | × | | | × | 9 |
| Peto | 3 | | | | | × | | × | | | × | | | | | | | | | | 9 |
| Mortimer | 1 | | | | | | | | × | | | | | | | | | | | | 9 |
| Poins | 3 | | × | | | × | | × | | | | | | | | | | | | | 10 |
| Northumberland | 1 | | | × | | | | | | | | | | | | | | | | | 10 |
| Westmorland | 4 | × | | | | | | | | | | | × | | | × | | | | × | 11 |
| Vintner | 1 | | | | | | | × | | | | | | | | | | | | | 11 |
| Chamberlain | 1 | | | | × | | | | | | | | | | | | | | | | 11 |
| Archbishop | 1 | | | | | | | | | | | | | | × | | | | | | 11 |
| Hostess | 2 | | | | | | | × | | | × | | | | | | | | | | 12 |
| Lady Mortimer | 1 | | | | | | | | × | | | | | | | | | | | | 12 |
| Sir Michael | 1 | | | | | | | | | | | | | | × | | | | | | 12 |
| Bardoll | 4 | | | | | × | | × | | | × | | × | | | | | | | | 13 |
| 2 Carrier | 1 | | | | × | | | | | | | | | | | | | | | | 13 |
| Servants/Mess./Ostler | 4 | | | | × | | × | | | | | × | | | | | × | | | | misc. |
| Travellers | 1 | | | | × | | | | | | | | | | | | | | | | misc. |
| | T | 1.1 | 1.2 | 1.3 | 2.1 | 2.2 | 2.3 | 2.4 | 3.1 | 3.2 | 3.3 | 4.1 | 4.2 | 4.3 | 4.4 | 5.1 | 5.2 | 5.3 | 5.4 | 5.5 | |

# APPENDIX 5

## THE Q0 FRAGMENT

The first edition of *1 Henry IV*, printed by Peter Short for Andrew Wise, survives only in a fragment now in the collection of the Folger Shakespeare Library. In a note dated 25 May 1867 on the inside cover of the bound fragment, J. O. Halliwell has written: 'These leaves were found at Bristol, some years ago, in the binding of a copy of Thomas' Rules of the Italian Grammar, Quarto, 1567.' A stained and creased single sheet (the four leaves of the 'C' signature), the fragment supplies copy for what most modern editions of the play indicate as 1.3.200–2.2.108. The reasonably well-printed text (see pp. 108–9) seems to have been produced in Short's printing house early in 1598, as the play was registered on 25 February of that year.

*of Henry the fourth.*

By heauen me thinkes it were an easie leape,
To plucke bright honor from the pale fac't moone,
Or diue into the bottome of the deepe,
Where fadome line could neuer touch the ground,
And plucke vp drowned honor by the locks,
So he that doth redeeme her thence might weare
Without corriuall all her dignities,
But out vpon this halfe fac't fellowship.

*Wor*. He apprehends a world of figures here,
But not the forme of what he should attend,
Good coosen giue me audience for a while.

   *Hot*. I cry you mercy.

   *Wor*. Those same noble Scots that are your prisoners.

   *Hot*. Ile keepe them all;
By God he shal not haue a Scot of them,
No, if a Scot would saue his soule he shal not,
Ile keepe them by this hand.

   *Wor*. You, start away,
And lend no eare vnto my purposes:
Those prisoners you shal keepe.

   *Hot*. Nay I wil, thats flat:
He said he would not ransome Mortimer,
Forbad my tongue to speake of Mortimer,
But wil find him when he lies asleepe,
And in his eare ile hollow Mortimer:
Nay, ile haue a starling shalbe taught to speake
Nothing but Mortimer, and giue it him
To keepe his anger stil in motion.

   *Wor*. Heare you cosen a word.

   *Hot*. All studies here I sollemnly defie,
Saue how to gall and pinch this Bullingbrooke,
And that same sword and buckler prince of Wales,
But that I thinke his father loues him not,
And would be glad he met with some mischance,
I would haue him poisoned with a pot of ale.

   *Wor*. Farewel kinsman, ile talke to you
when you are better temperd to attend.

                             C.j.          *North*.

*The Hystorie*

*North.* Why what a waspe-ſtung and impatient foole
Art thou, to breake into this womans moode,
Tying thine eare to no tongue but thine owne.

*Hot.* Why looke you? I am whip and ſcourgd with rods,
Netled, and ſtung with piſmires, when I heare
Of this vile polititian Bullingbrooke,
In Richards time, what do you cal the place?
A plague vpon it, it is in Gloceſterſhire;
Twas where the mad-cap duke his vnckle kept
His vncle Yorke, where I firſt bowed my knee
Vnto this king of ſmiles, this Bullingbrooke:
Zbloud, when you and he came backe from Rauenſpurgh.

*North.* At Barkly caſtle.

*Hot.* You ſay true.
Why what a candy deale of curteſie,
This fawning greyhound then did proffer me,
Looke when his infant fortune came to age,
And gentle Harry Percy, and kind cooſen:
O the diuel take ſuch cooſoners, god forgiue me,
Good vncle tel your tale, I haue done.

*Wor.* Nay, if you haue not, to it againe,
We wil ſtay your leiſure.

*Hot.* I haue done iſaith.

*Wor.* Then once more to your Scottiſh priſoners,
Deliuer them vp without their ranſome ſtraight,
And make the Douglas ſonne your onely meane
For Powers in Scotland, which for diuers reaſons
Which I ſhal ſend you written, be aſſur'd
Wil eaſely be granted you my Lord,
Your ſonne in Scotland being thus emploied,
Shal ſecretly into the boſome creepe
Of that ſame noble Prelat wel belou'd,
The Archbiſhop.

*Hot.* Of Yorke, is it not?

*Wor.* True, who beares hard
His brothers death at Briſtow the lord Scroop,
I ſpeake not this in eſtimation,

A͛

*of Henry the fourth.*

As what I thinke might be,but what I knowe
Is ruminated,plotted,and set downe,
And onely stayes but to behold the face
Of that occasion that shal bring it on.

*Hot.* I smell it. Vpon my life it will do well:

*Nort.* Before the game is afoote thou still letst slip.

*Hot.* Why, it cannot chuse but be a noble plot,
And then the power of Scotland,and of Yorke,
To ioyne with Mortimer, ha.

*Wor.* And so they shall,

*Hot.* In faith it is exceedingly well, aimd.

*Wor.* And tis no little reason bids vs speed,
To saue our heades by raising of a head,
Or beare our selues as euen as we can,
The king will alwayes thinke him in our debt,
And thinke we thinke our selues vnsatisfied,
Till he hath found a time to pay vs home,
And see alreadie how he doth begin
To make vs strangers to his lookes of loue.

*Hot.* He does,he does,weele be reuengd on him.

*Wor.* Coosen farewell,No further go in this,
Then I by letters shall direct your course
When time is ripe,which will be suddenly,
Ile steale to Glendower,and Lo:Mortimer,
Where you and Douglas,and our powers at once,
As *I* will fashion it shall happily meete,
To beare out fortunes in our owne strong armes,
Which now we hold at much vncertaintie.

*Nor.* Farewell good brother,we shall thriue *I* trust.

*Hot.* Vncle adieu:O let the houres be short,
Till fields,and blowes,and grones,applaud our sport. *Exeunt.*

*Enter a Carrier with a lanterne in his hand.*

*1 Car.* Heigh ho.An it be not foure by the day ile be hangd,
Charles-waine is ouer the new Chimney, and yet our horse not
packt. What Ostler.

*Ost.* Anon, anon.

C ñ. *1 Car.*

## The Hyftorie

1 *Car.* I preethe Tom beat Cuts faddle, put a few flockes in
the point, poore iade is wroong in the withers, out of all ceffe.

*Enter another Carier.*

2 *Car.* Peafe and beanes are as danke here as a dog, and that
is the next way to giue poore iades the bottes : this houfe is turned vpfide downe fince Robin Oftler died.

1 *Car.* Poore fellow neuer ioyed fince the prife of Oates rofe,
it was the death of him.

2 *Car.* I thinke this bee the moft villainous houfe in all London road for fleas, I am flung like a Tench.

1 *Car.* Like a Tench, by the Maffe there is nere a King chriften could be better bit then I haue bin fince the firft cocke.

2 *Car.* Why, they will allowe vs nere a Iordan, and then
we leake in your Chimney, and your chamber-lie breedes fle :
like a loach.

1 *Car.* What Oftler, come away and be hangd, come away.

2 *Car.* I haue a gammon of bacon, and two razes of Ginger, to be deliuered as farre as Charing Croffe.

1 *Car.* Gods bodie, the Turkies in my Panier are quite ftarued: what Oftler? a plague on thee, haft thou neuer an eie in thy
heade: canft not heare, and twere not as good deed as drinke to
breake the pate on theo, I am a verie villain, come and be hangd,
haft no faith in thee ?

*Enter Gadfhill.*

*Gadfhill.* Good morrow Cariers, whats a clocke?

*Car:* I thinke it be two a clocke.

*Gad:* I preethe lend me thy lanterne, to fee my gelding in the
ftable.

1 *Car:* Nay by God foft, I knowe a trike worth two of that
I fayth.

*Gad:* I pray thee lend me thine.

2 *Car.* I when canft tell? lend mee thy lanterne (quoth he)
marry ile fee thee hangd firft.

*Gad.* Sirtha Carier, what time do you meane to come to
London?

2 *Car.* Time enough to go to bed with a candle, I warrant
thee, fome neighbour Mugs, weele call vp the Gentlemen,
they

## *of Henrie the fourth.*

hey will along with companie, for they haue great charge.

  *Enter Chamberlaine,*       *Exeunt.*

 *Gad.* What ho : Chamberlaine.

 *Cham.* At hand quoth pickepurse.

 *Gad.* Thats euen as faire as at hand quoth the Chamberlaine: for thou variest no more from picking of purses, then giuing direction doth from labouring: thou layest the plot how.

 *Cham.* Good morrow maister Gadshil, it holdes currant that *I* tolde you yesternight, ther's a Frankelin in the wild of Kent hath brought three hundred Markes with him in golde, *I* heard him tell it to one of his companie last night at supper, a kinde of Auditor, one that hath abundance of charge too, God knowes what, they are vp alreadie, and call for Egges and Butter, they will away presently.

 *Gad:* Sirrha, if they meete not with Saint Nicholas clearkes, giue thee this necke.

 *Cham.* No, ile none of it, *I* pray thee keepe that for the hang-man, for *I* know thou worshippest Saine Nicholas, as trulie as man of falshood may.

 *Ga.* What talkest thou to me of the hagman: if *I* hang, ile make a fat paire of Gallowes : for if *I* hang, olde sir *Iohn* hangs with me, and thou knowest he is no starueling : tut, there are other Troyans that thou dreamst not of, the which for sport sake are content to do the profession, some grace, that would (if matters should be lookt into) for their owne credit sake make all whole. I am ioyned with no footland rakers, no long-staffe sixpennie strikers, none of these mad mustachio purplehewd maltworms, but with nobilitie, & tranquilitie, Burgomasters & great Oneyres, such as can hold in such as wil strike sooner then speak, and speake sooner then drinke, and drinke sooner then pray, and yet (zoundes) I lie, for they pray continually to their Saint the Common-wealth, or rather not pray to her, but pray on her, for they ride vp and downe on her, and make her their bootes.

 *Cham.* What, the Common-wealth their bootes ? will shee hold out water in foule way?

 *Gad.* She will, she will, Iustice hath liquord her: wee steale as in a Castell cocksure: we haue the receyte of Ferneseede, wee

        C iii.       walke

## The Hystorie

walke inuisble;

*Cham*: Nay by my faith, I thinke you are more beholding to the night then to Ferneseed, for your walking inuisble.

*Gad.* Giue me thy hand, thou shalt haue a share in our purchase, as I am a true man.

*Cham.* Nay rather let me haue it as you are a false theefe.

*Gad.* Go to, *homo* is a common name to al men, bid the Ostler bring my gelding out of the stable, farewell you muddye knaue.

*Enter Prince, Poynes, and Peto &c.*

*Po.* Come shelter, shelter, I haue remoude Falstalffes horse, and he frets like a gumd Veluet.

*Pr.* Stand close:    *Enter Falstalffe.*

*Fal.*Poynes, Poynes, and be hangd Poynes.

*Pr.* Peace yee fat-kidneyd rascall, what a brawling dost thou keepe?

*Fal.* Wheres Poynes, Hall?

*Pr.* He is walkt vp to the top of the hill, Ile go seeke him.

*Fal.* I am accurst to rob in that theeues companie, the rascall hath remooued my horse, and tied him I know not where, if I trauell but foure foote by the squire further a foote, I shall breake my winde . Well, I doubt not but to die a faire death for all this, if I scape hanging for killing that rogue. I haue forsworne his companie hourly any time this xxii:yeares, and yet I am bewitcht with the rogues companie. If the rascall haue not giuen mee medicines to make me loue him, ile be hangd. It could not be else, I haue drunke medicines.Poynes, Hall, a plague vpon you both, Bardol, Peto, ile starue ere ile robbe a foote further, and twere not as good a deed as drinke to turne trueman, and to leaue these rogues, I am the veriest varlet that euer chewed with a tooth. Eight yeards of vneuen ground is threescore and ten myles a foote with mee , and the stonie hearted villiaines knowe it well enough, a plague vpon it when theeues cannot be true one to another.

*They whistle.*

Whew, a plague vpon you all, giue mee my horse you rogues, giue me my horse and be hangd;

Peace

*Pr.* Peace yee fatte guts, lie downe, lay thine eare close to the grounde, and liſt if thou canſt heare the treade of trauay-lers.

*Falſt.* Haue you any leauers to liſt me vp againe being downe, zbloud ile not beare my owne fleſh ſo farre a foote againe for all the coyne in thy fathers Exchequer : What a plague meane ye to colt me thus ?

*Pr.* Thou lieſt, thou art not colted, thou art vncolted.

*Falſt.* I preethe good prince, Hall, helpe me to my horſe, good kings ſonne.

*Pr.* Out ye rogue, ſhall I be your Oſtler?

*Falſt.* Hang thy ſelfe in thine owne heire apparant garters, if I be tane, ile peach for this : and I haue not Ballads made on you all, and ſung to filthie tunes, let a cuppe of Sacke bee my poyſon, when a ieaſt is ſo forward, and a foote too I hate it.

*Enter Gadſhill.*

*Gad.* Stand. *Fal.* So I do againſt my will.

*Po.* O tis our ſetter, I knowe his voice. Bardoll, what newes.

*Bar.* Caſe ye, caſe yee on with your vizardes, theres mony of the kings comming downe the hill, tis going to the kinges Exchequer.

*Fal.* You lie, ye rogue, tis going to the kings tauerne.

*Gad.* Theres enough to make vs all.

*Fal.* To be hangd.

*Pr.* Sirs, you foure ſhall front them in the narrowe lane : Ned Poynes and I will walke lower, if they ſcape from your encoun-tur, then they light on vs.

*Peto.* How many be there of them ?

*Gad.* Some eight or ten.

*Fal.* Zounds will they not rob vs ?

*Pr.* What, a coward ſir Iohn paunch.

*Falſt.* Indeed I am not Iohn of Gaunt your grandfather, but yet no coward Hall.

*Pr.* Well, we leaue that to the proofe.

*Po.* Sirrha Iacke, thy horſe ſtandes behinde the hedge, when thou needſt him, there thou ſhalt find him : farewel & ſtand faſt.

*Falſt.* Now can not I ſtrike him if I ſhould be hangd.

Pr.

*Pr.* Prince, wheere are our diguises:

*Po.* Here, hard by, stand close.

*Falſt.* Now my maiſters, happie man be his dole, ſay I, euerie man to his buſineſſe.                    *Enter the trauailers,*

*Trauel.* Come neighbour, the boy ſhal lead our horſes down the hill, weele walke a foote a while and eaſe our legs.

*Theeues.* Stand. *Trauel.* Ieſus bleſſe vs.

*Falſt.* Strike, downe with them, cut the villaines throates, a horeſone Caterpillers, bacon-ſed knaues, they hate vs youth, downe with them, fleece them.

*Tra.* O we are vndone, both we and ours for euer.

*Fal.* Hang ye gorbellied knaues, are yee vndone, no ye fatte chuffes I woulde your ſtore were here: on bacons on, what yee knaues yong men muſt liue, you are grand iurers, are ye, weele iure ye faith.

*Here they rob them and bind them.     Exeunt.*

*Enter the Prince and Poynes.*

*Pr.* The theeues haue bounde the true men, nowe coulde thou and I rob the theeues, and go merrily to London, it woulde be argument for a weeke, laughter for a month, and a good ieaſt for euer.

*Po.* Stand cloſe, I heare them comming.

*Enter the theeues againe.*

*Fal.* Come my maiſters, let vs ſhare and then to horſe before day, and the prince and Poynes bee not two arrant cowardes theres no equitie ſtirring, theres no more valour in that Poynes, then in a wilde ducke.

| | |
|---|---|
| *Pr.* Your money. | *As they are ſharing the prince & Poins ſet vpon them, they all runne away, and Falſtalſſe after a blow or two runs away too, leauing the bootie behind them.* |
| *Po.* Villaines. | |

*Prin.* Got with much eaſe, now merrily to horſe: the theeues are al ſcattered, and poſſeſt with feare ſo ſtrongly, that they dare not meete each other, each takes his fellowe for an officer, away good Ned, Falſtalſſe ſweates to death, and lards the leane earth as he walkes along, wert not for laughing I ſhould pittie him.

*Po.* How the fat rogue roard.                    *Exeunt.*

*Enter*

# ABBREVIATIONS AND REFERENCES

Quotations and references to Shakespeare plays other than *1 Henry IV* are from *The Arden Shakespeare Complete Works*, ed. Richard Proudfoot, Ann Thompson and David Scott Kastan, rev. edn (2001). Biblical quotations are from the Geneva Bible unless otherwise indicated. In all references, place of publication is London unless otherwise stated.

## ABBREVIATIONS

### ABBREVIATIONS USED IN NOTES

| | |
|---|---|
| * | precedes commentary notes involving readings altered from the two quarto editions of 1598 upon which this edition is based |
| c | corrected state |
| conj. | conjectured by |
| n. | (in cross-references) commentary note |
| n.d. | no date |
| n.s. | new series |
| om. | omitted in |
| RSC | Royal Shakespeare Company |
| SD | stage direction |
| SP | speech prefix |
| subst. | substantially |
| this edn | a reading adopted for the first time in this edition |
| TLN | through line numbering in *The Norton Facsimile: The First Folio of Shakespeare*, prepared by Charlton Hinman (New York, 1968) |
| t.n. | textual note |
| u | uncorrected state |

# WORKS BY AND PARTLY BY SHAKESPEARE

| | |
|---|---|
| *AC* | *Antony and Cleopatra* |
| *AW* | *All's Well That Ends Well* |
| *AYL* | *As You Like It* |
| *CE* | *Comedy of Errors* |
| *Cor* | *Coriolanus* |
| *Cym* | *Cymbeline* |
| *DF* | *Double Falsehood* |
| *E3* | *King Edward III* |
| *Ham* | *Hamlet* |
| *1H4* | *King Henry IV, Part 1* |
| *2H4* | *King Henry IV, Part 2* |
| *H5* | *King Henry V* |
| *1H6* | *King Henry VI, Part 1* |
| *2H6* | *King Henry VI, Part 2* |
| *3H6* | *King Henry VI, Part 3* |
| *H8* | *King Henry VIII* |
| *JC* | *Julius Caesar* |
| *KJ* | *King John* |
| *KL* | *King Lear* |
| *LC* | *A Lover's Complaint* |
| *LLL* | *Love's Labour's Lost* |
| *Luc* | *The Rape of Lucrece* |
| *MA* | *Much Ado about Nothing* |
| *Mac* | *Macbeth* |
| *MM* | *Measure for Measure* |
| *MND* | *A Midsummer Night's Dream* |
| *MV* | *The Merchant of Venice* |
| *MW* | *The Merry Wives of Windsor* |
| *Oth* | *Othello* |
| *Per* | *Pericles* |
| *PP* | *The Passionate Pilgrim* |
| *PT* | *The Phoenix and the Turtle* |
| *R2* | *King Richard II* |
| *R3* | *King Richard III* |
| *RJ* | *Romeo and Juliet* |
| *Son* | *Sonnets* |
| *STM* | *Sir Thomas More* |
| *TC* | *Troilus and Cressida* |
| *Tem* | *The Tempest* |
| *TGV* | *The Two Gentlemen of Verona* |
| *Tim* | *Timon of Athens* |
| *Tit* | *Titus Andronicus* |
| *TN* | *Twelfth Night* |

| | |
|---|---|
| *TNK* | *The Two Noble Kinsmen* |
| *TS* | *The Taming of the Shrew* |
| *VA* | *Venus and Adonis* |
| *WT* | *The Winter's Tale* |

# REFERENCES

## EDITIONS OF SHAKESPEARE COLLATED

| | |
|---|---|
| Alexander | *William Shakespeare: The Complete Works*, ed. Peter Alexander (1951) |
| Ard | *The Arden Shakespeare: Complete Works*, ed. Richard Proudfoot, Ann Thompson and David Scott Kastan, rev. edn (2001) |
| Ard¹ | *The First Part of King Henry the Fourth*, ed. R. P. Cowl and A. E. Morgan (1914) |
| Ard² | *The First Part of King Henry IV*, ed. A. R. Humphreys (1960) |
| Bell | *Bell's Edition of Shakespeare's Plays, as they are performed at the Theatres Royal in London*, 9 vols (1773–4) |
| Boswell–Malone | *Plays and Poems*, ed. James Boswell, 21 vols (1821) |
| Cam | *Works*, ed. William George Clark, John Glover and William Aldis Wright, 9 vols (Cambridge, 1863–6) |
| Cam¹ | *The First Part of the History of Henry IV*, ed. J. Dover Wilson (Cambridge, 1946) |
| Cam² | *The First Part of King Henry IV*, ed. Herbert Weil and Judith Weil (Cambridge, 1997) |
| Capell | *Comedies, Histories, and Tragedies*, ed. Edward Capell, 10 vols (1767–8) |
| Collier | *Works*, ed. J. P. Collier, 8 vols (1842–4) |
| Collier³ | *Works*, ed. J. P. Collier, 8 vols (1878) |
| Collier MS | MS annotations once thought to be by an 'Old Corrector' but probably by J. P. Collier, in Collier's copy (the Perkins–Collier–Devonshire copy) of F2 in the Huntington Library, and entered by Collier in his own copy of the first of his editions, now in the Folger Shakespeare Library |
| Davison | *The First Part of King Henry the Fourth*, ed. P. H. Davison, New Penguin Shakespeare (Harmondsworth, England, 1968) |
| Delius | *Shakespeares Werke*, ed. Nicolaus Delius, 7 vols (1857) |
| Dering | *The History of King Henry the Fourth, as Revised by Sir Edward Dering, Bart.*, ed. George Walton Williams and G. Blakemore Evans (Charlottesville, Va., 1974) |

| | |
|---|---|
| Dyce | *Works*, ed. Alexander Dyce, 6 vols (1857) |
| Dyce[2] | *Works*, ed. Alexander Dyce, 9 vols (1864–7) |
| F1 | *Comedies, Histories and Tragedies*, The First Folio (1623) |
| F2 | *Comedies, Histories and Tragedies*, The Second Folio (1632) |
| F3 | *Comedies, Histories and Tragedies*, The Third Folio (1663) |
| F4 | *Comedies, Histories and Tragedies*, The Fourth Folio (1685) |
| Folg[2] | *Henry IV, Part 1*, ed. Barbara A. Mowat and Paul Werstine, New Folger Library Shakespeare (New York, 1994) |
| GD | *King Henry IV, Part I: from the Acting Copy with remarks by G[eorge] D[aniel]* (1830) |
| Hanmer | *Works*, ed. Thomas Hanmer, 6 vols (1743–4) |
| Hanmer[2] | *Works*, ed. Thomas Hanmer, 6 vols (Oxford, 1771) |
| Hemingway | *Henry the Fourth, Part I*, ed. Samuel Burdett Hemingway, New Variorum (Philadelphia and London, 1936) |
| Hinman | *Henry IV: The Quarto of 1598*, ed. W.W. Greg and Charlton Hinman (Oxford, 1966) |
| Johnson | *Plays*, ed. Samuel Johnson, 8 vols (1765) |
| Johnson, T. | *A Collection of the Best English Plays*, 16 vols (The Hague, 1720–2) |
| Kittredge | *The First Part of King Henry the Fourth*, ed. George Lyman Kittredge (Boston, 1940) |
| Mack | *The History of Henry IV*, ed. Maynard Mack, Signet Classic Shakespeare (New York, 1965) |
| Malone | *Plays and Poems*, ed. Edmond Malone, 10 vols (1790) |
| Oxf | *Complete Works*, ed. Stanley Wells and Gary Taylor (Oxford, 1986) |
| Oxf[1] | *Henry IV, Part 1*, ed. David Bevington (Oxford, 1987) |
| *Poems* | *Poems* (1640) |
| Pope | *Works*, ed. Alexander Pope, 6 vols (1723–5) |
| Q0 | *The History of Henry the Fourth*, sigs C1$^r$–4$^v$ (1598) |
| Q1 | *The History of Henry the Fourth*, The First Quarto (1598) |
| Q2 | *The History of Henry the Fourth*, The Second Quarto (1599) |
| Q3 | *The History of Henry the Fourth*, The Third Quarto (1604) |
| Q4 | *The History of Henry the Fourth*, The Fourth Quarto (1608) |
| Q5 | *The History of Henry the Fourth*, The Fifth Quarto (1613) |

| | |
|---|---|
| Q6 | *The History of Henry the Fourth*, The Sixth Quarto (1622) |
| Q7 | *The History of Henry the Fourth*, The Seventh Quarto (1632) |
| Q8 | *The History of Henry the Fourth*, The Eighth Quarto (1639) |
| Q9 | *King Henry IV with the Humours of Sir John Falstaff: A Tragi-comedy*, The Ninth Quarto (1700; Betterton's acting version) |
| Riv | *The Riverside Shakespeare*, ed. G. Blakemore Evans (Boston, 1974) |
| Rowe | *Works*, ed. Nicholas Rowe, 7 vols (1709) |
| Rowe³ | *Works*, ed. Nicholas Rowe, 8 vols (1714) |
| Singer | *Dramatic Works*, ed. Samuel W. Singer, 10 vols (1856) |
| Staunton | *Plays*, ed. Howard Staunton, 3 vols (1858–60) |
| Steevens | *Plays*, ed. Samuel Johnson and George Steevens, 10 vols (1773) |
| Steevens² | *Plays*, ed. Samuel Johnson and George Steevens, 2nd edn, 10 vols (1773) |
| Steevens⁴ | *Plays*, ed. Samuel Johnson and George Steevens, 4th edn, 15 vols (1793) |
| Theobald | *Works*, ed. Lewis Theobald, 7 vols (1733) |
| Thirlby MS | Styan Thirlby's MS notes on *Henry IV, Part 1*, published posthumously in Johnson (1765) |
| Walter | *King Henry IV, Part One*, ed. J. H. Walter (1961) |
| Warburton | *Works*, ed. William Warburton, 8 vols (1747) |
| White | *Works*, ed. R. G. White, 12 vols (1859) |

### OTHER WORKS CITED

| | |
|---|---|
| Abbott | E. A. Abbott, *A Shakespearian Grammar*, 3rd edn (1870) |
| Addenbrooke | David Addenbrooke, *The Royal Shakespeare Company: The Peter Hall Years* (1974) |
| Ainger | Alfred Ainger, *Lectures and Essays*, 2 vols (1905) |
| Arber | *A Transcript of the Registers of the Company of Stationers of London, 1554–1640 AD*, ed. Edward Arber, 5 vols (1876) |
| Ashley | Robert Ashley, *Of Honour*, ed. Virgil Heltzel (San Marino, Calif., 1947) |
| Auden | W. H. Auden, *Lectures on Shakespeare*, ed. Arthur Kirsch (Princeton, NJ, 2000) |
| Auden, *Dyer's* | W. H. Auden, *The Dyer's Hand and Other Essays* (New York, 1962) |
| Bacon | Francis Bacon, *The Advancement of Learning*, ed. Michael Kiernan, The Oxford Francis Bacon, IV (Oxford, 2000) |

| | |
|---|---|
| Baker | Richard Baker, *Chronicle of the Kings of England* (1643) |
| Bakhtin | Mikhail Bakhtin, *Rabelais and his World*, tr. Helene Iswolsky (Bloomington, Ind., 1984) |
| Baldwin | Thomas Whitfield Baldwin, *The Organization and Personnel of the Shakespearean Company* (New York, 1961) |
| Bale | John Bale, *The Pageant of Popes* (1574) |
| Barber | C. L. Barber, *Shakespeare's Festive Comedy* (Princeton, NJ, 1959) |
| Basse | William Basse, *Sword and Buckler, or Serving-man's Defence* (1602) |
| Beaumont & Fletcher | Francis Beaumont and John Fletcher, *Comedies and Tragedies* (1647) |
| Bentley | Gerald Eades Bentley, *Shakespeare and Jonson: Their Reputations in the Seventeenth Century Compared*, 2 vols (Chicago, 1945) |
| Berry | Edward Berry, *Shakespeare and the Hunt* (Cambridge, 2001) |
| Bevington | *'Henry the Fourth, Parts I and II': Critical Essays*, ed. David Bevington (New York and London, 1986) |
| Bishops' Bible | *The Holy Bible . . . Authorised and Appointed to be read in Churche*s (1588) |
| Bland | Mark Bland, personal communication |
| Bloom | Harold Bloom, *Shakespeare: The Invention of the Human* (New York, 1998) |
| Blount | Thomas Blount, *Glossographia* (1656) |
| *Blurt* | Thomas Middleton, *Blurt, Master-Constable* (1602) |
| Boorde | Andrew Boorde, *Dietary of Health* (1542), EETS, 10 (1870) |
| Bowers | *The Dramatic Works in the Beaumont and Fletcher Canon*, ed. Fredson Bowers *et al.*, 10 vols (Cambridge, 1966–96) |
| Bowers, 'Poins' | Fredson Bowers, 'Establishing Shakespeare's text: Poins and Peto in *1 Henry IV*', *SB*, 34 (1981), 189–98 |
| Bowers, 'Theme' | Fredson Bowers, 'Theme and structure in *King Henry IV, Part I*', *The Drama of the English Renaissance: Essays for Leicester Bradner*, ed. Elmer B. Blistein (Providence, RI, 1970), 42–68 |
| Bradley | David Bradley, *From Text to Performance in the Elizabethan Theatre: Preparing the Play for the Stage* (Cambridge, 1992) |
| Breton | *The Works in Prose and Verse of Nicholas Breton*, ed. Alexander B. Grosart, 2 vols (1879) |
| Brome, *Five* | Richard Brome, *Five New Plays* (1653) |
| Brome, *Northern* | Richard Brome, *The Northern Lass* (1632) |
| Brome, *Queen's* | Richard Brome, *The Queen's Exchange* (1657) |

| | |
|---|---|
| Brooks & Heilman | Cleanth Brooks and Robert B. Heilman, *Understanding Drama* (New York, 1948) |
| Browne | *The Prose of Sir Thomas Browne*, ed. Norman Endicott (New York, 1967) |
| Bullokar | John Bullokar, *An English Expositor: Teaching the Interpretation of the Hardest Words in our Language* (1616) |
| Bullough | *Narrative and Dramatic Sources of Shakespeare*, ed. Geoffrey Bullough, 8 vols, vol. 4 (1966) |
| Burckhardt | Sigurd Burckhardt, *Shakespearean Meanings* (Princeton, NJ, 1968) |
| Burke | Edmund Burke, *A Philosophical Enquiry into the Origin of Our Ideas of the Sublime and Beautiful*, ed. Adam Phillips (Oxford, 1990) |
| Camden | William Camden, *Remains Concerning Britain*, ed. R. D. Dunn (Toronto, 1982) |
| Campbell | Lily B. Campbell, *Shakespeare's 'Histories': Mirrors of Elizabethan Policy* (San Marino, Calif., 1947) |
| Capell, *Notes* | Edward Capell, *Notes and Various Readings to Shakespeare* (1779) |
| Carlson | David R. Carlson 'The writings and manuscript collections of the Elizabethan alchemist, antiquary, and herald Francis Thynne', *Huntington Library Quarterly*, 52 (1989), 203–72 |
| Cawdrey | Robert Cawdrey, *A Table Alphabetical . . . of Hard Usual English Words* (1604) |
| Cercignani | Fausto Cercignani, *Shakespeare's Works and Elizabethan Pronunciation* (Oxford, 1981) |
| Chambers | E. K. Chambers, *William Shakespeare: A Study of Facts and Problems*, 2 vols (Oxford, 1930) |
| Chambers, *Stage* | E. K. Chambers, *The Elizabethan Stage*, 4 vols (Oxford, 1923) |
| Chapman | *The Plays of George Chapman: The Comedies*, ed. Allan Holaday (Urbana, Chicago and London, 1970) |
| Chaucer | *The Riverside Chaucer*, 3rd edn, ed. Larry D. Benson (Oxford, 1987) |
| Chettle & Kemp | Henry Chettle, *Kind Heart's Dream* (1592), and William Kemp, *Nine Days' Wonder* (1600), Elizabethan and Jacobean Quartos, ed. G. B. Harrison (Edinburgh, 1966) |
| Childers & Hentzi | *The Columbia Dictionary of Modern Literary and Cultural Criticism*, ed. Joseph Childers and Gary Hentzi (New York, 1995) |
| Chrétien | *Les Romans de Chrétien de Troyes*, 1: *Erec et Enide*, ed. Mario Roques (Paris, 1952) |

| | |
|---|---|
| Cibber | Colley Cibber, *Apology*, ed. R. W. Lowe (1889) |
| *Civil Wars* | Samuel Daniel, *The Civil Wars between the Two Houses of Lancaster and York* (1595) |
| Coleridge | *Coleridge's Writings on Shakespeare*, ed. Terence Hawkes (New York, 1959) |
| Coles | Elisha Coles, *An English Dictionary* (1676) |
| Collinson | Patrick Collinson, *The Elizabethan Puritan Movement* (1967; Oxford, 1990) |
| Collinson, 'Field' | Patrick Collinson, 'John Field and Elizabethan Puritanism', in Patrick Collinson, *Godly People: Essays on English Protestantism and Puritanism* (1983), 335–70. |
| *Complete Peerage* | *The Complete Peerage of England, Scotland, and Ireland* by G. E. C[ockayne], rev. edn, ed. Vicary Gibbs (1913) |
| Corbin & Sedge | *The Oldcastle Controversy: 'Sir John Oldcastle, Part I' and 'The Famous Victories of Henry V'*, ed. Peter Corbin and Douglas Sedge (Manchester and New York, 1991) |
| Cotgrave | Randle Cotgrave, *A Dictionary of the French and English Tongues* (1611) |
| Council | Norman Council, *When Honour's At The Stake: Ideas of Honour in Shakespeare's Plays* (1973) |
| *Country* | Richard Surflet and Gervase Markham, *Maison rustique; or, The Country Farm* (1616) |
| Craven | Alan C. Craven, 'The compositors of the Shakespeare quartos printed by Peter Short', *PBSA*, 65 (1971), 393–7 |
| Cross | Claire Cross, *Church and People, 1450–1660: The Triumph of the Laity in the English Church* (Glasgow, 1976) |
| *CSP Ireland* | *Calendar of State Papers, Ireland* (1860–1905) |
| *CSPD* | *Calendar of State Papers, Domestic Series, of the Reign of Elizabeth* (1856–72) |
| Daniel, G. | *The Poems of George Daniel, esq., of Beswick, Yorkshire*, ed. A. B. Grosart, 4 vols (privately printed, 1878) |
| Daniel, S. | Samuel Daniel, *The Complete Works*, ed. A. B. Grosart, 5 vols (1885–6; New York, 1963) |
| Davenant | *The Dramatic Works of Sir William D'Avenant*, ed. James Maidement and W. H. Logan, 5 vols (1872–4; New York, 1964) |
| Davenport | Robert Davenport, *A New Trick to Cheat the Devil* (1639) |
| Davies | Sir John Davies, *The Poems*, ed. Richard Krueger (Oxford, 1975) |
| Davies, *DM* | Thomas Davies, *Dramatic Miscellanies: Consisting of Critical Observations on Several Plays of Shakspear*, 3 vols (1784) |

| | |
|---|---|
| de Grazia & Wells | *The Cambridge Companion to Shakespeare*, ed. Margreta de Grazia and Stanley Wells (Cambridge, 2001) |
| Dean | Paul Dean, 'Forms of time: some Elizabethan two-part history plays', *Renaissance Studies*, 4 (1994), 410–30 |
| Dekker | *The Dramatic Works of Thomas Dekker*, ed. Fredson Bowers, 4 vols (Cambridge, 1953–61) |
| Dent | R. W. Dent, *Shakespeare's Proverbial Language: An Index* (Berkeley, Los Angeles and London, 1981) |
| Dent, *PLED* | R. W. Dent, *Proverbial Language in English Drama Excluding Shakespeare, 1495–1616: An Index* (Berkeley, Calif. 1984) |
| Dessen | Alan C. Dessen, *Recovering Shakespeare's Theatrical Vocabulary* (Cambridge, 1995) |
| Digges | Thomas Digges and Dudley Digges, *Four Paradoxes, or Politic Discourses* (London, 1604) |
| *DNB* | *Dictionary of National Biography* |
| Dobin | Howard Dobin, *Merlin's Disciples; Prophecy, Poetry, and Power in Renaissance England* (Stanford, Calif., 1990) |
| Douce | Francis Douce, *Illustrations of Shakespeare and of Ancient Manners* (1839) |
| Drayton | Michael Drayton, *Poly-Olbion* (1612) |
| Dryden | *The Works of John Dryden*, ed. H. T. Swedenberg, Jr, and Vinton A. Dearing, 20 vols (Berkeley and Los Angeles, 1956–96) |
| Dutton | Richard Dutton, 'Shakespeare and Lancaster', *SQ*, 49 (1999), 1–21 |
| Earle | John Earle, *Micro-Cosmography* (1628) |
| EETS | Early English Text Society |
| *ELH* | *English Literary History* |
| *ELN* | *English Language Notes* |
| Engle | Lars Engle, *Shakespearean Pragmatism: Market of His Time* (Chicago, 1993) |
| Erskine-Hill | Howard Erskine-Hill, *Poetry and the Realm of Politics: Shakespeare to Dryden* (Oxford, 1996) |
| Evans | G. Blakemore Evans, 'Shakespeare's *1 Henry IV* and Nashe', *NQ*, series 7, 6 (1959), 250 |
| Evans, 'Behaviourism' | Gareth Lloyd Evans, 'The twentieth century and "behaviourism"', *SS 20* (1967), 133–42 |
| Evans, *Supplement* | *Supplement to Henry IV, Part 1: A New Variorum Edition of Shakespeare*, ed. G. Blakemore Evans (n.p., 1956) |
| Everett | Barbara Everett, 'The fatness of Falstaff', *PBA*, 76 (1991), 109–28 |
| *Faerie Queene* | Edmund Spenser, *Faerie Queene*, ed. J. C. Smith, 2 vols (Oxford, 1909) |

| | |
|---|---|
| *Fair Maid of the Inn* | John Fletcher and William Rowley, *The Fair Maid of the Inn*, in Webster |
| *Family of Love* | Thomas Middleton, *The Family of Love* (1608) |
| *Famous Victories* | *The Famous Victories of Henry V* (1598), in Corbin & Sedge |
| Fehrenbach | Robert J. Fehrenbach, 'When Lord Cobham and Edmund Tilney "were att odds": Oldcastle, Falstaff, and the date of *1 Henry IV*', *SSt*, 18 (1986), 87–101 |
| Fennor | William Fennor, *Fennor's Descriptions* (1616) |
| Fiehler | Rudolph Fiehler, 'How Oldcastle became Falstaff', *MLQ*, 16 (1955), 16–28 |
| Field, *Amends* | Nathan Field, *Amends for Ladies* (1618) |
| Field, *Weathercock* | Nathan Field, *A Woman is a Weathercock* (1612) |
| Fischer | Sandra K. Fischer, '"He means to pay": value and metaphor in the Lancastrian tetralogy', *SQ*, 40 (1989), 149–64 |
| Fleming | John Caius, *Of English Dogs*, tr. Abraham Fleming (1576) |
| Florio | John Florio, *A World of Words, or Most Copious Dictionary in Italian and English* (1598) |
| Florio, *Second* | John Florio, *Second Fruits*, 1591 |
| Ford | John Ford, *'Tis Pity She's a Whore*, ed. Brian Morris (London, 1968) |
| Foxe | John Foxe, *Acts and Monuments of these Latter and Perilous Days* (1583) |
| Freeman | Arthur Freeman, 'The "Tapster Manuscript": an analogue of Shakespeare's *Henry the Fourth, Part One*', *English Manuscript Studies 1100–1700*, 6 (1997), 93–105 |
| French | A. L. French, 'Henry VI and the ghost of Richard II', *English Studies* (Anglo-American supplement), 50 (1960), xxxvii–xliii |
| Freud | *The Standard Edition of the Complete Psychological Works of Sigmund Freud*, tr. and ed. James Strachey, 24 vols (1953–74) |
| Fuller | Thomas Fuller, *The Church History of England* (1655) |
| Fuller, *Worthies* | Thomas Fuller, *Worthies of England*, ed. John Freeman (1952) |
| Garrard | William Garrard, *The Art of War* (1591) |
| Gayton | Edmund Gayton, *Pleasant Notes upon Don Quixote* (1654) |
| Geneva Bible | *Holy Bible* (first translated 1560; edition cited, 1582) |
| Gerard | John Gerard, *The Herbal, or General History of Plants* (1597) |
| Goldberg | Jonathan Goldberg, 'The commodity of names: "Falstaff" and "Oldcastle" in *1 Henry IV*', *Reconfiguring* |

|  | *the Renaissance: Essays in Critical Materialism*, ed. Jonathan Crewe (Lewisburg, Pa., 1992), 76–88 |
| Gosson | Stephen Gosson, *The School of Abuse* (1579) |
| Gould | J. D. Gould, *The Great Debasement* (Oxford, 1970) |
| Grady | Hugh Grady, 'Falstaff: subjectivity between the carnival and the aesthetic', *MLR*, 96 (2001), 609–23 |
| Green | William Green, *Shakespeare's Merry Wives of Windsor* (Princeton, NJ, 1962) |
| Greenblatt | Stephen Greenblatt, *Shakespearean Negotiations: The Circulation of Social Energy in Renaissance England* (Berkeley, Calif., 1988) |
| Greene, *Alphonsus* | Robert Greene, *Alphonsus* (1587) |
| Greene, *Quip* | Robert Greene, *A Quip for an Upstart Courtier* (1592) |
| *Greene's Tu Quoque* | J. Cooke, *Greene's Tu Quoque; or, the City Gallant*, ed. Alan J. Berman, Renaissance Imagination, 8 (New York, 1984) |
| Grosart | *The Non-Dramatic Works of Thomas Dekker*, ed. A. B. Grosart, 5 vols (1884–6) |
| Guilpin | Edward Guilpin, *Skialetheia; or, a Shadow of Truth in Certain Epigrams and Satires* (1598) |
| GWW | George Walton Williams, personal communication |
| Hall | *The Poems of Joseph Hall*, ed. Arnold Davenport (Liverpool, 1969) |
| Hardyng | *The Chronicle of John Hardyng* (1543) |
| Harington | John Harington, *The Most Elegant and Witty Epigrams* (1618) |
| Harrison | William Harrison, *The Description of England* (1587), ed. Georges Edelen (Washington, DC, 1968) |
| Harvey | Gabriel Harvey, *Four Letters and Certain Sonnets* (1592) |
| Hawkins | Sherman Hawkins, '*Henry IV*: the structural problem revisited', *SQ*, 33 (1982), 278–301 |
| Hay | *Lincoln and the Civil War in the Diaries and Letters of John Hay*, ed. Tyler Dennett (New York, 1939) |
| Hazlitt | William Hazlitt, *Characters of Shakespear's Plays*, ed. Sir Arthur Quiller-Couch (1912; 1962) |
| Hazlitt, *Works* | *The Complete Works of William Hazlitt*, ed. P. P. Howe, 21 vols (1930–4) |
| Helgerson | Richard Helgerson, *Forms of Nationhood: The Elizabethan Writing of England* (Chicago and London, 1992) |
| Henslowe | *Henslowe's Diary*, ed. R. A. Foakes and R. T. Rickert (Cambridge, 1961) |
| Herbert | *The Dramatic Records of Sir Henry Herbert, 1623–1673*, ed. Joseph Quincy Adams (New York, 1917) |
| Heywood, *Apology* | Thomas Heywood, *An Apology for Actors* (1612) |
| Heywood, *Captives* | Thomas Heywood, *The Captives*, ed. Arthur Brown with R. E. Alton, Malone Society Reprints (Oxford, 1953) |

Heywood, *Fair Maid*    Thomas Heywood, *The Fair Maid of the West*, Parts 1 and 2, ed. Robert K. Turner, Jr (Lincoln, Nebr., 1967)

Heywood, *Wise-Woman*    Thomas Heywood, *The Wise-Woman of Hogsdon* (1638)

Heywood & Brome    Thomas Heywood and Richard Brome, *The Late Lancashire Witches* (1634)

Hodgdon    Barbara Hodgdon, *The End Crowns All: Closure and Contradiction in Shakespeare's Histories* (Princeton, NJ, 1991)

Hogan    Charles Beecher Hogan, *Shakespeare in the Theatre, 1701–1800: A Record of Performances in London*, 2 vols (Oxford, 1952–7)

Holinshed    Raphael Holinshed, *The Chronicles of England, Scotland, and Ireland*, 3 vols, 2nd edn (1587)

Honigmann    E. A. J. Honigmann, 'Sir John Oldcastle: Shakespeare's martyr', *Fanned and Winnowed Opinions: Shakespearean Essays Presented to Harold Jenkins*, ed. John W. Mahon and Thomas A. Pendleton (1987)

Honigmann, *Lost*    E. A. J. Honigmann, *Shakespeare: The 'Lost Years'* (Manchester, 1985)

Honigmann, *Texts*    E. A. J. Honigmann, *The Texts of 'Othello' and Shakespearian Revision* (1996)

Howard & Rackin    Jean Howard and Phyllis Rackin, *Engendering a Nation: A Feminist Account of Shakespeare's English Histories* (1997)

*Humour's Blood*    Samuel Rowlands, *The Letting of Humour's Blood in the Head-Vein* (1600)

Hunter    William B. Hunter, 'Prince Hal, his struggle toward moral perfection', *SAQ*, 50 (1951), 86–95

Hunter, G. K.    G. K. Hunter, '*Henry IV* and the Elizabethan two-part play', *RES*, n. s. 5 (1954), 236–48

Jackson, 'Copy'    MacD. P. Jackson, 'The manuscript copy of the quarto (1598) of Shakespeare's *1 Henry IV*', *NQ*, ser. 7, 33 (1986), 353–4

Jackson, 'Two'    MacD. P. Jackson, 'Two Shakespeare quartos: *Richard III* (1597) and *1 Henry IV* (1598)', *SB*, 35 (1982), 173–91

James    *The Poems Etc. of Richard James, B.D.*, ed. A. B. Grosart (1880)

Jenkins    Harold Jenkins, *The Structural Problem in Shakespeare's 'Henry the Fourth'* (1956)

Jones    J. T. Jones, 'Shakespeare's pronunciation of Glendower', *English Studies*, 43 (1962), 248–50

Jonson    *Ben Jonson*, ed. C. H. Herford and P. and E. Simpson, 11 vols (Oxford, 1925–52)

| | |
|---|---|
| Jorgensen | Paul A. Jorgensen, *Redeeming Shakespeare's Words* (Berkeley, Calif., 1962) |
| Joseph | Sister Miriam Joseph, *Shakespeare's Use of the Arts of Language* (New York, 1947) |
| Jowett | John Jowett, 'The thieves in *1 Henry IV*', *RES*, n.s. 38 (1987), 325–33 |
| Kastan, *Companion* | *A Companion to Shakespeare*, ed. David Scott Kastan (Oxford, 1999) |
| Kastan, *SAT* | David Scott Kastan, *Shakespeare after Theory* (1999) |
| Kastan, *Shapes* | David Scott Kastan, *Shakespeare and the Shapes of Time* (1982) |
| Kelliher | Hilton Kelliher, 'Contemporary manuscript extracts from Shakespeare's *Henry IV, Part I*', *English Manuscript Studies 1100–1700*, 1 (1989), 144–81 |
| Kelly | Robert L. Kelly, 'Shakespeare's Scroops and "the Spirit of Cain"', *SQ*, 20 (1969), 71–80 |
| King | T. J. King, *Casting Shakespeare's Plays: London Actors and Their Roles, 1590–1642* (Cambridge, 1992) |
| Knowles | *Shakespeare and Carnival: After Bakhtin*, ed. Ronald Knowles (Basingstoke, England, 1998) |
| Lander | Jesse Lander, 'Crack'd crowns and counterfeit sovereigns: the crisis of value in *1 Henry IV*', *SSt*, 30 (2002 forthcoming) |
| Lang | Matheson Lang, *Mr Wu Looks Back* (1941) |
| Lee | Nathaniel Lee, *Ceasar Borgia: Son of Pope Alexander the Sixth: A Tragedy* (1680) |
| Leiter | Samuel L. Leiter, *Shakespeare around the Globe: A Guide to Notable Postwar Revivals* (New York, 1986) |
| Lentricchia & McLaughlin | *Critical Terms for Literary Study*, ed. Frank Lentricchia and Thomas McLaughlin (Chicago, 1990) |
| Levin | Harry Levin, 'Falstaff uncolted', *MLN*, 61 (1946), 305–10 |
| Levine | Nina Levine, 'Extending credit in the *Henry IV* plays', *SQ*, 51 (2000), 403–31 |
| Lily & Colet | William Lily and John Colet, *A Short Introduction of Grammar* (1549), Scolar Press facsimile (Menston, England, 1970) |
| Limon | Jerzy Limon, *Dangerous Matter: English Drama and Politics 1623–4* (Cambridge, 1986) |
| Long | William Long, 'Stage-directions: a misinterpreted factor in determining textual provenance', *TEXT*, 2 (1985), 121–38 |
| Lupton | Donald Lupton, *London and the Country Carbonadoed and Quartered into Several Characters* (1632) |

| | |
|---|---|
| Lyly | *The Complete Works of John Lyly*, ed. R. Warwick Bond, 3 vols (Oxford, 1902) |
| McCulloch | *A Select Collection of Scarce and Valuable Tracts on Money*, ed. John R. McCulloch (1856; New York, 1966) |
| McGinn | Donald J. McGinn, *John Penry and the Marprelate Controversy* (New Brunswick, NJ, 1966) |
| McKeen | David McKeen, *A Memory of Honour: The Life of William Brooke, Lord Cobham*, 2 vols (Salzburg, 1986) |
| McManaway | James G. McManaway, *Studies in Shakespeare, Bibliography, and Theater* (New York, 1969) |
| McMillin | Scott McMillin, *Shakespeare in Performance: 'Henry IV, Part One'* (Manchester and New York, 1991) |
| Macready | *The Diaries of William Macready, 1833–1851*, ed. William Toynbee, 2 vols (1912) |
| Maguire | Laurie E. Maguire, *Shakespearean Suspect Texts: The 'Bad' Quartos and Their Contexts* (Cambridge, 1996) |
| Mahood | Molly M. Mahood, *Shakespeare's Wordplay* (London, 1957) |
| Marlowe | *The Complete Works of Christopher Marlowe*, ed. Roma Gill and Richard Rowland, 5 vols (Cambridge, 1990–6) |
| Marmion | Shackerley Marmion, *Holland's Leaguer* (1632) |
| Marston | *The Plays of John Marston*, ed. H. H. Wood, 3 vols (Edinburgh, 1934–9) |
| Marston, *Dutch* | John Marston, *The Dutch Courtesan*, ed. Peter H. Davison (Berkeley, Calif., 1968) |
| Marston, *What You Will* | John Marston, *What You Will* (1607) |
| Martin | R. W. F. Martin, 'A Catholic Oldcastle', *NQ*, n.s. 40 (1993), 185–6 |
| *Martin's Month's Mind* | *Martin's Month's Mind by Marphoreus* (1589) |
| Massinger | *The Poems and Plays of Philip Massinger*, ed. Philip Edwards and Colin Gibson, 5 vols (Oxford, 1976) |
| *Meeting* | *The Meeting of Gallants at an Ordinary* (1604) |
| Melchiori | *The Second Part of King Henry IV*, ed. Giorgio Melchiori (Cambridge, 1989) |
| Meres | Francis Meres, *Palladis Tamia* (1598) |
| Mills | *A Dictionary of English Place-Names*, ed. A. D. Mills (Oxford, 1998) |
| Milton | John Milton, *The Complete Prose Works of John Milton*, ed. Don M. Wolfe, 10 vols (New Haven, Conn., 1953–82) |
| Minsheu | John Minsheu, *Ductor in Linguas, the Guide into the Tongues* (1617) |

| | |
|---|---|
| *Mirror* | *The Mirror for Magistrates* (1559), ed. Lily B. Campbell (Cambridge, 1938) |
| *Misogonus* | *Misogonus*, in *Early Plays from the Italian*, ed. R. Warwick Bond (Oxford, 1909) |
| *MLR* | *Modern Language Review* |
| *MLQ* | *Modern Language Quarterly* |
| *MLN* | *Modern Language Notes* |
| Monsarrat | Gilles Monsarrat, 'Shakespeare's Ravenspur(gh)', *NQ*, 243 (1998), 316–17 |
| More | Thomas More, *Utopia*, tr. Ralph Robinson, ed. J. Rawson Lumby (1883) |
| Morgann | Maurice Morgann, *Shakespearian Criticism*, ed. Daniel A. Fineman (Oxford, 1972) |
| Moryson | Fynes Moryson, *An Itinerary* (1617), 4 vols (Glasgow, 1907) |
| *MP* | *Modern Philology* |
| Mullin | Michael Mullin, 'Emrys James: on playing Henry IV', *Theatre Quarterly*, 7 (1977), 15–23 |
| Nashe | *The Works of Thomas Nashe*, ed. R. B. McKerrow, 5 vols (Oxford, 1904–10) |
| Neale | J. E. Neale, *Elizabeth I and Her Parliaments 1584–1601*, 2 vols (New York, 1966) |
| Noble | Richmond Noble, *Shakespeare's Biblical Knowledge and Use of the Book of Common Prayer* (1935) |
| North | *The Lives of the Noble Grecians and Romans, ... by Plutarch*, tr. Thomas North (1595) |
| *NQ* | *Notes and Queries* |
| Nuttall | A. D. Nuttall, *A New Mimesis: Shakespeare and the Representation of Reality* (1983) |
| Odell | George C. D. Odell, *Shakespeare from Betterton to Irving*, 2 vols (New York, 1921) |
| *OED* | *Oxford English Dictionary*, 2nd edn, prepared by J. A. Simpson and E. S. C. Weiner (Oxford, 1989) |
| Ogden | D. H. Ogden, 'The 1962 season at Stratford, Connecticut', *SQ*, 13 (1962), 537–40 |
| Onions | C. T. Onions, *A Shakespeare Glossary* (1911), rev. Robert Eagleson (Oxford, 1986) |
| Ornstein | Robert Ornstein, *A Kingdom for a Stage: The Achievement of Shakespeare's History Plays* (Cambridge, Mass., 1972) |
| Orrell | John Orrell, 'The London stage in the Florentine correspondence, 1604–1618', *Theatre Research International*, 3 (1977–8), 157–76 |
| Overbury | Sir Thomas Overbury, *New and Choice Characters of Several Authors* (1615) |

| | |
|---|---|
| Patterson | Annabel M. Patterson, *Reading Holinshed's Chronicles* (Chicago, 1994) |
| *PBA* | *Proceedings of the British Academy* |
| *PBSA* | *Papers of the Bibliographic Society of America* |
| Pendleton | Thomas Pendleton, '"This is not the man": on calling Falstaff Falstaff', *Analytical and Enumerative Bibliography*, n.s. 4 (1990), 59–71 |
| Pepys | *The Diary of Samuel Pepys*, ed. Robert Latham and William Matthews, 11 vols (Berkeley and Los Angeles, 1970–83) |
| Platter | *Thomas Platter's Travels in England*, tr. Clare Williams (1937) |
| Pliny | *The History of the World, Commonly Called, The Natural History of C. Plinius Secundus*, tr. Philemon Holland (1601) |
| Poole | Kristen Poole, *Radical Religion from Shakespeare to Milton* (Cambridge, 2000) |
| *Promos and Cass.* | George Whetstone, *Promos and Cassandra* (1578) |
| P.T. | P.T., 'Observations on Shakespeare's Falstaff', *Gentleman's Magazine*, 22 (October 1752), 459–61 |
| Pugliatti | Paola Pugliatti, *Shakespeare the Historian* (Basingstoke, England, 1996) |
| Puttenham | George Puttenham, *The Art of English Poesy* (1589) |
| Rackin | Phyllis Rackin, *Stages of History: Shakespeare's English Chronicles* (Ithaca, N.Y., 1990) |
| *Ram-Alley* | Lording Barry, *Ram-Alley; or, Merry Tricks* (1611) |
| *REED: Bristol* | *Records of Early English Drama: Bristol*, ed. Mark C. Pilkington (Toronto, 1996) |
| *REED: Somerset* | *Records of Early English Drama: Somerset*, ed. James Stokes and Robert Joseph Alexander, 2 vols (Toronto, 1996) |
| *Rehearsal* | George Villiers, Duke of Buckingham, *The Rehearsal* (1672) |
| *RES* | *Review of English Studies* |
| Ribner | Irving Ribner, *The English History Play in the Age of Shakespeare* (Princeton, NJ, 1957) |
| Romei | Annibale Romei, *The Courtiers' Academy*, tr. John Kepers (n.d., 1598?) |
| Rossiter | A. P. Rossiter, *Angel with Horns: Fifteen Lectures on Shakespeare*, ed. Graham Storey (1961) |
| Rothschild | Herbert Rothschild, 'Falstaff and the picaresque tradition', *MLR*, 68 (1973), 14–21 |
| RP | Richard Proudfoot, personal communication |
| Saccio | Peter Saccio, *Shakespeare's English Kings*, 2nd edn (Oxford, 2000) |

| | |
|---|---|
| Salgado | Gamini Salgado, *Eyewitnesses of Shakespeare: First Hand Accounts of Performances 1590–1890* (1975) |
| Sams | Eric Sams, 'Oldcastle and the Oxford Shakespeare', *NQ*, n.s., 40 (1993), 180–5 |
| Sanderson | James L. Sanderson, ' "Buff jerkin": a note to *1 Henry IV*', *ELN*, 4 (1966), 92–5 |
| *SAQ* | *South Atlantic Quarterly* |
| *SB* | *Studies in Bibliography* |
| Schoenbaum | Samuel Schoenbaum, *William Shakespeare: A Documentary Life* (Oxford, 1975) |
| Scot | Reginald Scot, *The Discovery of Witchcraft* (1584) |
| Scoufos | Alice-Lyle Scoufos, *Shakespeare's Typological Satyre: A Study of the Falstaff–Oldcastle Problem* (Athens, Ohio, 1978) |
| *Scourge* | John Davies of Hereford, *A Scourge for Paper-Persecutors; or, Paper's Complaint* (1624) |
| Selden | *The Table-Talk of John Selden*, ed. Samuel Harvey Reynolds (Oxford, 1892) |
| Shaaber, 'Problems' | M. A. Shaaber, 'Problems in the editing of Shakespeare's text', *English Institute Essays 1947* (New York, 1948) |
| Shaaber, 'Unity' | M. A. Shaaber, 'The unity of *Henry IV*', *Joseph Quincy Adams Memorial Studies* (Washington, DC, 1948), 217–27 |
| Shaheen | Naseeb Shaheen, *Biblical References in Shakespeare's History Plays* (Newark, NJ, 1989) |
| Shaw | George Bernard Shaw, *Shaw on Shakespeare*, ed. Edwin Wilson (New York, 1961) |
| Shirley | James Shirley, *Poems* (1646) |
| Siddons | *Memoirs of Mrs Siddon*, ed. J. Boaden (1827) |
| Sidney | *Sir Philip Sidney*, ed. Katherine Duncan-Jones, Oxford Authors (Oxford, 1989) |
| Sidney, *Prose* | *The Miscellaneous Prose of Sir Philip Sidney*, ed. Katherine Duncan-Jones and J. A. Van Dorsten (Oxford, 1973) |
| Sisson | C. J. Sisson, *New Readings in Shakespeare*, 2 vols (Cambridge, 1956) |
| Skelton | John Skelton, *Pithy, Pleasant and Profitable Works* (1568) |
| Smith | *Elizabethan Critical Essays*, ed. G. G. Smith, 2 vols (Oxford, 1904) |
| Smythe | *Certain Discourses, Written by Sir J. Smythe, Knight: concerning the forms and effects of divers sorts of weapons and other very important matters military* (1590) |

| | |
|---|---|
| *South Sea* | *The Observations of Sir Richard Hawkins Knight, in His Voyage into the South Sea, Anno 1593* (1622) |
| Speed | John Speed, *The Theatre of the Empire of Great Britain* (1611) |
| Sprague, *Actors* | Arthur Colby Sprague, *Shakespeare and the Actors* (Cambridge, Mass., 1944) |
| Sprague, 'Gadshill' | Arthur Colby Sprague, 'Gadshill revisited', *SQ*, 4 (1953), 125–37 |
| Sprague, *Stage* | Arthur C. Sprague, *Shakespeare's Histories: Plays for the Stage* (London, 1964) |
| Spurgeon | Caroline Spurgeon, *Shakespeare's Imagery and What It Tells Us* (1935) |
| *SQ* | *Shakespeare Quarterly* |
| *SS* | *Shakespeare Survey* |
| *SSt* | *Shakespeare Studies* |
| Stoll | E. E. Stoll, 'Falstaff', *MP*, 12 (1914), 65–108 |
| Stow | John Stow, *Annals; or, a General Chronicle of England. Begun by John Stow: continued … by Edmund Howes* (1592) |
| Stow, *Chronicles* | John Stow, *Chronicles of England* (1580) |
| Strohm | Paul Strohm, 'Shakespeare's Oldcastle: another ill-framed knight', *Theory and the Pre-Modern Text* (Minneapolis, 2000), 132–48 |
| Stubbes | Phillip Stubbes, *The Anatomy of Abuses* (1583) |
| Suckling | *The Works of Sir John Suckling*, ed. Thomas Clayton and L. A. Beaurline, 2 vols (Oxford, 1971) |
| Suetonius | Suetonius, *The History of Twelve Caesars*, tr. Philemon Holland (1606) |
| Sutcliffe | Matthew Sutcliffe, *The Practice, Proceedings and Laws of Arms* (1597) |
| Tanner | J. R. Tanner, *Tudor Constitutional Documents* (1922; Cambridge, 1951) |
| Taylor G., 'Cobham' | Gary Taylor, 'William Shakespeare, Richard James, and the House of Cobham', *RES*, n.s. 38 (1987), 334–54 |
| Taylor, G., 'Fortunes' | Gary Taylor, 'The Fortunes of Oldcastle', *SS 38* (1985), 85–100 |
| Taylor, J., *Carriers* | John Taylor, *The Carriers' Cosmography* (1637) |
| Taylor, J., *Penniless* | John Taylor, *The Penniless Pilgrimage* (1618) |
| Taylor, J., 1630 | *All the Works of John Taylor the Water Poet* (1630) |
| Taylor & Jowett | Gary Taylor and John Jowett, *Shakespeare Reshaped 1606–1623* (1993) |
| Thomas | Thomas Thomas, *Dictionarium Linguae Latinae et Anglicanae* (1587) |
| Thorn-Drury | George R. Thorn-Drury, *More Seventeenth-Century Allusions to Shakespeare and His Works Not Hitherto Collected* (London, 1924) |

| | |
|---|---|
| Tilley | M. P. Tilley, *A Dictionary of the Proverbs in England in the Sixteenth and Seventeenth Centuries* (Ann Arbor, Mich., 1950) |
| Tillyard | E. M. W. Tillyard, *Shakespeare's History Plays* (1944) |
| *TLS* | *Times Literary Supplement* |
| Tottel | *Songs and Sonnets*, ed. Richard Tottel (1557) |
| Towse | J. R. Towse, *Sixty Years of the Theater* (New York, 1916) |
| Traversi | Derek Traversi, *Shakespeare: From 'Richard II' to 'Henry V'* (Stanford, Calif., 1957) |
| Trussler | *The Royal Shakespeare Company 1980–81*, ed. Simon Trussler (1982) |
| Tucker Brooke | C. F. Tucker Brooke, *The Tudor Drama: A History of English National Drama to the Retirement of Shakespeare* (Boston and New York, 1911) |
| Turberville | George Turberville, *The Book of Hunting* (1576; Oxford, 1908) |
| *TxC* | Stanley Wells and Gary Taylor, with John Jowett and William Montgomery, *William Shakespeare: A Textual Companion* (Oxford, 1987) |
| Tyler | J. Endell Tyler, *History of Monmouth*, 2 vols (1838) |
| Tyllney | Edmond Tyllney, *Topographical Descriptions, Regiments, and Policies*, ed. W. R. Streitberger (New York, 1991) |
| Tynan | Kenneth Tynan, *He That Plays the King* (1950) |
| Upton | John Upton, *Critical Observations on Shakespeare*, 2nd edn, with alterations and additions (1748; New York, 1973) |
| Van Doren | Mark Van Doren, *Shakespeare* (New York, 1939) |
| *Varieties* | David Person, *Varieties, or a Survey of Rare and Excellent Matters* (1635) |
| Vaughan | William Vaughan, *The Golden Grove* (1600) |
| Vickers | Brian Vickers, *Shakespeare: The Critical Heritage*, 6 vols (1974–81) |
| Walker | Alice Walker, 'The Folio text of *1 Henry IV*', *SB*, 6 (1954), 45–59 |
| Wallack | Lester Wallack, *Memories of Fifty Years* (New York, 1889) |
| Walsingham | Thomas Walsingham, *Historia Anglicana*, ed. H. T. Riley, 2 vols (1863) |
| Walton | Isaac Walton, *The Compleat Angler; or, the Contemplative Man's Recreation* (1653) |
| Waugh | W. T. Waugh, 'Sir John Oldcastle', *English Historical Review*, 20 (1905), 434–56, 637–58 |
| Webbe | William Webbe, *A Discourse of English Poetry*, in Smith |
| Webster | *The Complete Works of John Webster*, 1–4, ed. F. L. Lucas (New York, 1937) |

Wells Stanley Wells, 'Revision in Shakespeare's plays', *Editing and Editors: A Retrospect*, ed. Richard Landon (New York, 1988), 67–97

Welsford Enid Welsford, *The Fool and His Social and Literary History* (1935)

West Gillian West, '"Titan", "Onyers", and other difficulties in the text of *1 Henry IV*', *SQ*, 34 (1983), 330–3

Wiles David Wiles, *Shakespeare's Clown* (Cambridge, 1987)

Wilkins George Wilkins, *Miseries of Inforst Marriage* (1607)

Williams Simon Williams, *Shakespeare on the German Stage*, 1: *1586–1914* (Cambridge, 1990)

Wilson John Dover Wilson, *The Fortunes of Falstaff* (Cambridge, 1943)

Wilson, 'Copy' John Dover Wilson, 'The Copy for *Hamlet*', *The Library*, 3rd series, 9 (1918), 153–85

Wilson, 'Origin' John Dover Wilson, 'The origin and development of Shakespeare's *Henry IV*', *The Library*, 26 (1945), 2–16

Wilson & Worsley John Dover Wilson and T. C. Worsley, *Shakespeare's Histories at Stratford* (1952)

Winter William Winter, *Shakespeare on the Stage: Third Series* (New York, 1916)

*Wits* *The Wits; or, Sport upon Sport*, ed. Robert Cox (1662)

Womersley David Womersley, 'Why is Falstaff fat?', *RES*, 47 (1996), 1–22

Wood & Clarke Roger Wood and Mary Clarke, *Shakespeare at the Old Vic* (1956)

Wylie James Hamilton Wylie, *History of England under Henry the Fourth*, 4 vols (1884–98; New York, 1969)

Yachnin Paul Yachnin, 'History, theatricality, and the "structural problem" in the *Henry IV* plays', *Philological Quarterly*, 70 (1991), 163–79

Yamada *The First Folio of Shakespeare: A Transcript of Contemporary Marginalia in a Copy of the Kodama Memorial Library of Meisei University*, ed. Akihiro Yamada (Tokyo, 1998)

Yeats W. B. Yeats, *Essays and Introductions* (1961)

Zimmerman Susan Zimmerman, 'The uses of headlines: Peter Short's Shakespearian quartos *1 Henry IV* and *Richard III*', *The Library*, 6th series, 7 (1985), 218–55

Zeeveld W. Gordon Zeeveld, 'The influence of Hall on Shakespeare's historical plays', *ELH*, 3 (1936), 317–56

# INDEX

Page numbers in *italics* refer to Figures.